Work-*Life* POLICIES

Also of interest from the Urban Institute Press:

Intergenerational Caregiving, edited by Alan Booth,
Ann C. Crouter, Suzanne M. Bianchi, and Judith A. Seltzer

Work-Life POLICIES

Edited by Ann C. Crouter and Alan Booth

THE URBAN INSTITUTE PRESS
WASHINGTON, DC

THE URBAN INSTITUTE PRESS
2100 M Street, N.W.
Washington, D.C. 20037

Library of Congress Cataloging-in-Publication Data

National Symposium on Family Issues (15th : 2007 : Pennsylvania State University)
  Work-life policies / edited by Ann C. Crouter and Alan Booth.
     p. cm.
  Papers presented at the 15th Annual National Symposium on Family Issues held at Penn State University in October 2007.
  Includes bibliographical references and index.
  Summary: "Sociological essays on policies that could help employees balance their workplace responsibilities with their other responsibilities. Policies examined encompass organizational policies, municipal policies, state policies, and federal policies. Workers studied include salaried professionals and low-wage part-time hourly workers"—Provided by publisher.
  ISBN 978-0-87766-748-3
  1. Work and family—United States—Congresses. 2. Corporate culture—United States—Congresses. 3. Flextime—United States—Congresses. 4. Hourly I. Crouter, Ann C. II. Booth, Alan, 1935-III. Title.

  HD4904.25.N385 2009
  306.3'60973—dc22

                                                        2008045635

Printed in the United States of America

13 12 11 10 09   1 2 3 4 5

THE URBAN INSTITUTE is a nonprofit, nonpartisan policy research and educational organization established in Washington, D.C., in 1968. Its staff investigates the social, economic, and governance problems confronting the nation and evaluates the public and private means to alleviate them. The Institute disseminates its research findings through publications, its web site, the media, seminars, and forums.

Through work that ranges from broad conceptual studies to administrative and technical assistance, Institute researchers contribute to the stock of knowledge available to guide decisionmaking in the public interest.

Conclusions or opinions expressed in Institute publications are those of the authors and do not necessarily reflect the views of officers or trustees of the Institute, advisory groups, or any organizations that provide financial support to the Institute.

Contents

Acknowledgments   xi

Preface   xiii

PART I: Workplace Policies: Opportunities to Improve Health and Well-Being

1   Work and Family Employment Policy for a Transformed Labor Force: Current Trends and Themes   3
Ellen Ernst Kossek and Brian Distelberg

2   Elaborations on a Theme: Toward Understanding Work-Life Culture   51
Cynthia A. Thompson and David J. Prottas

3   Union Strategies for Work-Family Issues: Collective Bargaining and Public Policies   61
Netsy Firestein

4   The Design of Work as a Key Driver of
    Work-Life Flexibility for Professionals   83
    Forrest Briscoe

PART II: **Intervening in the Corporate Workplace**

5   Learning from a Natural Experiment: Studying
    a Corporate Work-Time Policy Initiative   97
    Phyllis Moen, Erin Kelly, and Kelly Chermack

6   The Tensions, Puzzles, and Dilemmas
    of Engaged Work-Family Scholarship   133
    *Shelley M. MacDermid, Mary Ann Remnet,
    and Colleen Pagnan*

7   Corporate Work-Life Interventions:
    A Multilevel Perspective   141
    Jeffrey H. Greenhaus

8   Energizing the Study of Work Policies   155
    Anisa M. Zvonkovic

PART III: **Making a Difference for
           Hourly Employees**

9   Making a Difference for Hourly Employees   169
    Susan J. Lambert

10 Flexibility for Whom? Inequality in
    Work-Life Policies and Practices   197
    Ruth Milkman

11   Challenges Experienced by Vulnerable
     Hourly Workers: Issues to Consider
     in the Policy Conversation   207
     Noemí Enchautegui-de-Jesús

12   Making a Difference for Hourly Workers:
     Considering Work-Life Policies in Social Context   219
     Maureen Perry-Jenkins

**PART IV: Future Directions for Research
          and Policies**

13   Work-Life Policies: Future Directions
     for Research   231
     Jennifer Glass

14   Policy Challenges and Opportunities for
     Workplace Flexibility: The State of Play   251
     Chai R. Feldblum

15   Work-Life Policies: A "Both/And" Approach   289
     Ellen Galinsky

16   Work-Life Policies: The Changing Landscape
     of Aging and Work   309
     Michael A. Smyer and Marcie Pitt-Catsouphes

17   Limited, Mismatched, and Unequal: Work-Life
     Policies and Practices in the United States   323
     Kelly D. Davis and Katherine Stamps Mitchell

About the Editors   343

About the Contributors   345

Index   351

Acknowledgments

The editors are grateful to the many organizations at Penn State University that sponsored the 2007 National Symposium on Family Issues and this resulting volume, including the Population Research Institute; the Children, Youth, and Families Consortium; the Prevention Research Center; the Center for Human Development and Family Research in Diverse Contexts; the Women's Studies Program, and the departments of Human Development and Family Studies, Labor and Employment Relations, Psychology, and Sociology. The editors also gratefully acknowledge essential core financial support in the form of a five-year grant from the National Institute of Child Health and Human Development (NICHD), as well as ongoing, substantive guidance and advice from Christine Bachrach and Rosalind King of NICHD and Lynne Casper, formerly of NICHD and now in the Department of Sociology at the University of Southern California. The ongoing support of all of these partners has enabled us to attract excellent scholars from a range of backgrounds and disciplines—the sort of group upon whom the quality and integrity of the series depends.

A lively, interdisciplinary team of scholars from across the Penn State University community meets with us annually to generate symposia topics and plans and is available throughout the year for brainstorming and problem solving. We appreciate their enthusiasm, intellectual support, and creative ideas. We also sincerely thank Jeanette N. Cleveland, David

Almeida, Jennifer Hook, and Robert Drago for presiding over symposium sessions.

The many details that go into planning a symposium and producing a volume cannot be overestimated. In this regard, we are especially grateful for the assistance of our administrative staff, including Tara Murray, Barbara King, and Sherry Yocum. Finally, we could not have accomplished this work without Carolyn Scott, whose organizational skills, commitment, and attention to the many details that go into organizing a good conference and edited book series make it possible for us to focus on the ideas.

Preface

In an era of soaring health care costs, reducing work-life stress is a potential win-win proposition for employers, employees, and their families. Workplace policies that provide employees with more autonomy and flexibility in matters such as where and when they work, time off to deal with health and family concerns, and assistance with child care, offer opportunities for employers to support employees' lives outside of work. Such policies may result in bottom-line payoffs for the employer in terms of enhanced recruitment, retention, productivity, and lower health care costs. The state of research knowledge in this area is sparse, however. Researchers are just beginning to move beyond correlational, descriptive studies into exciting, rigorous intervention research that evaluates the consequences of changes in workplace policies. These new investigations pay attention not only to the effects of formal policies, but to the implications of changes in the informal culture of the workplace, for employers, employees, and employees' families. As this new wave of research gets off the ground, it is timely to ask how the research community can inform workplace policy in this important area.

The contributions to this volume are based on papers presented at the 15th Annual National Symposium on Family Issues held at Penn State University in October 2007, "Work-Life Policies that Make a Real Difference for Individuals, Families, and Organizations." This edited volume is the culmination of two days of stimulating and provocative presentations and discussions.

This volume is organized into four sections, each of which addresses a distinct goal. Each section includes a chapter by lead authors, followed by shorter chapters by discussants. Care has been taken to bring together perspectives from diverse disciplines in each section. The volume concludes with an integrative commentary.

The volume begins with a comprehensive overview by industrial and organizational psychologists Ellen Ernst Kossek and Brian Distelberg (Michigan State University) of family-friendly workplace policies in the United States, including estimates of their prevalence and data about their effectiveness. These themes are elaborated in subsequent chapters by authors from other perspectives. Cynthia A. Thompson of the Zicklin School of Business, Baruch College, City University of New York, and David J. Prottas of Adelphi University emphasize the role played by organizational culture in shaping employees' perceived access to policies and actual use of them. The access to and relevance of many of these policies for hourly workers is questioned in Netsy Firestein's chapter. Firestein, a labor organizer and director of the Berkeley-based Labor Project for Working Families, introduces important questions about the likelihood that corporations will be responsive to the needs of low-income workers and their families. Their chapters are complemented by a chapter from organizational sociologist Forrest Briscoe of Penn State's Smeal College of Business, highlighting the need for research on such organizational dimensions as size.

The lead chapters anchoring the second and third sections of the volume each focus on a different workplace intervention study. The focal chapter of the second section is Phyllis Moen, Erin Kelly, and Kelly Chermack's distillation of insights from an ongoing evaluation of the impact of the results-only work environment (ROWE) at Best Buy's corporate headquarters. This team of organizational and life-course sociologists has conducted a pathbreaking longitudinal study of participants in the intervention and provides empirical evidence that their primarily middle-class, professional sample benefited from their newfound flexibility in when and where work takes place. Three chapters discuss the Moen, Kelly, and Chermack chapter and offer additional insights. Shelley M. MacDermid, Mary Ann Remnet, and Colleen Pagnan from Purdue's Department of Child Development and Family Studies elaborate on some of the methodological challenges involved in evaluating field interventions like ROWE.

From the field of management, Jeffrey H. Greenhaus of Drexel University brings insights from a career of research on corporate managers. In the final chapter of this set, Anisa M. Zvonkovic, a developmental scholar from the Department of Human Development and Family Studies at Texas Tech University, adds additional nuances from her own research on the implications of work-related travel for employees and their families.

The focus of the third section of the volume moves from an examination of corporate work settings to a careful consideration of the workplace challenges faced by hourly employees and their families. The lead chapter by Susan J. Lambert, a sociologist in the School of Social Service Administration at the University of Chicago, describes the early stages of a workplace policy–oriented intervention in the retail sector that involved providing more predictable work hours for sales associates. The chapter includes a rich array of insights about the ways in which a "just in time" work culture makes it difficult for employees to have any control over their schedules, wreaking havoc with life off the job. Complementing the lead chapter, sociologist Ruth Milkman, formerly of the Institute of Industrial Relations at the University of California, Los Angeles, contributes insights from her policy-oriented studies of initiatives such as the effort to enact paid family medical leave in California. Noemí Enchautegui-de-Jesús from the Department of Psychology at Syracuse University adds findings from her own qualitative study of hourly employees in a university context. In the final chapter of this group, Maureen Perry-Jenkins, a family scholar in the Department of Psychology at the University of Massachusetts, Amherst, weaves in findings from her longitudinal study of the transition to parenthood and back to work for a sample of working-class couples. The experiences of these husbands and wives resonate with those in the Lambert study, but in this research, we see what this work is like from the perspective of married dual-earner couples dealing with the challenges of working-class hourly jobs, marriage dynamics, and child rearing.

In the fourth section of the volume, the focus turns to policymaking. The lead chapter by sociologist Jennifer Glass of Cornell University puts the United States in an international perspective and provides a sobering assessment of the social and economic forces working against the possibility of change. The three discussant chapters each take different tacks. Chai R. Feldblum, an attorney at the Georgetown University Law Center, brings insights from her role as codirector of Workplace Flexibility 2010, a campaign funded by the Alfred P. Sloan Foundation's National

Initiative on Workplace Flexibility to support the development of a comprehensive national policy on workplace flexibility. Ellen Galinsky's chapter provides examples from the many innovative work-family projects she has conducted in her role as president of the Families and Work Institute, a think tank focused on the changing nature of the work-family interface. Finally, Michael A. Smyer and Marcie Pitt-Catsouphes, codirectors of the Center on Aging and Work at Boston College, focus attention on the rapidly aging workforce in our society, one consequence of which may be a new emphasis on workplace flexibility as aging baby boomers flex their collective muscle and negotiate for more control over work in return for delaying retirement.

The final chapter is an integrative commentary by Kelly D. Davis and Katherine Stamps Mitchell, graduate students at Penn State University in Human Development and Family Studies and in Sociology, respectively. This interdisciplinary team deftly summarizes the themes woven throughout the volume and suggests next steps for research.

PART I
Workplace Policies
Opportunities to Improve Health and Well-Being

1

Work and Family Employment Policy for a Transformed Labor Force

Current Trends and Themes

Ellen Ernst Kossek and Brian Distelberg

Over three decades ago, the U.S. Department of Health, Education, and Welfare (now Health and Human Services) commissioned a report on the state of work in America, "Work and Health" (O'Toole 1973). The report identified the competing trends of growing numbers of employed mothers and prevailing societal ambivalence over whether to increase employer support of child care (Kossek 2006). At about the same time, sociologist Rosabeth Kanter (1977) noted the cultural myth of separate worlds between work and home. Her critical observation implied that the workplace continues to be designed with a storybook assumption that workers do not have families competing for energy, identity, and time.

Now we are well into the first decade of the 21st century; yet workplaces really have not changed all that much in how they are designed, even though workers and families have. What has changed dramatically is the emergence of "work and family" as a defined and mainstreamed employment issue. "Work and family" is no longer seen as an issue limited to individuals who have no choice but to combine breadwinning with caregiving, such as single working mothers in the 1950s. Most employed individuals in the United States will cope with managing caregiving for elders, children, family, or themselves at various points during their working lifetimes. The societal problem of conflicts between employment and family demands has not been remedied, and is rising in scope and intensity for virtually every demographic and occupational group (Kossek 2006). We face a growing structural mismatch between the design of jobs and career systems and a transformed workforce. In order to begin closing this gap, it is important to understand current trends and themes to facilitate the development of change strategies for employment policy innovation.

Chapter Goals

The goal of this chapter is to give an overview of current U.S. trends in employer supports for the work and family interface, upon which a future agenda for research and policy can be built. Toward this end, the following questions are explored: What does the overall approach to employer support for work and family look like in the United States? What are key work and family developments in the labor force and implications for the employment relationship? What kinds of supports are most likely to be available and by which employers? What kinds of occupations and jobs are likely to have access? What are worker experiences with these policies and practices?

This chapter addresses these questions, and in each section a summary theme is provided. The authors' review leads to an ultimate argument that the United States needs to develop more effective and wide-reaching coordinated work-family policy through both federal-state and public-private partnerships. If it does not, the failure to move our country toward some new collective cultural solutions for work-family conflicts could eventually impact U.S. economic competitiveness and the workforce and family resilience of our nation (Kossek 2006).

Employer Work and Family Supports

From an organizational perspective, "work and family" includes a three-legged stool of employer supports that shape the degree to which the workplace is designed to reduce work-family conflicts (Kossek 2006). These include (1) formal human resource policies related to work and family; (2) informal occupational and organizational culture and norms; and (3) job conditions and the structure of work, namely job design, work hours, and terms and conditions of employment. Overall, this review will show that despite increased employer interest in work and family policies, formal workplace policy support is uneven in availability and implementation. Further, linkages between these policies and job design, working conditions, and cultural norms are often ineffective. Without systematic integration between formal policies and the actual work context (e.g., job conditions and informal practices, organizational and departmental culture), policies available on paper either go underutilized or result in negative consequences for users.

To date, most policymakers have focused on employer adoption of formal human resource policies to enhance the ability to engage in paid employment while managing family demands. Such policies may include, but are not restricted to, those providing flexibility in working time, place, or load; information and resource and referrals; and employer provision of direct or subsidized services for child care, elder care, illness, or self-care. Yet adopting policies is just a first step. They will not necessarily reduce work-family conflict, if they are not supported by organizational cultural norms or if supervisors do not support their use. Worse, policies will not be helpful if they are not linked to other employment policies such as discipline for absenteeism, job security, pay and promotions, or core work hours.

Theme 1. Employer support of work and family involves a three-legged stool of formal policies, informal culture, and favorable job conditions. These areas often are not well linked in research or practice, and more study is needed on their interrelationships and connections to worker, family, and organizational effectiveness.

A Minimalist Market-Based Approach to Employer Work and Family Policy

Over recent decades the United States has gradually become more supportive of women's participation in paid employment and of fathers' involvement in early child care (Lewis and Haas 2005). Yet its overall approach to work and family policy remains much more limited and private-employer centered than other major industrialized countries. The United States is the only industrialized country that does not provide federal paid leave or public child care support for the general population (Stebbins 2001). Yet, for example, in Canada, workers can now go on leave with full or partial pay for up to a year and have job protection. In the European Union, mothers typically receive 14 weeks paid leave, with additional partial paid parental leave available if fathers share in care-giving. Provision of child care for children under 3 is considered a public service in many European Union countries where the government can be in the business of training, employing, and subsidizing child care workers (Kelly 2006).

In contrast, the United States' employment policy regarding work and family is predominately voluntary and private based. Scholars refer to this as "a minimalist market-based employer approach," where employers have wide latitude to voluntarily determine the manner and extent to which they will choose to financially support workers' family needs (Block, Berg, and Belman 2004). This policy approach emanates from leanings toward an individualistic societal culture. The United States values a limited role for government regulation, with caregiving decisions left up to the dis-cretion of individual employees and employers (Kossek 2006).

Some see this cultural proclivity and wariness of publicly funded work and family mandates as a barrier to policy innovation (Block et al. 2004). After all, the United States eventually mandated innovative civil rights protections in employment, such as the U.S. Civil Rights Act of 1964, which many countries have mirrored as a model. Why not follow this employer progressiveness for work and family policy? Yet currently, most United States employers have no policy requirements to support work and family other than the Family Medical Leave Act's (FMLA) minimal requirement that employers must provide up to 12 weeks of *unpaid leave* to care for a child, elder, or oneself in any calendar year. (It should be noted that a few states, such as Washington and California, now have mandated employer paid leave to dovetail with the FMLA.)

Even with the good intentions of the FMLA, policy gaps remain. For example, low- and middle-income workers may not be able to afford to take an unpaid leave of absence or may not have the resources to sue if employers are not supportive (Kossek 2006). Also, employers with fewer than 50 employees do not need to provide unpaid leave. They also can exempt senior employees in key jobs from leave authorization. With restrictions such as these, in practice the FMLA covers only 58 percent of workers (Cantor et al. 2000). The Employee Income Retirement Security Act of 1974 (ERISA), which regulates voluntary pensions, is another exam-ple of a policy gap. ERISA has a threshold of at least 1,000 hours per year for coverage. This prevents many part-timers from receiving pensions. Only 21 percent have pensions.[1]

For another example, take the Fair Labor Standards Act of 1938, which regulates work hours and pay. It recently was revised to redefine what is considered an exempt employee, to increase the number of exempt workers. The end result is that more workers do not have to be paid overtime for working more than a standard workweek, or granted vacations or holidays.

It should also be noted that Americans work the longest hours of any industrialized country. Dual-earner families in the United States work much longer hours than similar families in Europe.[2] In the United States, full-time work is commonly considered to be at least 40 hours per week, with full-time professional jobs often stretching to 60 hours a week or more (Williams and Calvert 2002). In some European countries, full-time work ranges from 35 to 39 hours per week, with a European Union policy limiting maximum weekly hours to 48 (Crosby, Williams, and Biernat 2004).[3] Thus, the United States' working-hour cultural norms about what is considered full- and part-time are also distinctive and have implications for work and family policy development.

Theme 2. The United States' minimalist free-market approach to work and family policy is distinctive compared to other industrialized countries. U.S. employers generally have far more latitude to determine work and family policy, few requirements to even offer policy support, and work cultures where employers often control work hours.

Surveys of Availability of Work and Family Policies

Most of the research in the literature has been on the availability of policies, and not necessarily on effectiveness. We researched the literature on the access and availability of several key policies to support work and family: flexibility policies, child and elder care, and leave for family reasons. One challenge we found was that there is no longitudinal, in-depth study of work-family policies that includes common measures of policies or workplaces.

Notwithstanding the fact that the surveys used different measures and widely different samples, we went to several sources and pulled data to identify trends from national studies (see tables 1.1, 1.2, 1.3, and 1.4). Table 1.1 shows summary data from four large national studies

Table 1.1. Workers with Access to Selected Work-Family Benefits by Worker and Establishment Characteristic, 2000, 2003, and 2006 (percent)

	Total	Employer Assistance for Child Care (2003) 2006			Adoption assistance (2000) 2006	Long-term care insurance (2000) 2006	Flexible workplace (2000) 2006
		Employer-provided funds	On-site and off-site child care	Resource and referral services			
Worker characteristics							
All	(14) 15	(3) 3	(5) 5	(10) 11	(5) 10	(7) 12	(5) 4
White-collar	(20) 20	(5) 4	(7) 7	(15) 15	(13)a 15	(16)a 17	(6)a 7
Blue-collar	(8) 8	(1) 1	(2) 2	(6) 7	(2) 7	(4) 7	(1) 1
Service	(8) 10	(2) 2	(4) 5	(5) 5	(2) 2	4	1
Full-time	(16) 16	(4) 4	(5) 6	(12) 12	(6) 12	(8) 13	(5) 5
Part-time	(8) 10	(2) 2	(4) 4	(5) 6	(2) 5	(2) 6	(2) 2
Union	(17) 19	(3) 3	(5) 6	(15) 17	(5) 14	(15) 15	(3) 3

Nonunion						
(14)	(3)	(5)	(10)	(5)	(6)	(5)
14	3	5	10	10	11	4
Average wage < $15 / hour						
(9)	(2)	(3)	(5)	(5)ᵃ	(6)ᵃ	(2)ᵃ
9	2		5	5	7	2
Average wage > $15 / hour						
(22)	(5)	(8)	(18)	(16)ᵃ	(19)ᵃ	(7)ᵃ
22	4	8	17	16	18	7
Establishment characteristics						
Goods producing						
(13)	(3)	(2)	(11)	(6)	(5)	(4)
13	2	3	10	11	10	4
Service producing						
(14)	(3)	(6)	(10)	(4)	(8)	(5)
15	3	6	11	10	12	4
1–99 workers						
(5)	(2)	(2)	(3)	(1)	(5)	(2)
5	1	2	3	10	11	10
100 workers or more						
(25)	(5)	(8)	(19)	(9)	(10)	(7)
26	5	9	19	17	20	5

Source: U.S. Bureau of Labor Statistics (2000, 2003, 2006).

a. Data from 2003 were used, due to a lack of inclusion or change in classification from 2000 to 2003 that would not allow for an appropriate comparison between the 2000 and 2006 values.

Table 1.2. Access to Selected Work-Family Benefits, 1992 and 2002 (percent)

Items in the National Study of the Changing Workforce	1992	2002
Access to elder care resources (or referral)		
Flextime	11	24
Able to set start and quit times periodically	29	43
Able to change start and quit times daily	18	23
Control over work hours		
Little control	44	39
Some control	27	25
Complete control	30	36
Supervisor support		
Supervisor is fair and does not show favoritism in responding to employees' personal and family needs.	79	82
Employees feel comfortable bring up personal and family issues.	65	73
There is an unwritten rule at my workplace that employees should not take care of family needs on company time.	36	32

Source: Bond et al. (2002).

on work-family policies based on several years of data from the Bureau of Labor Statistics' National Compensation Survey. Tables 1.2 and 1.3 summarize results over 10 years from the Families and Work Institute's National Study of the Changing Workforce (Bond et al. 2002). During the review below, we also will pull data periodically from the companion survey of the National Study of the Changing Workforce (NSCW), the National Study of Employers (Bond et al. 2005). Table 1.4 presents results from the Total Rewards Professional Census (WorldatWork 2007a). This survey reflects the view that some companies see access to work and family policies as another form of compensation in a "total rewards approach."

Comparing these surveys over the next sections, we will first discuss general trends and then turn to results for specific policies such as flexibility policies, child and elder care, and leaves. Although these studies all address the same issue (availability of employer supports for work and family), they vary significantly in their findings. Some of this variance can be accounted for by the sampling procedures used.

Table 1.3. High Levels of Employee Attitudes by Workplace Flexibility Option (percent)

	Low	Medium	High
		Flexibility	
Job satisfaction	30	49	65
Commitment to employer	24	27	39
Retention	54	62	73
		Supervisor support	
Job satisfaction	19	48	70
Commitment to employer	13	26	47
Retention	42	65	75
		Supportive work-life culture	
Job satisfaction	23	45	70
Commitment to employer	18	27	42
Retention	41	63	77

Source: Bond et al. (2002).

Table 1.4. Work-Life Policies as a Reward by Job Level (percent)

Work-life policy option	Executive/ officer/top level	Senior	Midlevel	Emerging	All
Flexible work schedule	44.4	62.4	67.0	57.4	64.3
Telecommuting/telework	33.3	39.0	38.8	24.6	37.1
Compressed workweek	11.1	10.0	17.6	17.5	15.4
Part-time schedule	5.6	9.1	14.9	13.1	13.0
Phased return from leave	5.6	6.3	10.2	8.2	8.8
Job sharing	0.0	3.3	6.2	3.8	5.0
Other/not specified	16.7	4.0	2.6	1.6	3.0
None	33.3	25.7	20.0	33.3	23.3

Source: WorldatWork (2007a).

The National Compensation Survey from the Bureau of Labor Statistics (BLS) is a representative survey of employees and employers, which uses a three-staged, stratified sample procedure. The first stage is identifying regional sectors. The second stage is identifying organizations within the sector (with an oversampling for larger organizations), and the final stage is obtaining a job list from the organization. Probability sampling is used to identify respondents.

The National Study of Employers (NSE) is conducted through the Families and Work Institute, a nonprofit organization dedicated to promoting work and family policy. It draws on a representative national sample of 1,092 for- and not-for-profit companies with 50 or more employees. The employers were selected from the Dun & Bradstreet lists. The study used stratified random sampling to ensure an equal representation of employees across companies, and to control for larger companies. Only one person, a company-identified representative, participates in the survey.

The NSCW was also conducted by the Families and Work Institute in 1992, 1997, and 2002. This is a telephone-based, random-digit-dial method survey of employees. It was structured as a regionally stratified, unclustered random probability sampling. Respondents were salaried or wage (2,810) and self-employed (694) employees.

The Total Rewards Professional Census is a web-based survey of 3,863 (mostly U.S.) respondents. Most respondents (81 percent) were members of WorldatWork, a compensation and benefit consulting association. WorldatWork members are "human resources professionals focused on attracting, motivating and retaining employees" (WorldatWork 2007a, 2). The vast majority of respondents (93 percent) had a bachelor's degree or higher. Two-thirds, or 63 percent, were women, and 60 percent had a professional designation, such as the CCP (Certified Compensation Professional). It should also be noted that WorldatWork recently merged with the Association of Work-Life Professionals.

Another reason for variation in findings is that some studies only measure actual access to specific policies, such as the BLS survey; while others, such as the NSCW, may also measure job-design characteristics, such as job control and ability to change start and stopping times without necessarily measuring linkages to formal policy. Also the NSCW measures elder care access while the BLS survey does not. In sum, these national surveys are all measuring different aspects of work and family supports.

Few surveys measure employee and employer views on access and use at the same time. Some of the surveys reported here, such as the NSE or the Total Rewards survey, sample either organizational leaders or human resource representatives on their organizations' characteristics. A drawback to this approach is that these self-reports may not represent most employees' experiences. Such approaches overmeasure policy availability on paper without assessing cultural support and informal practices that affect use.

Still another problem is that some surveys ask whether a policy is generally available to all, while others simply measure whether it exists. Also most surveys ask whether *any* employee can use a policy, while others ask whether workers *in general* can use a policy. Some surveys use a very restrictive definition of the policies, as we will illustrate below in discussing flexiplace, while others do not.

Such lack of comparability on survey data can lead to a popular cultural view that can be a little misleading on the availability of work and family policies. U.S. employer support for work and family, particularly via policies, may have been overstated in the popular media. Most studies are done at large employers, yet 80 percent of U.S. firms have fewer than 100 employees (U.S. Census Bureau 2001), which are far less likely to have formal supports. Or even when a policy is available, it doesn't mean that the workplace culture or the job demands and conditions of employment facilitate actual use.

After reading the business press or even research articles, one might assume that the mere existence of employer work-family policies leads to positive outcomes for employers and employees (Ryan and Kossek 2007). Perhaps this is partly because many articles have the problem that the studies they are reporting do not always clarify whether they are based on employer self-report of available policies. This reinforces the public relations adoption value of these policies without scrutinizing use, access, and effectiveness from workers' views. Even when articles are based on workers' responses, studies may self-report on perceived availability without reporting on users' actual experiences with policies or delve into why policies may not be used at all (Kossek, Berg, and Misra 2007).

Brief Overview of General Trends

The BLS data in table 1.1 show that only 15 percent of all workers have access to any form of child care assistance including on-site care, subsidies, or resources and referrals. This is up from 9 percent in 1999. However, this increase is somewhat misleading in the degree of support actually being provided. The most common type of assistance is simply information: resources and referrals are offered by 11 percent of firms, which do little to increase the availability of quality child care or help with the expenses. Only 5 percent of workers have actual on-site or near-site employer-sponsored child care access, with only 3 percent receiving subsidies. Telecommuting is also somewhat stagnant. Only 4 percent of all workers had access to telecommuting in 2006, down from 5 percent in 2000. So for these areas, there has been little growth in the diffusion of employer adoption of these policies over the past few years.

An exception to this trend is that increases can be seen in the diffusion of policies from 2000 to 2006 in adoption assistance, which is currently at 10 percent (up from 5 percent), and long-term care insurance (12 percent, up from 7 percent). Turning to another survey, the NSCW, (table 1.2) elder care assistance has increased over the past 10 years; nearly 24 percent of employee respondents have access compared to only 11 percent a decade ago.

Theme 3. Although national data on work and family policies is uneven and somewhat lacking, a review of available surveys over the last several years shows flat or only modest increases in employer support for family (e.g., child care assistance or flexible workplace policies, such as telecommuting). The vast majority of U.S. workers (85 percent) lack access to any formal paid work-family policies. Small increases in policy adoption are being seen in the availability of elder care, adoption assistance, and access to long-term care insurance, which are now available to about 1 in 10 workers.

What Predicts Employer Adoption

Nearly half of the companies in the NSE (47 percent) report that the main reason for implementing work-life policies and programs is to recruit and retain employees (Bond et al. 2005). One-fourth (25 percent) report productivity and job commitment as the main rationale for policy adoption, and 6 percent also mentioned other specific reasons, such as meeting organizational needs for flexible scheduling, reducing absenteeism, and lowering costs.

Although most NSE companies report implementing these programs, policies, and practices for business reasons, about two-fifths (39 percent) also claim to implement these policies and programs to help employees and their families. Another one-fifth (19 percent) gave altruistic organizational culture reasons—"we are a caring organization," "it's the right thing to do," and "we are a family organization, and it's the way we do things."

Theme 4. Half of all employers with work and family policies note recruitment and retention as the main reason for adoption.

Discussion of Trends Based on Specific Policies

Flexibility Policies

Employer Perspective of Flexibility Availability

Many of the surveys we examined did not make the definitions of flexibility as clear as would have been helpful for this review. This term has many meanings. For example, flexibility policies can range from having different start times, to working from home, to telecommuting. Thus, what we are reporting as the availability of flexibility policies can vary greatly depending on how one defines flexibility. We would like to see national standard definitions on flexible workplace policies and work and family benefits developed.

The 2006 BLS uses the most restrictive definition of the surveys we reviewed. The use of a flexible work-site location policy is the BLS's only measure of "flexible workplace." The specific definition is "arrangements permitting employees to work at home several days of the workweek. Such arrangements are especially compatible with work requiring the use of computers linking home to the central office." Such a definition suggests that the current state of access to flexible work locations has hovered between 3 and 5 percent since 1999 (U.S. Bureau of Labor Statistics 1999; 2000; 2003; 2007).

Similar to the BLS findings, only 3 percent of NSE employers allow most or all of their employees the option of working offsite occasionally (Bond et al. 2005). While the option to work from home or another location can be considered a *flexibility option,* it is not the only option available for a flexible workplace. The NSE provides additional measures for measuring worker access to flexibility. The NSE offers a different perspective due to including more basic forms of flexibility on the survey, such as vacation time and starting and quitting times, in addition to measuring the availability of alternative work schedules. In addition, the NSE survey also includes larger, more progressive employers than the BLS. NSE statistics show that over two-thirds (68 percent) of employers allow some of their employees the option to change starting and quitting times *periodically.* One-third (34 percent) of employers allow employees to change starting and quitting times on a *daily* basis. The NSE also reports one-third (34 percent) of employers allow some of their employees the option of working either at home or at another location occasionally, with 31 percent providing this option on a regular basis. It is also important to assess frequency of access. For example, NSE reports that 33 percent offer a periodic change in schedule, while 13 percent offer a daily change in schedule to all of their employees. This availability of the ability to change schedules is stagnant. It has not significantly increased in prevalence since 1998.

Regarding compressed workweeks, the NSE reports that 39 percent of employers allow some of their employees to work a compressed workweek for a part of the year, and 39 percent allow some employees to work a compressed workweek occasionally. Again, very few employers offer this option to all of their employees. Three percent allow all employees to work a compressed workweek occasionally.

There are also many other options presented by employers that may be considered a form of flexibility but are often left out of national studies on flexibility. The NSE has a number of interesting measures. It reports that employers offer the following forms of flexibility to *most or all* of their employees:

- Over half (53 percent) allow employees to have control over when they take breaks.
- Over one-fourth (28 percent) offer a phased retirement.
- More than one-quarter (28 percent) offer a sabbatical of six months or more with a return to a comparable job.
- Over one-fifth (21 percent) offer employees the ability to move from full-time to part-time and back again while remaining in the same position or level.
- One-fifth (20 percent) give employees control over which shifts they work.
- Fourteen percent offer control over paid and unpaid overtime hours.
- Thirteen percent allow job sharing.
- Ten percent work a compressed workweek for at least part of the year.

We appreciate the wording on the NSE survey, which focuses on policies being available to most or all workers as a measure of the extent of policy availability across the workforce. For nearly all flexibility categories, significant increases in access to flexibility were shown over a 10-year period.

Theme 5. We often lack common definitions and standards of employer policies and practices, which makes measurement of availability on a national level difficult. Flexibility, in particular, needs much more fine-grained measurement ranging from basic forms, such as control over breaks, to teleworking.

Employee Perspective on Flexibility Availability

Below are data from two of the surveys, highlighting several other trends found when employee surveys are added to the review. One trend is that there is often a gap between what employers say and what employees say when it comes to work and family policy access. Another is that samples of workers in occupations such as human resources (HR) may "bias report" much higher access to flexibility forms than surveys based on the general population.

For example, the report "Telework Trendlines for 2006" defines telework as "perform[ing] all of one's work from any remote location—either for an outside employer or through self-employment" (WorldatWork 2007b, 1). The definition implies access to resources to do this work, such as computers and the Internet.

Based on this survey definition, nearly half (44.8 percent) of HR experts who are members of WorldatWork report some use of telework (WorldatWork 2007a, b). It is estimated that the total number of employees allowed to work at least one day a month from home jumped from 9.9 million in 2005 to 12.4 million in 2006 (WorldatWork 2007b). This represents a 25 percent increase in 2006, which was preceded by a 63 percent increase from 2004 to 2005.

Further, this study found that when we include contracted and self-employed individuals together with employees working full- or part-time, the percentage of individuals without access to telework options has decreased 24 percent since 2005. The number of individuals who use a telework option almost every day is currently estimated at 14.7 percent, which is an increase of 20 percent since 2005 (WorldatWork 2007b). Only

10.3 percent of employees surveyed by WorldatWork do not use telework options at all. The percentages stated here do not even take into account those employees who do work from home as a spillover effect associated with increased technology availability. For example, more than one-third of all employees from the NSCW use computers to check work e-mails or to do work-related tasks outside of what they consider "work hours" (Bond et al. 2002).

Based on these surveys, employees are reporting much higher use of teleworking than the employer surveys. We are unsure if this is because employees are informally logging into e-mail after hours and taking work home, or if many supervisors are permitting this but HR departments do not formally know the actual extent of use. It is also difficult to ascertain whether telework is occurring as a part of job demands that is employer driven or whether employees are working in this way by choice.

A second example of a gap between employee and employer views is that employees are much less likely than employers to believe they can change starting and quitting times. For example, although 68 percent of employers report in NSE that employees have the option to change starting and quitting times periodically, only 42 percent of workers believe they can. While these are different samples, it is difficult to reconcile a finding in which 68 percent of employers say they have this specific flexibility policy and only 42 percent of employees say they can use it.

Theme 6. Employers tend to report higher access to flexibility, such as control over starting and stopping times, than employees. An exception may be use of e-mail and the Internet while not on the job, but it is unclear if this is by worker "choice" or is employer driven.

Demographics Associated with Availability and Access

Access to flexibility varied systematically by organizational size, occupation, and other demographics. As the summary of BLS survey data shows in table 1.1, workplaces with fewer than 100 employees offer significantly better access to flexibility options when compared to organizations that employ more than 100 people. The percentage of these smaller organizations that offer flexibility options has moved from 2 percent in 2003 to 10 percent in 2006, whereas larger organizations have dropped access from 7 percent in 2003 to 5 percent in 2006. Surprisingly, there were no significant differences between employers in goods-producing or service industries in whether they provided telecommuting.

BLS data also showed that white-collar workers are far more likely than blue-collar or even service workers to have access to flexibility. For example, 7 percent of all white-collar workers have access to telecommuting compared to only 1 percent of blue-collar workers. Full-time employees and employees who earn more than $15 an hour are more than two or three times as likely to have access to a flexible workplace. Union workers are more likely to have child care benefits than nonunion workers (19 percent compared to 14 percent).

Employee hierarchical status is also related to flexibility access. Turning to table 1.4, the Total Rewards Professional Census shows a curvilinear relationship. Executive and entry-level positions have the least access to flexibility options and mid- and senior-level employers fair better (WorldatWork 2007a). For example, top-level executives are more likely to report no access to flexibility options (33.3 percent) when compared to senior-level (25.7 percent) and midlevel (20.0 percent) employees. Midlevel employees seem to have the greatest access to flexibility options such as the compressed workweek (17.6 percent) job sharing (6.2 percent), and part-time work (14.9 percent) compared to lower levels. Then availability downshifts again at the senior or top executive levels, suggesting it is more difficult to have flexibility access at these higher levels. For telecommuting, only a quarter of new hires have access compared to more than one-third of mid- and senior-level employees. This suggests employers are more likely to grant telecommuting access to employees with a proven track record.

Theme 7. Access to flexibility systematically varies depending on who you work for and the nature of your job and occupation or level. For example, small employers appear to be more willing to give access to flexible workplace than larger firms. Midlevel employees have more flexibility access than many other levels. Full-time workers, white-collar workers, and workers earning more than $15 an hour have greater flexibility access than comparison groups.

Employer Benefits of Providing Flexibility

The research on the use of flexibility policies, while at least 30 years old, is still unclear about the benefits and costs of policies such as employee control over hours worked, compressed workweeks, and telecommuting.

Whole books could be written on each of these topics. Therefore, this section will highlight only a few broad costs and benefits for employees with the assumption that much more can be said about this topic.

First, there seem to be some benefits to organizations for providing flexibility access. As table 1.3 shows, the NSCW did find that employees with more access to flexibility policies had higher levels of job satisfaction (Bond et al. 2002). Specifically, less than one-third (30 percent) of employees who reported low levels of flexibility also reported a high level of job satisfaction. In contrast, two-thirds (65 percent) of employees who reported high levels of flexibility reported high levels of job satisfaction. Employees with higher levels of flexibility also had higher commitment to their employers and were less likely to turn over than those with lower access to flexibility.

A meta-analysis found similar results. The use of flexible schedules was positively associated with job satisfaction (Baltes et al. 1999). The literature also suggests that flexible policies, such as compressed workweeks and flexible start and stop times, are often used to supplement, or as a tradeoff for, higher wages (Baughman, DiNardi, and Holtz-Eakin 2003). Thus, flexibility policies can be used not only for recruitment, but also as a way for employers to reduce overhead costs. Access to flexibility is significantly related to reduced absenteeism (Dalton and Mesch 1990) and increased retention (Pavalko and Henderson 2006), and can have a positive effect on productivity such as willingness to help out at work (Eaton 2003).

The costs and benefits of offering flexibility clearly require more research focusing on the employee and family side of the equation. The NSCW found that flexibility is associated with lower levels of interference between job and family (Bond et al. 2002). Only 19 percent of employees with low access to flexibility policies report no interference, compared to 32 percent of employees with high access to flexibility policies reporting no interference. The study also found flexibility access was associated with lower negative spillover from job to home, lower levels of mental health problems, and overall higher levels of life satisfaction.

More research needs to be done on flexibility in terms of effects in the direction of the family, as results have been mixed. For example, Christensen and Staines (1990) found that flextime did not increase employees' satisfaction with their family lives. Similarly, Baltes and colleagues' 1999 review found that flexibility access did not necessarily reduce work-family conflict for professionals. Professionals have strong occupational cultures that demand working as long as needed to get the job done, or they already have some autonomy built into their jobs, making the policies irrelevant. Clark (2000) suggests that flextime may result in porous borders between work and home that allow work to spill into the home more than home spills into work, which could explain the lack of improvement in satisfaction.

Other important effects of the outcomes of flextime for employees and family life need to be studied further. These include the distribution of household work and caretaking responsibilities within families (Rau 2003). One recent study has taken a step in this direction. Noonan, Estes, and Glass (2007) found that the use of flexibility policies has a *net* effect. This means that mothers who work part-time spend more time in domestic labor, while their husbands spend less. Similarly, mothers who telecommuted spent more time in child care tasks. But women who used flextime, which changed only starting and stopping times, did fewer household tasks than their spouses. Thus, more research is needed on the costs and benefits of specific types of flexibility and other work-family policies with respect to family effectiveness.

One way to consider the benefit of flexibility policies is through the Alternative Work Schedules Act (AWSA, formally known as the Federal Employees Flexible and Compressed Work Schedules Act), which is a federal law that applies to all employees of federal agencies (U.S. Office of Personnel Management 2007). This allows federal agency employees the opportunity to use flexible or compressed work schedules as long as the use of these policies does not interfere with efficient operations of the organization. This law is an older sibling of the FMLA. Many governmental reports over the last decades have documented many beneficial aspects of the AWSA for employees and their families. These benefits include decreased commuter stress, accommodation of religious observations, flexibility to attend to children's needs and medical appointments, improved worker morale, increased productivity, increased ability to recruit and retain high-quality employees, diversity in the workforce, and increased hours of operation (Gore 1997; U.S. General Accounting Office 1994, 2001; U.S. Office of Personnel Management 2003).

AWSA's success can be seen as a road map for implementing controversial policies. The history of this legislation shows the importance of family advocacy, time, persistent effort, and links to boarder support (Liechty and Anderson 2007). Liechty and Anderson outline the history of this legislation from its beginning as an energy conservation act to decrease the traffic and the gasoline used in downtown Washington, D.C., to a family-friendly advocacy act. Arguments that highlighted AWSA's broad and systemic benefits won it support from conservationists as well as work-life advocates.

Theme 8. Demonstrating broad and systemic benefits of providing increased access to work and family policies, such as flexibility, is more likely to result in policy adoption.

Child Care Assistance

Employer Perspective on Availability

Previously noted was the fact that the BLS reports that 15 percent of employers offer some form of assistance for child care, up from 9 percent in 1999. This 15 percent is divided into three categorizes, with most of the support given in terms of information for resources or referrals (11 percent) (U.S. Bureau of Labor Statistics 2006). Only 3 percent of employers actually provide funds to employees for child care, and 5 percent provide either on-site or off-site child care.

Turning to the NSE, we find that employers are more likely to provide low- or no-cost child care options (Bond et al. 2005). This includes dependent care assistance plans (45 percent), which are programs for employees to pay into with pretax dollars, or child care resources and referrals (34 percent). Among employers with 50 or more employees, only 7 percent provide child care at or near the worksite.

Employee Perspective on Availability

The NSCW reports that there has been little change in employee perceptions of access to child care policies since 1992 (Bond et al. 2002). Currently, employees with children under 13 years of age (and, therefore, most likely to know about child care services) report that only 10 percent of employers offer any child care services. In 2002, only 0.3 percent of parents with preschool-age children reported using an employer-sponsored or -operated child care center as their main arrangement for their youngest preschool children while at work.

Demographics Associated with Availability and Access

According to the NSE, large employers are significantly more likely to offer child care options. They are significantly more likely to offer child care resources and referrals, dependent care assistance plans, and on- or near-site child care services (Bond et al. 2005). Only the latter option (on- or near-site child care) has significant direct costs for employers, so it might be expected to be more common among large employers that have greater resources and enough employee demand to justify an investment in on- or near-site child care. There are few differences between large and small employers in the likelihood of offering financial assistance for child care and vacation child care for school-age children, the incidence of which is very low (Bond et al. 2005). According to the BLS, employees who are white-collar, full-time workers and make more than $15 an hour are more likely to have access to any child care option (U.S. Bureau of Labor Statistics 2006).

Employer Benefits of Child Care Assistance

Baughman and her coauthors (2003) found that child care assistance does decrease turnover. The study also found that these programs were traded off for the cost of higher wages for entry-level workers. Studies also show child care increases retention (Lee 2004) and women's workforce attachment (Henry, Werschkul, and Rao 2003). Some studies based on over 40 years of studies found that child care programs with preschool services benefit the larger society by reducing crime rates and by increasing education, housing quality, and earnings of children in these programs versus those not in these programs (Schweinhart 2004).

Theme 9. Employer interest in increasing direct or financial support of child care has not risen substantially in recent years. Most activity has been in the area of information and referral.

Elder Care

Elder care can range from providing paid assistance to employees who are caring for elderly family members to providing access to information about resources. Elder care leave for some family members (e.g., in-laws) is not required by FMLA.

Employer Perspective on Availability

According to the NSE, a vast majority (79 percent) of employers say that they provide paid or unpaid time off for employees to provide elder care without jeopardizing their jobs (Bond et al. 2005). Another 29 percent provide employees with information about elder care services. Only 6 percent provide direct financial support for local elder care programs. Employers in 2005 were more likely (34 percent) to report that they offered elder care resource and referral services than employers in 1998 (23 percent). While unpaid leave for elder care is the norm, Pavalko and Henderson (2006) found that unpaid leave does have a large positive effect on the psychological well-being of employees with elder care needs.

Employee Perspective

According to the NSCW, 35 percent of employees have provided "special attention or care for a relative or in-law 65 years old or older, helping them with things that were difficult or impossible for them to do themselves." This study found that 13 percent of all employees take time off to care for a relative over the age of 65. In stark contrast to the employer survey, only 24 percent of those employees report any form of elder care resources at work, which is up from 11 percent in 1992.

Demographics Associated with Availability and Access

Based on the NSE, small and large employers are equally likely (81 percent) to allow employees time off to provide elder care without jeopardizing their jobs (Bond et al. 2005). Similar to the trend for the provision of child care resource and referral services, small employers are significantly less likely (25 percent) than large employers (50 percent) to provide these services. Fewer employers in general provide information about elder care (29 percent) than child care (34 percent). Perhaps this trend is because sometimes the same community agencies or vendors provide both child care and elder care resource and referral services. However, small employers may not have the additional staff to add this service or even be aware of the existence of such community services or government services (such as area agencies on aging). Perhaps they are also less likely to use national vendors to purchase these services as a package.

Theme 10. There is a perceptual gap between employees and employers regarding the availability of elder care, with employers reporting much higher availability than employees.

Maternity Leave

Employer Perspective on Availability

We have noted that the United States is unusual because the government does not either pay employees itself or require employers to pay workers while they are on leave (Waldfogel 1998, Williams and Calvert 2002). As a result, fewer than half of all employed women received any paid leave during the first 12 weeks of their children's lives and only 7 percent of employers offered any paid paternity leave (U.S. Office of Personnel Management 2001). The issue of paid or unpaid leave policies has a direct tie to the FMLA (U.S. Department of Labor 1993). Studies of employment leave often reflect the guidelines of this law.

In 2006, the U.S. Department of Labor conducted an inductive study of the progress of this federal policy. The result was a large ($N = 15,000$) qualitative study of employer and employee experience of the FMLA (U.S. Department of Labor 2007). Responses substantiated that many employees and employers are not having noteworthy FMLA-related problems. According to this study, "the FMLA is working as intended . . . the FMLA has succeeded in allowing working parents to take leave for birth or adoption of a child, and in allowing employees to care for family members with serious health conditions." However, employers voiced concern about their ability to manage business operations and attendance-control issues, particularly when unscheduled, intermittent leave is needed for *chronic* health conditions.

It appears that some gaps still remain in implementation. The NSE survey reports 22 percent of organizations offer less than 12 weeks of unpaid leave for maternity leave, 29 percent for paternity leave, 22 percent for adoption or foster care leave, and 21 percent to care for a child with a serious illness (Bond et al. 2005). Interestingly, 30 percent of organizations that have between 50 and 99 employees at one location (and, therefore, fall under the FMLA), do not offer the federally mandated 12 weeks of leave. Few organizations go above and beyond the FMLA by offering more than 12 weeks of leave, even if unpaid, for a family- or medical-related case. Only 29 percent do so for maternity leave, 19 percent for paternity leave, 19 percent for adoption or foster care, and 19 percent for care of a seriously ill child.

There has been one significant change in the use of employment leave since 1998. The average maximum job-guaranteed leave for a man following the birth of his child has increased from 13.1 weeks in 1998 to 14.5 weeks in 2005. Yet some studies show many fathers may not take parental leave because their right to use the policy has not been communicated clearly (Powell 1999).

Other issues that are not directly tied to the FMLA but fall under the leave practices are important to look at, also. For example the NSE found that two-thirds (67 percent) of employers allow employees a gradual return to work after childbirth or adoption, 60 percent offer time off for important personal and family needs without loss of pay, 57 percent offer extended career breaks for caregiving or other family or personal responsibilities, and 55 percent take time for education and training to improve skills.

It is important to note that, according to the NSE, nearly half (46 percent) of employers offer some form of replacement pay for maternity leave. Replacement pay is pay that does not count against vacation or sick leave. Yet only 13 percent provided replacement pay for paternity leave. Also, very few (7 percent) employers offer replacement pay for women taking leave following maternity leave for maternity-related disabilities (Bond et al. 2005). Over half of employers (51 percent) report providing replacement pay for a few days to care for a mildly ill child. While the prevalence of replacement pay has remained unchanged since 1998, the number of individuals who receive their full pay during a period of maternity-related leave has decreased from 27 percent in 1998 to 18 percent in 2005. The authors of this study associate this decrease to the increasing cost of health care, as the majority of replacement pay reported by employers comes from a general temporary disability insurance plan (79 percent).

Employee Perspective of Availability

According to the National Compensation Survey (U.S. Bureau of Labor Statistics 2006), only 8 percent of employees report that they receive some form of paid family leave. Over half (57 percent) report availability of paid sick leave, and over three-fourths (77 percent) report paid vacations. Additionally, half (50 percent) receive paid leave for childbirth, 43 percent for adoption or foster care, and 55 percent for the care of a family member with a serious health condition (U.S. Bureau of Labor Statistics 2000).

Many employees try to align their paid leave, if available, with use of FMLA so they are able to have some financial support, even if partial, during leaves. According to the 2006 U.S. Department of Labor Request for Information qualitative study (U.S. Bureau of Labor Statistics 2007), most employees are not having noteworthy FMLA-related problems. However, the report did identify some key areas for future study. Some employees expressed a desire for a greater leave entitlement. Secondly, it appears that the single most serious area of friction between employers and employees seeking the use of FMLA is the prevalence with which unscheduled intermittent FMLA leave would be taken in certain workplaces or work settings by individuals, such as those with chronic health conditions. These "certain" workplaces include work settings where business operations have a highly time-sensitive component, for example, delivery, transportation, transit, telecommunication, health care, assembly-line manufacturing, and public safety sectors.

The study also found a lack of education for employees regarding their rights in the FMLA (U.S. Bureau of Labor Statistics 2007). Many employees (even employees that possessed a general awareness of the FMLA) did not know how the FMLA applied to their situation.

These findings point to the need for informal practices fostering greater employer support of FMLA. Only 27 percent of employers reported to the NSE that supervisors make a real and ongoing effort to inform employees about assistance for balancing work and family (Bond et al. 2005). It is likely that employees are left to research the FMLA on their own and advocate for their rights based on information available from the government. This situation is further substantiated by the 30 percent of employers in noncompliance of the FMLA (Bond et al. 2005) and the overall confusion of employee rights found in the Request for Information on the FMLA (U.S. Bureau of Labor Statistics 2007). The gap between employee access and availability is supported by a study by Baum (2006). The study found that while the FMLA does not have an effect on wages and leave-taking practices of employees, it does increase the portion of employers offering family leave. This suggests that while FMLA has changed employers' policies, many employees may not be taking advantage of leave policies.

Finally, many employees express a desire to expand the FMLA beyond its current boundaries (U.S. Department of Labor 2007). The most frequently addressed expansions include paid time off, more time off, coverage of additional family members, lowering the 50-employee threshold, and increasing the 75-mile radius test for defining employer size. These revisions have also been suggested by Baum (2006).

Demographics Associated with Availability and Access

The most important trends for the availability of leaves in general, whether FMLA-related or not, are the difference between full- and part-time employment and whether one works for a small or large employer. According to the BLS statistics in table 1.1, part-time employees have significantly less access to all forms of leave, including family leave. Employees who work for larger employers are also significantly more likely to have access than those who work for small firms. This variation could be partly tied to the FMLA requirement that only organizations with more than 50 employees must comply (U.S. Department of Labor 1993). Although larger organizations are more likely to offer leave, the rate of replacement pay for that leave is very similar in small organizations (6 percent) and larger organizations (10 percent) (U.S. Bureau of Labor Statistics 2006).

Overall, the rate of replacement pay for leave is low regardless of demographics. White-collar workers report the highest levels of access to paid (11 percent) and unpaid (86 percent) family leave (U.S. Bureau of Labor Statistics 2006). Geography also matters. Employees in metropolitan areas are more likely to have access to paid leave than those in nonmetropolitan areas. Even the state in which the worker lives accounts for a great deal of the variance in access to paid leave. Currently, only five states offer short-term disability programs for maternity leave (California, New Jersey, Rhode Island, Hawaii, and New York) (Grant, Hatcher, and Patel 2005). Employees in these states have better access to paid leave options. The National Partnership for Women and Families has issued a report card for every state (Grant et al. 2005). The report has given 19 states a failing grade on parental leave policies, as there is generally less employee access to leaves in these states.

Employer Benefits

The gold standard for leaves has been California's passage of the Unemployment Insurance Code in 2002. The California law amends the State Disability Insurance Program to pay for up to six weeks of wage replacement (55 percent of salary up to $882 in 2007) to bond with a new child or to care for a seriously ill family member. The program is entirely funded by contributions from employees. This costs the employer very little, as this program is funded between the employee and the state. Other states such as Washington, New Jersey, and Massachusetts are examining this policy as well (Gault and Lovell 2006).

Research suggests maternity leaves offer an alternative to quitting and, thereby, reduce turnover (Glass and Riley 1998; Waldfogel 1998). An economic analysis of potential consequences of introducing paid family leave in California predicts reduction in turnover costs, benefiting employers (Dube and Kaplan 2002; U.S. Department of Labor 1996). Some studies go as far as to note that fathers on parental leave may learn skills that make them better managers (Haas 2003; Haas, Allard, and Hwang 2002).

Regarding the effects of leave policies on health and well-being of family members, some studies conclude that taking leaves benefits the health of mothers and newborn children (Hyde et al. 1996; Smolensky and Gootman 2003). A few studies have shown that the availability of leave policies increases the father's involvement in household and child care duties (Heymann 2002; Seward, Yeatts, and Zottarelli 2002). The later may not necessarily benefit employers in the short term, but may have long-term health cost and mental health benefits.

Theme 11. More research is needed to untangle the interaction between the FMLA and employee access to employer policies on paid and unpaid family leave.

Informal Support: Supervisor Practice and Cultures Regarding Ideal Workers

Having addressed policies, we need to briefly examine informal supports at the workplace for policies. Eaton (2003) defined informal supports as "flexible policies that are not official and not written down but are still available to some employees even on a discretionary basis." This is often a direct result of supervisor support. We expand her definition by specifically focusing on any work-life action, behavioral or cultural norms, values, and rules that are not official policies but work directly to affect the work-life domain.

Considerable research has indicated that supervisor support plays a key role in the experience of work-family conflict (Allen 2001; Barrah et al. 2004; Casper and Buffardi 2004; Casper et al. 2004; McManus et al. 2002; O'Driscoll et al. 2003). Supervisors are the gatekeepers to effective implementation of work and family policies. Supervisors (1) often have final approval as to whether employees can use an optional work-life policy such as reduced work load, telework, and flextime; (2) influence whether employees are cross-trained and able to back each other during absences or periods of heavy workload; (3) affect whether policies are well publicized and well understood; and (4) lead in the creation of norms supporting use of existing policies (Hopkins 2005). A supervisor's support of an employee's efforts to manage multiple roles may be directly related to whether a policy helps reduce strain (see Hopkins 2005 for a review). The following section will review what we know about the effects of supervisor support and related work-culture support taken from large national studies.

Supervisor Support

Supervisor support can be defined as the supervisor's willingness or accessibility in adapting the organizational structure and policies to fit the unique demands of employees' lives outside of their employment. Research consistently shows that supervisor support is linked to reduced work-family conflict (O'Driscoll et al. 2003; Thomas and Ganster 1995). Reviews show that many studies have found that when employees have supervisors who support work-family balance, job satisfaction is higher and work-family conflict is lower (Kossek and Ozeki 1999; Thomas and Ganster 1995). Eaton (2003) found that work-family policies affected organizational commitment, but only to the extent that employees felt free to use them without negative consequences to their work lives (e.g., damage to career-development opportunities or workplace relations). Any assessment of the effectiveness of policies must measure how proactive a supervisor is in providing resources or advice to employees regarding these policies.

Employer Perspective on Availability

The NSE (Bond et al. 2005) reports that a majority (63 percent) of employers believe supervisors are supportive of employees with family needs. A majority (53 percent) also encourage employees to openly discuss their needs for flexibility with their supervisors and treat men and women equally in regards to flexibility (76 percent). Two-thirds (62 percent) of employers believe that their supervisors assess requests for flexible work arrangements equitably.

Yet, only one-fourth (27 percent) of employers report that their supervisors or organizations make a real and ongoing effort to inform employees of available assistance for managing work and family responsibilities. Less than half (46 percent) of employers believe the importance of working and managing flexibly is clearly communicated throughout the organization.

Employee Perspective on Supervisor Support

We noted some discrepancies between perceived supervisor support by employees and employers. Comparing the NSE (Bond et al. 2005), which surveys employers, and the NSCW (Bond et al. 2002), which surveys employees directly, we found some perceptual gaps. From the NSE, only 9 percent of company representatives felt that the use of flexible time and leave policies jeopardizes employees' opportunities for advancement. In contrast, based on the NSCW, 39 percent of employees felt somewhat or strongly that using flexible schedules and taking time off for family reasons would impede their job advancement. Although the questions are not exactly identical in the two surveys, they are substantively the same, and the difference between employers' and employees' views is large enough to suggest that there is a perceptual gap.

The researchers behind the NSE (Bond et al. 2005), saw the discrepancy between supervisor support in the NSE and the NSCW (Bond et al. 2002), and decided to go back to the NSCW and pull apart some demographic issues that may help explain the discrepancy. What they found was that employees in smaller organizations were significantly more likely to report the presence of both a supportive supervisor and a supportive work-life culture (Bond et al. 2005).

Employer Benefits

Based on the NSCW, employees who report having a supportive supervisor also report much higher levels of job satisfaction and higher levels of loyalty, which was defined as a willingness to work harder than required to help their employers succeed (Bond et al. 2002). Supervisor support was related to reduced interference between job and family. For example, one-fifth (20 percent) of employees with lower supervisor support had no interference between job and family, while 37 percent of employees with higher supervisor support reported no interference between job and family. Higher supervisor support was also significantly related to fewer mental health problems, reduced negative spillover from job to home, and higher levels of general life satisfaction. These results were also mirrored in measures of having a positive work-life culture, which supervisors help shape. Employees who report a highly supportive culture in their organizations also report higher levels of job satisfaction, commitment, and retention; lower levels of mental health problems; less interference between job and family; less spillover from job to home; and higher levels of general life satisfaction.

Cultural Images of Ideal Workers: Growing Gender and Societal Tensions

A 2007 article by Joan C. Williams in the *American Prospect* reads, "Women aren't forsaking careers for domestic life. The ground rules just make it impossible to have both."[4] Williams argues that the U.S. labor force has an outdated image of the *ideal worker*. The ideal worker has been defined as a worker "who starts to work in early adulthood and works full time and full force for 40 years straight, taking no time off for childbearing and child rearing" (Crosby et al. 2004). Good jobs are still defined around an ideal worker who tends to be male, in Williams's view, pointing to gender inequity. Workplace ideals are still defined around men's bodies and life patterns, since men need no time off for childbirth and American women still do 70 to 80 percent of the child rearing.[5]

Williams sees many policy solutions as not being culturally supported. "Part-time work is often seen as part committed and sometimes as part competent" (Williams and Calvert 2002). The most desirable jobs are not part-time, essentially keeping mothers who are involved in child rearing from access. Defining workplace ideals in such a way, in Williams's view, is tantamount to sex discrimination. Crosby and her coauthors (2004, 678) argue, "Is it not discriminatory, for example, to refuse benefits to part-time workers while giving them to full-time workers? What can justify a refusal to prorate benefits? Isn't this form of economic disenfranchisement sex discriminatory?"

Bianchi (2000) reports that most mothers in the United States (95 percent) work less than the long workweek required in higher-paying jobs. Among mothers age 25 to 44, 95 percent work less than 50 hours a week year round (Bianchi 2000). Katha Pollitt reports that in the United States, most mothers who work outside the home do so for an average of 30 to 35 hours per week.[6] The discrepancy between their hours and the 40-plus hours required by most professional jobs demonstrates the urgent need for more jobs in the 30 to 35 hours per week range. Kossek and Lee (2005) have identified many employer benefits from offering reduced or customized workloads as a retention tool for high-performing employees, but to date these arrangements are not widely available at all levels. Increased availability of such jobs could result in increased maternal well-being, since employment has been shown to benefit women's health and well-being (Barnett and Rivers 1996), but not if long hours and inflexibility about when and where those hours are worked reduce employee control over work (Thomas and Ganster 1995).

Some argue that mothers' disadvantaged workplace position is due to the fact some mothers opt out for the good of their families.[7] Echoing Williams's statistics noted above, other studies report women still do 65 to 80 percent of child care (Sayer 2001), an average of 3.5 hours of child care per workday compared with 2.7 hours per workday for fathers (Bond et al. 2002). Women also conduct more than 70 percent of elder care (National Alliance for Caregiving and AARP 2004).

Men are not free from gender discrimination from their use of work and family policies. Almer, Cohen, and Single (2004) conducted a study that originally was focused on the interaction effect between gender and the use of family policies. The researchers found that when senior staffers read vignettes about employees with workplace flexibility, they judged fathers using flexible work arrangements to have less commitment to their organizations and be more likely to leave the organizations than mothers with flexible work arrangements. We still need to build support for both men and women to have access to flexibility policies.

Davis, Crouter, and McHale (2006) found that mothers who worked irregular shifts reported more intimacy with adolescents, while fathers who worked the same shifts knew less about their adolescent children. Maume (2006) found that men equate the use of vacation as a negative factor in career success. In contrast, mothers equate unused vacation time as a detriment to their family roles. The most significant predictor of unused vacation time was commitment to coworkers and commitment to organization.

Theme 12. Supervisory and societal cultures regarding ideal workers continue to be barriers to policy use and create gender differences in policy experiences.

Closing and a Future Agenda

This chapter has demonstrated the following main themes:

- Compared to other industrialized countries, the United States is unique in providing very limited public supports for the overall labor forces' work and family demands (Kossek 2006).

- Many workers lack access to policies and many improvements can be made in implementation.
- Access to policies systematically varies by employer and worker characteristics.
- Employee views of access are systematically lower compared to views of employers.

We should avoid "one size fits all" solutions. Policy workplace solutions and research need to not only be broad-brushed and comprehensive, but also implemented in ways that can be customized to empower and meet the special needs of individuals and particular labor market sectors. Perhaps the first step is to broaden the U.S. work-family policy agenda.

Broaden Policy Discourse to Reconnect with a Transforming Workforce

Kossek (2005) notes that many organizations, early in developing work and family polices, define "work-family" very narrowly, usually starting out by adopting policies focused on the most visible family needs such as parental roles. Over time, as employers become more experienced, they typically widen the range of policies to support participation in many nonwork roles (e.g., elder care, community service, school-age children's extracurricular activities and supervision, personal health care and fitness, the military, political and religious activities, domestic partnerships, and household care).

Some of the most effective companies define work and family issues broadly, as this helps them develop a performance, rather than a police, culture on monitoring access to flexibility and other supports. A greater focus on results and equality of access is more likely to ensue when employers define work and family broadly to support many key nonwork roles. We see public policy in some ways being stifled by this similar narrow view of work and family.

Naomi Gerstel, Dan Clawson, and Robert Zussman echo this sentiment for a broader discourse on what is considered a "work and family issue":

> The relatively little attention that policymakers and researchers have given to diverse family forms and class issues has had a significant effect on both families and workplaces. . . . This type of restrictive focus severely limits the effectiveness of policy and contributes to the continued rejection of underrepresented and diverse family forms. . . . Higher minimum wage is family policy. Immigration policy, wel-

fare policy, and health benefits are family policy, but people don't talk about them that way. . . . We need to reshape public discourse . . . Instead of advocating minor reforms, which often serve employers more than employees, researchers need to broaden the discussion. We need to look at job hours, living wage, family leave, and elder care as work-family issues. We need to think more broadly about what is family and what families need and ask broader questions.[8]

And, indeed, as table 1.5 shows, the problem of effectively managing breadwinning with caregiving has become a critical concern that addresses many broad employment issues across the entire U.S. workforce. Kossek (2006) notes that the workforce has transformed such that many of its segments are simultaneously facing cross-cutting yet distinct issues. Common workforce issues include (1) the cultural mainstreaming of work-family tensions for a majority of workers, (2) growing financial costs of child and elder caregiving, (3) perceptions of time shortages and schedule conflict, (4) increasing workloads on the job and at home, and (5) blurring boundaries between work and nonwork life. Distinctive issues focused on specific labor market segments are (1) the degree to which workers experience control over work hours and schedules, (2) disparities in access to work-family supports, and (3) the widening effects of these discrepancies on physical and mental health, employment-market readiness and participation, and effectiveness on and off the job.

Theme 13. The discourse and framing of U.S. work and family research and policy generally have been narrow and overly simplified. Yet most labor market segments are simultaneously facing complex issues requiring both cross-cutting and customized solutions. This disconnect has generally resulted in policy that often is neither broad enough to serve mainstream worker issues, nor tailored enough to address the needs of unique workforce segments.

Improve Policy Research

Many studies focused on these policies have the limitation that they wrap numerous policies into one variable or do not use common definitions, fail to use group randomization, or use misleading simplistic methods that do not account for complex relationships in policy implementation. Weak research hurts policy innovation and the study of the costs and benefits of new initiatives.

Another method that is important to consider is the use of structural models, or structural equation modeling (SEM). By using SEM, Frye and

Table 1.5.   Trends in Labor Force Transformation

Trend	Supporting statistics
Transformation of families' economic configuration	The dual-earner family is now the modal American family. Employment status of parents with children under 18: • two parent, dual earner (41%) • single mother, employed (16%) • two parent, husband sole earner (21%) • unemployed, single mother (7%) • single father, employed (5%) • two parent, mother sole earner (4%) • unemployed, two parent (4%) • unemployed, single father (1%) (CPS, Bianchi, and Raley 2005)
Growth in nontraditional families	A majority of adults will cohabit with another adult at some time. One-third of all births now occur outside of marriage. Before age 18, 40% of children will live in a cohabiting family and 50% of children will live in a single-parent household, most with their mothers (Cohen 2002). 15% of the workforce 40–65 years old are "sandwich generation" employees, who must manage care for both aging parents and financially dependent children or grandchildren (Ingersoll-Dayton, Neal, and Hammer 2001; Nichols and Junk 1997).
Increase in employee caregiving responsibilities	80% of U.S. wage and salaried workers live with family members and have immediate day-to-day family responsibilities when away from the workplace (Bond et al. 2002). 43% of workers report they have a child under 18 living at home at least half the year. 35% had significant elder care demands in the past year (reported by equal proportions of men and women) (Bond et al. 2002).

Table 1.5. *(Continued)*

Trend	Supporting statistics
Population decline in replacement workers: from pyramids to pillars	One of the fastest growing U.S. population segments is over 55 years old; a workforce shortage is predicted as baby boomers are reaching retirement. A 2003 SHRM report indicates that over the 10 years leading up to 2010, the number of workers 25–54 will increase 5%, and the number of workers over 55 will increase 46.6%; U.S. fertility rates declined to 1.9 children in 2003 compared with 3.1 in 1976 (Farnsworth Riche 2006).
Rise in work hours, work loads, work-family conflicts, and intensification	Couples in dual-earner households averaged 3,932 hours of work in 2000, an increase of 300 hours (7.5 additional workweeks per year) since 1989 and equal to more than two full-time EU jobs (Mishel, Bernstein, and Boushley 2003). U.S. workers worked an average of 1,978 hours per year in 2001 (Berg et al. 2004). America has the longest work hours in the world except for South Korea (OECD 2004). 38% of NSCW respondents state they must choose between advancing in their jobs or devoting attention to their families (Bond et al. 2002).
Increase in participation of women in labor force and key occupations, but with variation in age of children and marital status	Since 1975 in the U.S., labor force participation of women with children under 18 has increased from 47% to 78% (U.S. Bureau of Labor Statistics 2004). 39% of professional and managerial positions are held by women, compared to 24% in 1977 (Bond et al. 2002). One-third of mothers with working husbands and with children under 6 did not work at all in 2002, compared to 80% of married women with children 5–18 years old (Farnsworth Riche 2006; U.S. Bureau of Labor Statistics 2003).

(continued)

Table 1.5. *(Continued)*

Trend	Supporting statistics
Increase in new work and career structures	There has been a growth in preferences for part-time or reduced-load work. For example, the NSCW shows that 25% of working women held part-time jobs or jobs with reduced schedules as their main job, compared to 9% of men. About two-thirds of women work part-time and half of men do so by choice, even though 61% of part-time jobs often received prorated health care and lower pay (Bond et al. 2002). Growing numbers of workers are delaying retirement or working part-time in second careers until their 60s or 70s, as opposed to an up-and-out-in-30-years career (Moen 2003).
Change in beliefs about gender roles and work-home relationships	A 2000 poll by Radcliffe Public Policy Center with Harris Interactive stated that over four-fifths of men in their 20s and 30s believed that a work schedule that allowed for family time was more important to them than a challenging or high-paying job, a dramatic shift from earlier generations. In 1977, 74% of NSCW men believed that men should earn the money and women should stay home to take care of the children and the house, compared to only 42% in 2002. In 1977, barely half (49%) of men surveyed in the NSCW believed that employed mothers could have just as good a relationship with their children as mothers who only work in the home. In 2002, that number had risen to nearly two-thirds of men surveyed (Bond et al. 2002). Men do 38%–40% of the domestic chores, if the statistic counts child care and not just housework (Lee and Waite 2005).

Table 1.5. *(Continued)*

Trend	Supporting statistics
Technology and 24/7 global work blurring boundaries between work and home	15% of employed workers work or telework from home at least once a week (U.S. Census Bureau 2002). There has been an increase in major U.S. companies operating work sites overseas (e.g., India, China).

Source: Kossek (2006), reprinted with permission.
CPS = Current Population Survey
NSCW = National Study of the Changing Workforce
SHRM = Society for Human Resource Management

Breaugh (2004) found that use of family-friendly policies, fewer hours worked per week, and a supportive supervisor were predictive of lower work-family conflict. This study demonstrates ways to account for multiple dimensions in their model and to examine interactions. Another example of how to look at complex models is the use of hierarchical linear modeling (HLM). Using HLM, Fuwa and Cohen (2007) studied household labor across 33 countries and found that having policies promoting gender equality does have an effect on the division of labor. They also found that countries with longer parental leaves have a more egalitarian gender division of housework. The researchers concluded that while family policies do allow more women to enter the labor force, these policies may increase the gender wage gap. By controlling for between-country differences, the researcher found that a level of gender-wage inequity does exist even in the presence of family policies. This notion is also supported by Mandel and Semyonov (2005). Others such as Premeaux, Adkins, and Mossholder (2007) also have offered more complex models for studying the relationship between work and family.

Move to Focus on Policy Implementation and Effectiveness

In particular, there needs to be better research on how to improve the practice of policy implementation. Overall this chapter shows that, although many employers have adopted policies to support the integration of work with personal and family life, expected positive gains due to enhanced workplace inclusion are not always realized. Ryan and Kossek (2007) argue that one reason for this gap is that practitioners and researchers often overlook how variations in policy implementation and use by different employee stakeholder groups foster a culture of inclusiveness. It is clear that the existence of a policy does not guarantee employee recruitment, satisfaction, or retention. As Sutton and Noe (2005) concluded in a review of family-friendly program effectiveness, many policies had either no relationship or a negative relationship to attraction of new employees, improvement of retention rates, reduction of stress, and enhancement of productivity. This gap may be related to the fact that more research is needed on how to develop standards for effective policy implementation.

Ryan and Kossek (2007) suggest that implementation should be looked at through four areas of inclusion: the level of supervisor support, universality of availability, negotiability, and quality of communication. These tenets could be used to develop training and best practices in policy implementation. Organizations could also measure whether supervisors encourage and support employees when they seek to use a specific policy, or if they remove any obstacles to policy implementation.

Employers could also measure universalism. Universalism refers to the degree to which policies are perceived as readily available for use by everyone in all levels and jobs, in contrast to any availability (Ryan and Kossek 2007). Measuring universalism would tap into the availability-versus-use gap we have identified.

Employers could also develop clearer standards on which policies should be negotiable and which should be available to all workers. Negotiability reflects both the degree to which an individual's policy use or practice can be negotiated with an organizational agent (e.g., supervisor, HR department, coworkers, and senior management) and the perceived fairness of the negotiation process. Some policies, like the ability to telecommute, may be negotiable and available based on good performance. However, control over when to take breaks or whether workers should work when they or a family member are seriously sick, perhaps, should not be negotiable.

Last, benchmarks and training could be developed to assess the quality of policy communication. Employers could assess the degree to which policies are effectively communicated to employees, which is critical in the effective implementation of policies. Studies have also shown that variability exists within organizations in the degree to which formal written work-life policies exist for different organizational units (Kropf 1999). Not having a written policy could be a key barrier to effective policy implementation. It impedes employee awareness and limits guidance on different possibilities in implementation. And, as shown in the earlier discussion of the FMLA, even written policies are sometimes poorly communicated, which also limits cognizance of the policy's availability and creates a lack of understanding of the policy's applicability to individual situations (Christensen 1999).

Studies show employees are not always aware of the availability of government policies like the FMLA (Baird and Reynolds 2004). Indeed, a U.S. Department of Labor survey (2007) found that FMLA regulations defining how organizations must communicate the policy were one major source of tension between employers and employees. The same survey showed that employees and employers were not sure how FMLA affected their individual situations. More communication from the government and from employers would limit a considerable amount of tension between the government, employers, and employees around FMLA and many other work and family policies.

Consider Advocacy Research

Joan Williams argues that more policy research focused on advocacy should be done (Williams, Calvert, and Cooper 2003). She offers 19 proposed measures based on the view that parents (men and women alike) should be supported in their attempts to access current policies. Her Program on WorkLife Law has identified between 20 and 30 cases involving family caregiving in which plaintiffs have won or been allowed to proceed to trial. Some cases have yielded substantial awards and settlements: roughly $625,000 in one case (*Walsh v. Nat'l Computer Sys. Inc.* 2002), $495,000 in another tentative settlement (*Knussman v. Maryland* 2001), and $667,000 in a third (Williams and Segal 2003).

In addition to the suggestions above and the policy implications integrated throughout this chapter, we close with some final policy suggestions. In the United States there is little quality research on the availability of work and family policies or even on workers' actual experiences. We would like to see national standard definitions on work and family policies developed and broadened, and studies conducted to determine policies' effects on employers, the economy, and workers. Academic and practitioner research on policies should be better classified to allow for critical analysis of differential results, samples, and levels of analysis. Just as we saw great differences in the policy surveys we reviewed in tables 1.1 through 1.4, we see similar problems in how the research is reported and measured at different levels and from different sources. Overall, there is a lack of linked research on multiple stakeholder views on work and family policies (e.g., workers, employers, families, society) or on effective relationships between policies, culture, job conditions, and legislation, which creates policy gaps.

Toward this end, we need higher-quality state and national databases and research on work and family policies and effectiveness. We also saw a gap at the state level of analysis in the academic literature. While we know a handful of state-level studies are available, given the patchwork U.S. system, more research is needed comparing leaves and other working conditions relevant to work and family, such as in states like California and Washington, which are beginning to innovate and set national examples. National surveys from workers' and employers' perspectives should be conducted on access to and effectiveness of these policies, both within and across occupations, jobs, and industries. Until steps such as these are taken, our knowledge will remain limited on how to overcome challenges in implementing policies to foster organizational change toward individual and organizational effectiveness.

NOTES

1. Mothers & More, 2007, http://www.mothersandmore.org/ (accessed July 2007).

2. Andrew Curry, "Why We Work," *U.S. News & World Report,* February 24, 2003, 49–52, 54–56.

3. See also "European Union Council Directive 93/104/EC Concerning Certain Aspects of the Organization of Working Time," *Official Journal of the European Union* L 307, December 13, 1993, and "European Union Council Directive 97/81/EC Concerning the Framework Agreement on Part-Time Work," *Official Journal of the European Union* L14/9-11, January 20, 1998.

4. Joan C. Williams, "The Opt-Out Revolution Revisited," *American Prospect,* March 3, 2007, A12–A15.

5. Joan C. Williams, "The Opt-Out Revolution Revisited," *American Prospect,* March 3, 2007, A12–A15.

6. Katha Pollitt, "Pride and Prejudice," *The Nation,* May 5, 2003. http://www.thenation.com/doc.mhtml?i=20030505&s=pollitt (accessed September 26, 2008).

7. Lisa Belkin, "The Opt-Out Revolution," *New York Times Magazine,* October 26, 2003, 42.

8. Sloan Work and Family Research Network, "Conversations with the Experts: Reshaping Public Discourse—A Conversation with Naomi Gerstel, Dan Clawson, and Robert Zussman," *Network News* 4(2), Summer 2002, 1–3.

REFERENCES

Allen, Tammy D. 2001. "Family-Supportive Work Environments: The Role of Organizational Perceptions." *Journal of Vocational Behavior* 58: 414–35.

Almer, Elizabeth D., Jeffrey R. Cohen, and Louise E. Single. 2004. "Is It the Kids or the Schedule? The Incremental Effect of Families and Flexible Scheduling on Perceived Career Success." *Journal of Business Ethics* 54(1): 51–65.

Baird, Chardie L., and John R. Reynolds. 2004. "Employee Awareness of Family Leave Benefits: The Effects of Family, Work and Gender." *Sociological Quarterly* 45(2): 325–53.

Baltes, Boris B., Thomas E. Briggs, Joseph W. Huff, Julie A. Wright, and George A. Neuman. 1999. "Flexible and Compressed Workweek Schedules: A Meta-Analysis of Their Effects on Work-Related Criteria." *Journal of Applied Psychology* 84: 496–513.

Barnett, Rosalind C., and Caryl Rivers. 1996. *She Works/He Works: How Two-Income Families Are Happier, Healthier, and Thriving.* San Francisco: Harper.

Barrah, Jamie L., Kenneth S. Shultz, Boris Baltes, and Heidi E. Stolz. 2004. "Men's and Women's Eldercare-Based Work-Family Conflict: Antecedents and Work-Related Outcomes." *Fathering* 3: 305–30.

Baughman, Reagan, Daniela DiNardi, and Douglas Holtz-Eakin. 2003. "Productivity and Wage Effects of Family-Friendly Fringe Benefits." *International Journal of Manpower* 24: 247–59.

Baum, Charles L., II. 2006. "The Effects of Government-Mandated Family Leave on Employer Family Leave Policies." *Contemporary Economic Policy* 24: 432–46.

Berg, Peter, Eileen Appelbaum, Tom Bailey, and Arne L. Kalleberg. 2004. "Contesting Time: International Comparisons of Employee Control of Working Time." *Industrial and Labor Relations Review* 57(3): 531–49.

Bianchi, Suzanne. 2000. "Maternal Employment and Time with Children: Dramatic Change or Surprising Continuity?" *Demography* 37(4): 401–14.

Bianchi, Suzanne M., and Sara Raley. 2005. "Time Allocation in Working Families." In *Work, Family, Health, and Well-Being,* edited by Suzanne M. Bianchi, Lynne M. Casper, and Rosalind Berkowitz King (21–42). Mahwah: NJ: Erlbaum.

Block, Richard N., Peter Berg, and Dale Belman. 2004. "The Economic Dimension of the Employment Relationship." In *The Employment Relationship: Examining Psychological and Contextual Perspectives,* edited by Jacqueline A-M. Coyle-Shapiro, Lynn M. Shore, M. Susan Taylor, and Lois E. Tetrick (94–118). Oxford: Oxford University Press.

Bond, James T., Erin Brownfield, Ellen Galinsky, and Stacy S. Kim. 2005. "The National Study of Employers." http://familiesandwork.org/site/research/reports/2005nse.pdf. (Accessed June 23, 2007.)

Bond, James T., with Cindy Thompson, Ellen Galinsky, and David Prottas. 2002. "Highlights of the National Study of the Changing Workforce: Executive Summary." No. 3. New York: Families and Work Institute.

Cantor, David, Jane Waldfogel, Jeffrey Kerwin, Mareena McKinley Wright, Kerry Levin, John Rauch, Tracey Hagerty, and Martha Stapleton Kudela. 2000. *Balancing the Needs of Families and Employers: The Family and Medical Leave Surveys.* 2000 Update, 2.2.2, Table 2.3. Washington, DC: U.S. Department of Labor.

Casper, Wendy J., and Louis C Buffardi. 2004. "Work-Life Benefits and Job Pursuit Intentions: The Role of Anticipated Organizational Support." *Journal of Vocational Behavior* 65(3): 391–410.

Casper, Wendy J., Kevin E. Fox, Tracy M. Sitzmann, and Ann L. Landy. 2004. "Supervisor Referrals to Work Family Programs." *Journal of Occupational Health Psychology* 9: 136–51.

Christensen, Kathleen, and Graham Staines. 1990. "A Viable Solution to Work/Family Conflict?" *Journal of Family Issues* 11(4): 455–76.

Christensen, Perry M. 1999. "Toward a Comprehensive Work/Life Strategy." In *Integrating Work and Family: Challenges and Choices for a Changing World,* 2nd ed., edited by Saroj Parasuraman and Jeffrey H. Greenhaus (25–37). Westport, CT: Praeger.

Clark, Campbell. 2000. "Work/Family Border Theory: A New Theory of Work/Family Balance." *Human Relations* 53(6): 747–70.

Cohen, Philip N. 2002. "Cohabitation and the Declining Marriage Premium for Men." *Work and Occupations* 29(3): 346–63.

Crosby, Faye J., Joan C. Williams, and Monica Biernat. 2004. "The Maternal Wall." *Journal of Social Issues* 60(4): 675–82.

Dalton, Dan R., and Debra J. Mesch. 1990. "The Impact of Flexible Scheduling on Employee Attendance and Turnover." *Administrative Science Quarterly* 35: 370–87.

Davis, Kelly D., Ann C. Crouter, and Susan M. McHale. 2006. "Implications of Shift Work for Parent-Adolescent Relationships in Dual-Earner Families." *Family Relations* 55: 450–60.

Dube, Arindrajit, and Ethan Kaplan. 2002. "Paid Family Leave in California: An Analysis of Costs and Benefits." Berkeley, CA: Labor Project for Working Families. http://www.paidfamilyleave.org/pdf/dube.pdf. (Accessed July 2007.)

Eaton, Susan C. 2003. "If You Can Use Them: Flexibility Policies, Organizational Commitment and Perceived Performance." *Industrial Relations* 42(2): 145–67.

Farnsworth Riche, Martha. 2006. "Demographic Implications for Work-Family Research." In *The Work and Family Handbook: Multidisciplinary Perspectives and Methods,* edited by Marcie Pitt-Catsouphes, Ellen Ernst Kossek, and Stephen A. Sweet (125–40). Mahwah, NJ: Erlbaum.

Frye, N. Kathleen, and James A Breaugh. 2004. "Family-Friendly Policies, Supervisor Support, Work-Family Conflict, Family-Work Conflict, and Satisfaction: A Test of a Conceptual Model." *Journal of Business and Psychology* 19: 197–220.

Fuwa, Makiko, and Philip N. Cohen. 2007. "Housework and Social Policy." *Social Science Research* 36(2): 512–30.

Gault, Barbara, and Vicky Lovell. 2006. "The Costs and Benefits of Policies to Advance Work-Life Integration." *American Behavioral Scientist* 49(9): 1152–64.

Glass, Jennifer L., and Lisa Riley. 1998. "Family Responsive Policies and Employee Retention Following Childbirth." *Social Forces* 76(4): 1401–35.

Gore, Al. 1997. *Turning the Key: Unlocking Human Potential in the Family-Friendly Federal Workplace.* Washington, DC: U.S. Government Printing Office. http://govinfo.library.unt.edu/npr/library/papers/bkgrd/tkcontents.html#offer. (Accessed July 23, 2007.)

Grant, Jody, Taylor Hatcher, and Nirali Patel. 2005. *Expecting Better: A State-by-State Analysis of Parental Leave Programs.* Washington, DC: National Partnership for Women & Families.

Haas, Linda. 2003. "Parental Leave and Gender Equality: Lessons from the European Union." *Review of Policy Research* 20(1): 89–114.

Haas, Linda, Karin Allard, and Philip Hwang. 2002. "The Impact of Organizational Culture on Men's Use of Parental Leave in Sweden." *Community, Work, and Family* 5(3): 319–42.

Henry, Colleen, Misha Werschkul, and Manita Rao. 2003. "Child Care Subsides Promote Mothers' Employment and Children's Development." Washington DC: Institute for Women's Policy Research.

Heymann, Jody. 2002. *Can Working Families Ever Win? A New Democracy Forum on Helping Parents Succeed at Work and Caregiving.* Boston: Beacon Press.

Hopkins, Karen. 2005. "Supervisor Support and Work-Life Integration." In *Work and Life Integration: Organizational, Cultural and Individual Perspectives,* edited by Ellen Ernst Kossek and Susan J. Lambert (445–68). Mahwah, NJ: Erlbaum.

Hyde, Janet S., Marion J. Essex, Roseanne Clark, Marjorie Klein, and Janis E. Byrd. 1996. "Parental Leave: Policy and Research." *Journal of Social Issues* 52(3): 91–109.

Ingersoll-Dayton, Berit, Margaret B. Neal, and Leslie B. Hammer. 2001. "Aging Parents Helping Adult Children: The Experience of the Sandwiched Generation." *Family Relations* 50(3): 262–71.

Kanter, Rosabeth M. 1977. *Work and Family in the United States: A Critical Review and Agenda for Research and Policy.* New York: Russell Sage Foundation.

Kelly, Erin. 2006. "Work-Family Policies: The U.S. in International Perspective." In *Work and Family Handbook: Multi-disciplinary Perspectives, Methods, and Approaches,* edited by Marcie Pitt-Catsouphes, Ellen Ernst Kossek, and Stephen A. Sweet (99–124). Mahwah, NJ: Erlbaum.

Kossek, Ellen Ernst. 2005. "Workplace Policies and Practices to Support Work and Families." In *Work, Family, Health, and Well-Being,* edited by Suzanne M. Bianchi, Lynne M. Casper, and Rosalind Berkowitz King (97–115). Mahwah, NJ: Erlbaum.

———. 2006. "Work and Family in America: Growing Tensions between Employment Policy and a Changing Workforce." In *America at Work: Choices and Challenges,* edited by Edward E. Lawler and James O'Toole (53–72). New York: Palgrave MacMillan.

Kossek, Ellen E., and Mary D. Lee. 2005. "Making Flexibility Work: What Managers Have Learned about Implementing Reduced-Load Work." Alfred P. Sloan Foundation Study Technical Report. New York: Alfred P. Sloan Foundation.

Kossek, Ellen E., and Cynthia Ozeki. 1999. "Bridging the Work-Family Policy and Productivity Gap: A Literature Review." *Community, Work & Family* 2(1): 7–32.

Kossek, Ellen E., Peter Berg, and Kaumudi Misra. 2007. "Implementing Flexibility in Unionized Environments: Adding a Collective Voice Perspective to Work-Life

Research." Presentation at Academy of Management annual meeting, Philadelphia, PA, Aug. 3–8.

Kropf, Marcia B. 1999. "A Research Perspective on Work-Family Issues." In *Integrating Work and Family: Challenges and Choices for a Changing World,* 2nd ed., edited by Saroj Parasuraman and Jeffrey H. Greenhaus (69–76). Westport, CT: Praeger.

Lee, Sunhwa. 2004. "Women's Work Supports, Job Retention and Job Mobility: Child Care and Employer Provided Health Insurance Help Women Stay on Jobs." Washington, DC: Institute for Women's Policy Research.

Lee, Yun-Suk, and Linda J. Waite. 2005. "Husbands' and Wives' Time Spent on Housework: A Comparison of Measures." *Journal of Marriage and Family* 67(2): 328–36.

Lewis, Sue, and Linda Haas. 2005. "Work-Life Integration and Social Policy: A Social Justice Approach to Work and Family." In *Work and Life Integration: Organizational, Cultural, and Individual Perspectives,* edited by Ellen Ernst Kossek and Susan J. Lambert (349–74). Mahwah, NJ: Erlbaum.

Liechty, Janet M., and Elaine A. Anderson. 2007. "Flexible Workplace Policies: Lessons from the Federal Alternative Work Schedules Act." *Family Relations* 56: 304–17.

Mandel, Hadas, and Moshe Semyonov. 2005. "Family Policies, Wage Structures, and Gender Gaps: Sources of Earnings Inequality in 20 Countries." *American Sociological Review* 70(6): 949–67.

Maume, David J. 2006. "Gender Differences in Taking Vacation Time." *Work and Occupations* 33: 161–90.

McManus, Kelly, Karen Korabik, Hazel M. Rosin, and E. Kevin Kelloway. 2002. "Employed Mothers and the Work-Family Interface: Does Family Structure Matter?" *Human Relations* 55: 1295–324.

Mishel, Lawrence, Jared Bernstein, and Heather Boushley. 2003. *The State of Working America: 2002/2003.* Ithaca, NY: IRL Press.

Moen, Phyllis, ed. 2003. *It's About Time: Couples and Careers.* Ithaca, NY: Cornell University Press.

National Alliance for Caregiving and AARP. 2004. *Family Caregiving in the U.S.: Findings from a National Survey.* http://www.caregiving.org/data/04finalreport.pdf. (Accessed August 9, 2007.)

Nichols, Laurie S., and Virginia W. Junk. 1997. "The Sandwich Generation: Dependency, Proximity, and Task Assistance Needs of Parents." *Journal of Family and Economic Issues* 18(3): 299–326.

Noonan, Mary C., Sarah Beth Estes, and Jennifer L. Glass. 2007. "Do Workplace Flexibility Policies Influence Time Spent in Domestic Labor?" *Journal of Family Issues* 28(2): 263–88.

O'Driscoll, Michael P., Steven Poelmans, Paul E. Spector, Thomas Kalliath, Tammy D. Allen, Cary L. Cooper, and Juan Sanchez. 2003. "Family-Responsive Interventions, Perceived Organizational and Supervisor Support, Work-Family Conflict and Psychological Strain." *International Journal of Stress Management* 10: 326–44.

O'Toole, James. 1973. "Work and Health." In *Work in America: Report of a Special Task Force to the Secretary of Health, Education and Welfare* (76–92). Cambridge, MA: MIT Press.

OECD. 2004. "OECD in Figures." http://ocde.p4.siteinternet.com/publications/doifiles/ 012004071B0G007.xls. (Accessed July 23, 2007.)

Pavalko, Elisa K., and Kathryn A. Henderson. 2006. "Combining Care Work and Paid Work: Do Workplace Policies Make a Difference?" *Research on Aging* 28: 359–79.

Powell, Gary N. 1999. "The Sex Differences in Employee Inclinations Regarding Work-Family Programs: Why Does It Exist, Should We Care, and What Should Be Done About It (If Anything)?" In *Integrating Work and Family: Challenges and Choices for a Changing World,* 2nd ed., edited by Saroj Parasuraman and Jeffrey H. Greenhaus (167–76). Westport, CT: Praeger.

Premeaux, Sonya F., Cheryl L. Adkins, and Kevin W. Mossholder. 2007. "Balancing Work and Family: A Field Study of Multi-dimensional, Multi-role Work-Family Conflict." *Journal of Organizational Behavior* 28(6): 705–27.

Radcliffe Public Policy Center with Harris Interactive. 2000. "Life's Work: Generational Attitudes toward Work and Life Integration." Cambridge, MA: Radcliffe Public Policy Center.

Rau, Barbara L. 2003. "Flexible Work Arrangements." *Sloan Work and Family Encyclopedia.* http://wfnetwork.bc.edu/encyclopedia_entry.php?id=240&area=business. (Accessed July 23, 2007.)

Ryan, Ann Marie, and Ellen E. Kossek. 2007. "Work-Life Policy Implementation: Breaking Down or Creating Barriers to Inclusiveness?" *Human Resource Management Journal* Special Issue on Diversity and Inclusion 47(2): 295–310.

Sayer, Liana C. 2001. "Time Use, Gender, and Equality: Differences in Men's and Women's Market, Nonmarket, and Leisure Time." Ph.D. diss., University of Maryland, College Park.

Schweinhart, Lawrence J. 2004. "The High/Scope Perry Preschool Study through Age 40. Summary, Conclusions, and Frequently Asked Questions." Ypsilanti, MI: High/ Scope Educational Research Foundation.

Seward, Rudy Ray, Dale E. Yeatts, and Lisa K. Zottarelli. 2002. "Parental Leave and Father Involvement in Child Care: Sweden and the United States." *Journal of Comparative Family Studies* 33(3): 387–99.

Smolensky, Eugene, and Jennifer Appleton Gootman, eds. 2003. *Working Families and Growing Kids: Caring for Children and Adolescents.* Washington, DC: National Academies Press.

Stebbins, Leslie F. 2001. *Work and Family in America: A Reference Handbook.* Santa Barbara, CA: Abc-Clio.

Sutton, Kyra L., and Raymond A. Noe. 2005. "Family Friendly Programs and Work-Life Integration: More Myth than Magic?" In *Work and Life Integration: Organizational, Cultural, and Individual Perspectives,* edited by Ellen Ernst Kossek and Susan J. Lambert (151–70). Mahwah, NJ: Erlbaum.

Thomas, Linda T., and Daniel C. Ganster. 1995. "Impact of Family-Supportive Work Variables on Work-Family Conflict and Strain: A Control Perspective." *Journal of Applied Psychology* 80: 6–15.

U.S. Bureau of Labor Statistics. 1999. *National Compensation Survey: Employee Benefits in Private Industry in the United States, 1999—Supplementary Tables.* Washington,

DC: U.S. Department of Labor. http://www.bls.gov/ncs/ebs/sp/ebtb0001.pdf. (Accessed July 23, 2007.)

———. 2000. *National Compensation Survey: Employee Benefits in Private Industry in the United States, 2000—Supplementary Tables.* Washington, DC: U.S. Department of Labor. http://www.bls.gov/ncs/ebs/sp/ebtb0002.pdf. (Accessed July 23, 2007.)

———. 2003. *National Compensation Survey: Employee Benefits in Private Industry in the United States, 2003.* Washington, DC: U.S. Department of Labor. http://www.bls.gov/ncs/ebs/sp/ebbl0021.pdf. (Accessed July 14, 2007.)

———. 2004. *Women in the Labor Force: A Databook.* Report 973. Washington, DC: U.S. Department of Labor. http://www.bls.gov/cps/wlf-databook.pdf. (Accessed July 14, 2007.)

———. 2006. *National Compensation Survey: Employee Benefits in Private Industry in the United States, March 2006.* Washington, DC: U.S. Department of Labor. http://www.bls.gov/ncs/ebs/sp/ebsm0004.pdf. (Accessed July 23, 2007.)

———. 2007. *National Compensation Survey.* Washington, DC: U.S. Department of Labor. http://www.bls.gov/ncs/. (Accessed June 2007.)

U.S. Census Bureau. 2001. *Number of Firms, Number of Establishments, United States, All Industries 2001.* Washington, DC: U.S. Government Printing Office.

———. 2002. "Table No. 578. Persons Doing Job-Related Work at Home: 2001." In *Statistical Abstract of the United States: 2002—The National Data Book, Section 12, Labor Force, Employment, and Earnings.* Washington, DC: U.S. Census Bureau.

U.S. Department of Labor. 1993. "The Family and Medial Leave Act." Washington, DC: U.S. Department of Labor. http://www.dol.gov/esa/regs/statutes/whd/fmla.htm. (Accessed July 23, 2007.)

———. 2007. *Family and Medical Leave Act Regulations: A Report on the Department of Labor's Request for Information—2007 Update.* Washington, DC: U.S. Department of Labor. http://www.dol.gov/esa/whd/FMLA2007Report/2007FinalReport.pdf. (Accessed July 23, 2007.)

U.S. Department of Labor, Commission on Leave. 1996. *A Workable Balance: Report to Congress on Family and Medical Leave Policies.* Washington, DC: U.S. Department of Labor.

U.S. General Accounting Office. 1994. *Alternative Work Schedules. Many Agencies Do Not Allow the Full Flexibility Permitted by Law—Report to Congressional Committees.* GAO/GGD-94-55. Washington DC: U.S. General Accounting Office. http://archive.gao.gov/t2pbat4/150995.pdf. (Accessed July 23, 2007.)

———. 2001. *The Use of Alternative Work Arrangements at GAO: Personnel Appeals Board.* Washington DC: U.S. General Accounting Office. http://archive.gao.gov/f0102/a01513.pdf. (Accessed July 23, 2007.)

U.S. Office of Personnel Management. 2001. "Paid Parental Leave." http://www.opm.gov/oca/leave/HTML/ParentalReport.htm. (Accessed August 5, 2007.)

———. 2003. "Negotiating Flexible and Compressed Work Schedules." Washington, DC: U.S. Office of Personnel Management. http://www.opm.gov/lmr/html/flexible.asp. (Accessed July 19, 2007.)

———. 2007. "Handbook on Alternative Work Schedules." Washington, DC: U.S. Office of Personnel Management. http://www.opm.gov/oca/aws/html/define.asp#AWS. (Accessed July 12, 2007.)

Waldfogel, Jane. 1998. "The Family Gap for Young Women in the United States and Britain: Can Maternity Leave Make a Difference?" *Journal of Labor Economics* 16(3): 505–45.

Williams, Joan C., and Cynthia T. Calvert. 2002. "Balanced Hours: Effective Part-Time Policies for Washington Law Firms—The Project for Attorney Retention." *William and Mary Journal of Women and the Law* 8(3): 357.

Williams, Joan C., and Nancy Segal. 2003. "Beyond the Maternal Wall: Relief for Family Caregivers Who Are Discriminated Against on the Job." *Harvard Women's Law Journal* 26: 77–162.

Williams, Joan C., Cynthia T. Calvert, and Holly Cooper. 2003. *Better on Balance? The Corporate Counsel Work/Life Report*. San Francisco: Center for WorkLife Law, University of California, Hastings College of the Law. http://www.pardc.org/Publications/BetterOnBalance.pdf. (Accessed July 23, 2007.)

WorldatWork. 2007a. "Census of the Total Rewards Profession." Research report, June. Scottsdale, AZ: WorldatWork. http://www.worldatwork.org/waw/adimLink?id=19980. (Accessed June 14, 2007.)

———. 2007b. "Telework Trendlines for 2006." Research report, August. Scottsdale, AZ: WorldatWork. http://www.worldatwork.org/waw/adimLink?id=17182. (Accessed July 2007.)

Elaborations on a Theme

Toward Understanding
Work-Life Culture

Cynthia A. Thompson and David J. Prottas

I n this volume, Ellen Ernst Kossek and Brian Distelberg discuss a "three-legged stool" of employer supports for work and family: (1) formal human resource policies related to work and family, (2) informal occupational and organizational culture and norms, and (3) job conditions and the structure of work, including job design, work hours, and terms and conditions of employment. They pointed out that the links between these three types of employer supports are often ineffective. We would argue that the linkages are almost nonexistent. While work-family researchers and policymakers need to spend more time thinking about the connections between these three areas, we first need to more fully examine and develop an understanding of each leg of the stool. Ellen Kossek and Brian Distelberg have done that for the policy area, and excellent work has been done by Lotte Bailyn, Monique Valcour, Shelley MacDermid, Forrest Briscoe, and Eileen Appelbaum on the job-design side. We would like to focus our comments on the "culture" leg of the stool.

Of the 13 themes Kossek and Distelberg described in their chapter, at least 3 of them relate to some aspect of work-life culture. The first theme described the three-legged stool and the need for more research on the interconnections between policies, culture, and the structure of work. The second theme described the United States' minimalist approach to work and family policy and how U.S. employers have work cultures where they control the hours of work. Another theme described supervisory and societal cultures regarding ideal workers as barriers to policy use. As these themes suggest, various aspects of organizational culture appear to play a role in the decision of employers to implement work-life policies and programs, as well as the decision of employees to use or not use the programs. What is *not* clear is what factors influence organizational cultures to be supportive or not supportive of work-life policy implementation and policy usage.

What Do We Know So Far?

Recent research has shown that outcomes for both employees and organizations are enhanced when employees feel they work in a family-supportive culture that respects the demands of their lives outside of work (see Andreassi and Thompson 2008 for a review). For example, we know that employees in family-supportive work environments have higher levels of job and life satisfaction, lower levels of stress and work-family conflict, and higher levels of commitment to their organizations. We also know that employees who work in supportive work cultures are more likely to actually use the policies and programs, and we know that employees who actually use work-family benefits tend to be more committed to their organizations and have lower intentions to quit (Allen 2001; Eaton 2003; Grover and Crooker 1995; Thompson, Beauvais, and Lyness 1999). Finally, we know that employees who work in unsupportive work cultures are often reluctant to take advantage of these programs for fear of committing career suicide (Eaton 2003; Fried 1998; Lewis 1997; Thompson et al. 1999).

It is also well established that the composition of the workforce has changed dramatically over the last 50 years, largely due to the increasing numbers of women who have entered the workforce. As a result, organizations that are tuned in to their environments know that one strategy that may increase their competitive advantage is to provide a family-supportive work environment. *Working Mother* magazine's highly competitive list of 100 best companies for working mothers is testament to the increasing interest in organizations to appear responsive to working parents' needs.

What Don't We Know?

We don't know what factors influence an organization's culture to be supportive (or not) of an employee's ability to integrate work and life. While work-life programs may offer employees help in integrating work

with other life roles, as well as allow organizations to reap the public relations benefits of appearing family friendly, these programs are often superficial solutions that, in fact, may inure management to the real sources
of work-life imbalance. More to the point, work-family initiatives rarely
solve the root cause of employee work-life imbalance (Sutton and Noe
2005; Thompson 2005). That is, the decision to offer work-life programs is
often made without consideration of deeper, more fundamental problems,
such as how jobs are designed, how work is coordinated, how organizational
rewards are determined, and how the culture supports or hinders work-
life balance (Batt and Valcour 2003; Glass and Estes 1997; Thompson,
Andreassi, and Prottas 2005). To begin to determine the root cause, we need
to answer two questions: (1) why do some organizations provide work-
life policies and programs while others do not, and (2) why do some
organizations attempt to create a supportive culture while others do not?
We will discuss each question in turn.

Why Do Some Organizations Provide Work-Life Policies and Programs While Others Do Not?

There has been surprisingly little research on factors related to firm
adoption of work-life policies and programs. In the few studies available,
researchers have examined several industry and organizational factors that
may influence firm adoption, using various frameworks such as institutional theory, resource dependence theory, and organizational adaptation
theory (Davis and Kalleberg 2006; Goodstein 1994; Goodstein 1995; Ingram
and Simons 1995; Osterman 1995; Wood, de Menezes, and Lasaosa
2003). For example, as would be predicted by institutional theory, both
Goodstein (1994) and Ingram and Simons (1995) found that the greater
the diffusion of the practice within an organization's industry, the more
likely the focal organization was responsive. In general, this research has
found that organizations that are large, have greater proportions of
female employees, are in the public sector, and are in industries with low
unemployment rates for women are more likely to adopt work-family
policies and programs (for an overview of this research, see Thompson,
Beauvais, and Allen 2006). While this research has contributed to our
understanding of factors that influence organizational responsiveness
to work-life needs of employees, it has focused solely on responsiveness
as defined as programs and policies. To date, no research has examined
factors that influence responsiveness as defined as a supportive work-
life culture.

Why Do Some Organizations Attempt to Create a Supportive Work-Life Culture While Others Do Not?

Previous research on work-family culture has focused primarily on individual-level consequences of family-supportive work cultures (e.g., employees' attitudes and behaviors such as job satisfaction, stress, and intentions to quit), with little or no attention given to possible antecedents of family-supportive work cultures. As in research on organizational adoption of family-supportive programs and policies, researchers need to determine which institutional and organizational factors influence an organization's culture to be supportive; that is, which factors influence whether an organization's culture supports or hinders the ability of employees to integrate work and family. We define work-family culture as the "shared assumptions, beliefs, and values regarding the extent to which an organization supports and values the integration of employees' work and family lives" (Thompson et al. 1999, 394). A supportive organization is one whose formal and informal policies and practices allow employees to allocate the amount of time and energy for work- and nonwork-related activities (including, but not limited to family interests) in a way that meets the demands of both work and family/personal life, without the employee feeling that he or she will suffer economically or socially within the work domain and without the employer losing productivity. A supportive work-family culture is one that proactively provides tangible and intangible support for leading a balanced life. Our conceptualization of a family-*un*supportive culture is one in which the organization is not only indifferent to employees' needs for balance but adapts norms that actively promote *work primacy* rather than balance.

To better understand an organization's reluctance to being more supportive of workers' family/personal activities, we should abandon one of the primary assumptions that seems to guide much research in the work-family arena: that practices, policies, and cultures that are *not* family supportive are dysfunctional and maladaptive vestiges of a prior era when the workforce was dominated by married men with stay-at-home wives caring for their children. We suggest a different point of departure for studying nonsupportive cultures that recognizes (1) the changed nature of the American workforce is no longer a new phenomenon and (2) most for-profit organizations are keenly tuned to their environments and opportunities to improve their performance and competitive position, and they know that at least some companies have chosen to increase their competitive advantage by providing a family-supportive work environment (Thompson et al. 2005).

We believe that it is possible that for some organizations, a non-supportive culture *is* functional and adaptive to environmental or institutional demands, or is at least perceived to be functional and adaptive for the organization's survival. As such, we must look for characteristics of these organizations and their environment that would contribute to the formation and maintenance of a culture that is unfriendly to the needs of its employees—or even to a subset of its employees. Understanding the antecedents of "functional" unsupportive cultures is essential if we are to understand the obstacles to effecting cultural changes that could benefit organizations, employees, and their families. This line of thinking is similar to Jennifer Glass's discussion of whether it is always economically rational to implement policies responsive to employees with child care responsibilities (Glass and Estes 1997). However, it is important to note that while various external and internal factors may constrain an organization's ability to be supportive, we are not proposing a determinism that should prevent (or excuse) organizations from attempting to meet the work-life needs of their employees.

Theoretical Approaches to Understanding Influences on Work-Family Culture

As a first step toward understanding what factors might influence the supportiveness of an organization's work-family culture, research on organizational responsiveness (as defined as formal work-life programs) may be instructive. As described earlier, this research has used various macro-level theories to guide hypothesis development, including institutional theory, resource dependence theory, and organizational adaptation theory. These theories might provide us with insights regarding possible exogenous factors that would influence work-family culture.

One approach to understanding what factors might influence work-family culture is institutional theory, which views organizational culture (or a unit's subculture) as being influenced and constrained by the social and economic environment in which it exists and the need to seek and maintain legitimacy in the eyes of its stakeholders, including industry competitors (DiMaggio and Powell 1983; DiMaggio and Powell 1991).

According to institutional theory, three types of pressure push an organization toward institutional isomorphism: coercive (e.g., government mandates to reduce commuting costs by allowing employees to telecommute), mimetic (e.g., adopting work-life programs to keep up with or "copy" competitors), and normative (e.g., developing norms of long work hours through norms and values acquired through professional associations). Because "culture is very difficult to control and manage, let alone imitate or copy" (Jones 2007, 214), it may be unlikely that mimetic factors influence an organization's culture. It also seems unlikely that coercive factors would influence an organization's culture to be supportive or not. Instead, normative pressures may be relevant. For example, among global financial service firms, norms of professional service often involve 24/7 availability, and firms that do not comply with this norm are viewed as less competitive.

As it is likely there are multiple competing institutional pressures (e.g., some competitors are implementing work-life policies and creating family-supportive cultures, while other competitors are expanding globally, requiring longer hours of their employees), to which pressures does an organization choose to conform? To answer that question, organizational adaptation theory builds on institutional theory by suggesting that top management has discretion over how it responds to environmental pressures (Milliken, Martins, and Morgan 1998; Oliver 1991) and may decide to acquiesce to, ignore, or defy certain pressures. Importantly, this theory incorporates the values of senior management, as well as the information that senior management has about environmental pressures (Wood et al. 2003), as influences on strategic decisions about how responsive to be. By extension, because culture is influenced by the characteristics of the people within the organization, especially the founder and his or her values and beliefs, organizational adaptation theory seems especially suited to suggest possible factors that might influence an organization's work-family culture.

Resource dependence theory suggests additional factors that may be relevant to understanding work-life culture. According to Pfeffer and Salancik (1978), organizations strive to reduce uncertainty for the firm and acquire resources necessary for the firm's survival. Further, firms develop strategies to increase control over supplies of resources and to increase dominance in the market for needed resources. For example, firms that need a steady supply of GenX talent may understand that it is not enough to simply provide work-life programs; they know they must also create a work environment of flexibility (Shen, Pitt-Catsouphes, and Smyer 2007).

Structural contingency theory (Donaldson 2001) is another possible framework for exploring internal and external factors that may influence the development of a work-primacy or a work-life supportive culture. According to this theory, organizations that adapt to important contingent factors will be more effective than those that do not. To survive, organizations need to accommodate those contingencies that are most critical to their effectiveness. Contingencies include internal factors such as organizational size, technology, and strategy, as well as external factors such as environmental uncertainty. According to Donaldson (2001), organizational accommodation is most often structural in nature. For example, if an organization's survival is contingent on a diversification strategy, then the organization might adapt by creating a divisional structure. In addition to modifying structure, adapting to a given contingency might also take the form of changes in organizational processes or culture. If, for example, the critical contingency is to attract and retain a workforce of highly talented workers who also value work-life balance, then having a work-life supportive culture might be functional. If the critical contingency is to execute a specific strategy (such as a first-mover or global strategy), then a work-primacy culture might be viewed as functional.

Using contingency theory as a framework would also suggest that, for other than small organizations, the proper level of analysis may be strategic business units or functional areas rather than the organization as a whole. Strategic business units within a large organization with specialized and differentiated functions might confront very different contingencies, such as strategy, technology, customer demands, or labor market conditions. In such instances, a culture (or subculture) might be functional for one business unit, yet dysfunctional for another. For example, a work unit within a large public accounting firm that provides audit services for multinational corporations would likely differ from a work unit that provides estate-planning services to individuals. Each area would likely use different technologies and confront different demands and expectations from their clients, and as a result, have different approaches to work-life culture.

Policy Implications

In addition to helping us better understand work-life culture, these theories suggest frameworks through which we can better understand which types of government policies might have an impact on work-life culture within organizations. To the extent that governmental work-life policies signal an expectation as to how organizations are supposed to behave with regard to respecting their employees' nonwork interests, institutional theory would suggest that organizational norms would be subject to pressures to conform with these expectations. For example, Kossek (2006) suggested that we need a national certification system in which companies are certified if they are deemed "family friendly"; this, in turn, may create normative pressures to develop more supportive work-life cultures. The pressures may be more pronounced if the policies include coercive elements, such as penalties for organizations that require employees to work more than 70 hours per week.

Resource dependency and contingency theories might predict that organizations dependent on the goodwill of governmental authorities (e.g., for federal grants), would be more responsive. To the extent that a supportive organizational culture would be viewed as necessary to comply with the spirit, rather than the letter, of work-life policies, then organizations with greater reliance on governmental contingencies or resources would be more likely to adapt by changing their norms to be more supportive.

Conclusion

Research to date suggests that a supportive work-family culture is related to important organizational outcomes such as increased commitment, higher job satisfaction, lower absenteeism, decreased work-family conflict, decreased psychological distress, fewer somatic complaints, and decreased role strain. To keep Kossek and Distelberg's three-legged stool from wobbling, we need to learn more about the "third leg" of cultural support for work-life balance. We need to determine what structural and technical factors at the institutional and organizational levels influence work-life culture and ultimately, the ability of employees to allocate time and energy to their various life roles as they see fit and in a way that allows both individuals and organizations to benefit. By drawing on institutional, resource dependency, and contingency theories to explore the factors that shape organizational culture to be supportive of work-life integration, we can begin to expand our understanding of work-life culture.

REFERENCES

Allen, Tammy D. 2001. "Family-Supportive Work Environments: The Role of Organizational Perceptions." *Journal of Vocational Behavior* 58: 414–35.

Andreassi, Jeanine K., and Cynthia A. Thompson. 2008. "Work-Family Culture: Current Research and Future Directions." In *Handbook of Work-Family Integration,* edited by Karen Korabik, Donna Lero, and Denise Whitehead (331–52). New York: Elsevier Press.

Batt, Rosemary, and Monique Valcour. 2003. "Human Resource Practices as Predictors of Work-Family Outcomes and Employee Turnover." *Industrial Relations* 42: 189–220.

Davis, Amy E., and Arne L. Kalleberg. 2006. "Family-Friendly Organizations? Work and Family Programs in the 1990's." *Work and Occupations* 33: 191–223.

DiMaggio, Paul J., and Walter W. Powell. 1983. "The Iron Cage Revisited: Institutional Isomorphism and Collective Rationality in Organization Fields." *American Sociological Review* 48: 147–60.

———. 1991. "Introduction." In *The New Institutionalism in Organizational Analysis,* edited by Walter W. Powell and Paul J. DiMaggio (1–40). Chicago: University of Chicago Press.

Donaldson, Lex. 2001. *The Contingency Theory of Organizations.* Thousand Oaks, CA: Sage Publications.

Eaton, Susan C. 2003. "If You Can Use Them: Flexibility Policies, Organizational Commitment, and Perceived Performance." *Industrial Relations* 42(2): 145–67.

Fried, Mindy. 1998. *Taking Time: Parental Leave Policy and Corporate Culture.* Philadelphia, PA: Temple University Press.

Glass, Jennifer L., and Sara Beth Estes. 1997. "The Family Responsive Workplace." *Annual Review of Sociology* 23: 289–313.

Goodstein, Jerry D. 1994. "Institutional Pressures and Strategic Responsiveness: Employer Involvement in Work-Family Issues." *Academy of Management Journal* 37: 350–82.

———. 1995. "Employer Involvement in Eldercare: An Organizational Adaptation Perspective." *Academy of Management Journal* 38: 1657–71.

Grover, Steven L., and Karen J. Crooker. 1995. "Who Appreciates Family-Responsive Human Resource Policies: The Impact of Family-Friendly Policies." *Personnel Psychology* 48(2): 271–98.

Ingram, Paul, and Tal Simons. 1995. "Institutional and Resource Dependence Determinants of Responsiveness to Work-Family Issues." *Academy of Management Journal* 38: 1466–82.

Jones, Gareth R. 2007. *Organizational Theory, Design, and Change,* 5th ed. Upper Saddle River, NJ: Pearson Prentice-Hall.

Kossek, Ellen Ernst. 2006. "Work and Family in America: Growing Tensions between Employment Policy and a Changing Workforce." In *America at Work: Choices and Challenges,* edited by Edward E. Lawler and James O'Toole (53–72). New York: Palgrave MacMillan.

Lewis, Susan. 1997. " 'Family Friendly' Employment Policies: A Route to Changing Organizational Culture or Playing About at the Margins?" *Gender, Work, and Organizations* 4: 13–23.

Milliken, Frances J., Luis L. Martins, and Hal Morgan. 1998. "Explaining Organizational Responsiveness to Work-Family Issues: The Role of Human Resource Executives as Issues Interpreters." *Academy of Management Journal* 41: 580–92.

Oliver, Christine. 1991. "Strategic Responses to Institutional Processes." *Academy of Management Review* 16: 145–79.

Osterman, Paul. 1995. "Work/Family Programs and the Employment Relationship." *Administration Science Quarterly* 40: 681–700.

Pfeffer, Jeffrey, and Gerald R. Salancik. 1978. *The External Control of Organizations.* New York: Harper & Row.

Shen, Ce, Marcie Pitt-Catsouphes, and Michael A. Smyer. 2007. "Today's Multi-generational Workforce: A Proposition of Value." Issue Brief 12. Chestnut Hill, MA: Center on Aging and Work/Workplace Flexibility at Boston College.

Sutton, Kyra L., and Raymond A. Noe. 2005. "Family-Friendly Programs and Work-Life Integration: More Myth than Magic?" In *Work and Life Integration: Organizational, Cultural, and Individual Perspectives,* edited by Ellen Ernst Kossek and Susan J. Lambert (151–70). Mahwah, NJ: Erlbaum.

Thompson, Cynthia A. 2005. "Work-Life Balance? Organizations in Denial." *Journal of Employee Assistance* 35: 7–9.

Thompson, Cynthia A., Jeanine K. Andreassi, and David J. Prottas. 2005. "Work-Family Culture: Key to Reducing Workforce-Workplace Mismatch?" In *Work, Family, Health, and Well-Being,* edited by Susan M. Bianchi, Lynn M. Casper, and Rosalind Berkowitz King (117–32). Mahwah, NJ: Erlbaum.

Thompson, Cynthia A., Laura L. Beauvais, and Tammy T. Allen. 2006. "Work-Life Balance: An Industrial-Organizational Psychology Perspective." In *The Work-Family Handbook: Multi-disciplinary Perspectives and Approaches,* edited by Marcie Pitt-Catsouphes, Ellen E. Kossek, and Stephen A. Sweet. Mahwah, NJ: Erlbaum.

Thompson, Cynthia A., Laura L. Beauvais, and Karen S. Lyness. 1999. "When Work-Family Benefits Are Not Enough . . . The Influence of Work-Family Culture on Benefit Utilization, Organizational Attachment, and Work-Family Conflict." *Journal of Vocational Behavior* 54: 392–415.

Wood, Stephen J., Lilian M. de Menezes, and Ana Lasaosa. 2003. "Family-Friendly Management in Great Britain: Testing Various Perspectives." *Industrial Relations* 42: 221–50.

3

Union Strategies for Work-Family Issues

Collective Bargaining and Public Policies

Netsy Firestein

Unions have a particular role in the work-family world, and this chapter addresses two ways to look at the impact of unions in this arena: (1) union collective bargaining language is the strongest way to secure work-family programs and benefits in individual workplaces and ensure that they are not eroded or abused by employers or lack of supervisor support, and (2) there is a need for public policies on work and family, and unions are playing a role in passing state and federal legislation.

Every day, working people are forced to choose between their jobs and their families. Take the bus driver who has to get her kids to child care by 5:00 a.m. because she cannot be even two minutes late for her shift; the home health aide who makes just above minimum wage and cannot afford quality child care; the secretary who cannot afford to take unpaid family leave to care for her seriously ill parent.

Current workplace practices and public policies make it extremely difficult for working people who need time and resources to care for their families. New work-family policies—policies like child and elder care benefits and subsidies, flexible work schedules, family leave, leave to care for a sick child, and the like—make a world of difference. Achieving these new policies, however, requires organized constituencies advocating for change.

Unions are committed partners in the push for such change. In both individual workplaces and the public policy arena, unions represent a large constituency of working families. In fact, with over 15 million members (U.S. Bureau of Labor Statistics 2007), they represent more working families than any other organization in the United States. They are, therefore, an important voice in the movement to help improve and expand the child care system, address the growing issue of elder care, win paid family leave, and assure flexible work schedules.

Working families today are facing several major problems: (1) the lack of affordable quality child care services and the limited availability of child care services, including after hours and weekends; (2) the absence of workplace policies supportive of parenting and caregiving, including family leave and flexible work schedules; and (3) the lack of elder care services.

Balancing Work and Family—Labor Strategies

Since the early days of the U.S. labor movement, family and children's issues have been union issues. As the former president of Service Employees International Union (SEIU) 1199 Dennis Rivera points out, issues such as child care cannot be isolated from other issues important to labor unions. "What's important," he states, "is (that) the labor movement be a source of meaningful improvement in people's lives."[1] The labor movement has to fight for progressive social policies and also provide direct help and assistance to working people.

Labor has generally used three main strategies in the struggle for better conditions for working families: collective bargaining, legislation, and organizing. This chapter will focus on collective bargaining and legislation as a strategy for improving work and family policies.

Bargaining

Unions often "set the bar" for benefits and programs by negotiating for workers who are not in the segment of the population that employers want to "recruit or retain" as well as those who are valued because they are highly skilled or well educated, such as janitors, nursing aides, retail clerks, and bus drivers. They broaden the class of workers that become entitled to child care benefits, paid family leave, or flexible hours. These policies are critically important to all workers, from highly paid attorneys and executives to the workers who do the filing and clean the toilets. Union-negotiated work and family benefits can level the playing field by ensuring these benefits for all levels of workers rather than only the "highly valued" ones employers seek to recruit and retain.

In addition, negotiated benefits and programs are those that have been hammered out at the bargaining table with workers and employers; so, we would hope that these are in fact the benefits and provisions that best suit workers. Once in the collective bargaining agreement, there is a process for a grievance resolution and even arbitration if the terms of the contract are being violated. Although these contract provisions do not always work perfectly, they rely less on the "kindness of others"—the luck of having a good or supportive supervisor—and more on the "letter of the law" of the contract. Once in the contract, an employer cannot eliminate or change the program or benefit because business is not good or there are changes in the company. The provisions are protected by the collective bargaining agreement.

Unions use collective bargaining to address work and family issues. These may include child care services, elder care programs, flexible or alternative work schedules, and a range of family leave options. No systematic study has yet been done that documents the number of union contracts with work-family provisions or the types of provisions covered in such contracts. A good source of data on union-won, family-friendly provisions is the Best Contracts database of the Labor Project for Working Families. This database, with about 300 contracts, catalogues union contracts in the areas of paid and unpaid family leave, short-term leave, leave to care for sick children, child care (sick, emergency, and off-hours care), elder care, and flexible work schedules. The following cases, drawn from this Best Contracts database, profile several examples of work-family programs that were collectively bargained (Labor Project for Working Families 2007).

Child Care

There are many examples in labor/management contract language that provide for child care assistance. One example is the SEIU 1199. In 1989, when 1199 was preparing for contract negotiations, it faced a number of critical issues. In meetings and conversations with union leaders, many 1199 members had been complaining about the lack of services for child care in their communities due to underfunding of the public school system and crumbling parochial schools. Also, the union was constantly dealing with workers for whom they had to file grievances to defend them for arriving late to work, leaving early, or otherwise responding to household issues. A union survey found that a significant percentage of union members identified child care as a priority for themselves and their families, and in 1989 the union bargained for an employer-paid child care trust fund.

Today, employers from over 400 institutions contribute a certain percent of their gross payroll to the SEIU 1199/Employer Child Care Fund, which is administered by a labor-management board of trustees. The fund now provides a wide range of benefits for children of all ages:

- two child care centers,
- cash vouchers for child care ($780–$3,900) and after-school care ($400–$800),
- child care resources and referrals,
- summer camp programs and subsidies,
- a holiday program,
- a cultural arts program,
- college prep and leadership programs for teenagers, and
- parenting workshops.

In 2006, the fund provided program benefits to over 13,000 children. The joint fund serves as a model for the provision of quality and affordable child care and children's programs (Labor Project for Working Families 2007).

Flexibility

The flexibility to control work schedules and hours allows workers to meet their responsibilities outside of the workplace. It is imperative that flexible working-time arrangements offer opportunities to work while safeguarding needs for security (i.e., wages, benefits, job, etc.). A recent report of the European Trade Union Confederation uses the term "flexicurity" (flexibility + security) as an important marker of a balanced and worker-friendly flexible working-time arrangement (Pilinger 2006).

Having a union contract ensures that the union has negotiated with the employer to ensure that workers' rights are protected, that they have some control over their work time, and that there is a mechanism through a grievance process to resolve problems.

A Life-Course Approach

Flexible arrangements need to incorporate a life-course approach so as to address the diversity of working-time needs over a person's lifetime. A life-course approach can help workers address unforeseen and ongoing personal and family needs and attain career flexibility with multiple points for entry, exit, and reentry into the workforce.

Such work arrangements allow workers flexibility in scheduling work hours (alternative work schedules and arrangements regarding shifts and break schedules), the number of hours worked (part-time work with benefits and job shares), and the place of work (working at home or at a satellite location).

An exemplary example of flexibility is the Harvard clerical union, an American Federation of State, County, and Municipal Employees local. The Harvard union contract focuses on work redesign and creating a workplace where workers resolve conflict but also build community. The union and the university have agreed to "build a framework for greater employee participation." The union has developed a process whereby most issues related to leave and flexibility can be addressed and resolved between supervisor and employee, and if not, then by local and regional problem-solving teams. Principles of this process hold that (1) workplace problems are best solved at the local level, (2) consensus building is the most effective approach to problem solving, (3) individuals involved in this process should be trained, and (4) the process is intended to be flexible and encourage employees to seek resolution.

The Harvard clerical union sees 1,000 problem-solving cases each year; generally only one is settled by a mediator. About one-half of these cases usually involve flexibility in scheduling. The forum for local employee participation in workplace issues is the Joint Council (JC) at each school or administrative department. Larger policy issues are dealt with at the JC level. The JC is meant to promote communication and consensus building between managers and staff. Individual problems are handled through a problem-resolution procedure (Labor Project for Working Families 2007).

Other types of flexibility language in the contact include the following:

- flexible work hours,
- compressed/flexible workweek,
- variable part-year schedules,
- voluntary furlough,

- shift swap,
- part-time with benefits,
- job-sharing with benefits,
- part-time return to work,
- limits on mandatory overtime,
- shorter workweek, and
- flexible time off in short increments.

Leave

Another huge area of bargaining in the work-family arena is family leave. During the course of a workers' work life, he or she may need to take time off to care for a baby or a sick family member. Unions negotiate many forms of leave:

- paid family leave,
- leave in short increments,
- leave for victims of domestic violence,
- stress leave,
- mentoring or school-related leave,
- sick time for family members,
- broad definition of family,
- donated leave, and
- expanding the Family and Medical Leave Act (FMLA) through the contract.

Public Policy

Years ago, I worked with a graduate student from Sweden who was pregnant. She was appalled at our lack of paid maternity leave and services for young children. She was going home to have her baby. Our lack of policies seemed barbaric. We need to remind ourselves how different the United States is from other countries for working women and families. A report by the Project on Global Working Families (Heymann 2004) found that the United States lags behind other countries in many areas, including leave policies and services for children. Consider the following:

- Of 173 countries surveyed, only 4 do not offer guaranteed paid leave to women in connection with childbirth—the United States, Liberia, Swaziland, and Papua New Guinea.

- At least 76 countries protect working women's right to breastfeed; the United States does not, despite breastfeeding having been shown to reduce infant mortality sevenfold.
- At least 96 countries around the world mandate paid annual leave (vacation); the United States does not.
- At least 84 countries have laws that fix the maximum length of the workweek; the United States does not have a maximum length of the workweek or a limit on mandatory overtime per week.
- The United States is 39th (and tied with Ecuador and Suriname) in enrollment in early childhood care and education for 3- to 5-year-olds.
- In the United States, eligibility for child care subsidies is set so low that often, even very low income workers do not qualify.

For over a century, unions have fought in the state and federal legislatures to improve the work and family lives of U.S. workers. From the five-day workweek to overtime compensation, from livable wages to retirement pensions, unions have pushed for and won vital work-family supports. Recently, unions have pushed for laws to limit mandatory overtime for health care workers, provide unemployment insurance due to child care responsibilities, expand FMLA, and allow workers to use paid sick leave to care for family members.

In 2006, legislation for some type of paid family leave had been proposed in 19 states. Labor-community coalitions in eight states (Washington, New Jersey, Maine, Massachusetts, Wisconsin, Georgia, New York, and California), working together as the Multi-State Working Families Consortium, have been actively pushing legislation to address various work-time issues. These coalitions involve state labor federations and various unions working with community-based organizations to activate union members and community activists on behalf of family-friendly policies. Each state has a slightly different focus, from expanding FMLA, to requiring employers to provide a minimum number of paid sick days that can also be used to care for families, to more comprehensive paid family leave laws.

In 2002, a labor-community coalition in California passed the first paid family leave law in the country. In the 2006 legislative session, Washington State became the second state—it passed a law for paid parental leave. Massachusetts introduced legislation requiring employers to provide a minimum of seven paid sick days that can be used for a worker's own illness or to care for a sick family member. Maine passed a bill that allows workers to use a portion of their sick days to care for family members, and New Jersey passed a paid family leave law in 2008 that builds on the State Temporary Disability Program (Paid Family Leave Collaborative 2007).

Paid family leave, affordable child care, and flexibility with safeguards are winning policy issues because they are important to everyone. We cannot do this workplace by workplace. Some companies will always be more enlightened than others and institute good policies, some will do it to get on the "100 Best Companies for Working Mothers" list, and still others will understand that it's good for business.

But most employers won't provide paid family leave or flexibility that is good for workers unless it is mandated through law. In September 2007, the MultiState Working Families Consortium released a report called "Family Values at Work: It's About Time! Why We Need Minimum Standards to Ensure a Family-Friendly Workplace" (Mendel 2007). It calls for expanding the U.S. minimum labor standards to include those policies that help workers to balance work and family.

It is critical that we make work and family issues public policy issues so they cover all workers and are not at the whim of the marketplace. What do workers need? They need good wages, safe jobs, health insurance for themselves and their families, and retirement benefits, but they also need affordable quality child care, paid sick days, paid family leave, flexible work schedules, and elder care resources.

These are not separate issues that we will win when we have won everything else; they are part of the fabric that is needed in today's workplaces, with today's workforce. No one is home baking chocolate chip cookies and taking grandma to the doctor, so we should stop acting like we all have full-time stay-at-home wives and make public policies and laws that reflect the lives we now lead. Unions often set the standards for the workplace through collective bargaining; now unions are setting the standards for good public policies so that workers do not have to choose between their jobs and their families.

Conclusion

In many ways, today's labor unions do indeed speak for America's working families. At the bargaining table and through legislation, unions are and have historically been a voice demanding affordable, quality care for children and promoting a balance between work and family.

Unions have bargained for innovative policies and benefits for all types of workers through union contracts. But we need to go beyond workplace by workplace, employer by employer. We need to step into the modern world and pass laws that allow men and women to have real choices to raise their children and care for their families—and not have to choose between a job and a family.

NOTE

This chapter is based on the testimony of Carol Joyner, member, National Advisory Board of the Labor Project for Working Families, given before the U.S. Equal Employment Opportunity Commission, May 23, 2007, and drafted by the author.

1. Personal interview, 1999.

REFERENCES

Heymann, Jody. 2004. "The Work, Family and Equity Index: Where Does the United States Stand Globally?" The Project on Global Working Families. Boston, MA: Harvard School of Public Health.

Labor Project for Working Families. 2007. "Labor Contracts Database." http://www.irle.berkeley.edu/library/index.php?page=3. Berkeley, CA: Institute for Research on Labor and Employment Library. (Accessed July 6, 2008.) [Note: This is commonly called the Best Contracts Database.]

Mendel, Richard A. 2007. "Family Values at Work: It's About Time! Why We Need Minimum Standards to Ensure a Family-Friendly Workplace." Milwaukee, WI: MultiState Working Families Consortium. http://www.9to5.org/familyvaluesatwork/. (Accessed July 6, 2008.)

Paid Family Leave Collaborative. 2007. "Paid Leave Activity in Other States." Berkeley, CA: Paid Family Leave Collaborative. http://www.paidfamilyleave.org/otherstates.html. (Accessed July 6, 2008.)

Pilinger, Jane, ed. 2006. Report of the European Trade Union Confederation Conference: Challenging Times—Innovative Ways of Organizing Working Time, the Role of Unions. Brussels: ETUC.

U.S. Bureau of Labor Statistics. 2007. "Union Membership (Annual)." Washington, DC: U.S. Department of Labor. http://www.bls.gov/news.release/union2.toc.htm. (Accessed October 1, 2007).

Union Bargaining Strategies for Family-Friendly Provisions

Table 3A.1. Child Care Services and Financing Bargaining Strategies

The strategy	About the strategy	Model contract examples[a]
Resource and referral services	Finding high-quality, reliable, affordable care can be very difficult for working parents. Resource and referral services can help match employees with appropriate and available child care providers, taking into consideration the special needs of each family. An employer may contract with an outside agency or handle referrals in-house. Resource and referral services also can help develop child care resources in an area if no appropriate child care exists.	International Brotherhood of Electrical Workers Local 1245 and Pacific Gas and Electric
Tax programs	A dependent care assistance plan or flexible spending account allows workers to set aside up to $5,000 of their earnings in a tax-free account to pay for child care or elder care. The only cost to the employer for this IRS plan is its administration.	International Union of Electrical Workers and General Electric
Child care funds	Child care funds offset the high cost of child care. A child care fund provides reimbursement for child care expenses or payment directly to a child care provider.	1199 Service Employees International Union, NYC, Child Care Fund and Contributing Employers

Employer-provided child care	Unions have negotiated for on-site and off-site child care centers, subsidized slots in existing centers, and networks of family day care homes. Setting up a child care center is a costly and time-consuming process. Before negotiating for a child care center, be sure to consider the needs of your members: Do they prefer in-home or center care? Are they willing to drive to an off-site center? What shifts do they work? Are their children preschool age?	International Association of Machinists District Lodge 751 and Boeing Co.
Backup and sick child care	Backup care can be provided for mildly sick children on days when normal care arrangements fall through or in other unusual situations, such as snow days. Parents of school-age children may need child care during summer vacations and on holidays. Backup care can be provided through a special program, such as employer subsidies for in-home care or a backup center, or by allowing parents to use their sick time to care for sick children.	Alameda County Employees Labor Coalition/Service Employees International Union Locals 535, 616 and 790, and Alameda County, California
Extended hours for child care	Many working parents need child care before 9:00 a.m. and after 5:00 p.m., including before- and after-school hours and during extended hours when parents are working shifts.	United Auto Workers and the Tonawanda Business Community Child Care Consortium

a. For actual contract language from these and other "best practices" contracts, contact the Labor Project for Working Families, 2521 Channing Way No. 5555, Berkeley, CA, 94720, (510) 643-0788, or view the Labor Project's web page at http://www.working-families.org/.

Table 3A.2. Elder Care Services and Financing Bargaining Strategies

The strategy	About the strategy	Model contract examples[a]
Resource and referral services	Finding high-quality, reliable, affordable care can be very difficult for working people. Resource and referral services can help match employees with appropriate and available care providers, taking into consideration the special needs of each family. Employers either contract with an outside referral agency or handle referrals in-house.	United Auto Workers and General Motors Corporation
Tax programs	A dependent care assistance plan or flexible spending account allows workers to set aside up to $5,000 of their earnings in a tax-free account to pay for child care or elder care. The only cost to the employer for this IRS plan is its administration.	International Union of Electrical Workers and General Electric
Elder care funds	Elder care funds offset the high cost of dependent care. Funds provide direct cash payments or a reimbursement for elder care expenses.	UNITE HERE Local 2 and San Francisco Hotel Multi-employer Group
Family leave	Time off to care for an elder or another dependent is a commonly used solution for working families' elder care needs.	United Food and Commercial Workers and Gallo Wines, Distillery Wine Division

Support services	Some unions directly provide or work with employers to provide information and support as a way of addressing members' elder care needs. This strategy can help working people with elder care responsibilities make decisions about elder care strategies and reduce personal stress. Such services include counseling, referral services, seminars, support groups, handbooks and videos, and work and family committees.	UNITE HERE
Long-term care	Long-term care can be provided directly, either through the union or by the employer.	United Auto Workers and Michigan Blue Cross–Blue Shield
Sick time for sick family members	Unions have negotiated to allow workers to use their own sick time to care for sick family members.	Harvard Union of Clerical and Technical Workers and Harvard University

a. For actual contract language from these and other "best practices" contracts, contact the Labor Project for Working Families, 2521 Channing Way No. 5555, Berkeley, CA, 94720, (510) 643-0788, or view the Labor Project's web page at http://www.working-families.org/.

Table 3A.3. Family Leave Bargaining Strategies

The strategy	About the strategy	Model contract examples[a]
Family leave	Family leave gives an employee the right to take time off from work to care for a newborn or newly adopted child, to care for a family member who is seriously ill, or sometimes, for other personal reasons.	United Steelworkers of America Local 12075 and Dow Chemical
Parental leave	Parental leave is taken by mothers and fathers to care for newborn, newly adopted, or foster care children. It is very effective in reducing turnover, training costs, and absenteeism. Five states provide temporary disability leave for women for pregnancy or childbirth. Some contracts also contain provisions offering this benefit. Temporary disability leave often is used in combination with parental leave. The best parental leave language provides for paid leave, but many contracts offer unpaid leave as well.	American Federation of Musicians Local 6 and the San Francisco Symphony Orchestra
Part-time return to work	Many new parents want to work part time after children are born or adopted. Unions have bargained for part-time return to work for new parents.	Northern California Newspaper Guild Local 52 and San Francisco Chronicle and Examiner
Short-term leave	Working families often need short periods of time off from work, such as a half day or a few hours. Unions have bargained contracts allowing time off for various personal reasons, including school-related activities and adoption proceedings.	Service Employees International Union Local 790 and the San Francisco Unified School District

Donated leave and leave banks	Some union contracts allow employees to donate their own leave directly to a leave bank or to another employee who has used all of her own leave. Leave of this sort may be reserved for workers having serious family or personal crises.	New York State Nurses Association and St. Luke's Roosevelt Hospital Center
Expanded definition of family	The traditional idea of family as composed of a mother, father, and children does not describe many of today's working families. The definition of family in leave clauses is being broadened to include many different kinds of relationships.	Public Employees, Local One, and the Unified School District of Berkeley
Paid time off (PTO)	PTO generally combines sick and personal leave time and is separate from other vacation time employees may have. It can be used for any personal reason, such as caring for a sick child or recuperating from one's own illness.	UNITE HERE Local 2 and S.F. Hotel Multi-employer Group
Time for sick family members	Unions have negotiated to allow workers to use their own sick time to care for sick family members.	United Auto Workers Local 2324 and United Front Child Development Programs
Leave for special causes	Sometimes working people need leave to deal with particular family-related issues. Unions have bargained for leave to be taken in special situations, such as for families suffering from domestic violence.	American Federation of State, County, and Municipal Employees, Service Employees Union, and the Commonwealth of Massachusetts

a. For actual contract language from these and other "best practices" contracts, contact the Labor Project for Working Families, 2521 Channing Way No. 5555, Berkeley, CA, 94720, (510) 643-0788, or view the Labor Project's web page at http://www.working-families.org/.

Table 3A.4. Family and Medical Leave Act Bargaining Strategies

The strategy	About the strategy	Model contract examples[a]
Making FMLA leave paid	Many working families cannot afford to take needed time off without pay. Receiving pay while on FML can make it possible to use rights given under the law.	American Federation of State, County, and Municipal Employees Local 11 and the State of Ohio
Building FMLA language	If an employer violates FMLA law in some way, the only recourse is to file a complaint with the Department of Labor or to hire a lawyer. Both strategies can be very time consuming. If the employer agrees in a union contract to abide by the FMLA, violations can be settled through the union's grievance procedure.	UNITE HERE Local 2850 and Concession Air Inc., Oakland International Airport
Expanding FMLA coverage	Not all employers are required to abide by the FMLA. For example, employers with fewer than 50 employees need not provide FMLA benefits. Contracts can assure the right to FMLA benefits for all members, regardless of whether the members or the employer meet eligibility guidelines of the FMLA.	Service Employees International Union Local 1021 and the Labor Project for Working Families
Expanding reasons for FML	FMLA leave can be taken only for an employee's own serious illness; for the birth, adoption, or foster care placement of a child; or to care for a seriously ill spouse, parent, or child. By defining family in a contract as including, for example, grandparents, domestic partners, and in-laws, unions expand the instances in which an employee can take FML.	Public Employees Local One and the Unified School District of Berkeley

Increasing length of leave	In some cases, 12 weeks is not enough time to deal with some family or medical situations. The length of FMLA leave can be increased through bargaining.	United Auto Workers Local 2324 and United Front Child Development Programs
Limiting employers' rights	Unions can bargain to limit employers' right to designate what kind of paid leave will be used for FML.	Service Employees International Union Local 1877 and Apcoa Inc.
Continuing benefits during leave	Under the FMLA, employers must continue to provide health benefits on the same basis as before the leave, but they are not obligated to provide any other benefits or to help an employee who becomes unable to afford to pay his or her share of health insurance premiums.	United Auto Workers and Ford Motor Company
Accruing seniority during leave	Under the FMLA, seniority accrues during leave only for the purposes of vesting and eligibility in pension and retirement funds. Unions can bargain for accrual of seniority for other purposes as well, such as for vacation time or scheduling.	UNITE HERE Local 2 and San Francisco Hotel Multi-employer Group
Returning to work after a birth	Intermittent leave is allowed under the FMLA only for a serious health condition of the employee or employee's spouse, child, or parent. Unions can expand this provision to allow new parents to work reduced or intermittent schedules.	American Federation of Teachers Local 3695 and the University of Connecticut

a. For actual contract language from these and other "best practices" contracts, contact the Labor Project for Working Families, 2521 Channing Way No. 5555, Berkeley, CA, 94720, (510) 643-0788, or view the Labor Project's web page at http://www.working-families.org/.

Table 3A.5. Alternative Work Schedules Bargaining Strategies

The strategy	About the strategy	Model contract examples[a]
Flextime	Flextime agreements allow employees to start and end work during some range of hours. All employees may be required to be present during a core period.	Communications Workers of America and BellSouth Telecommunications
Part-time work with benefits	Part-time work can give people flexibility to take care of family needs; however, a part-time schedule may be unworkable if it does not come with health care and other benefits. Unions have bargained to provide part-time employees with benefits.	International Brotherhood of Electrical Workers Local 1245 and Pacific Gas and Electric
Telecommuting	Telecommuting means working from a site other than the central work site, usually at home. Unions have traditionally opposed this because work done at home is difficult to regulate and can easily become "sweatshop" labor. Also, workers who telecommute can become isolated and are difficult to organize. However, telecommuting can offer workers a great deal of flexibility and many union members favor it.	Service Employees International Union Local 660 and Los Angeles County
Job sharing	Under a job-share agreement, two part-time employees share one full-time job. The employees divide the full-time salary according to hours worked. Benefits and seniority often are prorated according to hours worked, although in some job-share situations both may receive full benefits and/or seniority. Union contracts can protect employees' right to enter into a job-share arrangement and can establish standards for job sharing.	American Federation of State, County, and Municipal Employees Local 2505 and Executive Department of the State of Oregon
Compressed workweek	Compressed work schedules allow full-time workers to work all their hours in fewer than five days per week. Common examples of these schedules allow workers to work four 10-hour days for an extra day off per week, or eight 9-hour days and one 8-hour day for an extra day off every two weeks.	International Brotherhood of Teamsters Local 830 and Philadelphia Coca-Cola Bottling Company

Making overtime voluntary	For many working families, being forced to stay at work past the regularly scheduled end time can be very stressful, particularly for working parents who do not have backup arrangements for child care. Provisions in union contracts making overtime voluntary protect employees from this loss of power over their daily schedules.	Washington-Baltimore Newspaper Guild Local 35 and Bureau of National Affairs
Shift swaps	A shift swap provision in a union contract allows workers to exchange shifts or workdays voluntarily to accommodate family needs, such as attending school events or medical appointments.	Association of Western Pulp and Paper Workers and Longview Fibre Company, Longview Mill
Shorter workweek	Unions have bargained for shorter workweeks for their members with full compensation. Some unions also have used shorter workweek provisions with less compensation as an alternative to layoffs.	Office and Professional Employees International Union Local 3 and S.F., Marin, and Sonoma Trade Union Health and Welfare and Pension Fund offices
Voluntary reduced time	Voluntary reduced time allows an employee to reduce the number of hours she or he works in a week in order to have extra time to take care of personal or family needs.	Service Employees International Union Local 715 and Santa Clara and San Mateo counties, California

Source: Labor Project for Working Families (2007).

Note: Some union names may have changed.

a. For actual contract language from these and other "best practices" contracts, contact the Labor Project for Working Families, 2521 Channing Way No. 5555, Berkeley, CA, 94720, (510) 643-0788, or view the Labor Project's web page at http://www.working-families.org/.

4

The Design of Work as a Key Driver of Work-Life Flexibility for Professionals

Forrest Briscoe

llen Kossek and Brian Distelberg (this volume) provide us with a useful and provocative review of the employer supports that help Americans reduce work-family conflict. They marshal evidence from the best survey data available to suggest that, in short, employers are mostly treading water in this area. Most workers lack access to any formal paid work-family policies, and voluntary adoption by employers is highly uneven across the economy. With regard to an emerging hot topic in work-family research, that of flexibility, Kossek and Distelberg find the data harder to interpret. There is little clarity across employers, across surveys, or across researchers on what this concept means, and it often combines temporal and spatial dimensions (e.g., schedule flexibility versus telecommuting). Nonetheless, with regard to flexibility as well as other employer supports, a recurrent theme is that even when employers offer relevant policies, workers do not report using them.

Building on earlier work by Kossek (2006), their chapter also offers a useful analytic framework to help us understand why this might be the case, based on a stool with three legs, each representing a feature of the workplace that affects work-life outcomes. The three legs are (1) human resources (HR) policies, (2) organizational culture and informal supports, and (3) the design of work. Kossek and Distelberg argue that all three legs of the stool matter for workers seeking flexibility, but by far, the most practically developed and studied one is the first. This imbalance has implications because it suggests that HR policies implemented without cultural and informal supports or consideration of the design of work may be less effective.

This chapter will focus on the third and least developed leg of that stool: the design (and, therefore, also the nature) of work itself. There are good reasons this leg is shorter than the rest. The design of work is often viewed as a core function of organizations that is central to their effectiveness and survival, making it difficult to critically study or alter for purposes of workers' own flexibility needs. Work also varies greatly across occupations, organizations, work groups, and individuals, making it difficult to conceptualize at any level of generality. Perhaps nowhere are these barriers greater than in professional occupations, in which work is highly complex and variable. Nevertheless, it can be argued that for many professional workers, the nature and design of work is an indispensable lever for flexibility, and one which is, in fact, already being manipulated in powerful and hopeful ways that should not be overlooked by work-family researchers. Using in-depth studies of one particular profession, this chapter will attempt to draw out themes related to work design that may be applied in other occupational contexts as well.

The Need to Understand
the Nature and Design of Work

To begin, consider the case of Susan K.—mother of two preschoolers, only child of ailing parents, and part of a dual-career household. Susan desperately wants the flexibility to adjust her work hours in order to respond to her family demands. What are the chances of Susan finding that flexibility? If Susan has an enlightened employer offering work-life HR benefits such as flextime, her odds should go up. If her supervisor also happens to be enlightened with regard to the value of accommodating subordinates' work-life needs, her odds should rise further.

But how does the story change if we learn that Susan is a physician? Her income will certainly help pay for nannies, babysitters, elder care, housecleaning, and other related services, partly alleviating her inherent need for flexibility. But the limits on her flexibility stemming from the nature of medical work are also formidable. Work schedules are very constrained by the need to treat patients who get sick at unpredictable and inconvenient times. In fact, the traditional medical practice for over a century has been organized around this need to respond to untimely patient illnesses (Starr 1982). In this situation, it appears that neither HR policies nor informal supports will do much to help Susan K. find flexibility. It is the nature of work that serves to constrain her flexibility, and therefore, the (re)design of work that holds potential for enabling her flexibility.

From society's point of view, the high price of medical services may be partly justified by the willingness of physicians to make themselves accessible to patients in this manner (Zerubavel 1979). Yet from the physician's point of view, such extreme levels of accessibility were only historically feasible with a family structure that buffered him from any need to be involved in parenting or other significant caregiving or household roles. In short, if the "ideal worker" of yesteryear was a male breadwinner with a stay-at-home wife who could insulate him from family demands (Acker 1990; Bailyn 1993; Williams 2000), the "ideal physician" fit that description to an even greater extent.

The disconnect between that "ideal" image and the current reality of physicians could not be more abrupt. The percentage of women entering the field of medicine has risen from 7 percent in 1970 to 49 percent in 2005 (AAMC 2006). Family structure also shifted over that time, such that dual-career families have become the norm in medicine, and in fact, dual-physician families are very common (Sobecks et al. 1999). These changes bring growing interest in schedule flexibility, nontraditional career options, and personal quality of life (Moody 2002).

Workplaces Where Physicians Actually Have Flexibility

Observing these trends, I set out to find which, if any, workplaces are better for physicians to obtain flexibility. In studying physicians—who lie at an extreme end of the occupational spectrum in terms of constraints on their flexibility—I also hoped to learn lessons that could be applied to professionals in other occupations with less extreme constraints. From June 2001 to May 2005 I gathered data on the work practices and careers of primary care physicians across a range of medical practice organizations in the United States. The research included two original surveys with a combined total of 588 respondents, more than 40 interviews combined with field observations in six medical practice organizations, and secondary analyses of two national surveys (Briscoe 2006, 2007, 2008).

What I found initially surprised me: physicians have more short-term schedule flexibility when they work in settings that are more bureaucratic—that is, characterized by standardizing rules and procedures. Not only this, but physicians in those more-bureaucratic contexts have greater *career* flexibility as well, reflected in their ability to take part-time stints ranging from months to years in length, during which they spend more time with families or pursue other kinds of work activities outside the clinic. Such part-time arrangements are notoriously difficult for physicians to achieve. More-bureaucratic medical practice organizations also tend to attract physicians whom one would anticipate valuing flexibility. The odds of practicing in a more bureaucratic organization rise for female physicians and for physicians of both sexes who identify themselves as primary caregivers within their families. Bureaucratic intensity also tends to correlate positively with workplace size, although subsequent analyses indicated that the enhanced flexibility derives from bureaucratization rather than size alone.

How Do Bureaucratized Workplaces Provide More Flexibility?

To understand why bureaucracy enables flexibility for physicians, it helps to start with a simple model of the physician's work. The constraint on physician flexibility stems from two features of that work: (1) patient needs appear unpredictably and urgently and (2) treatment often depends on knowledge and trust forged in an earlier encounter between physician and patient. The confluence of those two conditions implies that when a physician's patients get sick, that physician has few options other than to attend to those patients personally, no matter what else he or she had previously planned to be doing at that time.

The bureaucratization of the medical workplace actually changes that second feature of medical work, reducing the need for treatment to be delivered by the same physician who was present in earlier patient encounters. In the bureaucratic workplace, rules and procedures have the effect of standardizing much about the way physicians approach patient symptoms, the way they record information about patients, and the way they set patients' expectations about the services they will receive. As a result, when a given patient becomes ill, the options for competently treating that patient are expanded to include not just the particular physician who treated him or her in the past, but also other physicians and caregivers in the same workplace. In the most bureaucratized settings, those physicians share standardized treatment protocols, use a common electronic medical record system, and have primed their patients to expect a team approach to medical services rather than an entirely personal one.

In short, standardization is increasing the scope for patient handoffs among physicians, and this appears to be the key for physicians to achieve flexibility. At an abstract level, the link between standardization and handoffs is something that organizational theorists from Frederick Taylor onward might have predicted. While details, motivations, and consequences of the movement to standardize medical work are certainly complex and contentious, nonetheless it is clear that those medical practice workplaces that are more standardized are also those in which physicians find more flexibility.

It is equally important to appreciate that flexibility for physicians is accompanied by tradeoffs. The bureaucratic intensification, which paradoxically enables flexibility, also represents a measurable loss of individual autonomy over work (Briscoe 2006). This is an important change for members of a profession known for individual autonomy (Starr 1982). Anecdotally, the bureaucratic settings also may be associated with lower prestige and income for physicians. Objective effects on the quality of patient care are also of obvious concern and need to be a subject of future research.

What the Case of Physicians May Tell Us about Other Professionals

If it generalizes, this analysis could offer insights into flexibility for a wider range of professionals. Flexibility in many other professional occupations is also critically limited by the core task of providing client service—clients demand timely attention, and there are nontrivial barriers preventing one professional from handing off client work to another person. When bureaucratic processes such as those outlined above serve to relax that constraint, they should also enable new options for flexibility. Occupations to which this logic might apply include many medical specialties, corporate lawyers, laboratory scientists, financial advisors, investment bankers, university professors, accountants, architects, management consultants, and advertising and design professionals. Indeed, work-family scholars are increasingly concluding that there must be distinctive sources of flexibility for such occupations (Epstein et al. 1999; Jacobs and Gerson 1998; Kossek, Lautsch, and Eaton 2005; Lee, MacDermid, and Buck 2000; MacDermid and Tang 2006; Wharton and Blair-Loy 2002).

The model may also generalize further beyond client-based occupations. For example, the project teams that are common in high technology require workers seeking flexibility to orient toward other team members, somewhat like the physician does her patients. That is, the worker has to be responsive to demands that arise from others on the team at unpredictable times and cannot easily hand off those demands to someone else. Similarly, internal service workers, like computer network administrators, endure constraints in the sense that they must be responsive to unpredictably timed demands that cannot easily be handed off. Here, too, greater bureaucratization may provide increased flexibility.

These professional and technical workers represent a large and growing swath of the overall economy. Depending on the definition used, professional and technical services constitute or directly influence between 15 and 25 percent of the United States' gross domestic product (GDP), and however measured, that share has been expanding over time (Barley and Orr 1997; Broschak 2004). Furthermore, bureaucratizing changes are taking place across many professional occupations, which parallel the case of medicine. For example, organizations employing lawyers, accountants, engineers, and consultants are adopting standardizing project management and knowledge management systems to coordinate work and transfer insights across projects and clients (Adler 2005; Hansen and Haas 2001; Morris 2001). Such developments could be creating similar conditions for enhancing workplace flexibility.

It is also worth noting how these findings contrast with the view that professional and technical workers can find flexibility by escaping the confines of bureaucratic organizations. Scholars have recently debated the possibility that flexibility might be gained through a career of relative independence from organizations, for example, through independent contracting (Arthur and Rousseau 1996; Evans, Kunda, and Barley 2004). The case of physicians suggests caution: when the constraints on flexibility stem from the work itself, the best hope for alleviating such constraints may come from being firmly embedded in an organizational context.

Implications for Research and Policy

The specific finding that bureaucratized workplaces enable flexibility speaks directly to recent attempts at conceptualizing flexibility. Work-family scholars have recently identified the need to disentangle flexibility over work content, location, and timing (Kossek et al. 2005; MacDermid and Tang 2006). This study's findings indicate that *for some important professional workers, losing control over work content is actually necessary in order to gain control over the timing of work.* Hence, empirically, physicians' job autonomy is negatively related to their schedule and career flexibility. Why? Because the nature of their work is the major constraint on their flexibility, and bureaucratized contexts, which reduce their control of work, also help minimize that constraint on flexibility. For a broader model of flexibility, this suggests the need to better incorporate the nature of work. One possible way to do that might be to better conceptualize sources of constraint, such as client or project-team interdependencies.

Other interesting questions arise from the convergence of professional bureaucratization and personal flexibility. First, how will future generations of professionals view the tradeoff between work autonomy and personal flexibility that is captured in this analysis? Does gaining flexibility mean losing the professional "calling"? This study's research suggests a more nuanced account: career satisfaction was not lower among physicians in the bureaucratized settings. Yet that raises another possibility— namely the emergence of new forms of stratification within the professions based on who is willing to make the tradeoff between autonomy and flexibility. This could happen if bureaucratized workplaces are disproportionately chosen by women or by family caregivers of either sex who seek flexibility (Drago 2007; Leicht and Fennell 1997). Hence a second question: will the many other dimensions that might differ between flexible and inflexible workplaces potentially create new forms of industry and labor market segmentation?

Returning to the three-legged stool, these findings suggest that for key groups of professional workers, focusing on HR practices alone is unlikely to improve flexibility. Neither are improvements in organizational culture or informal supports if they are not accompanied by attention to the way work design hampers or enables flexibility. In other words, the third leg of the stool may be the most important one for supporting these workers' access to flexibility.

Because the design of work is a core feature of organizations and occupations, policy efforts to encourage redesign are likely to be fraught with controversy. To date few organizations of any type have agreed to make major changes in the design of core work processes for the purpose of addressing work-family issues, with a few notable exceptions (Moen, Kelly, and Chermack this volume; Perlow 1999; Rapoport et al. 2002). Yet *current changes in the design of work, which are spreading across professional organizations, represent a valuable natural experiment for researchers to study the links between work and workplace variation and flexibility outcomes for professional workers.* Such links may not be immediately recognized by practitioners or scholars who are focused largely on organizational performance outcomes. Research aimed at understanding these linkages will require painstaking field observation (Perlow 1999), a high level of engagement with practitioners (Rapoport et al. 2002), and a deep understanding of occupation and industry.

Many of Kossek and Distelberg's recommendations for advancing research and policy apply equally to the realm of professional work and the focus on work design. For instance, they highlight the importance of tracking organizational outcomes from work-life policies. Though establishing the costs and benefits of changes in work design is a daunting task, it is of great importance here as well. To illustrate, there is a possibility that increasing flexibility for physicians by enabling patient handoffs will adversely affect patient care. In the professional context more broadly, it will be critical to capture impacts of flexible work design on occupationally specific outcomes, such as the ability to effectively solve client problems and meet project goals.

Two final policy implications arise from the history of how medical organizations began offering this physician flexibility in the first place. The changes in physician work that enable flexibility were forged as a byproduct of efforts to reform health care delivery (Briscoe 2006; Laffel and Blumenthal 1989; Starr 1982). The effects on physician flexibility were an unanticipated consequence of those efforts. In fact, such changes might not have emerged at all if they had been framed in terms of work-family needs. That would likely have drawn opposition from traditionally minded physicians who did not want professional commitment (the "calling") to be diluted by personal family considerations. But, instead of being cast as a work-family issue, the innovations that enhanced flexibility were rooted in efforts to improve patient care. Perhaps just as important, their use was not limited to physicians who were mothers; others also took advantage of flexibility options to pursue a range of work and nonwork activities that were unrelated to their family needs. As a result, skeptics could not dismiss the flexibility options as the domain of only a narrow group of workers. This account suggests that work-family advocates should attend carefully to those changes in work design that alter or improve flexibility unintentionally. Secondly, whether intended or not, changes that improve flexibility may face less resistance in many professional workplaces when they are framed as broad developments that address a wider range of worker and organizational needs beyond those linked to family.

REFERENCES

Acker, Joan. 1990. "Hierarchies, Jobs, Bodies: A Theory of Gendered Organizations." *Gender & Society* 4: 139–58.

Adler, Paul. 2005. "The Evolving Object of Software Development." *Organization* 12(3): 401–35.

American Association of Medical Colleges (AAMC). 2006. "AAMC Data Book." http://www.aamc.org/data/databook/start.htm. (Accessed October 2007.)

Arthur, Michael, and Denise Rousseau. 1996. *The Boundaryless Career*. New York: Oxford University Press.

Bailyn, Lotte. 1993. *Breaking the Mold: Women, Men, and Time in the New Corporate World*. New York: The Free Press.

Barley, Stephen, and Julian Orr. 1997. *Between Craft and Science: Technical Work in U.S. Settings*. Ithaca, NY: Cornell University Press.

Briscoe, Forrest. 2006. "Temporal Flexibility and Careers: The Role of Large-Scale Organizations in the Practicing Physician Labor Market." *Industrial and Labor Relations Review* 60(1): 67–83.

———. 2007. "From Iron Cage to Iron Shield? How Bureaucracy Enables Temporal Flexibility for Professional Service Workers." *Organization Science* 18(2): 297–314.

———. 2008. "The Upside of Bureaucracy? Unintended Benefits for Careers in Professional Services." In *The White Collar Workplace: New Models for the 21st Century*, edited by Peter Cappelli (223–56). Cambridge: Cambridge University Press.

Broschak, Joseph. 2004. "Managers' Mobility and Market Interface: The Effect of Managers' Career Mobility on the Dissolution of Market Ties." *Administrative Science Quarterly* 49(4): 608–40.

Drago, Robert. 2007. *Striking a Balance: Work, Family, Life.* Boston: Dollars and Sense.

Epstein, Cynthia Fuchs, Carroll Seron, Bonnie Oglensky, and Robert Saute. 1999. *The Part-Time Paradox: Time Norms, Professional Lives, Family, and Gender.* New York: Routledge.

Evans, James, Gideon Kunda, and Stephen Barley. 2004. "Beach Time, Bridge Time, and Billable Hours: The Temporal Structure of Technical Contracting." *Administrative Science Quarterly* 49(1): 1–38.

Hansen, Martine, and Morten Haas. 2001. "Competing for Attention in Knowledge Markets: Electronic Document Dissemination in a Management Consulting Company." *Administrative Science Quarterly* 46: 1–28.

Jacobs, Jerry, and Kathleen Gerson. 1998. "Who Are the Overworked Americans?" *Review of Social Economy* 56(4): 442–59.

Kossek, Ellen Ernst. 2006. "Work and Family in America: Growing Tensions between Employment Policy and a Changing Workforce." In *America at Work: Choices and Challenges,* edited by Edward E. Lawler and James O'Toole (53–72). New York: Palgrave MacMillan.

Kossek, Ellen Ernst, Brenda Lautsch, and Susan Eaton. 2005. "Flexibility Enactment Theory: Implications of Flexibility Type, Control, and Boundary Management for Work-Family Effectiveness." In *Work and Life Integration: Organizational, Cultural, and Individual Perspectives,* edited by Ellen Ernst Kossek and Susan J. Lambert (234–62). Mahwah, NJ: Erlbaum.

Laffel, Glenn, and David Blumenthal. 1989. "The Case for Using Industrial Quality Management Science in Health Care Organizations." *Journal of the American Medical Association* 262: 2869–73.

Lee, Mary Dean, Shelley MacDermid, and Michelle Buck. 2000. "Organizational Paradigms of Reduced Load Work: Accommodation, Elaboration, Transformation." *Academy of Management Journal* 43(6): 1211–26.

Leicht, Kevin, and Mary Fennell. 1997. "The Changing Organizational Context of Professional Work." *Annual Review of Sociology* 23: 215–31.

MacDermid, Shelley, and Chiung Ya Tang. 2006. "Flexibility and Control: Does One Necessarily Bring the Other?" Manuscript presented at Brigham Young University Families and Work Research Conference, Provo, UT, March 20–22.

Moody, Jennifer. 2002. "Recruiting Generation X Physicians." *New England Journal of Medicine, Recruiting Physicians Today* 10(1): 1–2.

Morris, Timothy. 2001. "Asserting Property Rights: Knowledge Codification in the Professional Service Firm." *Human Relations* 54(7): 819–38.

Perlow, Leslie A. 1999. "The Time Famine: Towards a Sociology of Work Time." *Administrative Science Quarterly* 44: 57–81.

Rapoport, Rhona, Lotte Bailyn, Joyce K. Fletcher, and Bettye H. Pruitt. 2002. *Beyond Work-Family Balance: Advancing Gender Equity and Workplace Performance.* San Francisco: Jossey-Bass.

Sobecks, Nancy W., Amy C. Justice, Susan Hinze, Heidi T. Chirayath, Rebecca J. Lasek, Mary-Margaret Chren, John Aucott, Barbara Juknialis, Richard Fortinsky, Stuart Youngner, and C. Seth Landefeld. 1999. "When Doctors Marry Doctors: A Survey

Exploring the Professional and Family Lives of Young Physicians." *Annals of Internal Medicine* 130(4): 312–19.

Starr, Paul. 1982. *The Transformation of American Medicine*. New York: Basic Books.

Wharton, Amy, and Mary Blair-Loy. 2002. "The Overtime Culture in a Global Corporation: A Cross-National Study of Finance Professionals' Interest in Working Part-Time." *Work and Occupations* 29(1): 32–63.

Williams, Joan C. 2000. *Unbending Gender: Why Family and Work Conflict and What to Do About It*. New York: Oxford University Press.

Zerubavel, Eviatar. 1979. "Private Time and Public Time: The Temporal Structure of Social Accessibility and Professional Commitments." *Social Forces* 58(1): 38–58.

PART II
Intervening in the Corporate Workplace

5

Learning from a Natural Experiment
Studying a Corporate Work-Time Policy Initiative

Phyllis Moen, Erin Kelly, and Kelly Chermack

When we (Erin Kelly and Phyllis Moen) applied for funding to establish the Flexible Work and Well-Being Center at the University of Minnesota (as part of a larger National Institutes of Health, Centers for Disease Control [NIH-CDC] initiative to create an interdisciplinary, collaborative network on work, families, and health), we saw an opportunity to engage in a real-world investigation of an actual private-sector policy *change* aimed at lessening work-family conflicts and strains. This would be far different from simply studying possible associations between an existing policy and various work-family outcomes. We were interested in both (1) the process of organizational change and policy implementation and (2) the impacts of policy shifts aimed at reducing work-family conflicts and enhancing employee well-being at different points over the life course. We were especially drawn to this NIH initiative because it focused on policies changing *work,* not on changing *employees* (by promoting their coping strategies or teaching them stress-reduction techniques, for example).

Although neither of us had previously initiated a true policy intervention, we have always been drawn to *engaged scholarship* bridging the divide between theory and practice (Van de Ven 2007). The request for applications from NIH and the National Institute for Occupational Safety and Health suggested just such a possibility, one that would permit scholars to address a real-world problem by partnering with practitioners and stakeholders in the private sector.

Our goal in crafting the proposal was to theorize a workplace intervention that could potentially have high impact on employees and their families. To do so, we drew on our combined knowledge from (1) our previous research on flexibility policies and practices in organizations and the adaptive strategies of working families across the life course (e.g., Kelly 2003; Kelly and Kalev 2006; Moen 2003; Moen and Roehling 2005), as well as (2) the broad literature on workplace policies, job characteristics, and employee and family well-being, and (3) ongoing discussions with human resources professionals in corporate settings. How did we go from this knowledge base to crafting our actual proposal?

Research Problem and Theory Formulation

First, we recognized that most working families and, indeed, most employees face escalating time pressures, suggesting their need for greater temporal flexibility on the job. But a reduced-hours intervention didn't make sense given the secondary status of part-time employees and the reality that most employees need a full-time income. It was equally clear that an organizational intervention based on existing flexibility policies would not be sufficient, since such policies often result in minimal options for employees (Kelly and Moen 2007; Still and Strang 2003). We did not want to invest our time and taxpayers' money in studying yet one more policy officially "on the books," but in fact *on the margins*. We had previously observed that flexibility policies are actually available to a relatively small number of employees, often those who are especially valued by their employers. Existing flexibility policies may sound promising, but are not really integrated and legitimated within the culture and structure of most employing organizations.

Second, we were impressed by evidence from occupational health psychology, especially Karasek and Theorell's (1990) findings on the importance of *job control* for health. Karasek and Theorell have spawned a large body of theory and research (Bosma, Siegrist, and Marmot 1998; Bourbonnais et al. 1996; Butler, Gasser, and Smart 2004; Butler et al. 2005; Cheng et al. 2000; de Jonge et al. 2000; Dwyer and Ganster 1991; Fox, Dwyer, and Ganster 1993; Hemingway and Marmot 1999; Kristensen 1995, 1996; Landsbergis et al. 1992; Schnall, Landsbergis, and Baker 1994). Such evidence is also congruent with theories of the importance for health of self-direction and control more generally (e.g., Bandura 1982;

Heckhausen and Schulz 1995; Rodin 1986). Still other studies report findings that do not support Karasek and Theorell's job strain model in certain populations or with certain health outcomes (Evans and Steptoe 2002; Marshall, Sayer, and Barnett 1997). Our own research (e.g., Kim, Moen, and Min 2003; Moen, Waismel-Manor, and Sweet 2003; Roehling, Moen, and Batt 2003) also pointed to the importance of employees having flexibility and control over the time and timing of their work. Taken together, this diffuse set of studies and theoretical developments, along with mounting evidence of the increasing time pressures on employees at work and at home, suggested that an ideal policy intervention in the corporate sector would be flexibility *plus,* with the "plus" being employees' *greater self-direction and control over their working time.*

Third, we knew that some employees—especially those higher up occupational status ladders—already have considerable control over where and when they work. Scholars have previously shown (in mostly cross-sectional research) that control over the time and timing of work matters in predicting some outcomes (e.g., work-family conflict, work-life balance, schedule control; see Baltes and Heydens-Gahir 2003; Day and Chamberlain 2006; Linzer et al. 2002; Madsen 2003; Tausig and Fenwick 2001; Valcour and Batt 2003), but is it because those who have control over their time are also advantaged in other ways?

After many discussions with colleagues and graduate students, Moen and Kelly keyed in on the *time and timing* of work as a critical issue for employees, especially those with family responsibilities. We theorized the importance of employees' control over the time and timing of their work as one—if not the most—important mechanism for reducing employees' work-family conflicts, strains, and overloads.

In Karasek's (1979) job strain model, job control refers to employees' skill discretion and decisionmaking authority, that is, their control over *how* the work is done. It does not attend to employees' control over *when* and *where* the work is done. We believe that *control over work time* is yet another dimension of control in the world of work, providing an important complement to the concept of job control. Control over work time (also called work-time control) is defined as the flexibility and discretion that employees have regarding the number of hours they work, the schedules (or timing) of their work, the predictability of their work hours if the employees are not choosing their schedules, and sometimes control over the location where they work, which affects their commuting time (Kelly and Moen 2007; Kim et al. 2003; Moen and Spencer 2008). This concept reaches beyond flextime to a broader understanding of employees' control over the temporal conditions of their work.

Moreover, while job control is traditionally theorized in the job strain model as especially important for employees facing high job demands (Karasek and Theorell 1990), work-time control may be particularly important for employees with high *family or job demands or both,* since it offers employees greater ability to organize their work hours and/or work location in response to family and personal needs *as well as* work demands. Based on the existing job control research and previous research on schedule control and flexibility (Barnett and Brennan 1995; Carayon and Zijlstra 1999; Kim et al. 2003; Kossek, Lautsch, and Eaton 2005; Roehling et al. 2003; Thomas and Ganster 1995), we proposed a policy intervention designed to enhance employees' control over the time and timing of their work, theorizing that greater work-time control should reduce the chronic stressors of work-family strains and conflicts, as well as time pressures on and off the job.

We proposed a multilevel intervention study grounded in an ecology of the life-course theoretical framing (Kelly and Moen 2007; Moen and Chesley 2008; Moen, Elder, and Luescher 1995; Moen, Kelly, and Magennis 2008), as well as stress process theory (Pearlin 1989, 1999; Pearlin et al. 1981). Our policy intervention would be framed in conjunction with stakeholders from a partnering firm and would be aimed at enhancing employees' *work-time control,* what we saw as a theoretically motivated yet pragmatic intervention goal.

We hypothesized that increasing employees' control over the time and timing of their work would be associated with less work-family conflict, greater time adequacy, and better health-related behavior and well-being outcomes, over and above other conditions characterizing employees' job and family ecologies. Moreover, we expected that employees in different job and family ecologies (including their team configurations, occupations, and supervisory statuses, as well as their family statuses, ages, and life stages) might well experience both greater need for and greater benefits from increased control over their work hours and schedules. This is because of the particular confluence of demands and resources at home and on the job for employees in different occupations and job levels, as well as at different points in their life courses. Specifically, we were (and are) interested in effects of greater work-time control on employees at different levels in the organizational hierarchy, as well as employees who differ by gender, family, age, and life stage: young single employees with no children, single parents, married mothers and fathers actively raising young children, and married employees with no children at home, as well as those caring for an aging, infirm parent or a child with special needs and older employees thinking about retirement. We are also interested in similarities and differences, within and across occupational levels and teams, in the implementation of such a policy offering employees greater control over their work time.

We theorized an intervention that challenges the existing temporal organization of jobs by encouraging working practices designed to increase *all* employees' degree of control over the time, timing, and scheduling of their work. This intervention would not, however, be a "one size fits all" policy or a single "treatment." Rather, it reflects a *process* of replacing institutionalized clockworks with an emphasis on the quality of the job done. We envisioned this process of rethinking the temporal organization of work as taking place at the work-group level. This process is, of necessity, clearly tailored to the requirements of the type of work being accomplished. Our "dream" policy initiative would move away from the metric of time (of equating being "at work" with working), rewarding employees for their productivity and accomplishments, not simply their presence. We hypothesized that such a policy shift would serve to legitimate a more family-friendly and flexible corporate environment that, in turn, could enhance the well-being and effectiveness of employees at home and at work, as well as life quality of their partners and children.

Research Design

Given that the goal of the first phase of the NIH-CDC collaborative network was to conduct pilot work, our stated aims were to pilot test the implementation and impacts of a work-time control intervention by conducting a field experiment involving longitudinal (before and after intervention) research, using a range of both qualitative and quantitative methods. We proposed to investigate the *implementation process* as well as the process by which scholars can develop and sustain a long-term research partnership with key stakeholders within a corporation.

We were (and are) aware of no previous studies of private-sector policy interventions that have the enhancement of employees' control over the time and timing of their work as their primary goal. Accordingly, we discussed several possible alternatives among ourselves and our graduate students and broached these ideas with several of our corporate human resource contacts in the Twin Cities area. As we prepared the proposal to be submitted to NIH, we faced two related challenges: developing a work-time control policy intervention that would be powerful enough to actually matter for employees and their families while simultaneously finding a corporate partner willing to launch such a broad-scale organizational design change *and* let us study the effects on employees. We aimed for a major reorganization and redesign of managing, moving away from clocking employees' time. Such a redesign could be legitimated as "the way we work here" at an organization willing to partner with us. Note that we recognized that such a private-sector business policy offering employees greater control over when (and sometimes where) they work comes with two important caveats: employers might reasonably cede some control over work time to employees, *provided* the specific changes were tailored to fit various types of jobs *and* employees remained productive, meeting or exceeding the requirements of their jobs.

Despite our underlying concerns about access, we were sufficiently networked into the corporate community in the Minneapolis-St. Paul region to feel that it might just be possible to develop, roll out, and study an innovative work-time policy that would actually make a difference to the quality of life of employees and their families.

Multiple Challenges

To summarize, our objective was to develop and undertake successful research in a corporate setting, focused on investigating an intervention that would increase employees' discretion over (or at least predictability about) when they work, and sometimes where they work and to do so within an ecology of the life-course framework. Only after receiving support for this project from the National Institute of Child Health and Human Development did we fully recognize its Janus-faced nature: the need for focusing on *good science* by maintaining the highest scholarly research standards, while simultaneously cooperating with our partners within a *corporate environment*.

In the following sections we draw on observational and interview materials (our own, as well as systematic field notes from graduate students on the research team, including Samantha Ammons and Kelly Chermack) to capture the challenges of this double focus. We describe some of the difficulties and accommodations but also some of the rewards and lessons learned from research in a corporate environment. These include (1) *gaining access* to a corporation willing to consider and pilot test an initiative offering employees greater work-time control, (2) dealing with multiple, often *conflicting timetables,* and (3) implementing a *rigorous research design* that can offer the best scientific evidence. We conclude with (4) a *brief overview* of some early findings and (5) the usefulness for good science of *engaged research* in corporate settings.

Gaining Access: Developing a Corporate Partnership

Serendipity

Robert Merton wrote about the importance of serendipity in research (see Merton and Barber 2004), along with the fact that scholars rarely explicitly acknowledge accidental discoveries or circumstances as key ingredients of the research process. Our experience gives credence to his serendipity thesis: being at the right place and the right time for the "accident" to occur. Early in 2005 (see timeline, figure 5.1) we (Moen and Kelly) were doing our "dog and pony" presentation to interest corporations in this project (should it be funded). Members of an informal "think tank" of work-life practitioners and researchers that we participate in were invited to come to a presentation by two members of this group, Cali Ressler and Jody Thompson, who were employed at the headquarters of Best Buy, a large retail corporation headquartered in the Twin Cities. We sat stunned as they laid out ingredients of what sounded very much like our ideal work-time control intervention. We dared not even look at one another across the room because we were at once startled, pleased, and excited about the fit between the Best Buy innovation called ROWE (results-only work environment) and our own thinking about the importance of enhancing employees' control over the time and timing of their work. Both of us were thinking, "What a lucky coincidence! Could ROWE be our intervention? Could the stakeholders of Best Buy become our partners?"

ROWE was developed as an internal organizational intervention at Best Buy. It was designed to move employees and supervisors from existing, implicit contracts about the expected amounts of *time at work* toward a more explicit contract based on what is *required by the job* and what are

Figure 5.1. Timelines for Results-Only Work Environment Study

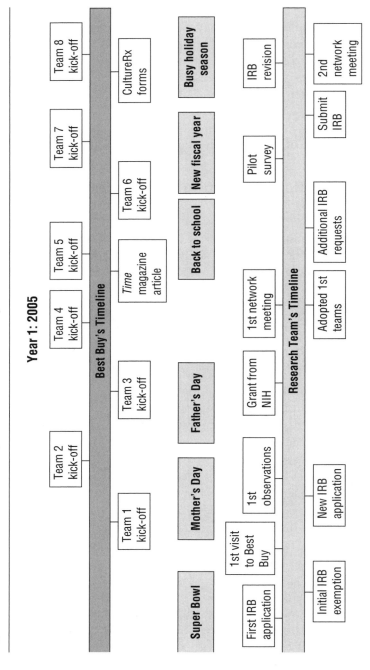

Figure 5.1. *(Continued)*

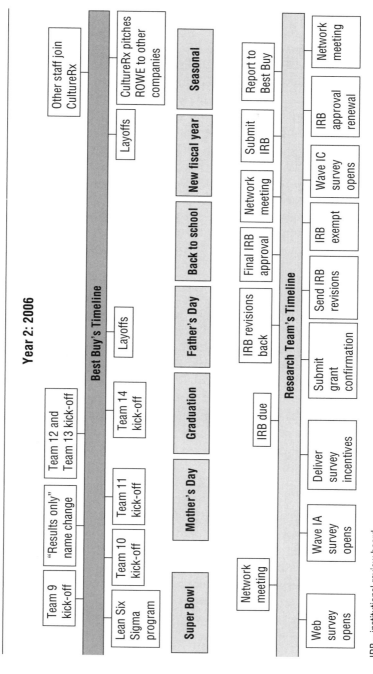

IRB = institutional review board
NIH = National Institutes of Health

appropriate measures of employees' *effectiveness in the job*. Teams transitioning from conventional time-based work practices to a ROWE arrangement aim to foster an environment where employees are free to complete their work whenever and wherever, provided they are productive and doing what works best to accomplish the tasks at hand, as well as each team's longer-term goals. This type of working environment shifts the spotlight away from time-oriented measures of work success (how many hours a worker put in last week; how much time she spent on a given task) to a completely results-based appraisal of productivity and accomplishment. With the ROWE innovation, Best Buy aims to change the temporal organization of work, shifting to an environment where employees have the tools (ways to roll over phone calls, etc.) they need to accomplish their assigned objectives while simultaneously giving them the freedom to accomplish their tasks with whatever type of work schedule is best for them. The participatory process in which teams create a new work environment—with new expectations, assumptions, and interaction practices—is called the ROWE "migration." Table 5.1 describes the differences between the ROWE innovation and existing ways most employees work. (See also Kelly and Moen 2007 for a discussion of how ROWE contrasts with common flexible work arrangements.)

Note that nowhere does the ROWE initiative mention *work-family* issues. This is deliberate on the part of its creators, as a way of *not* pigeonholing ROWE as yet another "mother" friendly or even "family" friendly initiative. Rather, the rationale for the ROWE innovation emphasizes better work results for the firm by moving away from working time as a gauge of effectiveness. It is an innovation meant to be applicable to all employees at all job levels, regardless of their family or personal circumstances, and to be understood as a strategy for recruiting and retaining a skilled workforce.

We immediately recognized the potential value of ROWE as a transformative policy challenging the existing temporal design of paid work and fostering an environment that might reduce employees' work-family conflicts and offer the possibility of greater work-family (or work-life) integration. As work-family, policy, and life-course scholars, we find ROWE particularly promising because, as Ellen Ernst Kossek and Brian Distelberg (this volume) write, it incorporates the "three-legged stool" of reducing work-family conflict through human resource policy, informal organizational culture, and rethinking the structure of work (see also Kossek 2006).

Table 5.1. What Is ROWE?

Results-only work environment. A transformation spotlighting and rewarding productivity and job requirements, not time at work or scheduling, and customized at the work-group level.

From	To
A focus on *work hours* (just being there or "face time")	A focus on *job requirements* (doing work well and on time)
Supervisor sets hours, schedules	Individual and team set hours, work times, schedules
Meetings are a regular part of work routine	Meetings held only as needed
Reliance on face-to-face interaction	Varied methods of virtual and transparent communication
A "reactive" orientation, dealing with crises as they occur	Proactive, early planning to avoid crises where possible
Flexibility arrangements negotiated between individual and supervisor	Flexibility is the norm. Team members cross-train to cover for one another and set schedules
If work needs are met, presence is still required	Customized work time and schedules aimed at achieving goals
Essential ingredient: *tracking employees' time spent working*	Essential ingredient: *defining specific nature of job and expectations*
Problematic: absenteeism, tardiness, presenteeism	Problematic: not meeting job deadlines, expectations

Timing

ROWE met all of the criteria that we had laid out for a potentially powerful intervention targeting employees' control over the time and timing of their work. We quickly met with the innovators at Best Buy (Jody Thompson and Cali Ressler, now of CultureRx) to discuss the feasibility of a possible research partnership. Our argument went like this: The research team from the University of Minnesota (UMN) could promise Best Buy an objective, outside assessment of ROWE, while Best Buy could serve as our corporate partner in our NIH-funded research. Because this partner had already developed what amounted to a work-time control policy innovation, this was truly an "experiment of nature" (Bronfenbrenner 1979), taking place whether or not we studied it. The frustration was that

Jody Thompson and Cali Ressler were ready to roll out ROWE before we could know if our proposal would be funded. We decided not to wait, hiring graduate students with funds from the Alfred P. Sloan Foundation (after seeking the approval of program director Kathy Christensen for this reallocation of existing support) in order to begin observing the ROWE migration right away.

But first we had to obtain the cooperation and buy-in of Best Buy management, someone at the senior level who could and would endorse the UMN/Best Buy partnership, including giving members of the research team access to the organization. We sought approval not only to interview and survey a sample of employees, but also to be allowed into the organization, permitted to attend ROWE sessions, and observe work groups. Our goal was not only to study the impact of ROWE on particular outcomes, but to capture the process of organizational transformation as ROWE was introduced, rolled out, interpreted, and implemented by work teams, individual employees, and supervisors.

We met with a vice president at Best Buy who signed off on the study and our access to the corporate headquarters. We were pleasantly surprised at the ease of our first entry, which was clearly facilitated by Ressler, Thompson, and their staff. As we discuss later on, there were some challenges once other officials from the two institutions (i.e., attorneys) got involved, but the initial entry and partnership was quite simple to negotiate.

Ongoing observation was key, given that ROWE involves a process of migration, not a one-shot treatment, and is implemented at the team level. We observed ROWE facilitators holding periodic meetings over a period of weeks: first with the leaders of a work group (team), then with all the members of the group, including the leaders. We were in the room when group members worked through what it would mean for their team, given its mission, to focus on results, not time at work. In these sessions we watched as employees and supervisors brainstormed about barriers and possibilities, as well as strategies to be more effective by getting rid of "low-value" work (such as regular meetings that have no real purpose) and focusing on the results expected of the team, as well as of each employee. Throughout the period of migration, employees and supervisors experimented and reported back in the ROWE sessions as they attempted to change the way they worked over a period of weeks. We regularly sat in on these sessions, following teams through the migration process and observing the transformation as it was taking place.

Throughout the research process we walked a fine line between creating an atmosphere of openness and trust while simultaneously keeping our distance. We remained somewhat friendly, but not friends, with people at Best Buy throughout the years of data collection. We knew and conveyed to our partners that, unlike some consultants they might hire, we were independent academic researchers, funded by the federal government, and would report findings based on the best scientific analysis, which might well include evidence they might not want to hear. That said, the trust that developed on both sides of the partnership was invaluable.

Even though we kept a degree of social distance, graduate student field researchers "adopted" teams to study in depth, developing much closer ties to team members. The development of relationships with employees they were observing and shadowing lead to enhanced communication, acceptance, and becoming "one of the team." There were many aspects of these relationships that made our graduate student researchers truly feel like participants as much as observers. They were invited to team lunches, team-development outings, off-campus meetings, birthday celebrations, and even a baby shower. This led to ongoing discussions among our research team about the process, ethics, and implications of participant-observation research.

The graduate student researchers also became closer to the leadership team rolling out ROWE. Two examples from field notes during observations of ROWE sessions show this:

> She [a facilitator, who worked with Thompson and Ressler] said hello to me and I said hi back. We did the usual, haven't seen you in a while deal and asked how things had been. She . . . commented to me that [two of the facilitators] are in Mexico and that [another facilitator] is really sick, so she'd be doing this session on her own and that she was pretty nervous. I told her not to worry, that she'd do fine and took a seat in the back of the room near the door.

> One thing that I found particularly interesting about this group was that [the facilitator] began to use the word "we" a lot. She would say things like, "we're going to show you a short video. . ." And, "look over at the charts we put up. . ." Since I've gotten in the habit of helping her figure out A/V issues and help put up and take down her giant stickies before the sessions, she has said to me a number of times that, "we make a good team . . . and she doesn't know what she would do without my help. . ."

This hands-on participant observation led to a fuller understanding of the social ecology of employees in teams transitioning to ROWE, as well as those in comparison-group teams who were not yet migrating.

Employees were able to share a tremendous amount of information because the graduate student interviewers already had insider knowledge and understanding of the dynamics of the team and each employee's unique time pressures. When the graduate students conducted semi-structured, in-depth interviews, several employees commented that it wasn't so much that they were being "interviewed" as it was having a long "chat" with a familiar individual.

Lesson 1: The Importance of Relationships

Our experience underscores the importance for conducting workplace research of seeking out and maintaining ongoing ties with professionals employed within corporations. We knew Thompson and Ressler only slightly prior to becoming Best Buy's research partner, but our participation in the local work-family network (of human resource professionals and academics) was key to even learning about their initiative. We had already envisioned this group as a potential source of partnerships, and this turned out to be the case.

Fostering trust and deeper connections with Ressler, Thompson, and other stakeholders at Best Buy was essential to gaining and maintaining access. We were up front about research progress and our inability to offer tentative findings early. Best Buy folks were equally open about the ROWE implementation. Relationships that we developed with other leaders in the organization, as well as with the employees who participated in the field research, provided valuable information and insight.

Managing Multiple Timetables

Even though we believed in and were studying ways people could loosen time constraints, our research team itself operated under considerable time pressures, exacerbated by multiple, overlapping, and sometimes contradictory timetables. Study design requirements necessitated collecting ethnographic evidence at Best Buy's corporate campus right away, because we wanted to capture the entire ROWE implementation process. Since our corporate partner was rolling out ROWE on their timetable, not ours, we had to fashion our research effort around their timetable (see figure 5.1).

Then there are the timetables related to good science. Before we could begin, we needed permission from the institutional review board (IRB) at the University of Minnesota, which required evidence that the proposed research would not harm human subjects. Did we need the IRB approval before we could even sit in on Best Buy meetings? We weren't sure, but thought we should proceed as if it were necessary, delaying our entry into the field. And then there was the research imperative of launching a pretest survey with our target sample *before* they were to undergo the ROWE migration, necessitating cobbling together a survey, which could not be launched prior to approval by the IRB. The Janus-faced aspects of this project in the form of conflicting timetables were becoming evident.

There were also the UMN's own timetables, requiring teaching and committee meetings for Kelly and Moen and classes for graduate students. We laughed at the contradictions of doing research on an innovation designed to give employees more work-time control, while the actual research process was creating layers of deadlines and time pressures for all the members of the research team.

The different cultures of research and business became even more evident when dealing with attorneys at UMN and at Best Buy who aimed to create a formal agreement for the research partnership. We had waited for IRB approval before beginning the study, but decided to let both legal representatives fashion the officially authorized nature of the research partnership even as we simultaneously moved into the field. We were wise to allow the attorneys to work this out, since their cautious pace would have seriously slowed the research.

There were also timetables related to employees' expectations. For example, people at Best Buy wanted to know "what we were finding" almost as soon as we started our observations. After each survey, several respondents asked what we "had found." We recognized that even as we knew little about organizational processes, employees knew little about research processes—the time it takes to clean and code survey data, much less to transcribe and code in-depth interviews and field notes. Employees in this corporation are used to brief internal surveys and equally brief descriptive summaries of findings that are available right away. They were amazed at how slow we were.

Lesson 2: Research Takes Place on a Moving Platform of Obligations, Expectations, and Change

As our timeline indicates (see figure 5.1), the researchers and the stakeholders (management, the innovation team, employee respondents) faced numerous pressures throughout the study period. Sometimes we found ourselves and our colleagues at Best Buy facing similar time pressures. But whether concurrent or staggered, these pressures affected the research process as we moved back and forth between business and academic timetables.

Moreover, the "targets" we were studying did not stand still. Best Buy was moving into new markets (such as China), dealing with external challenges, and designing new stores and delivery systems. There was one bout of extensive layoffs. The lives of employees were similarly in flux, with 45 members of our sample voluntarily leaving the corporation. Those who stayed experienced a plethora of life changes in the six months between our two surveys (see figure 5.2).

Implementing a Rigorous Research Design

The proposal we submitted to NIH called for a multi-method field experiment, including two waves of surveys completed by employees and managers in both ROWE and comparison teams. The objectives of the surveys are to assess the potential impacts of a work-time control intervention on a range of possible outcomes, including changes in employees' perceptions of work-time control; their actual behavior regarding when and where they work; employees' work-family conflicts and other aspects of the work-family interface; employees' health and health-related behaviors; and employees' job satisfaction, commitment, turnover expectations, involvement, and perceptions of the organization. These two computer-based surveys would constitute the main data source for outcome measures.

We also requested access to administrative data collected by the corporation, which would permit us to capture any "harder" outcomes, such as changes in actual health care usage and costs and changes in productivity measures or turnover. We were eventually able to obtain some institutional health records and turnover statistics from Best Buy, but the organization was unwilling to share other data related to productivity.

Our research design also called for analysis of the organizational process of implementation. We did this by observing the implementation of ROWE through daily team observations including shadowing and by doing in-depth interviews with team members. Since understanding the actual process of ROWE implementation required ethnographic observations (as well as in-depth interviews) over time, four study-team members (the authors and two graduate students, Kelly Chermack and Samantha

Figure 5.2. Life Changes of Employees in the Six Months between Surveys (percent)

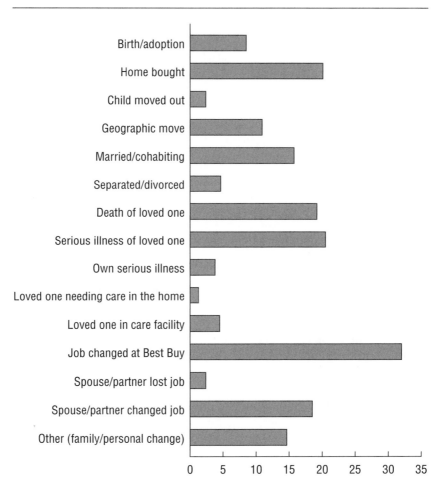

Birth/adoption
Home bought
Child moved out
Geographic move
Married/cohabiting
Separated/divorced
Death of loved one
Serious illness of loved one
Own serious illness
Loved one needing care in the home
Loved one in care facility
Job changed at Best Buy
Spouse/partner lost job
Spouse/partner changed job
Other (family/personal change)

0   5   10   15   20   25   30   35

Source: Authors' data and calculations.

Ammons) sought and obtained regular access to the headquarters campus. Our 16 months of fieldwork and interviewing at Best Buy was a unique experience. As Susan Lambert (this volume) discusses, such workplace field research allows for important insights into the everyday work of employees, insights crucial to our understanding of the work environment and its challenges. Our multi-method approach provided us with a vast knowledge of workers' daily tasks, behaviors, attitudes, and experiences that we would not have otherwise been able to comprehend, further enabling our understanding of the impacts of the work-time control innovation.

Confidentiality was absolutely crucial to the research process, both for ethical reasons and to maximize the validity of our evidence. All respondents (surveyed, interviewed, or shadowed) received written and oral assurances of full confidentiality. We guaranteed that any information we collected would be kept strictly confidential. Not only would we use pseudonyms for employees in publications, but we assured respondents that no identifying information would make it back to their supervisors or colleagues. We feel that our assurances of confidentiality, together with the climate of trust we actively fostered, allowed many of our study sample, particularly those who completed in-depth interviews, to really open up and share their perspectives without the worry of potential job penalties. The research also benefited from the company's identity as an organization that values transparency and open communication. While employees did not always experience the cooperation of their managers as open and transparent, they had been repeatedly exposed to the idea that it is part of Best Buy's culture to be open and transparent.

Our original research design mapped nicely onto the ROWE innovation, with the important exception that we were *not* able to randomize employees into an experimental and a control group. Rather than launching a true field experiment (e.g., Willer and Walker 2007), we were privileged to observe what Bronfenbrenner (1979; see also Bronfenbrenner and Crouter 1983) calls an "experiment of nature," or what Van de Ven (2007) terms a "quasi-experiment," occurring ready-made at Best Buy without any involvement on our part.

The process of choosing teams to observe, survey, interview, and shadow required both patience and persistence. The basic order of events began with Thompson and Ressler identifying teams that might soon undergo the ROWE migration, as well as teams whose ROWE migration was not imminent, so these teams could serve as comparison groups. Usually after the researchers had tentatively selected a team, Thompson or Ressler would approach the team manager and the relevant vice president to see whether they might be willing to have their unit participate in the research. If the manager and the vice president were willing to cooperate, a meeting between them, Thompson and Ressler, and our UMN team was then arranged. During this meeting, the UMN team was able to meet with these parties to ascertain whether there was a fit and an agreement from all parties. We then set up another meeting with the manager and employees in that team and our graduate student researchers so they could all get to know one another, and the researchers could introduce the informed consent and participation requirements in more depth. For the most part, everyone—vice presidents, managers, and line employees—was cooperative and very willing to participate. We had a few vice presidents who expressed some concern over just how much of their employees' time we would consume. Aside from that, we experienced very little hesitation or resistance on the part of employees, supervisors, or corporate leaders.

Fitting In

In April of 2005, we were able to begin our observations. Although the timelines for starting the study sometimes felt slow and frustrating, this was only four months after we first learned about ROWE. When we received our electronic badges we were allowed to come and go at the Best Buy headquarters campus as we pleased, using the employee entrance and not being considered visitors (who had to be escorted) anymore. It was exciting to be somewhat "official." Our badges were green, indicating that we were independent contractors, not regular employees. But they were legitimate, giving us a sense of legitimacy as well. Still, *getting in* did not mean *fitting in*. Because we knew that we were interlopers, we felt that everyone else must know it too. Our field notes underscore this discomfort.

> *Attending a leadership panel.* We arrived a little early and entered into the ramp. After chatting a while in the car, we headed into the north entrance. My badge worked fine and Phyllis's set off the alarm but a crowd of 4 or 5 people deliberately set off the alarm as a joke, pointing at a woman in their group with big smiles when the guards looked up. So Phyllis's alarm wasn't too obtrusive. She got her badge easily, and we chatted about the thrill of being semi-official and free in the corporate setting. We waited a few minutes, and I felt awkward because we weren't going anywhere or working in the public spaces. So even though there is plenty of room to "hang out," hanging out and looking around makes me feel unproductive and awkward.
>
> *Observing in the common areas.* It feels weird and kind of thrilling to be walking around in the building without an escort. I am excited to have my green badge but still feel that it must be obvious to everyone that I don't really belong there. As we

sat there, I felt awkward because we were not talking enough to be "normal" in that space. Sam (graduate student) was looking around with more intention than I was. I was aware of the security guard who could see us and seemed, to me at least, to be watching us and our note-taking. I realized I had a half smile plastered on my face . . .

Another challenge that we faced as academics being thrust into a large corporate organization was getting a grasp of its organizational culture. From our first visit to Best Buy, we faced the task of learning about the organizational culture through our own observations and experiences. We had to grow accustomed to their rhythm of work. For example, there is the "seven-minute rule." We would arrive at a scheduled session on time, only to watch employees file in between six and seven minutes late.

We also had to learn an entirely new vocabulary. During ROWE training and subsequent team adoption sessions, we took notes while simultaneously trying to understand the process and terminology. "Drivebys" (coworkers randomly stopping by an employee's cube) and "firedrills" (last-minute deadlines that require employees to drop what they are currently working on and "put out the fire") are examples of aspects of this culture that we could only learn by watching and listening. But learning their language and culture was key to conducting optimal in-depth interviews because respondents assumed correctly that we "knew" their daily work lives and routines and what they were talking about.

Ambiguous Identities

Early in the process, collecting data sometimes seemed awkward because we did not have any official role at meetings. Even though we planned to introduce the study at each session and the facilitators agreed to give us two minutes to do so, we were not always introduced, and even when we were it sometimes felt awkward. Whether it was being ignored or being put on the spot, we often felt the anxiety of being different from everyone else. Examples abound from notes about attending various sessions.

> I was looking around the room and caught Tyler looking at me once and then quickly glancing away when he noticed I saw him. I took fewer notes than I usually did and tried to fade away into the wall as much as possible. I felt REALLY uncomfortable.
>
> We're already way into this meeting and Jody has not asked me to introduce myself. Obviously the group knows I don't belong there, but no one asks me who

I am. Half of the time Jody and Cali forget to have me introduce myself, but with a group this small, it's a little awkward. I'm never sure what I should do though, so I continue to sit there quietly.

I feel like everyone expects us to take notes during the sessions, we're there to observe those sessions. But, I feel weird about writing notes before and after sessions or during the casual conversation that Sam and I witnessed with Jody and the HR staff . . . I'm not sure which is better, to witness the conversation and then try and get down as many notes as possible after, or risk writing during the conversation, knowing that people may be more likely to say less and censor their comments with us in the room writing.

Sometimes we felt very visible, as when our security badges expired because of a computer error and no longer granted us access to the organization.

I'm entering the parking ramp at 8:30 and I have a ton of cars behind me, and my badge won't let me in. I thought about pushing the red button and asking to be let in, but I wasn't sure what to say or if they'd even let me in . . . I wasn't sure what to do, and I was contemplating just going home. But, this was the day I was supposed to shadow Dick and I had already rescheduled once and didn't want to bail on this day. I got out my cell phone and called 411 and asked for the Best Buy corporate office. When the operator at Best Buy answered, I asked for Corinne (she's always here this early) and told the operator that I couldn't remember her extension. She gave me the number and then offered to connect me . . . Corinne answered, thank god, and I told her the situation. She said to just come to the visitor's entrance and then she'd come down and get me, which is what I was going to ask her to do. I apologized to her and she said that "you're funny" and that it would be no problem to come and get me. I parked in the visitor's lot and headed to that entrance.

Events like this reminded us that our access was a "gift" and could be rescinded at any time.

In an effort to reduce the amount of employees' time we consumed, we tried to be accommodating to their schedules, keeping the interviews as short as possible. However, it took about an hour for the interviews for those in the comparison groups, and an hour to an hour and a half to interview members of the treatment groups. We interviewed everyone twice, before and after the ROWE migration. Paying special attention to employees' needs and time constraints sometimes meant splitting up the interview into two parts or ending the interview and resuming it later if need be. We made every effort to be sensitive and responsive to time pressures.

Dick, a 27-year-old white male buyer, had told me beforehand that, although we'd reserved an hour for this interview, it was really difficult for him to give that amount of time right now. I thought about rescheduling, but it had been difficult to schedule with him in the first place and I didn't want to risk it. So I decided that we could go ahead and do this interview now, even if it ends up being short. I did feel a little rushed to read a question, wait for a brief answer, and then move to the next question.

We also tried to be sensitive about having graduate students shadowing employees: spending an entire day with an individual, attending his or her meetings, observing desk work, having lunch with him or her, and so on. Our goal was to garner as much information as possible during our limited time at Best Buy while interfering with employees' daily work as little as possible. As an example from shadowing notes shows, we made every effort to observe employees in their work environments in an unobtrusive way.

> Seriously, when do these people use the restroom? Maybe it's just because I drink a lot all day, but they never seem to go. Daphne, a 35-year-old white female buyer, told me once before that sometimes she just doesn't have the time to go; I can't even imagine that!!!

As we, the researchers, and our subjects, the employees, became more comfortable, being there became even easier. After a while, the graduate student researchers were just another part of the usual scenery and were able to ask questions, participate in water-cooler gossip, and attend meetings and lunches just as if they belonged there. Once it seemed normal to have us there, our own stress at feeling intrusive slowly disappeared.

Shadowing employees proved to be simpler than we had thought. Most employees were happy to have us follow them around. In fact, a number of them found it comforting to have an unbiased individual to confidentially "vent" to throughout the day. Most of the time, employees would share their own commentaries and thoughts about how a meeting went or how much they liked or disliked a coworker or supervisor. This gets back to the importance of trust. Some of the employees tried to skirt the shadowing, but eventually everyone we needed agreed to participate. There were also employees who, at the mention of the possibility of being shadowed, could not wait for it to happen. One of our researchers spent the day with Grant, a 27-year-old man who was a demand planner in marketing, for instance, when another employee actually asked if she could also be shadowed.

> When we were done with copies, we swung by Reese's desk so that she could take a look at the finished handouts. Reese actually remembers my name and exactly

what I'm doing here. I'd only met her a couple of times, and I was impressed. Grant told her about how I was shadowing him today. "I want you to follow me!" she said.

In relation to our own sensitivities about their time, we began to notice when employees were under a great deal of time pressure and stress. The marketing teams especially had weekly deadlines and updates for which they were responsible. This created stress and used up a large amount of their time, and the process was repeated week after week. The teams in marketing faced unique weekly time pressures, aside from the cyclical stress of holiday preparations and quarterly and annual reports. On a weekly basis they spent most of the day on Monday preparing reports on sales from the previous week and adjusting their forecasts for the upcoming week. They also encountered increased stress on Friday when they had stores calling for last-minute increases in shipments for the weekend. We attempted to be sensitive to the ebb and flow of their time pressures and worked with their schedules as best we could. This meant extending our stay with some teams to be sure we had gathered all the data we needed. Rescheduling interviews and shadowing, as well as rescheduling our own meetings, tended to draw out this process longer than we had expected.

This is part of the balance required with any study partnership. There are obvious goals for and challenges to both parties. And we were acutely aware of the tenuousness of our situation. At any moment, the organization, the teams, or the people we were observing could withdraw from the research process, or even kick us out of the organization entirely. This awareness made us even more sensitive about our presence on campus and our level of intrusiveness. There was, however, never an instance of our legitimacy being questioned. We were never told that we could not do something. The cooperation that we experienced was incredible.

Lesson 3: Aim at Minimal Intrusiveness

It is often said that the business of business is business. Just being on the Best Buy campus reinforced this fact; people were there to do their jobs, *not* to participate in our study. While research was of course our priority, it was not theirs. Accordingly, we tried to reduce our visibility and "footprint" by being minimally intrusive and accommodating our research needs to employees' availability.

Does ROWE Make a Difference? Early Survey Findings

Recall that the aim of the UMN study was to assess whether working in a ROWE environment changes the nature and quality of employees' work experiences, reduces conflict between employees' work and their family or personal lives, affects employees' health and health-related behaviors, and alters their commitment to and perceptions of the organization. We briefly summarize early findings from two surveys of 658 employees conducted six months apart. Characteristics of this sample are shown in table 5.2.

The sample is divided roughly equally between employees whose teams began the ROWE migration just after the first survey and a comparison group of employees in teams who were not yet slated for ROWE at the time the surveys were launched. We compare differences between the ROWE and comparison-group respondents in terms of any changes employees experienced in the six months spanning the period before and after the ROWE migration.

We find no statistically significant differences between ROWE and comparison-group respondents in terms of changes (in the six months between pre- and post-study surveys) in the hours they put in on the job, their income adequacy, or any positive spillover from work to family or from family to work. Neither do we see any meaningful difference in the shifts between waves in the level of negative spillover from family to work. Analysis to date has also not detected significant ROWE effects on changes in employees' satisfaction with their managers or coworkers, in their assessments of their own individual and their teams' performance, or in their decision authority on the job. Not significant, as well, are ROWE versus comparison-group changes in employees' overall assessment of their health, their psychological distress or well-being, their emotional exhaustion, their sense of mastery, or their number of physical symptoms.

We do, however, find evidence that ROWE has statistically significant impact on changes in employees' sense of control over their work time, their decisions about where and when they work, their sense of work-family conflict, some aspects of their health and wellness, and their work pressures and commitment. The evidence is particularly convincing because we examine *changes within people* over the six-month period, finding different patterns of change for ROWE and comparison employees.

Table 5.2. Sample Characteristics of Those Participating in Two Survey Waves (percent)

Characteristic	Total $N = 658$	Men $n = 339$ (51.5%)	Women $n = 319$ (48.5%)
Family situation			
Not married, no children	30.2	30.1	30.4
Married, no children (or none at home)	34.8	34.2	35.4
Children at home (mostly married)	35.0	35.7	34.2
Age group			
20–29	45.3	42.4	48.5
30–39	39.2	40.9	37.3
40–60	15.5	16.7	14.2
Job level			
Individual contributor	66.3	63.4*	69.3
Manager	19.8	19.8	19.7
Senior manager	14.0	16.8	11.0
Exempt status			
Exempt	95.0	97.0**	92.8
Nonexempt	5.0	3.0	7.2
Education			
High school or less	1.6	0.9	2.2
Some college	12.8	14.6	10.8
Bachelor's degree	73.2	70.4	76.1
Graduate or professional degree	12.5	14.0	10.8
Tenure at Best Buy			
Less than 1 year	18.8	17.3	20.5
1–5 years	46.7	45.2	48.3
Longer than 5 years	34.5	37.5	31.2

Source: Authors' data and calculations.

*$p < .10$; **$p < .05$

Summarizing statistically significant changes in work-time control and working patterns, we find the following.

- Fewer ROWE employees than comparison employees have had their commute times to and from work increase.
- More ROWE employees than comparison employees have greater control over where and when they work, choose to work at home or off campus more frequently, and have greater variability in their work hours and schedules each week.

We also find changes in the work-family interface.

- More ROWE employees than comparison employees experience a decline in work-family conflict; have less negative spillover from work to family; report more time adequacy in terms of doing their work, family, and personal observations; and describe the Best Buy culture as more family friendly.

There were also significant changes in some health and health-related behavior outcomes, specifically, by the second survey.

- Fewer ROWE employees than comparison employees come to work on campus when sick.
- More ROWE employees than comparison employees sleep more than seven hours a night, see improvements in the quality of their sleep, now go to the doctor when sick, exercise more frequently (three or more times a week), and report gains in energy.

Finally, we document some changes in work conditions and effectiveness between the two survey waves.

- Fewer ROWE employees than comparison employees do low-value (unnecessary) work, have high turnover intentions, experience interruptions at work, and feel pressure to work overtime.
- More ROWE employees than comparison employees view the work culture as being family friendly, have greater organizational commitment, and report more job satisfaction.

Our findings suggest that ROWE may be a realistic work-time inno-vation with potential for broad adoption and impact. It was developed in a company rather than by academics, providing it with the legitimacy that may aid in its diffusion to other organizations. At the same time, it also makes sense in light of theory and research findings on work-family time pressures and the importance of a sense of control for health, well-being, and effectiveness.

But our evidence comes with certain caveats. First, this initiative occurred in the headquarters of a major corporation with primarily white-collar and professional employees. ROWE in a retail setting, where employees' jobs require their physical presence, would take different forms and require different types of strategies to increase employees' work-time control. Second, six months between surveys is a short period in which to capture changes in work-family and health arenas, and yet funding constraints made it impossible to field a third survey later on.

Our next steps will be to assess the impact of this workplace intervention within particular family and job ecologies. We also want to develop an understanding of the implementation process through comparisons within and across work units.

Summing Up: Getting to the Science

ROWE is what Bronfenbrenner (1979) called an ecological transition—a fundamental change in the setting in which a role (that of employee) is played out. It is truly an experiment of nature as Bronfenbrenner and Crouter defined changes that occur naturally (i.e., without the intercession of researchers). As such, it is ideal for the study of the effects of environmental change "with a built-in, before/after design in which each subject can serve as his own control" (Bronfenbrenner and Crouter 1983, 381).

Our field observations and investigations of this quasi-experiment in a corporate setting have taught us more about work, family, and organizations—and organizational policy change—than we could ever learn from the analysis of a random sample of adults working for various employers. We have offered our lessons learned from this study: about the importance of *relationships* with key stakeholders, the need to recog-nize and respond to *multiple timetables* (of employees, leadership, and researchers), and the value of being *minimally intrusive* in work settings. We conclude with a fourth lesson.

Lesson 4: Recognize and Accommodate Gaps between Ideal Research Design and Corporate Realities

An "experiment of nature" has many built-in strategic advantages. For instance, the design of and the case for the policy innovation have been made by those in the corporate setting and do not need to be developed or argued by the research team.

Still, there are undeniable drawbacks. We previously raised the issue of the impossibility of random assignment in this natural experiment setting, a factor making this a quasi- rather than a true experiment. Other modifications and accommodations were also necessary. For example, in our proposal we noted that our ecology of the life-course approach would include analysis of older workers and their work-time needs and wants as they move toward retirement, but Best Buy's workforce is relatively young, providing insufficient numbers of older workers to undertake such analysis. There is also the issue of "generalizability"— including how ROWE would operate in other industries, with other workforces. That question can only be addressed through replication. For us, these modifications and accommodations were clearly worth it as part of our effort to get rich and detailed data about the process of organizational change and the impact of work-time control on employees.

Two other challenges to traditional research design—a lack of consistency in the treatment or intervention and the problem of contamination across work groups—puzzled us more and became the subject of many conversations. We have not reached firm conclusions yet, but we share our thinking here.

No control over timing of intervention and no way to keep intervention "the same." We all know that ideally an intervention delivery should be consistent, but even as we entered the corporate environment in order to learn about organizational change, so too did the organization continue to learn from itself. This meant that the change process itself adapted and innovated over the course of our study. This raises a number of potential challenges because the specific content of ROWE shifted over time. We responded by carefully tracking and monitoring these changes, by attending well over 100 ROWE sessions and taking detailed field notes in each. For example, the following excerpts from our field notes track changes in the session that prepares department leaders for ROWE:

> Jody and Cali started the slide show, and [their phrase] "results-*oriented* work environment" has now become "results-*only* work environment." Jody said that

oriented was "too wimpy" and that "results-only is stronger." She explained that they changed it because the "new teams are getting savvy."

The changes I noticed since the last leadership session I'd seen were the glossy slides and also the guideposts are shown and then there is a section with each guide-post and "What it is" and "What it isn't."

She (Jody) mentioned that they were doing sludge [a way of having employees recognize how traditional time-related work expectations creep into conversations] a little differently now. . . . a script change that they were trying out.

Moreover, ROWE is less a one-shot intervention than a process of participatory change. Not all employees receive the same exposure, since the intervention specifically encourages teams to make it their own. The result? Different "pockets" of ROWE where individual teams developed their own version of how ROWE would look and "rules" to accompany their version. We believe that ROWE has powerful effects in part because of this participatory process, allowing employees and teams to experiment with new ways of working that meet their personal needs and the needs of the business. However, this change strategy requires that researchers be vigilant in capturing and analyzing those experiments across both individuals and teams.

No way to prevent contamination. Good science requires that the comparison (control) group should be totally separate and independent from the "treatment" group, something nearly impossible among employees working in the same building. Best Buy is known for its cross-functionality and teamwork, and prides itself on developing relationships. In fact, one internal measure of success is the high number of employees who report having "a best friend at work." With cross-functional work networks and highly developed social networks, we found that at least some information about ROWE was known by employees in different parts of the organization. Whether it was factual information or just a rumor, employees were talking. This meant teams that were beginning ROWE or teams that were considering adopting ROWE often had preconceived and sometimes misguided perceptions early in the process. We also found that as teams learned that they would begin ROWE in the near future, they sought out information and best practices from other teams that were already in the ROWE environment.

These information flows were not ideal for the research and were also viewed as problematic by Thompson and Ressler. They found it more difficult to implement ROWE in teams that had already planned how they might change or assumed they had prior knowledge regarding what to expect and how to incorporate ROWE within their teams. Yet, considering the information that they were able to access through regular organizational communication channels or sought out themselves, every team that we studied had at least some prior expectations going into the ROWE migration.

Why Engaged Research Is an Optimal Design for "Basic" Science

Urie Bronfenbrenner (1979) always said that if you want to understand something, try and change it. Bronfenbrenner also said that nothing was more useful to furthering basic, theory-driven scholarship than research on a particular policy. What have we learned?

The three years we have been engaged in this research project at Best Buy have demonstrated in concrete ways the absence of life-course "fit" between occupational and family clocks (Moen and Kelly forthcoming; Moen and Roehling 2005) and the way this lack of fit plays out in the day-to-day lives of employees. The costs to employees, their families, and business of this chronic, systemic misfit between the two most fundamental institutions for human development—work and family—are evident to the observer but not always tangible in the ways that other costs are calculated.

Studying the process of implementation of a temporal policy shift at Best Buy provided ample evidence that trying to alter some aspect of the engrained, taken-for-granted clockworks of work is extremely difficult. We had not expected the degree of difficulty employees experience in trying to think of work as outcomes, not time put in at a desk or elsewhere. Neither had we anticipated the degree of pushback from others made uncomfortable with this new definition that changes basic assumptions about the "right" way to work. We had hypothesized that employees experiencing the ROWE innovation would report less time pressure and work-family conflicts, and that was the case. But we were surprised that a corporate policy innovation such as ROWE could make a difference on such a range of outcomes.

We have not yet had a chance to think about and process unanticipated consequences. For example, Best Buy believes that having a "best friend" at work is good for employee productivity, and some leaders wondered if working at different times and places might lessen such social network ties. We also want to look at the outcomes for midlevel managers, who may feel they are losing control over their work because they are no longer in charge of scheduling their employees' time and have to monitor results rather than attendance.

This hands-on research experience has led us to question the value of the cross-sectional research that we and other scholars typically engage in. Finding so many changes in outcomes and other descriptive variables over even a short six months challenges the scientific value of evidence showing an association between two or more variables at a single point in time. People live, work, and raise their families in a dynamic, ever-changing environment in which nothing is static—except perhaps the outmoded policies limiting their options.

Urie Bronfenbrenner was right: evaluating a real-world (as opposed to hypothetical) policy change *as it is implemented* is difficult, even messy, but remains essential for good science and theory development. Despite its departures from the ideal experimental design, we are grateful for the opportunity to investigate ROWE, since the payoffs of studying such an experiment of nature, a ready-made policy change in an actual corporate setting, far outweigh any costs or disadvantages. It is also fundamental for developing real-world solutions to the work, family, and health challenges confronting most of today's workforce, solutions that are both feasible and effective.

NOTE

This research was conducted as part of the Work, Family and Health Network, which is funded by a cooperative agreement through the National Institutes of Health and the Centers for Disease Control and Prevention: National Institute of Child Health and Human Development (Grant U01HD051217, U01HD051218, U01HD051256, U01HD051276), National Institute on Aging (Grant U01AG027669), Office of Behavioral and Social Sciences Research, and National Institute of Occupational Safety and Health (Grant U01OH008788). The contents of this publication are solely the responsibility of the authors and do not necessarily represent the official views of these institutes and offices. Special acknowledgment goes to Extramural Staff Science Collaborator Rosalind Berkowitz King, Ph.D. (NICHD) and Lynne Casper, Ph.D. (now of the University of Southern California) for design of the original Workplace, Family, Health and Well-Being Network Initiative. Persons interested in learning more about the Network should go to https://www.kpchr.org/workplacehealth/ (accessed July 2, 2008). We also thank the Alfred P. Sloan Foundation for additional support of this research, Best Buy, CultureRx, and especially the employees who participated in the study.

REFERENCES

Baltes, Boris B., and Heather A. Heydens-Gahir. 2003. "Reduction of Work-Family Conflict through the Use of Selection, Optimization, and Compensation Behaviors." *Journal of Applied Psychology* 88: 1005–18.

Bandura, Albert. 1982. "Self-Efficacy Mechanism in Human Agency." *American Psychologist* 37: 122–47.

Barnett, Rosalind C., and Robert T. Brennan. 1995. "The Relationship between Job Experiences and Psychological Distress: A Structural Equation Approach." *Journal of Organizational Behavior* 16: 259–76.

Bosma, Hans R., Peter J. Siegrist, and Michael G. Marmot. 1998. "Two Alternative Job Stream Models and the Risk of Coronary Heart Disease." *American Journal of Public Health* 88: 68–74.

Bourbonnais, Renee, Chantal Brisson, Jocelyne Moisan, and Michel Vézina. 1996. "Job Strain and Psychological Distress in White Collar Workers." *Scandinavian Journal of Work, Environment and Health* 22: 139–45.

Bronfenbrenner, Urie. 1979. *The Ecology of Human Development: Experiments by Nature and by Design.* Cambridge, MA: Harvard University Press.

Bronfenbrenner, Urie, and Ann C. Crouter. 1983. "The Evolution of Environmental Models in Developmental Research." In *Handbook of Child Psychology,* vol. 1, edited by Paul H. Mussen (357–414). New York: John Wiley and Sons.

Butler, Adam, Michael Gasser, and Lona Smart. 2004. "A Social-Cognitive Perspective on Using Family-Friendly Benefits." *Journal of Vocational Behavior* 65: 57–70.

Butler, Adam B., Joseph G. Grzywacz, Brenda L. Bass, and Kirsten D. Linney. 2005. "Extending the Demands-Control Model: A Daily Diary Study of Job Characteristics, Work-Family Conflict, and Work-Family Facilitation." *Journal of Occupational and Organizational Psychology* 78: 155–69.

Carayon, Pascale, and Fred Zijlstra. 1999. "Relationship between Job Control, Work Pressure, and Strain: Studies in the USA and in the Netherlands." *Work and Stress* 13(1): 32–48.

Cheng, Yawen, Ichiro Kawachi, Eugenie Coakley, Joel Schwartz, and Graham Colditz. 2000. "Association between Psychosocial Work Characteristics and Health Functioning in American Women: Prospective Study." *British Medical Journal* 320: 1432–36.

Day, Arla L., and Trina C. Chamberlain. 2006. "Committing to Your Work, Spouse, and Children: Implications for Work-Family Conflict." *Journal of Vocational Behavior* 68: 116–30.

de Jonge, Jan, Hans Bosma, Peter Richard, and Johannes Siegrist. 2000. "Job Strain, Effort-Reward Imbalance and Employee Well-Being: A Large-Scale Cross-Sectional Study." *Social Science and Medicine* 50: 1317–27.

Dwyer, Deborah J., and Daniel C. Ganster. 1991. "The Effects of Job Demands and Control on Employee Attendance and Satisfaction." *Journal of Organizational Behavior* 12(7): 595–608.

Evans, Olga, and Andrew Steptoe. 2002. "The Contribution of Gender-Role Orientation, Work Factors and Home Stressors to Psychological Well-Being and Sickness Absence in Male- and Female-Dominated Occupational Groups." *Social Science and Medicine* 54: 481–92.

Fox, Marilyn L., Deborah J. Dwyer, and Daniel C. Ganster. 1993. "Effects of Stressful Job Demands and Control on Physiological and Attitudinal Outcomes in a Hospital Setting." *Academy of Management Journal* 36: 289–318.

Heckhausen, Jutta, and Richard Schulz. 1995. "A Life-Span Theory of Control." *Psychological Review* 102: 284–304.

Hemingway, Harry, and Michael Marmot. 1999. "Evidence-Based Cardiology: Psychosocial Factors in the Etiology and Prognosis of Coronary Heart Disease: Systematic Review of Prospective Cohort Studies." *British Medical Journal* 318: 1460–67.

Karasek, Robert A., Jr. 1979. "Job Demands, Job Decision Latitude, and Mental Strain: Implications for Job Redesign." *Administrative Science Quarterly* 24: 285–308.

Karasek, Robert A., Jr., and Torez Theorell. 1990. *Healthy Work: Stress, Productivity, and the Reconstruction of Working Life.* New York: Basic Books.

Kelly, Erin L. 2003. "The Strange History of Employer-Sponsored Child Care: Interested Actors, Uncertainty, and the Transformation of Law in Organizational Fields." *American Journal of Sociology* 109: 606–49.

Kelly, Erin L., and Alexandra Kalev. 2006. "Managing Flexible Work Arrangements in U.S. Organizations: Formalized Discretion or 'A Right to Ask'." *Socio-economic Review* 4(3): 379–416.

Kelly, Erin L., and Phyllis Moen. 2007. "Rethinking the Clock Work of Work: Why Schedule Control May Pay Off at Work and Home." *Advances in Developing Human Resources* Special Issue on Work-Life Integration 11(9): 487–506.

Kim, Jungmeen E., Phyllis Moen, and Hyunjoo Min. 2003. "Well-Being." In *It's About Time: Couples and Careers,* edited by Phyllis Moen (122–32). Ithaca, NY: Cornell University Press.

Kossek, Ellen Ernst. 2006. "Work and Family in America: Growing Tensions between Employment Policy and a Changing Workforce." In *America at Work: Choices and Challenges,* edited by Edward E. Lawler and James O'Toole (53–72). New York: Palgrave MacMillan.

Kossek, Ellen Ernst, Brenda A. Lautsch, and Susan C. Eaton. 2005. "Flexibility Enactment Theory: Implications of Flexibility Type, Control, and Boundary Management for Work-Family Effectiveness." In *Work and Life Integration: Organizational, Cultural, and Individual Perspectives,* edited by Ellen Ernst Kossek and Susan J. Lambert (243–62). Mahwah, NJ: Erlbaum.

Kristensen, Tage S. 1995. "The Demand-Control-Support Model: Methodological Challenges for Future Research." *Stress Medicine* 11: 17–26.

———. 1996. "Job Stress and Cardiovascular Disease: A Theoretical Critical Review." *Journal of Occupational Health Psychology* 1: 246–60.

Landsbergis, Paul A., Peter L. Schnall, Diane Deitz, Richard Friedman, and Thomas Pickering. 1992. "The Patterning of Psychological Attributes and Distress by 'Job Strain' and Social Support in a Sample of Working Men." *Journal of Behavioral Medicine* 15: 379–405.

Linzer, Mark, Martha Gerrity, Jeffrey A. Dougles, Julia E. McMurray, Eric S. Williams, and Thomas R. Konrad. 2002. "Physician Stress: Results from the Physician Work-Life Study." *Stress and Health* 18: 37–42.

Madsen, Susan R. 2003. "The Effects of Home-Based Teleworking on Family Conflict." *Human Resource Development Quarterly* 14: 35–58.

Marshall, Nancy L., Aline Sayer, and Rosalind C. Barnett. 1997. "The Changing Workforce, Job Stress and Psychological Distress." *Journal of Occupational Health Psychology* 2: 99–107.

Merton, Robert K., and Elinor Barber. 2004. *The Travels and Adventures of Serendipity: A Study in Sociological Semantics and the Sociology of Science.* Princeton, NJ: Princeton University Press.

Moen, Phyllis, ed. 2003. *It's About Time: Couples and Careers.* Ithaca, NY: Cornell University Press.

Moen, Phyllis, and Noelle Chesley. 2008. "Toxic Job Ecologies, Lagging Time Convoys, and Work-Family Conflict: Can Families (Re)gain Control and Life-Course 'Fit'?" In *Handbook of Work-Family Integration: Research, Theory, and Best Practices,* edited by Donna S. Lero, Karen Korabik, and Denise L. Whitehead (95–118). Toronto: Academic Press.

Moen, Phyllis, and Erin Kelly. Forthcoming. "Working Families under Stress: Socially Toxic Job Ecologies and Time Convoys." In *Handbook of Families and Work,* edited by E. J. Hill and D. R. Crane. Lanham, MD: University Press of America.

Moen, Phyllis, and Patricia V. Roehling. 2005. *The Career Mystique.* Boulder, CO: Rowman and Littlefield.

Moen, Phyllis, and Donna Spencer. 2008. "Cycles of Control: Job and Home Demands, Work-Time Control, Job Security and Personal Mastery at Different Life Stages." Unpublished draft.

Moen, Phyllis, Glen H. Elder Jr., and Kurt Luescher. 1995. *Examining Lives in Context: Perspectives on the Ecology of Human Development.* Washington DC: American Psychological Association.

Moen, Phyllis, Erin Kelly, and Rachel Magennis. 2008. "Gender Strategies: Socialization, Allocation, and Strategic Selection Processes Shaping the Gendered Adult Course." In *Handbook of Research on Adult Development and Learning,* edited by M. Cecil Smith and Thomas G. Reio Jr. Mahwah, NJ: Erlbaum.

Moen, Phyllis, Ronit Waismel-Manor, and Stephen Sweet. 2003. "Success." In *It's About Time: Couples and Careers,* edited by Phyllis Moen (133–52). Ithaca, NY: Cornell University Press.

Pearlin, Leonard I. 1989. "The Sociological Study of Stress." *Journal of Health and Social Behavior* 30: 241–56. Reprinted in W. C. Cockenham, ed., 1995, *The Sociology of Medicine,* Cheltenham, UK, Edward Elgar Publishing.

———. 1999. "The Stress Process Revisited." In *Handbook of the Sociology of Mental Health,* edited by Carol Anehensel and Jo C. Phelan (395–415). New York: Kluwer Academic/Plenum.

Pearlin, Leonard I., Morton A. Lieberman, Elizabeth G. Menaghan, and Joseph T. Mullan. 1981. "The Stress Process." *Journal of Health and Social Behavior* 22: 337–56.

Rodin, Judith. 1986. "Aging and Health: Effects of the Sense of Control." *Science* 233: 1271–76.

Roehling, Patricia V., Phyllis Moen, and Rosemary Batt. 2003. "Spillover." In *It's About Time: Couples and Careers,* edited by Phyllis Moen (101–21). Ithaca, NY: Cornell University Press.

Schnall Peter L., Paul A. Landsbergis, and Dean Baker. 1994. "Job Strain and Cardiovascular Disease." *Annual Review of Public Health* 15: 381–411.

Still, Mary C., and David Strang. 2003. "Institutionalizing Family-Friendly Policies." In *It's About Time: Couples and Careers,* edited by Phyllis Moen (288–309). Ithaca, NY: Cornell University Press.

Tausig, Mark, and Rudy Fenwick. 2001. "Unbinding Time: Alternate Work Schedules and Work-Life Balance." *Journal of Family and Economic Issues* 22(2): 101–19.

Thomas, L. T., and Daniel C. Ganster. 1995. "Impact of Family-Supportive Work Variables on Work-Family Conflict and Strain: A Control Perspective." *Journal of Applied Psychology* 80: 6–15.

Valcour, P. Monique, and Rosemary Batt. 2003. "Work-Life Integration: Challenges and Organizational Responses." In *It's About Time: Couples and Careers,* edited by Phyllis Moen (310–32). Ithaca, NY: Cornell University Press.

Van de Ven, Andrew H. 2007. *Engaged Scholarship: A Guide for Organizational and Social Research.* New York: Oxford University Press.

Willer, Davis, and Henry A. Walker. 2007. *Building Experiments: Testing Social Theory.* Stanford, CA: Stanford University Press.

6

The Tensions, Puzzles, and Dilemmas of Engaged Work-Family Scholarship

Shelley M. MacDermid, Mary Ann Remnet,
and Colleen Pagnan

Engaged scholarship is messy. "Messy" is not a very scientific term, but any scientist reading the chronicle of Moen, Kelly, and Chermack's study cannot help but empathize with the challenges and envy the opportunities they confronted. My role as a discussant gave me a great opportunity to participate in a lively discussion of the chapter with my two student author colleagues, whose contributions I gratefully acknowledge. My goal in this discussion is to highlight some of the key tensions embedded in this study from a methodological perspective, identify some puzzles to be solved for the future, and recognize some of the ongoing dilemmas of work-family research. I hope that doing so will assist researchers who hope to conduct workplace-based engaged scholarship in the future, and both researchers and policymakers who aim to improve the quality of life for workers and their families.

Tensions

Perhaps the most obvious tension documented in the chapter is the tension in the study between *control* and *chaos*. Any good scientist recognizes the importance of controlling extraneous sources of variation that might lead to false conclusions about the impact of an intervention. The classic randomized experiment is designed to assure precise similarity between control and intervention groups—except for the presence of the intervention. In workplaces, however, it is rarely possible to randomize or control. Workplaces face external pressures from the global marketplace, regulators, and competitors who hire good workers away, as well as internal pressures from supervisors who do not want competition for workers' attention and various administrative departments that want to push particular agendas for organizational change in such things as business practices, financial policies, or methods of innovation. Even if a researcher could control these things, to do so would reduce the ecological validity of the study.

What strategies do we see in this chapter for keeping chaos at bay? First, longitudinal data and comparison groups are key—the best available strategies for trying to isolate the effects of an intervention when randomization is not possible. Second, the approach described in the chapter includes thorough and careful documentation of the process of both the research and the intervention. Attention to the circumstances that emerge while the research and intervention are being conducted can reveal potential mediating and moderating factors that should be examined empirically when assessing impact of the intervention. For example, the benefits of flexibility could be reduced during a period of heavy workload, such as the week before the Super Bowl in the case of the retailer studied here. The challenge for the researcher is to pick which of the thousand specific circumstances to attend to and to figure out how best to measure them in order to take them into account.

Another tension evident in the chapter is that between *skeptical scrutiny* and *collaborative cooperation*. Researchers are supposed to be skeptical, always looking for flaws in data or methods, but work-family researchers need access to research sites and to get that they collaborate effectively with their corporate colleagues. Notable in this study is that the researchers participated regularly with a group of corporate colleagues long before any research project was undertaken. When the opportunity for ROWE emerged, they had already built up sufficient credibility to be considered trustworthy enough by the prospective partner to gain a hearing for their proposal. More importantly, the researchers had clear goals for their research program but also recognized ways that they could adapt their goals to meet the logistical demands of the ROWE opportunity when it emerged. It is very important to be in the right place at the right time, but it is even more important to be able to recognize when that has occurred. Similarly notable, the research team made an explicit distinction between being friendly and being friends with their corporate partners. This is a very difficult but important balance to maintain. Of course there is the risk of researcher bias, which is hopefully minimized by some emotional distance between the partners. Even more difficult is making sure that researchers' own hopes that the intervention will be successful do not cloud any of the methods or rigor of the study.

Another important consideration is that research takes a very long time when judged according to corporate clocks, and there is relatively little chance that the research project will finish with the corporate point of contact with whom it began. Embedded researchers must make sure their fortunes are not tied too tightly to one particular person within the organization, so if that person leaves or is promoted, or if the position is reorganized, the relationship with the organization is not severed. Sustaining this continuity requires considerable effort on the part of researchers, who must establish and maintain rapport, trust, and accountability with multiple members of the organization.

The final tension I will recognize is that between the utility of the research to the *client* versus the utility to *science*. Corporate practitioners who manage "family-friendly" programs live in a world with very short-term time horizons. Their work has a less obvious connection to organizational revenue generation than that of line managers, and so, every day, they must focus on justifying the expense of their programs and thus, their continued existence. Their mission is to make a rapid, measurable difference that improves performance of the organization in a meaningful way, by improving morale, decreasing costs, increasing retention, or—even better—raising revenue. Researchers, of course, have very different goals that play out according to a very different timeline. It takes time for interventions to play out and for the eventual impacts to be visible to researchers. In the meantime, revealing too much about what is being learned could change the ultimate impact—for better or worse—and make the results less about the intervention itself and more about the relationship between the researcher and the organization. Researchers are faced with the unenviable challenge of being responsive to their corporate partners—who are functionally their clients—without compromising the impact they hope to observe.

Puzzles

I'm going to shift my focus now to puzzles, which I think of as matters that are going to have to be addressed in order to implement control over work schedules on a large scale and to successfully achieve meaningful improvement in working conditions. Here I speak largely to policymakers, a group that includes individuals who design and implement not only public policies at various levels of government, but also those who do so within the private worlds of corporate and not-for-profit employers.

In my judgment, all the literature on job flexibility and schedule control is based on the unacknowledged assumption that job demands are held constant. But if increased schedule control is to have the desired effect, we have to push on this assumption. What would supervisors do if it became impossible to require workers to maintain particular work hours or schedules and if workers were to be evaluated only on the basis of the results they produced? I think some supervisors would make sure their subordinates had such long task lists that they would never be finished with their tasks. Even if wish lists of results were initially reasonable, I wonder whether they would expand beyond anything that schedule control could accommodate. To facilitate schedule control in a large-scale implementation, we will need some regular system for monitoring the results required in particular jobs to ensure that they are reasonable for the level, training, compensation, and other parameters of the job and the worker.

A second puzzle we have to address is how to deal with individual variation in the ability to produce results in given periods of time. Workers are diverse in their intellectual and physical abilities and in the numbers and kinds of demands they face away from the job, both of which can affect their abilities to produce results in given periods of time. Workers who tend to produce more slowly than average may actually find that their work hours increase when they are solely evaluated according to results.

Third, we must figure out how to manage work results that are not easily measurable or at first glance do not appear to be results at all. A few minutes spent chatting in the coffee room may do nothing to improve the quality of a report but may foster collaborative working relationships, putting important social capital "in the bank" that can be called upon during a future crisis. Focusing exclusively on measurable individual results could make it very difficult to foster the development of strong collaborative relationships and effective teamwork. But focusing too much on team results could lead to social pressure among workers that ramps up the pace of work to undesirable levels. This all comes home to roost when raises are being considered. Most employers use a merit-based system to award pay increases and incentive bonuses. If timely delivery of results becomes the measurable indicator of performance, would employers eventually slip into a model of defining merit according to early completion and thus encouraging workers to constantly strive to work harder and faster? Suddenly, we are back to having little control over time.

Fourth, we have the challenge of how to administer benefits in a results-only world. Personally, I find the idea of a results-based vacation very appealing—I would not have to return to work until I was completely relaxed! But the reality is that many workers now have benefits that are defined by time—such as paid vacation, sick days, holidays, and bereavement days. In a completely results-oriented workplace, perhaps it would be unnecessary to define these as benefits because workers could come and go when they needed to. But once again I catch myself assuming that expectations for results will not rise steeply.

In a completely results-oriented workplace, even the definition of "employee" is thrown into question because federal laws about contractors and employees are based in part on how time is allocated and managed. Would moving toward a results-oriented model hasten the advent of a labor force made up completely of independent contractors? In this case the question becomes how to equitably provide workplace benefits to contractors. Is this a problem, and if so, how would the statutes need to be revised?

The final puzzle I'll mention is how to fit the idea that workers should have greater ability to control their schedules with a world where consumers are told many times each day that they deserve to have whatever they want, whenever they want it. Considering that vast labor forces of workers around the world are poised at every moment of every day to work longer for less money than workers in industrialized countries, perhaps our best hope here is the accelerating popularity of "asynchronous commerce," or the ability to find and acquire goods and services without requiring live persons to interact in real time.

Dilemmas

I will close this chapter by focusing briefly on some dilemmas of work-family research. I suspect these will prove to be long-term challenges. It has long been recognized, but incompletely acted upon, that there is a bias in the work-family research literature toward a focus on white-collar, educated workers who have ample work to do and often ample pay to do it. Their problem is an overabundance of work. A case could be made, and several of the authors in this volume could make it far better than I, that these members of the workforce are statistically not the norm. A large and growing population of blue-collar and white-collar workers lives an everyday reality of less-than-ample work or tenuous work that could disappear at any moment. Schedule control is essential for many of those workers who juggle multiple jobs, face mandatory overtime, and experience other severe time challenges. I wonder whether many of those workers are less worried about controlling their schedules than they are about getting enough work hours—even from multiple jobs—to pay the rent or mortgage.

I also wonder whether focusing on the control side of the demand-control equation, as is the case in Moen, Kelly, and Chermack's chapter, will merely delay an inevitable need to tackle the demand side. There is a point at which schedule control cannot compensate for excessive demands. Today there are many jobs in which workers have more schedule control than they can exercise, because the workload is so heavy. Likewise, as it becomes more common and perhaps fashionable to be constantly in demand, are workers becoming less able to resist the social pressure to take their BlackBerries to the beach? As jobs become more tenuous, are workers hesitating more to speak up about unreasonable demands? What should we, as researchers concerned about quality of life, be saying and doing about the demand side?

The last dilemma I wish to raise is the dilemma of what work-family researchers should be studying. For the past several years, I have had the honor of chairing the international committee of the Rosabeth Moss Kanter Award for Excellence in Work-Family Research. This committee annually selects the best work-family study published in more than 70 peer-reviewed scientific journals from around the world. Along with colleagues at Purdue's Center for Families, the Boston College Center for Work and Family, and the Alliance of Work-Life Progress, I write summaries of the top 20 articles and tabulate their topic foci. I then make presentations about the results of the studies to corporate practitioners, on each occasion trying to distill the key take-home messages of the research for their work.

My unintentional role as a cultural translator has given me the opportunity to observe that researchers and practitioners are typically focused on quite different problems. The dilemma for researchers who want to have impact is how to find the research problem that is worthy of scientific study but also addresses a practical problem. This to me is the fundamental mission of engaged scholarship and the mission to which many of the people writing in this volume are devoted. Nonetheless, the most popular topics of the top studies in the Kanter competition are an imperfect reflection of the issues that preoccupy practitioners. For example, wage differentials according to gender, parental status, or occupation are some of the most popular topics of Kanter-nominated research but topics that I have rarely seen addressed by corporate work-life practitioners, because they are usually governed by a completely different department of the organization that may not have parental status and these other issues on its radar screen. Often, corporate practitioners are very focused on the best ways to implement new programs and practices, such as providing lactation rooms, reducing absenteeism due to child care breakdowns, or encouraging new mothers to expeditiously return to work for their original employers. Corporate work-life practitioners are a key audience for researchers who wish to affect the quality of life for workers and their families, but they often do not have sufficient authority to address the large-scale structural challenges in organizations that preoccupy researchers. This is a fundamental, but little-discussed, dilemma yet to be addressed.

7

Corporate Work-Life Interventions
A Multilevel Perspective

Jeffrey H. Greenhaus

S ubstantial research on the work-family interface has emerged over the past 25 years, spurred by an increasing participation of dual-earner partners and single parents in the workforce, a blurring of gender roles and boundaries between work and family domains, and a shift in employee values toward achieving greater balance in life (Greenhaus and Foley 2007). Because extensive conflict between work and family roles can produce dissatisfaction within the work and family domains, life stress, and poor health (Bruck, Allen, and Spector 2002; Carlson and Kacmar 2000; Frone 2003; Greenhaus, Allen, and Spector 2006; Kossek and Ozeki 1998), much of the research has examined the factors that produce or alleviate work-family conflict in employees' lives.

Not surprisingly, a considerable amount of research has been devoted to understanding the impact of employers' work-life initiatives and family-supportive cultures on employees' work-family stress, work attitudes, job performance, and retention in the organization (Greenhaus and Foley 2007). This literature suggests that work-life practices (such as flexible work hours and employer assistance with child care) and family-supportive cultures can promote positive work attitudes, enhance job performance, and reduce work-family conflict, stress, absenteeism, and turnover (Allen 2001; Glass and Finley 2002; Lobel 1999), although the findings are far from consistent and conclusive (Greenhaus and Foley 2007).

In short, although there is evidence that employer work-life initiatives can help employees manage their work and family responsibilities, there is much to learn about the factors that contribute to an initiative's success, especially the manner in which the initiative is introduced into an organization. In their chapter in this volume "Learning from a Natural Experiment: Studying a Corporate Work-Time Policy Initiative," Moen, Kelly, and Chermack address this gap in the literature by examining the impact of the introduction of a work-life intervention on individual and team outcomes.

In this chapter, I discuss my reaction to Moen, Kelly, and Chermack's study, propose additional research questions and analyses at the levels of work teams and individual employees, and suggest future research that adopts a decisionmaking perspective on employer work-life initiatives. I hope to demonstrate the importance of considering the interacting effects of organizational interventions with team dynamics and individual characteristics on employees' well-being and effectiveness in their work and family roles.

Assessment of the Best Buy Study

Moen, Kelly, and Chermack examined the impact of a results-only work environment (ROWE) intervention at Best Buy that was intended to change the organization's culture from an emphasis on hours of work and "face time" to an emphasis on the quality of job performance. The focus on job performance was accompanied by enhanced flexibility, greater control by individuals and teams over customized work schedules to achieve performance goals, proactive planning to avoid crises, and improved and timely communication (see table 5.1). The researchers used qualitative and quantitative data to compare the attitudes and performance of employees in ROWE teams with those in teams that had not yet undergone migration to the results-oriented culture. The Moen team's study was impressive in a number of respects.

The Concept

The researchers sought to examine a *change* in employer practices designed to reduce employees' work-family conflicts and strains. Because most research focuses on the effects of existing work-life initiatives, their decision to examine the introduction of a new intervention has the potential to provide insights into the change process and the factors that promote effective change.

Moreover, the particular type of change they envisioned studying—an intervention that replaced "institutionalized clockworks with an emphasis on the quality of the job done" (Moen et al. this volume)—is theoretically grounded in the literature. Prior research has demonstrated that a family-supportive culture that provides employees with increased control over their work time and eliminates the requirement of face time can reduce the severity of work-family conflict and strain (Allen 2001; Thompson, Beauvais, and Lyness 1999). Importantly, Moen, Kelly, and Chermack extended Karasek's (1979) notion of control over how a job gets done to control over the time and timing of the work.

Especially salient is the researchers' expectation that increased control over the timing of work would "potentially enhance the well-being and effectiveness of employees at home and at work" (Moen et al. this volume). The focus on well-being and effectiveness in *both* domains—work and family—is consistent with what I believe to be a crucial issue for many employees: how they can derive substantial satisfaction and effectiveness from those roles in life that matter to them (Greenhaus and Foley 2007). Therefore, individuals who value both roles need opportunities to experience effectiveness and satisfaction in work and family life, and a shift from a time-oriented culture to a results-oriented culture has the potential to provide employees with these opportunities.

Access to a Corporate Work-Life Intervention

It is one thing to want to study the introduction of a work-life initiative; it is another to actually gain permission from the employer to do so. Although the researchers observed that the establishment of the collaborative partnership between them and Best Buy was "quite simple to negotiate," I suspect that their reputations, credibility, and high-quality research plan had a great deal to do with the approval they received. After all, their research required more than simply administering a one-shot survey, but rather involved their observing teams in planning sessions, interviewing team members, and "shadowing" some employees during the course of their daily work. The approval that the research team received to immerse themselves in the culture transformation process is a credit to the researchers and to Best Buy.

Flexibility

It is perhaps ironic that the key feature of the ROWE intervention—increased flexibility—was also required by the researchers themselves. They noted many instances that required flexibility and adaptability on their part in dealing with conflicting timetables and goals, understanding the organization's culture and language, living with ambiguous identities, and other realities of conducting research in organizations in the midst of change. The researchers' ability to "go with the flow" was, I believe, a critical ingredient to the success of their project.

Collection of Quantitative and Qualitative Data

Although the use of multiple methods of data collection is frequently recommended, it is not frequently achieved. Moen's team not only collected quantitative data through the administration of pre- and post-intervention surveys, but also gathered qualitative data through observations of team meetings, interviews, and job shadowing during the change process. Particularly impressive was the use of graduate students as participant-observers of individuals and teams as they migrated to the new culture.

Interesting Findings

The researchers reported a number of interesting and important differences between employees in teams undergoing ROWE migration and employees in comparison teams over a six-month period. For example, in contrast to the comparison teams, the ROWE teams experienced heightened levels of the following:

- control over time,
- health and wellness,
- time adequacy,
- perception of the culture of Best Buy as family friendly,
- organizational commitment, and
- job satisfaction.

The ROWE teams also experienced reduced levels of the following:

- work-family conflict,
- negative spillover from work to family,

- low value (unnecessary) work, and
- turnover intentions.

Moen, Kelly, and Chermack also observed a number of areas in which differences between ROWE teams and comparison teams did *not* emerge, such as positive spillover between work and family, negative spillover from family to work, satisfaction with managers or coworkers, self-reported individual and team performance, decision authority on the job, and a sense of mastery on the job. Because the ROWE migration did not have all of its expected effects, it is likely that additional analyses on the dataset can provide further insight into the factors that determined the consequences of this work-life intervention. I now discuss two types of additional analyses that can be conducted.

Additional Research Questions and Analyses on the ROWE Intervention

The Impact of Team Processes on Outcomes

Inherent in the ROWE migration process is the power that each team was granted to develop its own version of how to implement the results-only philosophy. Moen's team rightfully recognized that this practice represents a gap from an "ideal" research design in which all individuals or groups exposed to a treatment (in this case, the ROWE intervention) receive the identical treatment. However, I suggest that the variation in teams' migration experiences be viewed as an opportunity rather than a problem—an opportunity to understand the effect of the change process on the outcomes achieved by teams and individuals undergoing the ROWE initiative. Therefore, I suggest that additional analyses be conducted only on the teams that migrated to the results-only culture to identify team characteristics that were associated with changes in outcomes at the conclusion of the migration process.

A framework for examining the impact of team characteristics during the change process is shown in figure 7.1. The model proposes that team characteristics affect two immediate outcomes of the intervention—control over time and the efficient design of team members' jobs—which in turn affect the extent to which team members are effective in their work and home domains. I selected control over time and an efficient job design as immediate outcomes because those seem to be the aims of the ROWE

Figure 7.1. A Framework for Examining the Impact of Team
Characteristics on Team and Individual Outcomes

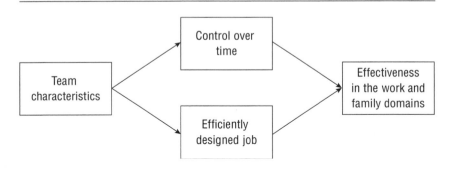

intervention: to enable employees to restructure their jobs in such a way
that promotes high-quality work while at the same time giving them more
control over the timing of their work. I selected effectiveness at work and
at home as the ultimate outcomes because, as mentioned earlier, I believe
that individuals want to be effective and fulfilled in significant life roles
(Greenhaus and Foley 2007).

Although many team characteristics can be examined, I suggest the
following (University of Victoria 2008):

- The clarity of the team's goals during the migration process. Do teams
  know what they want to accomplish in the migration process? Teams
  that have clear, specific, and challenging goals to which they are
  committed should experience more control over the timing of their
  work and design their jobs in a more efficient manner than teams who
  do not have clear, specific, and challenging goals or are not committed
  to these goals.
- The *structural mechanisms* developed and used by the team to
  address their goals or to make decisions regarding their migration
  to a results-only work environment. I propose that teams that
  participatively develop clear procedures for deciding how migration decisions get made, how conflicts get resolved, and how tasks
  get accomplished experience more control over the timing of their
  work and design their jobs in a more efficient manner than teams
  that do not have clear procedures or have not developed them
  participatively.

- The quality of the *interpersonal interactions* within the team. Teams that foster high involvement and inclusion in decisionmaking; capitalize on the diversity of skills, knowledge, and perspectives of team members in making decisions; engage in active listening and nonthreatening communication; promote trust; and use task-focused communication (rather than personal attacks) to resolve conflicts and disagreements should experience more control over the timing of their work and design their jobs in a more efficient manner than teams that do not engage in these positive interactions.
- *Leadership* within the team. I suggest that teams whose leaders inspire team members to develop a vision of what a future results-only environment can be and help them develop team norms of cooperation by practicing shared leadership, monitoring the group process, and teaching and role modeling problem-solving skills experience more control over the timing of their work and design their jobs in a more efficient manner than teams without such leaders.

In summary, I encourage Moen's team to focus some of their additional analyses on team characteristics. To the extent to which the researchers' observations of team meetings and interviews of team members enable them to assess goal setting, decisionmaking mechanisms, interpersonal interactions, and leadership, I suggest they examine the impact of these team characteristics on the outcomes specified in figure 7.1, as well as other outcomes deemed relevant to the ROWE intervention.

The Impact of Individual Employee Characteristics on Outcomes

In addition to examining the role of team characteristics in the migration process, it would be useful to determine how characteristics of individual employees influence the success of the ROWE intervention. The examination of individual differences as moderators of relationships between inputs and outcomes has a rich history in organizational behavior. It is not unreasonable to believe that the effectiveness of the ROWE intervention is dependent upon a range of individual difference factors.

Figure 7.2 proposes that individual difference variables can influence the effectiveness of the ROWE intervention in two ways. First, they may moderate the relationships of exposure to ROWE with control over

Figure 7.2. A Framework for Examining the Moderating Effects
of Individual Difference Variables

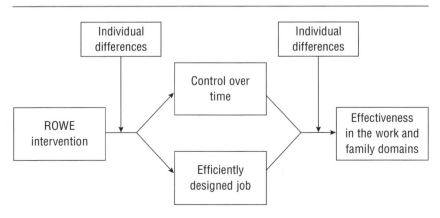

ROWE = results-only work environment

time and an efficient job design; that is, the ROWE intervention may
have a stronger impact on control and job design for some individuals
than for others. Second, they may moderate the relationships of control over time and an efficient job design with effectiveness in the work
and family domains. In other words, enhanced control and an efficiently
designed job may promote domain effectiveness more strongly for some
individuals than others. Box 7.1 contains examples of three types of
individual difference variables (job characteristics, family characteristics, and personal characteristics) that may be relevant to the ROWE
process.

The first moderator effect suggests that some employees may experience
more control over their work time and a more efficiently designed job
than other employees following the introduction of ROWE. For example, it is possible that employees whose jobs require extensive boundary
spanning (that is, interactions with others outside their department or
outside Best Buy) may benefit less from the ROWE intervention because
they need to respond to pressures from other stakeholders who have little
control or flexibility in their own jobs. Or perhaps employees in some
job functions benefit less than others because their jobs are more difficult
to restructure in a way that affords them greater control over the timing
of their work.

Box 7.1. Illustrations of Individual Difference Variables

Job characteristics
- job function and level
- job scope (e.g., variety, autonomy, feedback)
- task interdependencies
- boundary-spanning activities

Family characteristics
- marital status
- responsibility for dependents
- family stage
- spouse employment characteristics

Personal characteristics
- sex
- salience of work, family, and personal roles
- advancement aspirations

The second moderator effect suggests that an increased control over work time and an efficiently designed job may influence effectiveness at work and at home more strongly for some employees than for others. For example, career-oriented employees with strong advancement aspirations may not take advantage of their newly found control and may continue to work extremely long hours, evenings, and weekends that detract from their effectiveness and satisfaction in the home. In theory they have more control over the timing of their work, but their desire to demonstrate their commitment to their job or to perform at extraordinarily high levels may restrict their participation, effectiveness, and satisfaction at home. As another example, employees who are dependent on other individuals (e.g., members of other departments, suppliers, clients) to perform their jobs may find that their effectiveness at work is more strongly influenced by the performance of others than by the efficient design of their own jobs.

The two types of moderator effects suggest that the impact of the ROWE intervention on control, job design, and ultimate effectiveness at work and at home may be contingent upon a wide range of factors. Therefore, I encourage the researchers to explore the extent to which a variety of job, family, and personal characteristics play a role in determining the effectiveness of the ROWE initiative.

Going beyond the Present Study:
A Decisionmaking Perspective

In the previous section, I encouraged the researchers to consider conducting additional analyses regarding the role of team characteristics and individual difference variables in the effectiveness of the ROWE intervention. In this section, I suggest a different stream of research going beyond the present study that links corporate work-life initiatives to individual decisionmaking.

The work-family literature has generally emphasized the environment (pressures and stresses arising in the work and family domains) as a major force that produces work-family conflict in employees' lives (Frone 2003; Voydanoff 2004). In fact, the implementation of corporate work-life initiatives rests on the assumption that providing flexibility and other resources will relieve some of the work-related constraints and pressures that ultimately reduce employees' work-family conflicts and strains.

Although environmental factors undoubtedly affect the intensity of the work-family conflicts that employees experience, the employees themselves also play a role in this process by virtue of the decisions they make or do not make in their daily lives (Poelmans 2005). Defining a "work-family decision" as a choice regarding participation in the work or family domain that is influenced by considerations in the other domain, Greenhaus and Powell (2007) have encouraged researchers to adopt a decisionmaking perspective to better understand the intersection of work and family. They propose that individuals often take one domain into account (e.g., family) when making a decision regarding the other domain (e.g., work) in order to avoid or reduce the level of work-family conflict in their lives.

Greenhaus and Powell (2007) identified four categories of work-family decisions: role entry, role participation, role boundary management, and role exit. Table 7.1 defines each type of work-family decision and provides two examples: one a decision in the work domain that is influenced by family considerations and the other a decision in the family domain that is influenced by work considerations.

The adoption of a decisionmaking perspective raises many interesting research questions: under what conditions do individuals take family (or work) considerations into account when making a decision regarding work (or family)? Are some individuals more prone than other individuals to take "extra-role" considerations into account when making a decision? Are certain decisionmaking styles (e.g., intuitive) more likely than other

Table 7.1. Four Categories of Work-Family Decisions

Category	Definition	Examples
Role entry	Decision regarding entering a role	*In the work domain* An individual accepts a job with flexible work hours so he can meet family responsibilities more effectively. *In the family domain* An individual decides not to get married so she can immerse herself in her career.
Role participation	Decision regarding investment of time and emotion in a role and participation in role-related activities	*In the work domain* An individual decides not to pursue a promotion because she believes that the additional stress, work hours, and travel associated with the promotion would intrude into her family life. *In the family domain* An individual decides not to attend a child's dance recital because an emergency project-team meeting has been called.
Role boundary management	Decision regarding the segmentation or integration of work and family roles	*In the work domain* An individual brings his child to the office because there is no school that day. *In the family domain* An individual decides not to take business calls at home.
Role exit	Decision regarding leaving a role	*In the work domain* An individual decides to quit a job because it interferes excessively with her family life. *In the family domain* An individual decides to leave a marriage because it interferes excessively with his career.

styles (e.g., rational) to consider family (or work) factors when making a decision regarding one's work (or family) life? How do individuals' life values affect their work-family decisionmaking?

One question that is especially relevant to Moen, Kelly, and Chermack's study and this volume is whether working in a ROWE-type culture affects the kinds of work-family decisions an employee makes. Does an emphasis on results rather than face time enable employees to make choices regarding participation in family (or work) activities that are less constrained by work (or family) responsibilities? For example, does an individual employed in a more supportive, flexible work environment conclude, "I don't have to avoid taking on a new work assignment because I can work on the assignment at a time that doesn't interfere with family responsibilities," or "I don't have to forgo participating in a family activity because I can still fulfill my work responsibilities later that day, over the weekend, or by passing my task on to a cross-trained colleague?"

I recommend that work-family scholars consider integrating research on organizational interventions with individual decisionmaking. This research should investigate the process by which individuals take extra-role considerations into account in making work-related and family-related decisions and should determine whether different types of organizational interventions influence the decisionmaking process.

Summary and Conclusions

Moen, Kelly, and Chermack's study is an ambitious and important piece of research. Its quantitative and qualitative assessments of teams and individuals represent a useful framework for examining the introduction of an organizational work-life intervention. Moreover, their data provide opportunities to conduct additional analyses on the impact of team characteristics on team and individual outcomes, as well as on individual differences that may moderate the effect of the intervention on outcomes.

This chapter has emphasized organizational, team, and individual phenomena because they capture the multiple foci of this research. However, it is important to recognize that the interrelationships among organizations, teams, and individual employees are contingent upon the larger cultural context in which employers conduct their business and employees enact their daily lives. Glass (this volume) has demonstrated the wide variation in work-family public policies in different countries and described the dominant orientation in the United States as a "free-market" approach that essentially leaves it up to individual employers to decide what, if any, assistance to provide to their employees in managing the intersection of their work and family lives.

An assessment of the advantages and disadvantages of the free-market approach is beyond the scope of this chapter. However, the extensive discretion afforded individual employers in a free-market culture highlights the importance of studying the factors that contribute to successful organizational interventions. Research that demonstrates that organizational work-life initiatives can promote the well-being of employees *and* employers and that guides organizations on how to increase the likelihood of these initiatives' success should encourage employers to introduce work-life initiatives to maintain their competitive advantage in the marketplace. Moen, Kelly, and Chermack's research takes an important step in that direction.

REFERENCES

Allen, Tammy D. 2001. "Family-Supportive Work Environments: The Role of Organizational Perceptions." *Journal of Vocational Behavior* 58: 414–35.

Bruck, Carly S., Tammy D. Allen, and Paul E. Spector. 2002. "The Relation between Work-Family Conflict and Job Satisfaction: A Finer-Grained Analysis." *Journal of Vocational Behavior* 60: 336–53.

Carlson, Dawn S., and K. Michele Kacmar. 2000. "Work-Family Conflict in the Organization: Do Life Role Values Make a Difference?" *Journal of Management* 26: 1031–54.

Frone, Michael R. 2003. "Work-Family Balance." In *Handbook of Occupational Health Psychology,* edited by James. C. Quick and Lois E. Tetrick (143–62). Washington, DC: American Psychological Association.

Glass, Jennifer L., and Ashley Finley. 2002. "Coverage and Effectiveness of Family-Responsive Workplace Policies." *Human Resource Management Review* 12: 313–37.

Greenhaus, Jeffrey H., and Sharon Foley. 2007. "The Intersection of Work and Family Lives." In *Handbook of Career Studies,* edited by Hugh Gunz and Maury Peiperl (131–52). Thousand Oaks, CA: Sage.

Greenhaus, Jeffrey H., and Gary N. Powell. 2007. "A Conceptual Analysis of Decision Making at the Work-Family Interface." Paper presented at the Second International Conference of Work and Family, IESE Business School, University of Navarra, Barcelona, Spain, July 8–10.

Greenhaus, Jeffrey H., Tammy D. Allen, and Paul E. Spector. 2006. "Health Consequences of Work-Family Conflict: The Dark Side of the Work-Family Interface." In *Research in Occupational Stress and Well-Being,* vol. 5, edited by Pamela L. Perrewe and Daniel C. Ganster (61–98). Amsterdam: JAI Press/Elsevier.

Karasek, Robert A., Jr. 1979. "Job Demands, Job Decision Latitude, and Mental Strain: Implications for Job Redesign." *Administrative Science Quarterly* 24: 285–308.

Kossek, Ellen E., and Cynthia Ozeki. 1998. "Work-Family Conflict, Policies, and the Job-Life Satisfaction Relationship: A Review and Directions for Organizational Behavior-Human Resources Research." *Journal of Applied Psychology* 83: 139–49.

Lobel, Sharon A. 1999. "Impacts of Diversity and Work-Life Initiatives in Organizations." In *Handbook of Gender and Work,* edited by Gary N. Powell (453–76). Newbury Park, CA: Sage.

Poelmans, Steven A. Y. 2005. "The Decision Process Theory of Work and Family." In *Work and Life Integration: Organizational, Cultural, and Individual Perspectives,* edited by Ellen Ernst Kossek and Susan J. Lambert (263–85). Mahwah, NJ: Erlbaum.

Thompson, Cynthia A., Laura L. Beauvais, and Karen S. Lyness. 1999. "When Work-Family Benefits Are Not Enough . . . The Influence of Work-Family Culture on Benefit Utilization, Organizational Attachment, and Work-Family Conflict." *Journal of Vocational Behavior* 54: 392–415.

University of Victoria. 2008. "Developing Effective Teams Workbook: Team Effectiveness Model." http://web.uvic.ca/hr/hrhandbook/organizdev/teammodel.pdf. (Accessed October 1, 2007.)

Voydanoff, Patricia. 2004. "The Effects of Work Demands and Resources on Work-to-Family Conflict and Facilitation." *Journal of Marriage and Family* 66: 398–412.

8

Energizing the Study
of Work Policies

Anisa M. Zvonkovic

I t was a pleasure to read the Moen, Kelly, and Chermack chapter. Unlike with many academic works, the reader absolutely gets a feeling for what it is like to be a researcher studying issues related to work-life initiatives. Engaged scholarship is well depicted; the authors position themselves as engaged at every step. My comments are structured from the broad—related to issues of ideology and philosophy—to the more specific—questioning the intervention of ROWE. I discuss what research such as this contributes to family scholarship and where families are positioned in this research program. I will close with a presentation of my own sagas in doing research on job demands and the ways I have applied the concept of job demands in my own research program.

Issues of Ideology and Philosophy

I very much appreciated that the National Institutes of Health (NIH) initiative "focused on policies changing *work*, not on changing *employees*" (Moen, Kelly, and Chermack this volume). There are ideological and philosophical issues associated with this stance. Such a stance requires the realization that the problem does not exist at the individual level, nor does it exist as a "mismatch" between jobs and people. Rather, the problem is structural, and the potential might exist to change the way we work.

When considering interventions in the workplace, particularly when they are designed and pitched as work changes with company buy-in, we must always be cognizant of whose interests are being served by the intervention. Research that has applied aspects in any form must account for potentially competing interests (McGraw, Zvonkovic, and Walker 2000), and research within a particular company places itself in an especially precarious position. There are clear benefits of a program like ROWE being developed at work sites, and therefore readily accepted at the workplace. Contemporary work sites, in times of labor shortages (at least of skilled workers in some occupational categories), have an interest in retaining highly valued workers (i.e., talent) so their interest in happy, committed workers could factor into their calculations of "what works" for them.

Such a program is likely to have a much larger impact on workers' well-being than any mild intervention that researchers might possibly convince an organization to test. The ROWE program in particular carries a potential drawback of actually increasing people's overwork (though that work might occur not at the office). On balance, ROWE's potential and its ingenious evaluations seem to outweigh concerns, though it is always important to air and account for the potential concerns.

Still, I think broad questions should be discussed: Do people actually work more hours under this type of intervention? Are they accessible 24/7 now, even if they are not physically in the office? Are there data on their heightened productivity? Might this higher productivity be because, indeed, they are spending more time doing work (even if not putting in "face time")?

As Hochschild elegantly wrote in *Time Bind* (1997), there is a difference between written policy (results only) and unspoken norms. Sometimes policies actually get enacted in such a way that the flexibility goes only one way (e.g., a workplace can demand that employees agree to irregular work schedules or to be constantly available, but employees cannot refuse these demands or ask the workplace for flexible schedules). Skeptical questioning of workplace-initiated policies must be posed, along the lines of (1) who defines workplace policies as working and (2) what tradeoffs might exist in different spheres of a worker's life—working for the company versus working in personal life (Hochschild 2003). Ellen Ernst Kossek and Brian Distelberg (this volume) recently found that heightened flexibility may increase family-to-work spillover because workers may need to negotiate and spend more time arranging their schedules, potentially increasing family conflict. Given that calendars are already a source of tension and concern for families (Arendell 2001), further pursuit of such issues is warranted.

In times of heightened job insecurity, how are programs and policies perceived? On the topic of heightened job insecurity, much data have been touted about how workers feel their jobs are more insecure. But these data make me think of a parallel in the field of family studies, and that is the nostalgia myth of a stable, harmonious past (Coontz 1992). Families yearn for a life like the past as they nostalgically envision it. I wonder if some degree of worker-perceived insecurity is similarly nostalgic: workers may be yearning for a past work life that was actually very rare. Certainly agrarian jobs were always income insecure. In this way and many others, the fields of family studies and the fields related to the study of work can cross-fertilize each other (MacDermid, Roy, and Zvonkovic 2005). Consider issues like time pressure and job insecurity and how people's perceptions of these issues may not jibe with the reality of historical and contemporary workplaces.

ROWE Intervention

I would like to read more about the actual ROWE intervention, and I am sure that Moen and Kelly and their colleagues will be reporting more about their project as time goes on. I understand and appreciate that the authors took their purpose to be explaining what the process was actually like, which was gratifying to read. I understand that ROWE enhanced employees' schedule control (1) when they worked and (2) where they worked. Moen and her colleagues make a convincing argument for schedule control, pitched for all employees.

I am curious about how ROWE actually changed what people did. The researchers' field notes on pre-ROWE conditions would be useful, to characterize how daily work changed. I appreciated the inclusion of stated policies in table 5.1, but as we know, there is commonly a mismatch between stated policies and what gets done. I was intrigued with the presentation that ROWE was "rolled out" in such a way that it was a major change in how business was done. The section on early survey findings provides some flavor of the quantitative data available to show what may have changed as a result of the ROWE policy, but I'm left wondering about presumed moderators or mediators of this intervention. One avenue of inquiry that I am especially eager to have the researchers pursue relates to family and personal life.

Where Is Family and Personal Life in This Research Program?

From a family or personal-life perspective, I wonder about the way that personal life is conceived in such work interventions. The early survey findings present some variables that were not significantly different and some encouraging significant tests between ROWE and non-ROWE groups (e.g., time control; time adequacy, work pressure; work-family conflict; commitment; perception of health and wellness; sleep; increased energy). As the authors point out, this analysis only spanned six months, and it may well be that other effects would take longer to emerge. It is easy to imagine that workers' engagement and commitment might be enhanced over the long run, and their perception of inability to fit into the "ideal worker" concept might be reduced (Blair-Loy 2004; Williams 2000).

Readers will be eager to have the researchers uncover the conceptual processes and reasons for these associations. Are there personality factors such as self-efficacy or confidence that might affect for whom interventions at work actually are effective? What types of models might best account for these associations? We could also conceive of family factors, many of which have been studied as either control or dummy variables: family structure, family status, parental status, having preschool children. These potential outcomes of the intervention help us understand how this intervention and others might work.

Working with Companies: Lessons from Moen, Kelly, and Chermack and My Own Research Program

I appreciated reading the details concerning working with a corporation. The sagas of corporate work, the moving platform, the tension between ideal research design and corporate realities were beautifully portrayed. These stories often go untold and unheard, yet they are so vital for researchers who are trying to study inside workplaces.

My current NIH-funded research project focuses on work travel. Not all workers travel, clearly, and not all employees of any given corporation travel; therefore, my focus requires me to have access into several companies. If one of my primary aims is to generalize to the population of traveling workers, then I need to proportionally sample across industry and occupational categories. Fortunately, I have analyzed secondary data that ask simple questions about travel (e.g., number of nights away), so I can identify the occupational and industrial categories that are most likely to include work travelers. For example, in analyses based on the 2002 wave of the National Survey of the Changing Workforce, individuals who traveled more nights were more likely to be employed in managerial/professional jobs, sales/technical jobs, and precision production/craft repair occupations than in other job categories.[1] Individuals who did not travel for work were more likely to be in a greater variety of jobs, such as education, administrative support, and service. As well, self-employed individuals were more likely to travel more nights than salaried individuals;[2] however, salaried workers were more likely to travel in general. Analyses of variance revealed that higher levels of job-related travel were associated with higher personal earnings,[3] higher family incomes,[4] and higher education levels.[5] Incomes and education levels jumped significantly once people started traveling.[6]

My task in approaching companies is arguably more complicated than the task of entrée to one company. I am working with multiple companies and focusing on particular work groups. What sagas and lessons can my project provide? And how do they relate to Moen, Kelly, and Chermack's work?

1. I, too, need champions to advance participation in my project, and I have found them from many places in the organizational structure: sometimes they are workers who are tired from travel, sometimes they are especially energized by it. Sometimes my champions are owners or long-term employees who have the respect of human resources and other groups. Cultivating champions has been a process of serendipity and flexibility. As Moen and her colleagues point out, the timetables of corporations are not conducive to academic work. Half of my cooperators, between the time I applied to the NIH and the time the funding came, had left their companies or were no longer heads of their work-life or human resources divisions. I have a full-time project director whose job it is to cultivate companies.

2. The strategies effective in obtaining participants from work sites differ. Therefore, I (and all other researchers who do this type of work)

have to wrestle with issues presented by Moen and her colleagues: the tension between the methodology of "good science" and what works in companies (issues of practicality).

3. It can be a challenge to make a pitch to businesses that does not position them as potentially exploitive of their workers or vulnerable to negative perceptions about corporate travel policies. In some companies, reimbursements, extra vacation, and comp time are really pressure (or pain) points. While it's important to study companies that are perceived to do travel well, it is more important to sample traveling workers thoroughly. Therefore, access to companies whose workers may feel less than positive about the effects of work travel can be a legitimate problem. It compromises validity if participants are overwhelmingly positive or negative due to sampling strategies.

Related to this point is how we account for heterogeneity in our research designs. It is typically the case that sampling happens at the family level in work-family research because certain family structures and ages of children have been associated with problems (Crouter 1994). I applaud this study of workplaces. I will give an example of work I have done that sampled for variation in family, from a qualitatively grounded theory project of women whose jobs required travel. Women were selected from three different occupations, very different in culture and in travel schedule. Within those groups, women also differed in family structure, that is, presence of an intimate partner, gender of the intimate partner, and presence of children. It was not easy to obtain this diversity. The issue to be discussed here is what you gain from focusing on one particular type of job, one particular company, or one particular family structure, and what you lose from not having variability. If a particular job demand or a particular intervention affects workers differently based on their family statuses, their place in the occupational hierarchy, and other such factors, then we need research that includes this variation.

4. As I have written before (McGraw et al. 2000), participants may feel that we will be in a position to improve their lives and may have unrealistic expectations of what participating will mean for changing their work policies.

5. As noted previously, the Moen, Kelly, and Chermack project was conducted within one organizational setting. They noted the chal-

lenges faced in maintaining their profile in the field as scientists and balancing that with the need to blend into the corporate environment and build rapport with the groups and individuals they were observing. The challenges related to the organizations in my project are different. Although participants in my study are recruited from organizations, data are collected outside the office environment, not only from the traveling workers but also from their families. Because of the nature of the data we are collecting, NIH and our university's internal review board require confidentiality, and we promise anonymity as far as participants' workplaces are concerned. However, when participants are asked to provide a preferred method of contact, many give us a work e-mail address or a company-provided cell phone number. The fact that monitoring of workplace communication is increasingly commonplace leaves us (the research staff) concerned. Are our participants divulging their participation simply by corresponding with us? Are they tacitly waiving their right to confidential participation if they choose to communicate with us via company-provided technology?

6. It strikes me that the Moen, Kelly, and Chermack project followed mixed methods, including online surveys and ethnographic methods. Like the authors, I tend to use multiple methods in my own research. In their chapter, the qualitative component comes through and is vividly presented in the "Lesson" sections, whereas the quantitative component is in a small section titled "Does ROWE Make a Difference? Early Survey Findings." It appears so far that the qualitative information gathered via ethnographic participant-observation methods concerns the organizational process of migrating to this ROWE intervention. The quantitative component relates to the comparisons between groups that had benefited from the ROWE intervention and those that had not yet encountered it. I suspect that the authors have qualitative information relative to the evaluation as well. It seems they have information on the interviews and shadowing, which could be used to address more than the process of the migration.

I, too, struggle with how to integrate qualitative and quantitative work, and I typically present the work gathered via different methods in different papers. In my current study, we have qualitative information, quantitative survey data, and a behavioral self-report process that gathers data via PDAs. It is a struggle to incorporate data gathered via multiple methods in the same paper, yet it is precisely this presentation that allows for triangulation. We will eagerly await more information from Moen's team.

Job Demands

The classic Karasek article in *Administrative Science Quarterly* (1979) defines job demands as composed of workload and stressors in the work environment. Typically, high workload and time pressures are considered in his scheme as markers of high job demands. Sociologists have studied job demands in several ways, primarily focusing on the time and timing of work—shift work (Presser 2003), part-time work (Hill, Märtinson, and Ferris 2004), overtime (Jacobs and Gerson 2001), and commuting couples (Gerstl and Gross 1984)—and in terms of the class-related demands on workers (Karasek 1979; Kohn 1977; Perry-Jenkins 2005). I insist that the ways work affects personal life can be most fruitfully understood through *specific* job demands, and I prefer to include measures that are proximal to the work being done as I assess job demands. My own work has focused on the job demand of work travel.

My working conceptual model, however, presents a variety of job demands, which often occur simultaneously, stemming *from* the work organization and affecting *personal* life (figure 8.1). I conceptualize policies and work culture as affecting how job demands are expressed, experienced, and sanctioned through a process I term "institution-to-employee spillover." We know that policies on the books are not necessarily used and not applied evenly across a work organization. For example, not just the number of work hours, but also the pattern of the work hours (e.g., day or night, regular or varying) are crucial, as are factors such as the workers' control over their schedules and the amount of flexibility in the schedule (e.g., ROWE). We might best be able to understand job demands by working with anthropologists and by doing ethnographic work.

It would be a serious mistake to ignore gender and other worker factors that structure workers' opportunities and constrain their work and personal contexts. Theory and practice in the area of work and personal life struggles with how to incorporate such factors. I do not minimize the importance of gender, social class, and other worker factors in accounting for people's work opportunities and experiences, as well as their personal

Figure 8.1. Conceptual Model of Job Demands and Work-Family Spillover

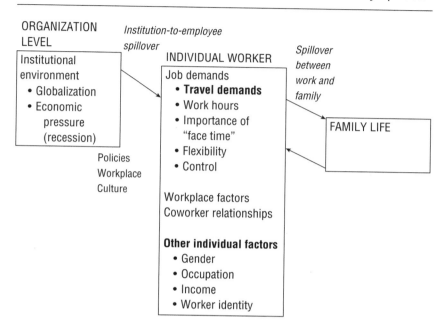

lives. I position these factors here so that we can demonstrate how institutional environments may react differently, for example, to women and men, to ethnic minorities and Caucasians, to their workers who are in the professional as compared to the working class. Similarly, when we get to the level of personal and family life, looking at gender, social class, ethnicity, and the interplay between these factors and income is important. The concept of intersectionality, which refers to the intersection of race, class, ethnicity, and gender, among other categories, applies to this effort (see Hill Collins 1998 and Mohanty 1999). Attempting to sample for diversity in these categories allows us to add variation and understand more about for whom and under what circumstances job demands affect personal life. As I have mentioned before, the factors under consideration in contemporary work and family scholarship have added much richness to the task of understanding how work and personal life are connected. Situating some of the factors that account for this richness in an organized model will, I hope, allow scholarship in the different disciplines to be integrated and provide ground for future scholarship. It will also allow us to answer with more richness, "What works? For whom? In what ways?"

Summary

Moen, Kelly, and Chermack express the challenge of studying work policies: "People live, work, and raise their families in a dynamic, ever-changing environment in which nothing is static—except perhaps the outmoded policies limiting their options." In the field of family studies, we have challenged other scholars and the consumers of our work to make explicit the outmoded "family theories we live by" (Daly 1996) and to be critical of them. When we try to intervene effectively in real problems experienced by real people, we need to bring outmoded ideologies of family and of work to the surface in order to identify and correct the problems these ideologies cause (MacDermid et al. 2005). Such an attempt would allow us to reveal the processes by which interventions are effective and for whom they are effective, and to examine critically how we define effectiveness. I am heartened by the transparency of Moen, Kelly, and Chermack's discussion of their project; their thoughtful delineation of the lessons they have learned should be helpful to future researchers.

NOTES

1. $\chi^2 (24, n = 3{,}291) = 281.68, p < .001$
2. $\chi^2 (3, n = 3{,}540) = 28.78, p < .001$
3. $F (3, 3194) = 33.85, p < .001$
4. $F (3, 3119) = 3.96, p < .01$
5. $F (3, 3533) = 69.53, p < .001$
6. Further data are available from the author.

REFERENCES

Arendell, Teresa. 2001. "The New Care Work of Middle Class Mothers: Managing Child-rearing, Employment, and Time." In *Minding the Time in Family Experience: Emerging Perspectives and Issues,* edited by Kerry J. Daly (163–204). Amsterdam: JAI.

Blair-Loy, Mary. 2004. *Work Devotion and Work Time.* New York: Russell Sage Foundation.

Coontz, Stephanie. 1992. *The Way We Never Were: American Families and the Nostalgia Trap.* New York: Basic Books.

Crouter, Ann C. 1994. "Processes Linking Families and Work." In *Exploring Family Relationships with Other Social Contexts*, edited by Ross D. Parke and Sheppard G. Kellam (9–28). Hillsdale, NJ: Erlbaum.

Daly, Kerry J. 1996. *Families and Time: Keeping Pace in a Hurried Culture.* Thousand Oaks, CA: Sage Publications.

Gerstl, Naomi, and Harriet Gross. 1984. *Commuter Marriage.* New York: Guilford.

Hill, E. Jeffrey, Vjollca K. Märtinson, and Maria Ferris. 2004. "Beyond the Mommy Track: The Influence of New-Concept Part-Time Work for Professional Women on Work and Family." *Journal of Family and Economic Issues* 25(1): 121–36.

Hill Collins, Patricia. 1998. *Fighting Words: Black Women and the Search for Justice.* Minneapolis: University of Minnesota Press.

Hochschild, Arlie R. 1997. *The Time Bind: When Work Becomes Home and Home Becomes Work.* New York: Henry Holt.

———. 2003. *The Commercialization of Intimate Life: Notes from Home and Work.* Berkeley: University of California Press.

Jacobs, Jerry A., and Kathleen Gerson. 2001. "Overworked Individuals or Overworked Families? Explaining Trends in Work, Leisure, and Family Time." *Work and Occupations* 28(1): 40–63.

Karasek, Robert A., Jr. 1979. "Job Demands, Job Decision Latitude, and Mental Strain: Implications for Job Redesign." *Administrative Science Quarterly* 24(2): 285–308.

Kohn, Melvin L. 1977. *Class and Conformity: A Study in Values, with a Reassessment.* Chicago: University of Chicago Press.

MacDermid, Shelley M., Kevin Roy, and Anisa M. Zvonkovic. 2005. "Don't Stop at the Borders: Theorizing Beyond Dichotomies of Work and Family." In *Sourcebook of Family Theory and Research*, edited by Vern L. Bengtson, Alan C. Acock, Katherine R. Allen, Peggye Dilworth-Anderson, and David M. Klein (493–516). Thousand Oaks, CA: Sage Publications.

McGraw, Lori A., Anisa M. Zvonkovic, and Alexis J. Walker. 2000. "Studying Postmodern Families: A Feminist Analysis of Ethical Tensions in Work and Family Research." *Journal of Marriage and the Family* 62(2): 68–77.

Mohanty, Chandra T. 1999. "Feminist Encounters: Locating the Politics of Experience." In *Social Postmodernism: Beyond Identity Politics*, edited by Linda Nicholson and Steven Seidman (68–86). Cambridge: Cambridge University Press.

Perry-Jenkins, Maureen. 2005. "Work in the Working Class: Challenges Facing Families." In *Work, Family, Health, and Well-Being*, edited by Suzanne M. Bianchi, Lynne M. Casper, and Rosalind Berkowitz King (453–72). Mahwah, NJ: Erlbaum.

Presser, Harriet B. 2003. *Working in a 24/7 Economy: Challenges for American Families.* New York: Russell Sage.

Williams, Joan C. 2000. *Unbending Gender: Why Family and Work Conflict and What to Do About It.* New York: Oxford University Press.

PART III
Making a Difference for Hourly Employees

9

Making a Difference for Hourly Employees

Susan J. Lambert

W orkers in low-level hourly jobs on average have less access to work-life supports than workers in higher-level managerial and professional positions. This is true of supports provided by employers (Glass and Estes 1997; Golden 2001, 2005; Lambert and Waxman 2005; Swanberg, Pitt-Catsouphes, and Drescher-Burke 2005) as well as through public policy (Acs, Phillips, and McKenzie 2001; Lambert 1993; Lambert and Haley-Lock 2004), because access to both often depends on characteristics of workers' employment. For example, many employers condition eligibility for employee benefits, such as health insurance and paid time off, on seniority, job status, and the number of hours worked—all qualities on which hourly workers come up short. Similarly, workers' eligibility for supports defined in U.S. public policies, such as Temporary Assistance for Needy Families (TANF), Unemployment Insurance (UI), and the Family and Medical Leave Act, is also conditioned on hours worked, job tenure, or both, leaving many hourly workers outside the public's safety net during times they may most need protection. Thus, a serious mismatch exists not only between today's workplaces and workforce (Bianchi, Casper, and King 2005), but also between today's workplaces and public policies.

A growing group of researchers and practitioners has become interested in increasing access to existing supports, those defined in both employer and public policy (e.g., Bond 2003; Booth, Crouter, and Shanahan 1999;

Dodson, Manuel, and Bravo 2002; Families and Work Institute 1999; Lambert 1999; Lambert and Henly 2007; Perry-Jenkins 2005; Swanberg 2005). In addition, and of primary focus in this chapter, workplace interventions are being developed that are targeted specifically at supporting employees in hourly jobs (e.g., Kim, Lopez, and Bond 2003; Litchfield, Swanberg, and Sigworth 2003; Swanberg et al. 2005). For any of these efforts to make a meaningful difference in the lives of employees and their families, they must reflect the practices found on the front lines of today's firms. Just as the traditional male-breadwinner model no longer fits the realities facing many of America's families (cf. Gornick and Meyers 2003), the traditional model of "standard" employment no longer fits the realities facing many of America's workers (cf. Bernhardt and Marcotte 2000; Presser 2003).

I begin this chapter with a discussion of the importance of researchers understanding how hourly jobs fit into firms' current business and labor strategies if workplace interventions are to achieve intended effects. I then highlight some of the features of hourly jobs that hold implications for the design of intervention research intended to improve the well-being of hourly employees and their families. I provide an example of an ongoing workplace experiment that evaluates the effects of an intervention targeted at improving scheduling practices on sales associates' well-being, performance, and access to public benefits. This experiment is used as a platform to discuss both the challenges and merits of incorporating features of hourly jobs and firms' frontline labor practices into intervention research.

Understanding the Place of Hourly Jobs in Firms' Labor Strategies

The field of human resource management is replete with language proclaiming the virtues of recruiting and retaining "talent," a term rarely used to refer to employees in hourly jobs. Instead, many firms view labor in hourly jobs as a cost to be contained, rather than an asset in which to invest. Many of today's hourly jobs are designed to keep labor costs flexible in order to reduce, if not minimize, labor costs (Appelbaum, Bernhardt, and Murnane 2003; Hacker 2006; Harrison 1997; Moss, Salzman, and Tilly 2005).

Minimizing labor costs is often accomplished through practices that allow employers to keep a tight link between labor costs and variations in consumer demand for service and products (Lambert 2008). Across industries, managers are held accountable for maintaining a particular ratio of labor costs to productivity. In retail, for example, frontline managers must staff within a particular number of hours derived from projected and ongoing sales or traffic. Such accountability requirements place enormous pressures on managers to reduce labor costs when sales are less than anticipated. In many stores, when sales go down, workers go home.

Pressures to contain labor costs can affect all workers (Hacker 2006). Cost containment pressures play out differently, however, for workers paid by the hour versus those paid with a salary (Lambert and Haley-Lock 2004). Salaried workers are more likely than hourly workers to come with fixed costs (e.g., benefits, salary). Thus, for salaried workers, labor costs are contained by keeping staffing levels (people on the payroll) low and requiring overwork during peak times. For hourly workers, labor costs are contained by matching work hours to variations in consumer demand. Staffing levels are often kept high to allow for absenteeism and turnover, which means that some hourly workers may get few hours during slow periods (Lambert 2008; Schlosser 2001).

Although employers may complain about high turnover and absenteeism in low-level hourly jobs, the practices they use to keep labor costs flexible ensure these outcomes (Appelbaum et al. 2000; Baron and Bielby 1980; Jacobs 1994; Lambert and Waxman 2005; Osterman 1999; Pfeffer and Baron 1988). While maintaining high turnover is a conscious strategy used by some employers to restrict labor costs (especially fixed costs such as benefits), other employers view high turnover as problematic (Hacker 2006; Lambert 2008; Tilly 1997). Regardless of whether it is intended or not, the high turnover and absenteeism caused by efforts to closely match labor costs to consumer demand mean that researchers and practitioners often work with a moving target when designing and evaluating interventions to support hourly workers. This complicates both the design of the intervention and its evaluation, as discussed below.

Realities of Hourly Jobs

In hourly jobs that serve the purpose of keeping labor costs flexible, common understandings of employment policies and statuses may not hold. Below, I summarize features of hourly jobs that hold implications for work-life research, especially intervention research. These features were gleaned primarily from a study of 88 low-level hourly jobs at 22 Chicago-area workplaces (all national corporations) in four industries (retail, hospitality, transportation, and financial services). I led the study between 1998 and 2004 (Lambert 2008; Lambert and Waxman 2005).[1]

Nonstandard Features Are Creeping into Standard Jobs

In the not-so-distant past, jobs were divided into broad categories that captured particular qualities of employment—temporary versus regular, part-time versus full-time. Today, the lines between many established categories are being blurred by everyday practices on the front lines of firms (Bernhardt and Marcotte 2000; Kalleberg, Reskin, and Hudson 2000). Most notably, in many low-level hourly jobs, job status (full-time versus part-time) is only loosely related to the number of hours that workers paid by the hour work week to week and season to season. Full-time hourly jobs do not always provide full-time hours, and part-time hourly jobs may require workers to regularly work beyond part-time limits (examples in Henly and Lambert 2005; Lambert and Waxman 2005). Moreover, "regular" jobs—so-called permanent positions filled directly by the firm—may look more like temporary positions given the high annual turnover rates characteristic of many low-level jobs (Lambert and Waxman 2005).

Similarly, job security can no longer be gauged by whether an employer has implemented formal layoffs. Although only two of the Chicago-area firms studied reported formal layoffs in the previous two years, all reported engaging in informal layoffs, called "workloading" or "workload adjustments." In times of workloading, workers are kept on the payroll roster and, thus, officially have a job, but they are not given any hours, and of course any pay, for weeks or even months.

A key lesson for both work-life and policy scholars is that jobs at the lower levels of today's firms may not correspond to their official labels (e.g., part-time or full-time) and might not be as stable as they first appear. For example, some firms are "always hiring" for certain jobs, which could indicate either that there is steady work for workers in these jobs or that high turnover results in a consistent flow of job openings. It is hard to get a handle on the exact nature of today's hourly jobs from national surveys that continue to rely on traditional employment distinctions. Surveys that ask workers in hourly jobs to report "typical hours" or that assume a full-time job provides 35 hours of employment a week, year round, may not accurately capture the job conditions experienced by many of today's hourly workers (Lambert and Henly 2007).

Nonstandard job features complicate the design of intervention research. It takes time for a change in practice to produce a measurable impact. In jobs with high turnover and quick hiring, workers incur different lengths of exposure to the intervention. If the intervention period is too long, few of the sample of workers involved in the study at its onset may be left at its close, which certainly complicates a pre- and post-intervention research design. Information on how periods of reduced and increased consumer demand are handled in hourly jobs can help one design an intervention that is robust to the kinds of instability hourly workers face today. The blurry distinctions of employment in today's low-level jobs are key reasons that work-life scholars and policy researchers need to work together to consider policy and practice options that meet the needs of hourly workers who may rotate among under-, over-, and unemployment because of employer practices.

Barriers to Access: Employment Status, High Turnover, and Benefit Waiting Periods

Research on employer-provided work-life supports provides strong evidence that policies do not always translate into practice and that workers at all levels face obstacles to accessing supports defined in employer policy (Kossek and Distelberg this volume; Kossek, Lautsch, and Eaton 2005). Even the same obstacles, however, can play out differently for hourly workers than salaried ones.

One example is how employment status serves as a barrier to accessing supports. Part-time jobs in general are often excluded from health insurance plans and paid time off (Kalleberg 2000; Tilly 1996). This is true for hourly jobs more than salaried positions, however. Professionals working less than full-time may not be categorized as working in a part-time job and instead are often given a different title, such as "reduced compensation *professional*." Such distinctions enable firms to extend benefits to salaried workers while simultaneously excluding hourly workers in part-time *jobs* from benefits, including training and tuition reimbursement programs, as well as health insurance (Lambert and Waxman 2005).

Even when covered by supports as a matter of policy, hourly workers face several obstacles to achieving eligibility and access. Particularly problematic are benefit waiting periods. Although benefits may start on the first day of employment or soon after for workers in salaried positions, most hourly workers become eligible after varying lengths of employment. In the Chicago study, benefit waiting periods ranged from 30 days to one year for personal health coverage and lasted up to 36 months for dependent coverage. Even the definitions of benefit waiting periods can be misleading. In some firms, a 30-day benefit waiting period does not mean that workers will be eligible for benefits 30 days from the point of hire; instead, the period can refer to 30 days of employment, which may take months for some workers to achieve. Moreover, the prorating of benefits for workers in part-time jobs can make the high cost of health insurance all the more prohibitive for those in low-income households. In the Chicago study, high turnover rates, coupled with lengthy benefit waiting periods, meant that only a small proportion of workers in many of the low-level jobs studied qualified for health insurance provided by their firms as a matter of stated policy (Lambert and Waxman 2005).

Benefit waiting periods can also interfere with the ability of workers in hourly jobs to access paid time off. Hourly workers eligible for paid time off may be able to begin accruing paid time off at the point of hire but are often restricted from using it until they have worked 90 days, and often six months. Again, these waiting periods may not be determined from point of hire but as a count of the number of days worked at the firm. Moreover, an increasingly common practice is for employers to implement penalty systems in which workers are given demerits when they take any "unplanned" time off, including times when workers use paid sick leave for which they are eligible (Lambert and Waxman 2005).

Work-life researchers are well aware that it is important to look beyond policy to see what supports are delivered to workers in everyday practice. This is all the more challenging in low-level hourly jobs because different rules may apply to hourly jobs than to salaried ones—rules that are outside many a researcher's professional and personal experience. To the extent cost containment is a goal in the targeted jobs, efforts to extend existing supports to workers may be undermined by everyday practices that mangers use to keep a tight link between labor costs and consumer demand, specifically by high turnover, as discussed above, and by variations in work hours, as discussed next.

Challenging Scheduling Practices

A key tool managers use to maintain a tight link between labor costs and consumer demand is scheduling practices (Lambert 2008). Many low-level hourly jobs are characterized by fluctuating hours in which both the number and timing of hours can change day to day, week to week, and season to season, at the discretion of management (Henly and Lambert 2005; Henly, Shaefer, and Waxman 2006). It is important to recognize that few firms guarantee a minimum number of hours to workers in part-time hourly jobs. In the Chicago study, none of the firms guaranteed a minimum number of hours to workers in hourly jobs—full-time or part-time.

The hours worked in part-time jobs were especially variable, ranging from zero hours some weeks to hours exceeding part-time limits during other weeks. But hourly full-time jobs are not immune from hour variations. A trend in the retail sector, for example, is a new job status called "full-time flex" in which hours in full-time hourly jobs can vary, commonly between 32 and 40 hours per week, at the discretion of management. Of course, hourly workers' incomes "flex" along with their hours.

Another problematic characteristic of scheduling practices in many hourly jobs is that schedules are posted with little advance notice—in most of the settings studied, the Wednesday or Thursday before the workweek that started on Sunday. Managers also readily make last-minute changes to schedules once posted, as well as real-time changes in which workers are sent home or called in when daily demand differs from projections.

The unpredictability in work schedules resulting from fluctuations in hours and last-minute posting of work schedules poses challenges for conducting workplace research. In a very practical way, it is hard to anticipate who will be on site when observing workplaces, to schedule interviews, and to craft intervention procedures that can be systematically implemented.

The nature of scheduling practices in low-level hourly jobs makes it especially difficult to conceive of how to extend flexibility options developed for professional and managerial workers to those in hourly jobs. Most existing flexibility options seek to "loosen up" rigid scheduling practices by, for example, offering hourly workers compressed workweeks, flexible starting and ending times, leaves of absence, and job sharing. Rather than being rigid, however, many hourly jobs are already "loose," requiring employees to work fluctuating and unpredictable hours. Thus, different interventions may be needed to improve scheduling practices in low-level hourly jobs than in professional and managerial salaried ones.

Stratification of the Hourly Workforce

The workforce in many hourly jobs is stratified by employer practices that concentrate instability onto particular groups of workers (Lambert 2008). Most often, instability is distributed on the basis of seniority, job status, or both. Specifically, the workers with the least seniority are most likely to be scheduled for fluctuating hours and during evenings and weekends, and to experience workloading. In the Chicago study, turnover among new hires was in many jobs 200 percent higher than that among workers with more seniority. In some settings, part-time jobs are used to absorb much of the fluctuation in consumer demand and thus, their workers are most at risk for fluctuating income.

Stratification of workers within hourly jobs creates a significant barrier to the uniform implementation of interventions and thus, adding new supports in the context of organizational stratification may in the end fuel, rather than smooth, inequality in the workplace. Gathering information on the mechanisms used to distribute instability among workers in hourly jobs can in turn be used to identify, a priori, barriers that might restrict the access of certain workers to supports defined in firm policy (Lambert and Waxman 2005). For example, learning about the roles that seniority and job status play in setting schedules for hourly workers may reveal pockets of employees who will not have the opportunity to fully benefit from new work-life initiatives. History, as well as research on employment outcomes, would suggest that these pockets are most likely to be filled by workers of color, women with young children, and those with limited educational credentials (Andersson, Holzer, and Lane 2005; Blank 1997; Carnevale and Rose 2001; Lambert 1998; Mishel, Bernstein, and Allegretto 2005).

Figuring out how to implement work-life interventions in ways that reach hourly employees on whom instability is concentrated is a key challenge for those of us interested in interventions that will make a meaningful difference in the lives of hourly workers. It is almost natural, and certainly easier, to concentrate efforts on those workers who tend to be a steady presence in the workplace, rather than taking steps to include those who are more likely to come and go. Yet, unless researchers and practitioners acknowledge and attend to stratification when developing work-life interventions, we can be assured that the working poor will continue to be "locked out" of work-life opportunities distributed through the workplace (Kossek et al. 1997; Lambert and Kossek 2005).

A Well-Intended Policy with Unintended Consequences: An Example

Even well-intended policies may result in unanticipated negative consequences if attention is not given to the realities of today's low-level hourly jobs. One example that has emerged from our research is how the lack of a guaranteed minimum number of hours can result in an earnings penalty when hourly workers claim control over the timing of work hours (Henly and Lambert 2005; Lambert and Henly 2007). For example, many retailers allow employees to "claim availability," which permits sales associates to declare the days and times they are available and unavailable for work. Although many employers ensure that associates will not be scheduled for work during unavailable times, they do not ensure that associates will be scheduled for work during available times. Without a guaranteed minimum number of hours, sales associates with limited availability get fewer hours than their counterparts with greater availability. Workers in low-level hourly jobs in all of the industries we have studied face a tradeoff between working enough hours and working preferred hours. In sum, the nature of today's hourly jobs—fluctuating work hours, no guaranteed minimum number of hours, benefit waiting periods, ambiguous job status, stratification of the workforce—can complicate and even undermine the successful implementation of work-life interventions intended to foster the well-being of hourly workers and their families.

Taking Firm-Level Labor Strategies and Practices into Account: The Scheduling Intervention Study

The Scheduling Intervention Study is a cluster-randomized experiment that assesses the effects of greater schedule predictability on workers' performance, daily family practices, health, and well-being.[2] Table 9.1 provides an overview of the study, which includes random assignment of stores to experimental and control conditions, extensive use of organizational documentation, and pre- and post-intervention surveys of managers and sales associates. In designing the Scheduling Intervention Study, we have tried to attend to the complicated nature of low-level jobs, the risk they pose to workers' earnings and well-being, and the business strategies found in the retail sector. Below, I discuss how information on key labor practices was used to inform the design of both the intervention protocol and the evaluation procedures.

Table 9.1. Overview of the Scheduling Intervention Study

Goal	To assess the effects of greater schedule predictability on hourly sales associates' work performance, daily family practices, health, and well-being.
Setting	National women's apparel retailer with stores concentrated in Midwestern and Eastern states.
Sample	The experiment is currently underway in the Chicago area (20 stores); implementation in the New York/New Jersey region (48–60 stores) is to follow. Stores are small (an average of 10 associates) and located primarily in urban and suburban strip malls. Managers and sales associates are almost exclusively female (99 percent), but the workforce is diverse in terms of race, ethnicity, and age.
Cluster-randomized experiment	In each region, stores are matched on sales and then randomly assigned to intervention and control conditions. The minimum is a two-month baseline period, followed by a four- to six-month intervention period.
Corporate data	
Personnel records	Corporate administrative data on employees in 153 stores (the 80 target stores and 73 additional stores selected for control purposes and possible study expansion) are used to track turnover month to month.
Weekly work schedules and hours	We collect the weekly schedule initially posted (which tells us when employees were scheduled to work), changes made to the initial schedule, and the timing and number of hours employees actually worked during the week (from the company's payroll system).
Associates' scheduling requests	Scheduling requests submitted to store managers are compared to associates' actual work hours to determine the extent to which managers incorporate requests into their scheduling practices. Comparisons of pre- and post-intervention payroll data allow us to estimate the effects of the intervention on timing as well as the number of hours associates work.
Sales data	Weekly sales information per employee and store are from corporate data management systems.
Telephone surveys of managers and sales associates	Telephone surveys of 139 store managers were conducted pre-intervention to document managers' scheduling challenges and practices. Telephone surveys are conducted with all personnel in the stores included in the experiment, both pre- and post-intervention, to gather information on work-family conflict, family practices, child care, well-being, and performance-related attitudes and behaviors.

Table 9.1. *(Continued)*

Return on investment (ROI)	The study is designed to track turnover and the ratio of labor costs to sales throughout baseline and intervention periods, allowing for the estimation of an ROI model at the store level.
Use of public supports	The study investigates the hypothesis that improving scheduling practices will improve workers' access to public benefits. The pre- and post-intervention employee interviews gather information on employees' eligibility for and use of specific public benefits (public assistance, food stamps, unemployment insurance, state health programs, and child care subsidies).

Developing the Intervention: The Role of Labor Strategies and Practices

The intervention evaluated in the Scheduling Intervention Study is intended to balance managers' goals—to tightly link staffing levels in the stores to variations in consumer demand—with employees' goals—to work enough hours at preferred times. The intervention protocol is based on interviews with store employees at multiple levels and on-site observations of store practices conducted over a two-year period. The full research protocol was refined based on feedback from store managers who piloted both the intervention and data collection methods for an additional nine-month period and on our analyses of pilot data.

Targets Considered for Intervention

We targeted scheduling practices for improvement and evaluation for several reasons. Employer scheduling practices are a well-documented source of employment instability that can impede worker performance and worker and family health and well-being (Crouter and McHale 2005; Henly and Lambert 2005; Hsueh and Yoshikawa 2007; Presser 2003). Yet, causal connections are unclear, as they are in much of the research on relationships among work, family, health, and well-being (Casper, Bianchi, and King 2005). Moreover, the policy literature currently gives much more attention to improving hourly wages than the distribution of hours, although income in hourly jobs is obviously a function of not only hourly wages but also hours worked, as is eligibility for many public benefits. Thus, targeting scheduling practices for rigorous evaluation holds the possibility of contributing new knowledge to the work-life field as well as informing public policy debates.

As explained more fully in the next section, the Scheduling Intervention Study focuses on improving scheduling predictability (i.e., advance notice). Several other aspects of scheduling in hourly jobs might have been targeted for improvement, including fluctuating hours, lack of control over timing of hours, nonstandard timing (weekends and evenings), and last-minute changes to work schedules.

Ample literature is available on two of these potential targets: work during nonstandard times and the lack of control over work hours. The former literature tends to focus on workers in hourly (nonexempt) jobs and the latter on workers in salaried (exempt) positions. Among salaried workers, such as managers and professionals, issues of work hours are primarily framed in terms of flexibility in the timing of work hours, that is, how much control workers have over when they work (e.g., Kossek et al. 2005; Moen, Kelly, and Chermack this volume). Among hourly workers, timing of work hours is more often framed in terms of the perils of working during "nonstandard" times (Hsueh and Yoshikawa 2007; Presser 2003). Harriet Presser estimates that "two-fifths of all employed Americans work mostly at nonstandard times," operationalized in her research as "working in the evening, at night, on a rotating shift, or during the weekend" at least half of the time (Presser 2003).

Research indicates that not only do employees often have little control over their schedules when working in jobs that incorporate nonstandard timing, many—though not all—would prefer a more standard arrangement. In their study of industry restructuring in electronics manufacturing, food service, financial services, and retail sales, Moss and his colleagues (2005) found "little employee-driven flexibility and much employer-driven flexibility" in entry-level jobs. They report that workers in service industries are especially likely to have variations in work hours imposed on them by employers. Notably, the majority of low-skilled unmarried mothers who work nonstandard schedules do so because their employer requires it (Presser and Cox 1997; Tausig and Fenwick 2001).

In the case of the Scheduling Intervention Study, reducing work during nonstandard times did not seem like a promising target for the intervention, given the general labor strategies found in today's retail sector. The retail sector is now a 24/7 operation. In the firm involved in the experiment, stores are open evenings and weekends, which requires that at least some employees be available for work during these times. It would be hard to make the case to reduce store hours during evenings and weekends since these are the times when sales peak.

Moen, Kelly, and Chermack (this volume) summarize well the numerous merits of developing interventions that increase workers' control over the time and timing of their work hours. However, given that our prior research suggested that exerting control may place hourly workers at risk of reduced earnings, making schedule control the primary target of the intervention seemed risky and even raised ethical issues for us. In the firm that is participating in the intervention, only store managers are paid by salary and fully 70 percent of hourly workers in the stores hold part-time positions for which there is no guaranteed minimum number of hours. Scheduled hours vary greatly in part-time positions, ranging from as few as 4 hours per week to as many as 30. Hours for full-time assistant managers and sales associates also vary, in most stores between 32 and 40 hours per week, depending on corporate policies and individual store practices.

We examined in more depth whether the risk to earnings is a real one in this setting through in-person interviews and structured telephone interviews with store managers in several regions of the United States ($N = 139$). The data substantiate our worry that an intervention that asks workers to put restrictions on their availability for work may have negative repercussions for their earnings. Fully 79 percent of the store managers surveyed either agreed or strongly agreed with the statement "I give more hours to sales associates who have greater availability," and 89 percent disagreed or strongly disagreed with the statement "I give more hours to sales associates who seem to really need the money."

As in other retail settings, the managers of the stores in this firm are held accountable for staffing within hour limits set by the corporation. The larger the staff in a store, the more people there are among whom to divvy up that week's hours. When asked to chose between two general labor strategies, 67 percent of the store managers surveyed chose the statement "I like to keep my sales associate staff on the large side so that I have several associates I can tap to work when needed," over the statement "I like to keep my sales associate staff on the small side to help ensure that workers get hours." Thus, the labor strategies expressed by the majority of managers of the stores targeted for the experiment suggest that increasing worker control over work hours as part of the intervention might have the unintended outcome of reducing at least some workers' earnings.

Given that a signature characteristic of many hourly jobs is fluctuations in the number and timing of work hours, increasing stability of hourly workers' schedules is also a possible target for intervention. As discussed before, however, a key business strategy not only in this firm but in many firms today is to keep a tight link between consumer demand and labor costs. If firms will not guarantee a minimum number of hours to workers in part-time jobs, they are unlikely to guarantee a particular shift week to week. This is true of the firm participating in the current study. Thus, increasing the stability of workers' hours in low-level retail jobs was an unrealistic target for intervention in this case.

The Intervention: Improving Predictability

The intervention developed and evaluated in the Scheduling Intervention Study is designed to increase the predictability of sales associates' work schedules by posting schedules further in advance than is the usual practice. I emphasize that we did not "settle" for this goal, but instead saw it as a meaningful target of intervention. A companion investigation to the study of Chicago-area employers of low-income mothers employed in retail jobs indicated that the last-minute posting of work schedules interfered with workers' ability to effectively structure and use the hours they were not at work (Henly and Lambert 2005; Henly et al. 2006). For example, the unpredictability of retail workers' schedules made it difficult to plan family meals, to adopt consistent homework and bedtime routines, and to volunteer at their children's schools. Limited advance notice of work days and shifts posed complications for child care as well. Henly found that parents who work unpredictable schedules make child care arrangements at the last minute or else set up arrangements in advance, only to cancel them when work times are different from what was expected. Moreover, in Henly's study, parents with unpredictable schedules relied disproportionately on relative providers and used a patchwork of arrangements to accommodate schedules. Some parents reported that problems with child care arrangements resulted in absenteeism and tardiness, limiting their ability to earn a stable and adequate income. Thus, changing the timeframe in which schedules are posted seemed a potentially effective strategy for supporting hourly workers and their families.

The Feasibility of Increasing Advance Notice

Interviews with store managers provided useful information on the accountability requirements they face day to day and on their current scheduling practices. This information allowed us to assess whether posting schedules further in advance is feasible in the firm and if so, to determine how far in advance it might be reasonable to post schedules.

Store managers report, and corporate officials corroborate, that managers receive their staffing hours for a full month at a time (January, February, and so forth), commonly 10 to 14 days in advance of the month. Although store managers are given their staffing hours a month at a time, corporate policy is that managers need only post schedules the Tuesday before the workweek that begins on Sunday. Interview and survey data indicate that most (64 percent) managers post one schedule at a time, for the upcoming week. Some, however, post two weeks at a time (30 percent) and a small minority (less than 1 percent) posts schedules for a full month. The fact that some managers are already posting schedules for multiple weeks provides additional evidence that posting schedules further in advance is feasible, although not common practice, for the store managers in this firm.[3]

In sum, the intervention—posting schedules for a full month at a time—is intended to enable managers to schedule within corporate guidelines while providing workers with longer advance notice than they currently receive. A store manager who completed a nine-month pilot of the intervention indicated that she will continue to post schedules a month at a time because "it is more efficient for me, and my associates like to be able to plan."

A Potential Caveat: Predictability or Rigidity?

The benefits of a predictable schedule for workers may be attenuated in situations where schedules are not sufficiently responsive to accommodate nonwork-related responsibilities. Indeed, schedule predictability may turn into rigidity if workers have limited input into their work schedules or if posted schedules are not amenable to change. Without any input into scheduling decisions, workers are likely to be scheduled during hours that they cannot work, which may interfere with their ability to retain the job in the long term. Yet, restricting workers' availability may result in reduced earnings, as discussed above. These conflicting pressures led us to look closely at how managers track workers' ongoing availability for work and record workers' requests for days off and other scheduling changes.

In-person interviews with store managers occurred at their stores, allowing us to see firsthand the process by which sales associates communicate scheduling requests and preferences. In most of the stores visited, informal systems were used by sales associates to indicate scheduling requests and changes to their availability (e.g., leaving a post-it note for the manager). The structured survey of store managers in multiple regions indicated that most stores follow similar practices, that is, communication around scheduling issues tends to take place informally. Managers report that these informal systems make it difficult for them to "keep on top of requests and preferences."

We thus saw merit in trying to improve the process by which employees communicate their scheduling requests and preferences to store managers by making it more systematic, and had planned to make this part of the intervention. Prior to the implementation of the experimental phase of the study, however, we learned that store managers in the Chicago region were adopting a system that allows sales associates to record their scheduling requests and preferences on a calendar. Store managers told us that they think the new protocol has improved communication with their staffs about work schedules and that they would be reluctant to give up this new system. As a result, the intervention we have implemented in Chicago stores does not include a component designed to formalize communication between sales associates and managers regarding scheduling requests and preferences. We may add this component back into the intervention when we move to additional regions to conduct the experiment, since the new calendar system is a local, rather than a corporate, initiative. This change in the design of the intervention highlights the importance of maintaining ongoing contact with research sites so that the intervention that is implemented complements daily management practices, which can change during the course of a study.

Issues of Generalizability

The fact that retailers vary in the timeframe in which they provide managers with the information they need to schedule staff raises issues of the generalizability of the intervention. "Generalizability" is primarily an issue when defined narrowly in terms of the exact replication of the intervention protocol. As explained above, posting schedules one month at a time fits with current management practices at the participating firm. In other firms, increasing predictability may need to be implemented differently. If managers receive their hours more than a month at time, an intervention protocol might be developed that provides workers even further advance notice. If managers are given staffing hours at the last minute, it may be impossible to deliver meaningful predictability to employees.

Intervention protocols that do not fit with everyday firm practices may not be implemented effectively, if at all. Employers are often reluctant to adopt policies that will require widespread changes to everyday practices found at the front lines of the firm. Perhaps even more worrisome is the circumstance when an intervention protocol is adopted, even when at odds with other frontline practices. For example, during our piloting of the intervention, we asked a manager to try out a different scenario in which, rather than posting schedules for a particular month, she posted schedules for four weeks at a time. This required that she post one new schedule each week (for four weeks out). Because of the timing of when managers receive their staffing hours, she had to develop some schedules before receiving word as to what her hour allocations were for those weeks. When hour reductions came down from the corporate level, she had to make severe modifications to the posted schedules, undermining the goal of providing greater predictability of work hours.

Broadening discussions of generalizability to focus more on concepts and goals than on specific intervention procedures helps prevent the problem of cookie-cutter solutions to complex organizational problems. Inattention to operational realities at the front lines of firms may help explain why many work-life policies look better on paper than in practice. When defined in terms of increasing schedule predictability, the generalizability of the current intervention looks better than when defined narrowly in terms of posting schedules a month at a time.

The firm participating in the Scheduling Intervention Study was recruited through our participation in the National Retailers' Work-Life Forum, a membership group of some of the nation's largest retail firms. Members concur with our assessment that unpredictable scheduling poses a serious challenge to workers (for example, by making child care arrangements difficult) and adds to the difficulties store managers face in maintaining adequate staffing levels. Moreover, they suggest that an emphasis on increasing scheduling predictability frames the discussion of scheduling problems in a way that encourages upper-management support for intervention, because it still allows employers to implement variations in work hours, does not entitle workers to guarantees about number of hours worked, and does not intervene with operational decisions of the firm. As one member of the Retailers' Work-Life Forum said after a presentation we made to that group, "Now this we can do something about." What each may be able to do, however, will and should vary by the realities found on the front lines of each firm.

Labor groups in other segments of the retail industry are beginning to focus on schedule predictability in their negotiations with employers. For example, the Puget Sound Share the Success initiative (targeted at improving working conditions for grocery workers) is emphasizing changes to the three-day advance posting of schedules that is standard practice in many stores, pointing out how such short notice interferes with workers' ability to plan time with their families.[4] Moreover, given that unpredictable scheduling practices (limited advance notice and frequent last-minute changes) were a typical employer strategy for managing fluctuations in consumer demand and were observed in all 22 workplaces studied in Chicago, the results of the intervention hold the potential to inform practices in industries in addition to retail.

Using Turnover Data to Inform the Intervention Period

As Bloom (2005) states, "Mobility is the Achilles' heel of place-based programs and of cluster randomization experiments." The entry and exit of individuals (employees) from randomized clusters (stores) undermine the ability to identify accurately the effects of an intervention, perhaps inflating estimates when effectiveness is judged on only those who stayed or underestimating effects when estimates include individuals who left before they received an adequate dose of the treatment.

Attrition of workers is especially a challenge for high turnover industries such as retail. Indeed, one reason employers may be interested in participating in a workplace intervention is to reduce turnover, and this is, in fact, one reason the women's apparel retailer is participating in the Scheduling Intervention Study. Because most of the targeted stores are located in strip malls, customers usually come purposefully to the stores rather than simply stopping by to shop as many customers do when walking through an enclosed mall. Although the merchandise and its pricing may be the main draw, relationships between customers and sales associates are also important to sales. In our in-person interviews, managers told us that some customers will ask for a particular sales associate and even call ahead to see when she is working. Retention of sales associates is a stated goal for this firm. Nonetheless, in the stores targeted for the intervention, the annual turnover rate is similar to other retailers we have studied (79 percent turnover between August 2006 and July 2007).

While turnover poses challenges to intervention research, it is also an important store-level dependent variable in this study. Analyses will examine the extent to which turnover is lower in the stores that implement the intervention when compared to the stores that continue usual scheduling practices. Turnover remains a threat to internal validity for analyses at the individual level, however. Stores, not individuals, are randomly assigned to experimental and control conditions for obvious reasons. Thus, hypotheses related to the effects of the intervention on certain types of workers (workers with children, for example) will be primarily addressed by comparing workers' responses on pre- and post-intervention surveys. Although the study design includes post-intervention surveys of all workers in the stores at baseline even if they have terminated employment (the intent-to-treat group), comparing pre- and post-intervention responses among workers who left the job undermines the usefulness of the survey data for evaluating the effectiveness of the intervention, as well as for examining other relationships between work conditions and worker performance and well-being.

At first glance, an annual turnover rate of 79 percent suggests that, were our intervention to last a year, only about 20 percent of the workers would be consistent throughout the intervention period. This would be the case were turnover equally distributed within the workforce. As noted earlier, however, many low-level hourly jobs are stratified, that is, instability is often concentrated on subsets of workers who turn over rapidly. Analyses of corporate data suggest that turnover is not equally distributed among employees in the target stores.

For over a year, we have been receiving lists of employees in all target stores so that we can examine who stays and who leaves and when. These data indicate that, during a one-year period, an average of 59 percent of employees has remained the same in the targeted stores, and 51 percent of the part-time sales associates are the same. As in many other workplaces, a core group of employees with longer seniority works alongside another group that tends to turn over rapidly, accounting for the higher cumulative turnover rate across the year. In this firm, younger workers (under 24 years of age), those with little seniority, and those in part-time jobs are least likely to continue employment month to month. Data we are also collecting on the timing and number of hours worked will allow us to assess the hypothesis that instability is being concentrated onto these groups of workers in the form of fluctuating work hours and nonstandard timing.

The patterns of continued employment tracked monthly show that turnover occurs quickly among part-time sales associates and those younger than 24—within the first month or two after hiring—and then tapers off. Restricting the intervention to a month or two, however, seems too short of a time to determine whether or not the intervention makes a difference, especially on workers' family routines and child care arrangements.

Our analyses suggest that a four-month intervention period better balances the risk to internal validity of inadequate exposure with the risk of attrition. A four-month intervention period shows continued employment rates between 74 and 81 percent among all store employees and between 68 and 78 percent in part-time sales associate jobs, depending on seasonal variations in staffing practices. These analyses allow us to estimate that, with a four-month intervention period, approximately 70 percent of employees who enter the intervention will still be employed at its close, unless the intervention has the unintended effect of reducing retention. A six-month intervention period brings the rate of continued employment to around 70 percent overall and around 60 percent among part-time sales associates. We will continue to assess continued employment to determine whether it is wise to extend the intervention to a six-month period in order to increase employees' exposure to the intervention.

In sum, an advantage of conducting workplace research is the possibility of securing information from the firm to inform elements of the research design that, in many studies, are based on researchers' assumptions rather than on analyses (Lambert 2006). For the Scheduling Intervention Study, we analyzed corporate personnel data to track patterns in continued employment, thus providing an empirical basis for establishing the intervention period. We have also used corporate administrative data to refine our power estimates of the number of stores needed to reliably identify the effect of the intervention on turnover. Of course, it remains an empirical question whether the estimates we have developed through our analyses of corporate data are accurate—specifically, whether four to six months is adequate to establish the effects of the intervention, if any, and whether our sample size is indeed large enough to reliably estimate these effects on worker- and store-level outcomes.

Conclusion

Researchers and practitioners face a challenging task when seeking to extend and develop interventions to support the well-being of workers in hourly jobs. Workplaces are often havens for inequality (Lambert and Haley-Lock 2004). Given the widening gap in the well-being of those at the top and bottom of the income distribution (Hacker 2006; Heymann 2000; Lewis and Smithson 2001), figuring out how to deliver supports to those most at risk of poverty is important work that will take the combined efforts of both the public and private sectors.

My goal in this chapter has been to help prepare researchers, practitioners, and policy analysts for this work. Knowledge of firms' labor strategies and practices can provide insight into some of the more problematic features of hourly jobs that, if ignored, can undermine the effectiveness of both well-intended workplace interventions and public policies. The more aware researchers, practitioners, and policymakers are of the daily accountability pressures confronted by frontline managers, the more likely it is they will develop interventions and policies that can be effectively implemented into everyday practice. Many low-level hourly jobs are designed to keep a tight link between variations in consumer demand and labor costs. Instability is thus structured into many hourly jobs through daily workplace practices, including fluctuating work hours, vague job status, informal layoffs, stratification of the workforce, and benefit waiting periods.

These workplace practices not only make it difficult for hourly workers to access supports defined in workplace policy, they also diminish the effectiveness of public policies. For example, the ability of TANF to serve antipoverty purposes is undermined by the week-to-week, season-to-season variations in income that accompany shifting schedules and rapid job loss. Qualifying for UI requires an involuntary termination, but workers experiencing workloading are still technically employed, and it is hard to distinguish between voluntary and involuntary terminations in jobs with excessive turnover rates. Even the effectiveness of living-wage initiatives is limited by the fact that higher wages will not reduce poverty unless jobs provide workers with enough hours. Thus, public policies that reflect the realities of today's hourly jobs are in short supply.

Workplace interventions that can improve work-life outcomes for workers in jobs designed for cost containment are sorely needed as well. The Scheduling Intervention Study attempts to take into account the everyday practices retailers use to match store staffing levels to variations in customer traffic and sales. The intervention and research design are both informed by analyses indicating that turnover is concentrated among sales associates who are young and new in the stores and that asking associates to put restrictions on their availability may place their earnings at risk. Rather than targeting worker control over the timing of work hours, the intervention targets improving the predictability of workers' schedules by posting schedules further in advance. This change may seem minor to those of us in managerial and professional positions, but even a small change can make a big difference in the everyday lives of working-class families. Knowing how much income they are going to earn in a month and when they will need child care is critical to the well-being of workers and their families. Of course, whether improving scheduling predictability constitutes enough of an improvement to sales associates' jobs to enhance their well-being and performance remains, at this time, an empirical question.

Although the research summarized here holds suggestions for researchers targeting hourly jobs for intervention, it does not hold all the answers. Notably, the Scheduling Intervention Study takes cost-containment strategies as a given. A basic goal of the larger project from which the study was developed is to identify ways to improve hourly jobs within today's business climate and practice models. In this study, we have made it a point to build on existing practices as much as possible in an effort to develop an intervention that can be implemented into everyday practice, rather than one that remains as a good idea "on the books."

In the end, making a real difference in the lives of hourly workers will require a much more ambitious intervention: improving the place of hourly jobs in firms' labor strategies and changing the strategies themselves. The literature suggests that firms with business models that base profits on cost containment are less likely to include lower-level workers in opportunity structures than are firms that seek profits through product differentiation, that is, higher-quality services and products (Hunter 2000; Osterman 1999; Tilly 1997). For example, most of the U.S. corporations included in the report by Litchfield and colleagues (2003) on model programs for hourly employees include "differentiation" reasons, such as improved customer service, in their list of benefits of the program to the firm itself.

Caution is warranted, however, in assuming that problems with hourly jobs will be solved were all firms to adopt differentiation strategies. Today's firms pursue multiple strategies that get translated into different practices at different operational levels. The mechanisms of stratification found in today's firms often operate to exclude low-level hourly jobs from opportunity structures, even in firms committed to pursuing profit through quality-enhancement strategies (Lambert 2008; Lambert and Waxman 2005). Notably, several of the companies included in the Chicago-area study have appeared on lists of the best companies to work for in America and yet, have hourly jobs that incorporate many of the problematic features identified earlier.

Fully integrating hourly workers into the opportunity structures of today's firms will require that jobs themselves be enhanced. Currently, many low-level hourly jobs are structured so that workers cannot add much value to the firms in which they work. For example, placing cash registers at the front of the store rather than in departments severs the link between customer service and sales; one cashier is about as good as the next and most sales occur without any service. It is no wonder that many retail jobs command little from the market. These jobs are *designed* to pay workers little.

The extent to which interventions to improve hourly jobs are effective in enhancing the well-being of workers and their families will depend on developments in the larger economy and in society. Hacker (2006) chronicles what he terms the "Great Risk Shift" in which a greater proportion of economic risk is now transferred directly to American families—and not just those headed by hourly workers—rather than pooled through insurance structures, both corporate and government. Thus, society has a larger problem to deal with if workers of all ilks are to stand a fair chance of earning a stable and adequate living. Cross-national comparisons make clear that instability is not a natural outcome of globalization, immigration, or other significant social changes but rather is determined by societal priorities and the daily decisions and practices found at the front lines of major societal institutions, both public and private (cf. Hacker 2002; Hacker 2006; Lewis and Smithson 2001; Moss et al. 2005).

In conclusion, broadening both research and public discourse to include the work-life challenges of hourly workers is essential if millions of low-income families are not to fall further behind in terms of income and well-being. Understanding how business models translate into frontline practices is essential if work-life interventions and public policies are to make a real difference in the lives of hourly workers, their families, and communities.

NOTES

The author thanks colleagues Evelyn Brodkin, Anna Haley-Lock, Elaine Waxman, and particularly, Julia Henly, for input on the ideas developed here and the studies drawn on as examples. She thanks as well Tianna Cervantes, Ellen Frank, Jessica Manvell, and Luke Shaefer for extraordinary effort as research assistants on the Scheduling Intervention Study.

1. The Study of Organizational Stratification was funded by the Ford Foundation through a grant to Susan Lambert and Evelyn Brodkin, coprincipal investigators.

2. Susan Lambert and Julia R. Henly are coprincipal investigators of the Scheduling Intervention Study. The study is supported with grants from the Ford Foundation, the Russell Sage Foundation, and the Annie. E. Casey Foundation.

3. Random assignment of stores to experimental and control conditions should balance out the effects of pre-intervention posting practices on study outcomes. We can also control for pre-intervention posting practices in analyses.

4. http://sharethesuccess.wordpress.com (accessed July 22, 2008).

REFERENCES

Acs, Gregory, Karen Ross Phillips, and Daniel McKenzie. 2001. "Playing by the Rules but Losing the Game: Americans in Low-Income Working Families." In *Low-Wage Workers in the New Economy,* edited by Richard Kazis and Marc S. Miller (21–44). Washington, DC: Urban Institute Press.

Andersson, Fredrik, Harry J. Holzer, and Julie I. Lane. 2005. *Moving Up or Moving On: Who Advances in the Low-Wage Labor Market?* New York: Russell Sage Foundation.

Appelbaum, Eileen, Annette Bernhardt, and Richard Murnane. 2003. "Low-Wage America: An Overview." In *Low-Wage America: How Employers Are Reshaping Opportunity in the Workplace,* edited by Eileen Appelbaum, Annette Bernhardt, and Richard Murnane (1–29). New York: Russell Sage Foundation.

Appelbaum, Eileen, Thomas Bailey, Peter Berg, and Arne Kalleberg. 2000. *Manufacturing Advantage: Why High-Performance Work Systems Pay Off.* Ithaca, NY: Cornell University Press.

Baron, James N., and William T. Bielby. 1980. "Bringing the Firms Back In: Stratification, Segmentation, and the Organization of Work." *American Sociological Review* 45(5): 737–65.

Bernhardt, Annette, and Dave Marcotte. 2000. "Is 'Standard Employment' Still What it Used to Be?" In *Nonstandard Work: The Nature and Challenges of Emerging Employment Arrangements,* edited by Francoise Carre, Marianne Ferber, Lonnie Golden, and Stephen Herzenberg (21–40). Ithaca, NY: Cornell University Press.

Bianchi, Suzanne, Lynne Casper, and Rosalind Berkowitz King, eds. 2005. *Work, Family, Health, and Well-Being.* Mahwah, NJ: Erlbaum.

Blank, Rebecca M. 1997. *It Takes a Nation: A New Agenda for Fighting Poverty.* New York: Russell Sage Foundation.

Bloom, Howard S. 2005. "Randomizing Groups to Evaluate Place-Based Programs." In *Learning More from Social Experiments: Evolving Analytic Approaches,* edited by Howard Bloom (115–72). New York: Russell Sage Foundation.

Bond, James T. 2003. "Information for Employers about Low-Wage Employees from Low-Income Families." Report W2003-03. New York: The Families and Work Institute.

Booth, Alan, Ann C. Crouter, and Michael J. Shanahan, eds. 1999. *Transitions to Adulthood in a Changing Economy: No Work, No Family, No Future?* Westport, CT: Greenwood Press.

Carnevale, Anthony P., and Stephen J. Rose. 2001. "Low Earners: Who Are They? Do They Have a Way Out?" In *Low-Wage Workers in the New Economy,* edited by Richard Kazis and Marc S. Miller (45–66). Washington, DC: Urban Institute Press.

Casper, Lynne, Suzanne Bianchi, and Rosalind Berkowitz King. 2005. "Forging the Future in Work, Family, Health, and Well-Being Research." In *Work, Family, Health, and Well-Being,* edited by Suzanne Bianchi, Lynne Casper, and Rosalind Berkowitz King (531–40). Mahwah, NJ: Erlbaum.

Crouter, Ann C., and Susan McHale. 2005. "Work, Family, and Children's Time: Implications for Youth." In *Work, Family, Health, and Well-Being,* edited by Suzanne Bianchi, Lynne Casper, and Rosalind Berkowitz King (49–66). Mahwah, NJ: Erlbaum.

Dodson, Lisa, Tiffany Manuel, and Ellen Bravo. 2002. "Keeping Jobs and Raising Families in Low-Income America: It Just Doesn't Work." The Across the Boundaries Project, Radcliffe Public Policy Center and 9 to 5 National Association of Working Women. Boston, MA: Radcliffe Institute for Advanced Study, Harvard University.

Families and Work Institute. 1999. "The Business Case for Employer Investment in Benefits Targeted to Low-Wage Workers." Report W99-01. New York: Families and Work Institute.

Glass, Jennifer L., and Sarah Beth Estes. 1997. "The Family Responsive Workplace." *Annual Review of Sociology* 23: 289–313.

Golden, Lonnie. 2001. "Flexible Work Schedules: Which Workers Get Them?" *American Behavioral Scientist* 44: 1157–78.

———. 2005. "The Flexibility Gap: Employee Access to Flexibility in Work Schedules." In *Flexibility in Workplaces: Effects on Workers, Work Environment and the Union,* edited by Isik U. Zeytinoglu (38–56). Geneva: IIRA/ILO.

Gornick, Janet C., and Marcia K. Meyers. 2003. *Families That Work: Policies for Reconciling Parenthood and Employment.* New York: Russell Sage Foundation.

Hacker, Jacob. 2002. *The Divided Welfare State: The Battle over Public and Private Social Benefits in the United States.* New York: Cambridge University Press.

———. 2006. *The Great Risk Shift: The Assault on American Jobs, Families, Health Care, and Retirement and How You Can Fight Back.* New York: Oxford University Press.

Harrison, Bennett. 1997. *Lean and Mean: Why Large Corporations Will Continue to Dominate the Global Economy.* New York: Guilford Publications.

Henly, Julia R., and Susan Lambert. 2005. "Nonstandard Work and Child Care Needs of Low-Income Parents." In *Work, Family, Health, and Well-Being,* edited by Suzanne Bianchi, Lynne Casper, and Rosalind Berkowitz King (473–92). Mahwah, NJ: Erlbaum.

Henly, Julia R., H. Luke Shaefer, and Elaine Waxman. 2006. "Nonstandard Work Schedules: Employer- and Employee-Driven Flexibility in Retail Jobs." *Social Service Review* 80: 609–34.

Heymann, Jody. 2000. *The Widening Gap: Why America's Working Families Are in Jeopardy—and What Can Be Done About It.* New York: Basic Books.

Hsueh, Joann, and Hirokazu Yoshikawa. 2007. "Working Nonstandard Schedules and Variable Shifts in Low-Income Families: Associations with Parental Psychological Well-Being, Family Functioning, and Child Well-Being." *Developmental Psychology* 43: 620–32.

Hunter, Larry. 2000. "What Determines Job Quality in Nursing Homes?" *Industrial and Labor Relations Review* 53: 463–81.

Jacobs, David. 1994. "Organizational Theory and Dualism: Some Sociological Determinants of Spot and Internal Labor Markets." *Research in Social Stratification and Mobility* 13: 203–35.

Kalleberg, Arne. 2000. "Nonstandard Employment Relations: Part-Time, Temporary, and Contract Work." *Annual Review of Sociology* 26: 341–65.

Kalleberg, Arne L., Barbara F. Reskin, and Ken Hudson. 2000. "Bad Jobs in America: Standard and Nonstandard Employment Relations and Job Quality in the United States." *American Sociological Review* 65(2): 256–78.

Kim, Stacy S., Marta Lopez, and James T. Bond. 2003. "Promising Practices: How Employers Improve Their Bottom Lines by Addressing the Needs of Lower-Wage Workers." Report W2003-02. New York: Families and Work Institute.

Kossek, Ellen Ernst, Barbara Lautsch, and Susan Eaton. 2005. "Flexibility Enactment Theory: Implications of Flexibility Type, Control, and Boundary Management for Work-Family Effectiveness." In *Work and Life Integration: Organizational, Cultural, and Individual Perspectives,* edited by Ellen Ernst Kossek and Susan J. Lambert (243–62). Mahwah, NJ: Erlbaum.

Kossek, Ellen E., Melissa Huber-Yoder, Domini Castellino, and Jacqueline Lerner. 1997. "The Working Poor: Locked Out of Careers and the Organizational Mainstream?" *Academy of Management Executive* 11: 76–92.

Lambert, Susan. 1993. "Workplace Policies as Social Policy." *Social Service Review* 67(2): 237–60.

———. 1998. "Workers' Use of Supportive Workplace Policies: Variations by Race and Class-Related Characteristics." In *Workforce Diversity: Issues and Perspectives,* edited by Alfreda Daly (297–313). Washington, DC: NASW Press.

———. 1999. "Lower-Wage Workers and the New Realities of Work and Family." *Annals of the American Academy of Political and Social Science* 562: 174–90.

———. 2006. "Both Art and Science: Employing Organizational Documentation in Workplace-Based Research." In *The Work and Family Handbook: Multi-disciplinary Perspectives and Approaches,* edited by Marcie Pitt-Catsouphes, Ellen Ernst Kossek, and Stephen A. Sweet (503–25). Mahwah, NJ: Erlbaum.

———. 2008. "Passing the Buck: Labor Flexibility Practices that Transfer Risk onto Hourly Workers." *Human Relations* 61(9): 1203–27.

Lambert, Susan, and Anna Haley-Lock. 2004. "The Organizational Stratification of Opportunities for Work-Life Balance: Addressing Issues of Equality and Social Justice in the Workplace." *Community, Work and Family* 7(2): 181–97.

Lambert, Susan, and Julia R. Henly. 2007. "Low-Level Jobs and Work Family Studies." In *Work and Family Encyclopedia,* edited by Patricia Raskin and Marcie Pitt Catsouphes. Boston: Sloan Work-Family Research Network, Boston College. http://wfnetwork. bc.edu/encyclopedia.php?mode=nav. (Accessed July 21, 2008.)

Lambert, Susan, and Ellen Ernst Kossek. 2005. "Future Frontiers: Enduring Challenges and Established Assumptions in the Work-Life Field." In *Work and Life Integration: Organizational, Cultural, and Individual Perspectives,* edited by Ellen Ernst Kossek and Susan Lambert (513–32). Mahwah, NJ: Erlbaum.

Lambert, Susan, and Elaine Waxman. 2005. "Organizational Stratification: Distributing Opportunities for Work-Life Balance." In *Work and Life Integration: Organizational, Cultural, and Individual Perspectives,* edited by Ellen Ernst Kossek and Susan Lambert (103–26). Mahwah, NJ: Erlbaum.

Lewis, Suzan, and Janet Smithson. 2001. "Sense of Entitlement to Support for the Reconciliation of Employment and Family Life." *Human Relations* 54: 1455–81.

Litchfield, Leon, Jennifer Swanberg, and Catherine Sigworth. 2003. "Increasing the Visibility of the Invisible Workforce: Model Programs and Policies for Hourly and Lower Wage Employees." Report 31. Boston College Center for Work and Family, Carroll School of Management. Boston, MA: Boston College.

Mishel, Lawrence, Jared Bernstein, and Sylvia Allegretto. 2005. *The State of Working America 2004–2005.* Washington, DC: Economic Policy Institute.

Moss, Philip, Hal Salzman, and Chris Tilly. 2005. "When Firms Restructure: Understanding Work-Life Outcomes." In *Work and Life Integration: Organizational, Cultural, and Individual Perspectives,* edited by Ellen Ernst Kossek and Susan Lambert (127–50). Mahwah, NJ: Erlbaum.

Osterman, Paul. 1999. *Securing Prosperity: The American Labor Market—How it Has Changed and What To Do About It.* Princeton, NJ: Princeton University Press.

Perry-Jenkins, Maureen. 2005. "Work in the Working Cass: Challenges Facing Families." In *Work, Family, Health, and Well-Being,* edited by Suzanne M. Bianchi, Lynne M. Casper, and Rosalind Berkowitz King (453–72). Mahwah, NJ: Erlbaum.

Pfeffer, Jeffrey, and James Baron. 1988. "Taking the Workers Back Out: Recent Trends in the Structuring of Employment." In *Research in Organizational Behavior,* edited by Barry Staw and Larry L. Cummings (257–303). Greenwich, CT: JAI Press.

Presser, Harriet B. 2003. *Working in a 24/7 Economy: Challenges for American Families.* New York: Russell Sage Foundation.

Presser, Harriet B., and Amy G. Cox. 1997. "The Work Schedules of Low-Educated American Women and Welfare Reform." *Monthly Labor Review* 120: 25–34.

Schlosser, Eric. 2001. *Fast Food Nation: The Dark Side of the All-American Meal.* New York: Houghton Mifflin.

Swanberg, Jennifer. 2005. "Job-Family Role Strain among Low-Wage Workers." *Journal of Family and Economic Issues* 26: 143–58.

Swanberg, Jennifer, Marcie Pitt-Catsouphes, and Krista Drescher-Burke. 2005. "A Question of Justice: Disparities in Employees' Access to Flexible Schedule Arrangements." *Journal of Family Issues* 26(6): 866–95.

Tausig, Mark, and Rudy Fenwick. 2001. "Unbinding Time: Alternate Work Schedules and Work-Life Balance." *Journal of Family and Economic Issues* 22(2): 101–19.

Tilly, Chris. 1996. *Half a Job: Bad and Good Part-Time Jobs in a Changing Labor Market.* Philadelphia, PA: Temple University Press.

———. 1997. "Arresting the Decline of Good Jobs in the USA?" *Industrial Relations Journal* 28: 269–73.

10

Flexibility for Whom?
Inequality in Work-Life Policies and Practices

Ruth Milkman

In both the academic and popular literatures on changing work arrangements, the word "flexibility" has a highly positive connotation. (Who, after all, would admit to preferring "rigidity"?) Sometimes the term refers to genuine efforts to give workers more control over their time and accommodate family care and other nonwork commitments. The Best Buy Results-Only Work Environment (ROWE) innovation described by Moen, Kelly, and Chermack in this volume is an excellent example. Here, a group of mostly white-collar and professional employees at Best Buy's corporate headquarters gained greater control over the "time and timing" of their work through a policy change that reduced work-family conflict and turnover while enhancing employee morale, productivity, and, presumably, the firm's profitability. Assuming the effects are lasting and significant beyond any short-term Hawthorne effect, the ROWE initiative is a clear "win-win" situation.

Lambert's contribution to this volume, however, tells a strikingly different tale. She provides a much-needed in-depth account of a rapidly growing form of service-sector employment in which work schedules are not fixed but instead fluctuate widely depending on consumer demand. In this case, the hourly workers involved have virtually no control over the "time and timing" of their work but are at the mercy of the market. In effect, this arrangement forces workers to shoulder market risks formerly absorbed by the firm. This represents a very different type of "flexibility," one designed entirely to serve the interests of employers. Far from reducing work-family conflict, this sort of "flexible" scheduling intensifies the daily difficulties that many of the hourly workers involved might face under standard scheduling arrangements. The practices Lambert documents, in short, take the word "flexibility" to a new level of corporate doublespeak.

The stark contrast between the ROWE case study and Lambert's findings is *not* one involving distinct economic logics or industries facing different sets of market constraints—Best Buy is a retail firm, and Lambert also studied retailers (along with other service-sector firms in the hospitality, transportation, and financial services industries). It would not be surprising if Best Buy itself used the kind of scheduling Lambert describes for the hourly employees in its retail stores—though Moen, Kelly, and Chermack do not report on this matter. The key point is that, as Lambert puts it, "many firms view labor in hourly jobs as a cost to be contained, rather than an asset in which to invest."

As the intervention Lambert describes illustrates, it is possible to improve the predictability of working hours—mainly by encouraging supervisors to plan ahead a bit more than they might otherwise. Certainly this practice should be encouraged whenever possible, but this is only tinkering at the margins as long as the corporate risk-shifting strategies embodied in this type of "flexible" scheduling are taken as given, rather than as something to be challenged in their own right. Lambert acknowledges this limitation explicitly and also notes that, in this particular case, "increasing the stability of workers' hours in low-level retail jobs was an unrealistic target."

If we take this observation seriously, one implication is that *the logic of the "business case" for family-friendly policies simply may not apply to the majority of the workforce.* It makes eminent "business sense" for employers to institutionalize work-life policies for salaried managers and professionals, especially those with firm-specific skills, insofar as such policies increase retention. But as Lambert notes, in the firms she studied, policies for salaried and hourly workers differ dramatically. In regard to the former, who receive benefits and are exempt from overtime premium pay requirements and the like, the best way to control total labor costs is to minimize staffing levels ("headcount") and to require that employees work longer hours as needed to cope with periods of peak demand. This is far cheaper for the firm than adding new salaried employees to the payroll, which would involve an investment in training and, also, add to the firm's fixed costs for both salaries and benefits.

By contrast, for hourly workers—who in this brave new world often receive no benefits whatsoever thanks to extended "waiting periods" for health insurance and other benefits that large firms once routinely offered to all their workers—staffing levels are deliberately kept high, so that a large pool of surplus, expendable labor is available to respond to variations in consumer demand. This arrangement requires workers to make themselves available as needed and to "flexibly" adjust their schedules on short notice to the hours offered. In practice, this often means working fewer hours than they desire or on schedules that are less than optimal for balancing the demands of work and family. Large numbers of these hourly workers end up working part-time—at one of the retail firms Lambert studied, the figure was 70 percent of all hourly workers.

Interesting sidelight: recall the observation in Kossek and Distelberg's chapter in this volume that many young mothers work less than full-time. The key issue, however, is the extent to which such part-time work is involuntary. While some workers, especially mothers, actively prefer part-time work, it is unlikely that many would choose the employer-controlled, unpredictable scheduling arrangement Lambert describes if they had any alternative options. Involuntary part-time work has grown as a proportion of all part-time work (Mishel, Bernstein, and Allegretto 2006), but the scheduling system Lambert documents for the retail sector suggests that the very categories of "part-time" (voluntary or not) and "full-time" work are becoming obsolete, for all practical purposes.

Lambert does not report wage rates for the hourly workers in the cases she studied, but the majority appear to be paid at or just above the legal minimum wage, with limited or nonexistent benefits. The inevitable result of such low levels of compensation is high turnover and absenteeism. While managers may sometimes express a real or imagined desire to reduce turnover at the rhetorical level, in practice any such rhetoric is radically undermined by the fluctuating and uncertain hours that result from the scheduling policies Lambert describes so vividly. Indeed, as she remarks, "in hourly jobs that serve the purpose of keeping labor costs flexible, common understandings of employment policies . . . may not hold."

Among the reasons that the disconnect between managerial rhetoric and the reality on the ground attracts so little notice is that those "common understandings"—not only in managerial circles but also in policy debates and in both academic and public commentary—all too often focus exclusively on the needs and dilemmas of the affluent. This phenomenon dates back at least to Friedan's (1963) *The Feminine Mystique*, which highlighted the anomie of college-educated homemakers in the post–World War II years, urging them to embrace careers to solve "the problem that has no name." Millions of women have followed Friedan's advice in the years since and indeed, today unprecedented numbers are employed in managerial and professional jobs. One result, ironically, is the widening of inequalities *within* the employed female population (Bianchi 1995; McCall 2001).

Today, while public and scholarly attention to the work-life dilemmas facing highly educated women in professional and managerial jobs is extensive, the far more difficult plight of the majority of the female work-force, concentrated in low-wage hourly jobs of the type Lambert describes in her chapter, remains far less visible. All too often, commentators generalize from the experience of women in the most privileged jobs to that of "everywoman" but in reality, work-life issues are quite distinctive for those in the upper reaches of the labor market.

That some of the companies Lambert studied, as she notes, actually appear on lists of the "Best Companies to Work for in America" and yet have hourly jobs that could hardly be less attractive, is a poignant illustration of this problem. As she stresses, the very same firms may adopt one set of strategies for hourly workers and an entirely different set for salaried managers and professionals. All too often only the latter are publicized. Such disparities are not new, but they have probably intensified in the past few decades as economic inequalities have grown.

Indeed, Lambert's findings parallel those of Jacobs and Gerson (2004), who show that managers and professionals (of both genders) in the United States typically work far longer hours than lower-level employees; those who aspire to successful careers in elite occupations face particularly intense time pressures. By contrast, as Jacobs and Gerson also observe, many nonsupervisory workers would prefer to work *more* hours than are available to them. They derive this conclusion from analysis of large-scale survey data on the time use and expressed preferences of the U.S. workforce. If, as seems likely, the employer strategies Lambert documents in her chapter were less widespread in the 1990s (when the data on which Jacobs and Gerson draw were collected) than today, disparities between salaried and hourly workers have only widened in the years since.

Similar disparities exist in regard to access to health insurance and retirement benefits, as well as paid time off for illness or family caregiving. All are far more often available to professionals and managers (albeit on a modest scale, by European standards), than to the rest of the workforce. There is an intermediate group, comprised of unionized and public-sector employees, but this sector of the workforce is shrinking rapidly as economic polarization continues to reshape the nation's political economy (Mishel et al. 2006).

Class inequalities are hardly a new phenomenon in the United States, but by virtually all available measures they have widened dramatically over the past three decades. The economic gap between managers and professionals and hourly workers—a gap widened by endogamous marriage patterns as well as greater marital stability among the affluent—has grown to the point where the two groups inhabit ever more distinctive social worlds.

As noted above, the dilemmas of managerial and professional women occupy center stage in much of the academic and public policy commentary on these issues, in part because of employers' efforts, at least in some high-profile fields, to retain the new cadres of highly trained women. Ironically, the escalating time demands on the nation's upper-tier employees emerged just when large numbers of highly educated women first gained access to elite jobs. Blair-Loy (2003) has poignantly exposed the hegemony of the "male model" at the highest levels of the corporate world, where family involvement for women (as well as men) is effectively precluded by a deeply entrenched culture that demands total 24/7 commitment to the firm. At the same time, the late–20th century ideology of "intensive mothering" (Hays 1996) has been disproportionately adopted by the nation's most affluent families, eager to reproduce their class position, as Lareau (2003) has beautifully documented; by contrast, working-class parenting takes a very different form.

The same contradiction, albeit in less extreme form, pervades the salaried ranks (not just the top echelon). Indeed, even when firms are putatively family friendly, available benefits often go underutilized by salaried workers for this reason (see Fried 1998; Hochschild 1997). And some women do respond by abandoning their fledgling careers or, alternatively, forgoing motherhood entirely (Blair-Loy 2003). As Stone (2007) argues, many of those who depart are, in effect, "pushed out," rather than "opting out," contrary to the media stereotype. Still, highly paid professionals and managers are also more able to afford the wide array of commodified services now available—from prepared meals to paid domestic labor and private child care—on which affluent families often rely to reconcile the conflicting demands of work and family care.

In sharp contrast, low-wage women workers—who are far more likely to be single mothers than their more affluent sisters—are often forced to choose between economic security and providing vital care for family members. For them, leaving the workforce is simply not an option. Public welfare provisions for the indigent have been radically restructured so as to require workforce participation from poor single mothers who once had access to state assistance while caring for their children at home (Reese 2005). And the growing workforce of undocumented immigrants is often unable or unwilling to access even the meager public provisions for work-life support that remain.

One recent survey found that two-thirds of low-income mothers (compared to slightly over one-third of middle- and upper-income mothers) lose pay when they miss work because a child is sick (Kaiser Family Foundation 2003). Apart from lost income, of course, missing work under such conditions often has other negative employment consequences. And regardless of whether they have traditional or "flexible" work schedules, hourly workers are far less likely than their managerial and professional counterparts to be offered employer-provided benefits like paid sick leave, paid vacations, or paid family leave. For example, between 1996 and 2000, whereas 59 percent of college-educated women who were employed during pregnancy received paid leave after the birth of their first child, only 18 percent of women with less than a high school education did so (Johnson and Downs 2005). With the important exception of unionized workers (a steadily declining group), professionals, managers, more-educated, and better-paid workers generally are far more likely than nonsupervisory, low-wage, less-educated workers to have access to any type of employer-provided paid leave benefits. Ironically, male employees are more likely to have formal access to such benefits than their female counterparts (Heymann 2000; Milkman and Appelbaum 2004).

One of the biggest advantages of government-sponsored work-life programs is that they can be social levelers, offering benefits to those who are most disadvantaged in the market. The 1993 federal Family and Medical Leave Act (FMLA) was not especially successful in this regard, however, since the leaves it guaranteed were unpaid and since a large proportion of the workforce was not even covered by the law. California's new paid family leave (PFL) program, passed in 2002 and in effect since mid-2004, is far more promising, at least in principle. It is nearly universal in coverage (public-sector workers and self-employed workers are largely excluded, although under certain conditions they too can participate in the program). Whereas before 2004, many salaried workers, managers, and professionals already had benefits superior to those that the new state program provides, now millions of workers who previously had no access to paid leave can draw on the PFL program for partial wage replacement for up to six weeks to care for a new child or a seriously ill family member.

Popular support for family leave legislation has been on the rise in the United States since at least the 1980s; poll after poll shows that measures like universal paid family leave and paid sick days are strongly supported by the vast majority of Americans. However, even the famously minimalist FMLA became law in the face of continual opposition from organized business interests that effectively blocked it for many years. Similarly, when California's PFL legislation was proposed in 2002 it faced intense opposition from the business lobby. The state chamber of commerce and other such organizations vigorously opposed the bill, directly echoing the claims of the business groups that had opposed the FMLA a decade earlier: any such program would impose excessive burdens on employers, especially small businesses (Koss 2003). With rare exceptions, indeed, employers can be relied upon to consistently resist—often on explicitly ideological, market-fundamentalist grounds—virtually all efforts to secure social legislation that would move the United States toward European-style family policies, as well as minimum- and living-wage laws.

Some work-family advocates have devoted a great deal of energy to advancing the "business case" for paid family leave and, more generally, for a "family-friendly" workplace. But Lambert's chapter confirms the sad reality that when it comes to the workers who need work-life support the most, namely low-wage hourly workers, business itself is moving in the precisely opposite direction of the one called for by these advocates. Even employers that do offer extensive family benefits to some or all of their own workers and who support family-friendly policies on the rhetorical level, generally stand in solidarity with the rest of the business community in opposing any legislative mandates in this area. The only way to overcome their well-financed and insistent opposition is to mobilize enough political support for work-family legislation to secure its passage in spite of business objections. That is how advocates finally won passage of both the FMLA (see Bernstein 2001; Martin 2000) and the California PFL law (see Labor Project for Working Families 2003).

Once business opposition is successfully overcome, employers pragmatically accept defeat, make the necessary adjustments in their day-to-day practices, and move on. This became apparent in the aftermath of both FMLA and the California PFL law. All the more reason for advocates to concentrate on struggling for state intervention, rather than seeking to persuade or placate organized business. But there is an additional problem which deserves mention, again tied to the theme of disparities between haves and have-nots, this time in regard to access to information.

A survey I conducted in fall 2003, about a year after the new law was passed, found that only 22 percent of adult Californians were aware of the PFL program's existence (Milkman and Appelbaum 2004). At that time it had been passed but was not yet available. In a follow-up survey in the summer of 2005, about a year after the program came into effect, the figure was a somewhat higher 30 percent. This figure was still well below the same respondents' awareness of FMLA, which was 59 percent in the initial 2003 survey and 57 percent in the 2005 follow-up. A third survey conducted in 2007 found that the level of awareness has actually fallen slightly since 2005. Crucially, those most in need of paid family leave—low-income persons, those with limited education, and immigrants—were disproportionately represented among those who were unaware of the state program. In 2005 for example, only 17 percent of respondents with household incomes of $25,000 or less knew of the program, less than half the level (38 percent) of those with household incomes over $75,000. The program's potential as a social leveler cannot be realized if those who stand to benefit most from it remain unaware of its existence.

The state of Washington passed a paid leave program in 2007 (although at this writing, funding is not yet provided), New Jersey followed in 2008, and a few other states are poised to pass similar legislation. As the political momentum builds, however, so will business opposition. A key lesson of Lambert's chapter is that advocates who seek to advance the work-family cause by appealing to economic rationality are fighting a losing battle, at least for hourly workers. Instead, out-organizing organized business in the political arena is the only viable path to success. Rather than framing the issue in terms of the "business case," advocates must simply insist that paid family leave proposals, and state-sponsored work-life policy generally, deserve support because they meet an urgent human need.

REFERENCES

Bernstein, Anya. 2001. *The Moderation Dilemma: Legislative Coalitions and the Politics of Family and Medical Leave.* Pittsburgh: University of Pittsburgh Press.

Bianchi, Suzanne. 1995. "Changing Economic Roles of Women and Men." In *State of the Union: America in the 1990s,* vol. 1, edited by Reynolds Farley (107–154). New York: Russell Sage Foundation.

Blair-Loy, Mary. 2003. *Competing Devotions: Career and Family among Women Executives.* Cambridge, MA: Harvard University Press.

Fried, Mindy. 1998. *Taking Time: Parental Leave Policy and Corporate Culture.* Philadelphia, PA: Temple University Press.

Friedan, Betty. 1963. *The Feminine Mystique.* New York: W. W. Norton.

Hays, Sharon. 1996. *The Cultural Contradictions of Motherhood.* New Haven: Yale University Press.

Heymann, Jody. 2000. *The Widening Gap: Why America's Working Families Are in Jeopardy—And What Can Be Done About It.* New York: Basic Books.

Hochschild, Arlie. 1997. *The Time Bind: When Work Becomes Home and Home Becomes Work.* New York: Metropolitan Books.

Jacobs, Jerry, and Kathleen Gerson. 2004. *The Time Divide: Work, Family, and Gender Inequality.* Cambridge, MA: Harvard University Press.

Johnson, Julia Overturf, and Barbara Downs. 2005. "Maternity Leave and Employment Patterns of First-Time Mothers: 1961–2000." Current Population Reports P70-103. Washington, DC: U.S. Census Bureau.

Kaiser Family Foundation. 2003. "Women, Work, and Family Health: A Balancing Act." http://www.kff.org/womenshealth/loader.cfm?url=/commonspot/security/getfile.cfm&PageID=14293. (Accessed November 7, 2007.)

Koss, Natalie. 2003. "The California Temporary Disability Insurance Program." *Journal of Gender, Social Policy & the Law* 11: 1079–1087.

Labor Project for Working Families. 2003. "Putting Families First: How California Won the Fight for Paid Family Leave." Berkeley: Labor Project for Working Families.

Lareau, Annette. 2003. *Unequal Childhoods: Class, Race, and Family Life.* Berkeley: University of California Press.

Martin, Cathie Jo. 2000. *Stuck in Neutral: Business and the Politics of Human Capital Investment Policy.* Princeton: Princeton University Press.

McCall, Leslie. 2001. *Complex Inequality: Gender, Race and Class in the New Economy.* New York: Routledge.

Milkman, Ruth, and Eileen Appelbaum. 2004. "Paid Family Leave in California: New Research Findings." *State of California Labor* 4: 45–67.

Mishel, Larry, Jared Bernstein, and Sylvia Allegretto. 2006. *The State of Working America 2006/2007.* Ithaca, NY: Cornell University Press.

Reese, Ellen. 2005. *Backlash against Welfare Mothers: Past and Present.* Berkeley: University of California Press.

Stone, Pamela. 2007. *Opting Out: Why Women Really Quit Careers and Head Home.* Berkeley: University of California Press.

11

Challenges Experienced by Vulnerable Hourly Workers

Issues to Consider in the Policy Conversation

Noemí Enchautegui-de-Jesús

"My supervisor asked me, 'Why don't you move [the family] to a safer neighborhood?' but how could I—we're barely making it," said Karen. "Where's the help for people that are working?" responded Amanda. Workers in low-level, hourly jobs confront many challenges to their ability to manage their families in the ways they want, while they also fulfill their working roles. Lambert pointed out elsewhere in this volume that these workers are the least likely to benefit from working conditions conducive to work-family or work-life supports. Moreover, it has been stated that workers most susceptible to instability in hourly jobs are "most likely . . . workers of color, women with young children, and those with limited educational credentials" (Lambert this volume). Because they face multiple challenges, the task of developing appropriate interventions or policies to address their needs seems an insurmountable one. The goal of this chapter is to elaborate on and illustrate some of these realities from the perspective of working mothers in low-level hourly jobs. In doing so, we are invited to consider what issues need to be part of a conversation about interventions and policy changes responsive to the challenges of low-wage workers.

One of the lessons we learn from Lambert and colleagues is the importance of talking to stakeholders to understand their perspectives before conceiving of a specific intervention. From a participatory action research approach, it is imperative to listen to those voices. To elaborate and illustrate the significance of attending to the challenges of work life for vulnerable hourly workers, in this chapter I share the perspectives of working-poor mothers about the realities of their work experience as captured in two studies. These are the New Hope Ethnographic Study and the Work-Family Focus Groups Study, both of which sought to hear the voices of working mothers belonging to the vulnerable segment of the hourly workforce described above. These studies are described next.

Description of Qualitative Studies

The New Hope Ethnographic Study (NHES), with Tom Weisner as principal investigator, was the qualitative component of the larger New Hope Child and Family Study. The principal investigators and coprincipal investigators of the larger study were Aletha Huston, Greg Duncan, Vonnie C. McLoyd, and Tom Weisner. The Child and Family Study was an experimental evaluation of the New Hope Project, an antipoverty program providing benefits to participants whose income was 150 percent of the federal poverty level and who were willing to work 30 or more hours per week. The sample of this larger study consisted of 745 parents who had one or more children between 1 and 11 years of age at the time of random assignment to the experimental or control group.

The ethnographic component, or the NHES, began in 1998 as the New Hope experiment was in its final year. For three years, fieldworkers visited 42 families randomly selected from the larger study. They visited families' homes or community settings approximately every 10 weeks, using open-ended interviews to elicit descriptions of their lives and routines (for more details see Yoshikawa, Weisner, and Lowe 2006). The ethnicity of the NHES sample was 50 percent African American, 32 percent Latina, and 18 percent white. The mean age of the participants was 34 years (SD = 6.7). Twenty-five percent were married or living with someone when they were interviewed five years after random assignment in the New Hope Project. NHES participants had an average of three children. The material described in the following pages is extracted from the notes of fieldworkers conducting the NHES visits. A larger set of challenges for low-wage working mothers is explored in an earlier analysis of the NHES (Enchautegui-de-Jesús, Yoshikawa, and McLoyd 2006).

The Work-Family Focus Groups Study was a project I conducted to understand the work-family spillover experiences of working mothers in different occupations within an organization. Participants had to have at least one child 9 to 17 years old. Sixteen mothers from administrative and clerical occupations and nine from food-service and custodian occupations participated in five focus groups. The ethnic distribution of the 25 participants was 20 percent African American, 68 percent European American, and 12 percent Latina. Seven of the eight women of color and two of the 17 European American women were employed in food-service and custodian jobs. Fifty-six percent of all participants were hourly employees.

In the next section, I draw from these studies to illustrate work-family challenges stemming from schedule predictability and communication between management and employees. These are the two issues that Lambert's intervention aimed to address.

Challenges of the Most Vulnerable Hourly Workers

Many work-family challenges were found in the NHES and the Focus Group studies. The focus of this section is on four of the most pressing issues closely tied to the stress produced by schedule predictability and communication between management and employees. These are (1) difficulty securing child care and supervision, (2) obstacles to take time off from work, (3) work schedules that conflict with family and transportation needs, and (4) rigidity of supervisors regarding workers' family-emergency needs.

Difficulty Securing Child Care and Supervision

In a 24/7 economy, nonparental care and supervision of children is needed at all times. It is difficult for working parents to find individuals they can trust and on whom they can rely to watch their children, especially on short notice. Thus, workers need a sense of predictability about their schedules, but also the ability to communicate with supervisors about times when it is not possible for them to secure the type of care they need for their children. These points are illustrated in the following scenarios from Rose and Samantha, as captured by NHES fieldworkers, and from Shelly, a participant in the Work-Family Focus Groups.

Rose would like to take advantage of more hours of work, but cannot do it if there is no one to babysit her children. Rose said "[the nursing placement agency] called me this afternoon to work the evening shift, but I can't just go off and work. I need time to arrange child care and figure out how I am going to get there." A second point highlighted in Rose's situation is access to transportation, which makes a difference in the opportunities available to low-income workers (Raphael and Stoll 2000) and impacts whether mothers can fulfill work responsibilities in jobs that require complicated commutes, depending on the location and schedule of the job, as will be addressed below.

Samantha is another working mother who had been trying to get her hours increased (at a video store). But she said the store will not do it unless she works the night shift from 9:00 p.m. to 1:00 a.m. Samantha said she is not going to do that because of the kids. She said that working one night a week was bad enough trying to find someone to watch the kids. This raises the question for policymakers of how working parents could be assisted in their need for child care during nonstandard hours, either evening or weekends.

Shelly, for example, was confronted with lack of child care on weekends. Her supervisor asked her to work on Saturdays but she said, "My boyfriend works on Saturdays. I have no babysitter for Saturday. I need Saturday off." Shelly's case also serves to illustrate the role of communication between workers and supervisors. Whereas others in the same job did not have a problem getting their supervisors to accommodate them, Shelly seemed to have a harder time because her supervisor was less flexible, an issue that will be addressed later in this chapter.

From stories like these, it is apparent that a conversation about policy and interventions regarding child care and supervision has to consider the hours and days when care is needed, as well as what type of supervision scenario would be acceptable for parents. Because parents' values and cultural beliefs shape the type of care in which they are willing to put their children, it would be inappropriate to propose a "one size fits all" intervention or policy model (Lowe and Weisner 2006).

Obstacles to Taking Time Off from Work

In the intervention described in Lambert (this volume), we are presented with an innovative strategy to open the communication channel that allows hourly employees to request time off. For hourly workers in many jobs, being able to take time off can be an onerous experience. They are challenged with extensive restrictions regarding how to take breaks during the work shift, how to get sick days or time off approved, and how long they have to be in the job to qualify for time off, especially if it is paid. The following scenarios from Karen and Amanda (focus group participants) and Inez (NHES participant) will illustrate some of these issues.

For workers like Karen and Amanda, who have their 13-year-old sons stay home after school in high-risk neighborhoods, a short break to call home and make sure their children are OK is very important to maintain their peace of mind at work. However, even a short break to make a phone call is difficult for hourly workers in very restrictive environments usually imposed by their supervisors. Karen, for instance, was not allowed to make calls on her cell phone except during her break. Because her break was too early, before the child was back from school, she had to sneak out to make a call every day, making sure her supervisor did not see her. Her rationale was, "I don't care, because if I come home and my child is dead, what can you possibly say to me?" Amanda was in a similar predicament: "My son gets out of school at 3:00 and at 3:10 I call home. I told my supervisor 'I don't care, but I have to make sure my son is at home.'" Other mothers reported how they had lost their jobs because they received phone calls regarding their children beyond what supervisors were willing to tolerate.

Many working parents described situations in which their time off work was used to attend to children that were ill. Unfortunately, they can get penalized for doing so. Frida's supervisor suspended her for three days because she was absent taking care of her sick daughter. In order to not be penalized for using time off, working parents in low-wage jobs have to submit themselves to more burdens, such as obtaining written notes from doctors to present as an excuse to their supervisors. For instance, when Inez's son got sick she did not qualify for sick days yet because she had only been permanent at her job for six months. Therefore, she had to get a written doctor's excuse. She lied about her son's temperature, saying it was higher than it was so that the doctor would give her an appointment and write her an excused absence.

The complications of supervisor-employee communication regarding scheduling and time off are clearly illustrated in the scenario that followed Inez's dealing with her son's illness. She had to take her son to a follow-up appointment. Inez told her boss that she would be leaving early on that date, but was told that it had to be approved. Inez said that her family came first, and she was going to do what she had to do to take care of them. The supervisor told Inez that she was messing up the schedule. But Inez said that she didn't care and, no matter what, she was leaving early on the date of the appointment. Inez said that she would only miss two hours of work anyway, and that she was prepared to make that time up. She also told her supervisor that if she did not approve the time off, the next time the supervisor needed someone to work on a Saturday, Inez would say no.

What these cases show us is the restrictive and burdensome practices hourly workers encounter when they want to take time off in the form of sick leave, personal time off, or just a short break to attend to matters pertaining to their families. A discussion of interventions and policies to address this matter would have to consider how the process can be facilitated so that workers are not penalized or have to incur more hassles to not lose their jobs. This conversation has to incorporate two pressing issues. One is that time off is often needed to take care of a family's health. The other is that, due to the low income of hourly workers, they need to be able to get paid for their time off. Unfortunately, existing federal policy (the Family and Medical Leave Act) falls short of meeting their economic needs, causing them to not take leave even if they need it most (Gerstel and McGonagle 1999).

Work Schedules that Conflict with Family and Transportation Needs

Scheduling is a major issue among hourly workers, as Lambert explained. Working parents are concerned with the predictability of their work hours because of arrangements they need to make regarding child care and supervision (as discussed above), but also because it affects the amount of money they receive with each paycheck. For example, Rose (a NHES participant) worked every week in a nursing placement agency, but she could not count on what exactly her total hours would be. Some weeks she would work 30 hours, but then the next week she might only work 12.

Beyond predictability, working parents are also looking for a schedule that fits their circumstances and how they want to manage their family demands (Hsueh 2006). Clerical workers in the Work-Family Focus Groups suggested that they would prefer to work from 9:30 a.m. to 2:30 p.m., so that they could be home when children leave for and come back from school. But this is only viable if they could be paid the full-time amount for a shortened work schedule. Others in the same study who worked in blue-collar positions suggested a different alternative, namely, completing a full-time work schedule in four longer daily shifts per week, because they wanted to be able to have a weekday to visit their children's schools and take their children to appointments or other activities.

In the NHES, L'Kesha is a working parent who has been able to accommodate her schedule to her needs. She has flexible hours at work. Although she generally works 9:00 a.m. to 5:00 p.m., she has been working 7:00 a.m. to 3:00 p.m. with no problem. The extent to which supervisors reduce or induce work-family conflict regarding time at work is discussed below. First, the stories of Faye and Katrina also provide a glimpse at how schedules can fit different preferences. The NHES fieldworkers noted that the major reason Faye is not happy with the job is the hours she works. The hours she is scheduled for are 3:00 to 8:00 p.m., but Faye does not want to work in the evening. She wants to be home in the evenings so she can keep an eye on the kids. Katrina is also unhappy with her schedule but, unlike Faye, she would prefer the second (evening) shift. However, Katrina works during the daytime and gets home from work late. She said she cannot get dinner together until 8:00 p.m., and she thinks that this is too late for her kids to eat. With a second shift position, she would be with her kids in the morning and, when the older three leave, she could drop her youngest son at day care, go to work, take a late lunch break to pick him up at day care, and then bring him home where the other kids could watch him.

Although workers seem to recognize that job opportunities are found at longer distances, they have a difficult time taking advantage of them due to complicated transportation arrangements and commuting hours. Karen said that many of the jobs are really far away and, as it is, she is already commuting over one hour each way for a $6 per hour job. An NHES participant, Geraldine, was working for a temporary service that sent people out to factories away from the city. She said she had to leave her house at 3:30 a.m. every day to catch the bus from her neighborhood and then would transfer from the city bus to a bus owned by the work-service company that took her and other workers to the factory. She said they didn't arrive at the factory until about 6:30 a.m. Geraldine definitely disliked having to commute so far and so early for work. She said she would try to sleep on the bus and wouldn't get home until after 6:00 p.m.

In light of the distances required to reach potential "good job" opportunities outside of the city, an important consideration for city residents deciding if they can pursue those jobs is the extensive amount of commuting time added to scheduled work hours. This is especially true when there is a lack of adequate public transportation to allow workers to reach the workplace and their homes in a timely fashion.

The scheduling experiences from working mothers presented above point to a number of concerns that need to be part of the policy conversation to ease schedule conflicts for hourly workers. These include enhancing schedule predictability, ensuring access to and availability of adequate transportation, providing options to work a shift that best fits family demands, and allowing some flexibility to create alternative shift hours. As I discuss next, the disposition and culture at the management level is a critical ingredient in the potential transformation that can be achieved regarding these and other challenges of hourly workers.

Rigidity of Supervisors Regarding Workers' Family-Emergency Needs

A common element found in the three challenges of hourly workers described so far is the role supervisors seem to play in exacerbating them. It appears that, even if formal policies were in place to address the issues mentioned above, the rigidity of supervisors regarding personal needs, especially emergency situations, created a work environment with little recourse for hourly workers. The personal stories described next paint a picture of confrontations and communication breakdowns between supervisors and employees. We also see what participants in both NHES and the Work-Family Focus Groups mentioned in the scenarios described above: they are willing to risk the job for the sake of their families and children.

L'Kesha described to the NHES fieldworker that she is only one of two people at her job with children, so coworkers and her boss don't understand what it is like to be a working parent. Therefore, there is usually a problem when L'Kesha wants or needs to leave because of her kids, be it to take them to the doctor or to register them in their new schools. The supervisor does not allow it. She said that the inability to get off work for family and child issues is very frustrating.

Lynnette took a preemptive approach in her job regarding what she would do in an emergency. When she first started working in an office processing insurance, she was asked what her weaknesses were. She told them that she has "but one weakness, that's my child. If something is wrong with my kid, I have to make sure he's OK. Kiss my butt, if he's wheezing and whatever, I need to jump up and get to him. I'm gone."

Fortunately, there are other stories that illustrate the opposite type of environment, in which supervisors do not impose this type of rigidity and seem more understanding of workers' needs. For instance, Rhonda described her boss as very understanding, someone who didn't give her any hassle when she had to go to the doctor. Jackie, too, described the management as very understanding; she can ask for days off in advance. Susan liked the fact that her job was flexible, and she could always call and cancel if something came up. Usually that meant she would have to go in on her day off and make up the hours, but they always had plenty of "fill-ins."

It is not only a matter of having policies in place, but of keeping a sense of civility and helpful disposition in the way supervisors treat workers. Michol asked her supervisor for more hours, but was told the supervisor did not need her to stay late. Michol said, "she doesn't *need* me, well am I only here when she needs me?" Michol would rather be treated with some more respect on this job, but she needs the hours. This issue has been repeatedly expressed in NHES and the Work-Family Focus Groups. In fact in the latter study, what emerged was a picture in which even within the same organization, some workers are able to enjoy tremendous flexibility in terms of getting or making calls from and to their families, taking time off, and arriving to work late or leaving early. All of it due to what they considered an "understanding" supervisor.

Unfortunately, the situation of workers in the lowest-level jobs in the Work-Family Focus Groups did not appear to be as positive. They seemed to receive the least understanding from their supervisors. The restrictions of time and close supervision were very stressful, in their view. As we look into policies and we consider individual- and job-centered changes, it is important to consider the role of attitudes and culture (Thompson and Prottas this volume). Lambert's intervention intended to change communication patterns, and this is a way to start changing attitudes. For this to work, it requires normative change, not just the individual supervisor's change; it has to become part of the culture of the workplace.

Conclusion

In conclusion, the challenges of the work experience in low-level hourly jobs are multiple and complex. This becomes more obvious as we consider the often conflicting goals of the economy, employers, and employees. Policies at the employer level show promise, especially when stakeholders can see the benefits and the change remains within the bottom line of the company, as Lambert explained.

The more difficult task for us is to consider how we could simultaneously tackle issues that can be addressed at the lower order, that is, the employer level, and issues that will require changes at the state or federal level given their complexity. Fortunately, the participatory approach in Lambert's chapter will serve us well as we think of ascertaining needs and creating solutions that are feasible. The next step is to take that model and advocate for more policy solutions that require bringing forth new working conditions and resources.

NOTE

Thanks to Tom Weisner for his generosity in giving me access to his data from the New Hope Ethnographic Study. In addition, I want to acknowledge the collaborative team assembled under the leadership of Hirokazu Yoshikawa, whose work resulted in the book *Making it Work: Low-Wage Employment, Family Life, and Child Development* (edited with Thomas S. Weisner and Edward D. Lowe, Russell Sage Foundation Publications, 2006). This collaboration was instrumental in providing the foundation for the review of qualitative data done for this chapter. Finally, I want to express my appreciation to Lisa M. Brennan and Deborah Nelson West of the Office of Human Resources at Syracuse University and to my undergraduate research assistants at Syracuse University for their invaluable help in the Work-Family Focus Groups Study.

REFERENCES

Enchautegui-de-Jesús, Noemí, Hirokazu Yoshikawa, and Vonnie C. McLoyd. 2006. "Job Quality among Low-Income Mothers: Experiences and Associations with Children's Development." In *Making It Work: Low-Wage Employment, Family Life, and Child Development,* edited by Hirokazu Yoshikawa, Thomas S. Weisner, and Edward D. Lowe (75–96). New York: Russell Sage Foundation Publications.

Gerstel, Naomi, and Katherine McGonagle. 1999. "Job Leaves and the Limits of the Family and Medical Leave Act: The Effects of Gender, Race, and Family." *Work and Occupations* 26(4): 510–34.

Hsueh, JoAnn. 2006. "Mothers at Work in a 24/7 Economy: Exploring Implications for Family and Child Well-Being." In *Making It Work: Low-Wage Employment, Family*

Life, and Child Development, edited by Hirokazu Yoshikawa, Thomas S. Weisner, and Edward D. Lowe (97–123). New York: Russell Sage Foundation Publications.

Lowe, Edward D., and Thomas S. Weisner. 2006. "Childcare and Low-Wage Employment." In *Making It Work: Low-Wage Employment, Family Life, and Child Development,* edited by Hirokazu Yoshikawa, Thomas S. Weisner, and Edward D. Lowe (235–55). New York: Russell Sage Foundation Publications.

Raphael, Steven, and Michael Stoll. 2000. "Can Boosting Minority Car-Ownership Rates Narrow Inter-racial Employment Gaps?" Working paper. New York: Russell Sage Foundation. http://www.russellsage.org/publications/workingpapers/Can% 20Boosting%20Minority%20Car-Ownership%20Rates%20Narrow%20Inter-Racial %20Employment%20Gaps/document. (Accessed June 24, 2008.)

Yoshikawa, Hirokazu, Thomas S. Weisner, and Edward D. Lowe. 2006. "Introduction: Raising Children Where Work Has Disappeared." In *Making It Work: Low-Wage Employment, Family Life, and Child Development,* edited by Hirokazu Yoshikawa, Thomas S. Weisner, and Edward D. Lowe (1–24). New York: Russell Sage Foundation Publications.

12

Making a Difference for Hourly Workers

Considering Work-Life Policies in Social Context

Maureen Perry-Jenkins

As work-family scholars have come to learn, and as is the case in most disciplines, the processes that link conditions of employment and family life differ by social context (Bianchi, Casper, and King 2005). Factors such as social class, race, ethnicity, gender, and age can all moderate the ways in which conditions of work are related to worker well-being and family relations. Thus, work-family or work-life policies designed as "one size fits all" will fail to benefit all employees equally and may, in fact, have unintended negative effects on some employees. As Lambert (this volume) so aptly points out, there is a serious mismatch between today's workplaces, today's workforce, and the public policies, or lack thereof, that support working families.

According to the Bureau of Labor Statistics, two-thirds of workers who fall into the low-income or working-poor strata are employed in three main occupational areas: (1) service occupations, (2) sales and office occupations, and (3) production, transportation, and material moving occupations (U.S. Bureau of Labor Statistics 2006). It is clear, due to the unique characteristics of work within each occupational area, that policies related to the timing of work hours, schedules, flexibility, and leave benefits would have to look quite different across work contexts. For example, retail sales workers' job characteristics would call for quite different types of interventions as compared to truck drivers'. Thus, a primary aim of my chapter is to focus on how the distinct characteristics of low-wage employment create unique social and ecological niches in which to explore work-family issues and policies. In the first section of this chapter, I will highlight some of the critical points made in Lambert's chapter regarding employers' perspectives on and goals for hourly jobs. I will further this analysis by considering these same issues through the eyes of low-wage workers and their family members. Second, using examples from data we have been collecting for the past 10 years on low-income working families, I will examine how the workplace intervention currently underway by Lambert and her colleagues could possibly affect the working parents and children in our study. In addition, I will address some of the unique methodological challenges that arise when studying low-income workers. Finally, I will close by sharing some thoughts about future interventions that might make a difference for hourly employees.

The "Place" of Hourly Jobs: The View from the Top and the Bottom

Lambert raises some key issues for consideration when understanding why low-level hourly jobs are quite different from salaried work. Specifically, she points out the distinction between the "recruiting and retaining talent" terminology used when human resource managers are hiring salaried, professional workers, as compared to the language of "cost containment" that is most often linked to hourly jobs. She highlights the fact that "many of today's hourly jobs are designed to keep labor costs flexible in order to reduce, if not minimize, labor costs." Thus, a major goal of management is to match work hours to times of greatest consumer demand.

One consequence of employers' primary goal being to meet consumer demand is what Lambert refers to as "nonstandard features . . . creeping into standard jobs." She notes that in many low-level hourly jobs the concept of job status (full- or part-time) is only loosely related to the hours an employee works. Workers may be kept on payroll rosters but be given no work hours (and pay) for weeks and months at a time. In our longitudinal research with working parents it is not unusual for workers to rotate between employment, underemployment, overemployment, and unemployment multiple times over the course of a year. At a very pragmatic level, this variability in work wreaks havoc with attempts to "operationalize" variables such as "average" work hours or a "typical" work schedule. More importantly, at the conceptual level it is clear that we have not yet developed the methods to capture the great degree of change and upheaval in work conditions that can occur on the lower rungs of the occupational hierarchy.

From the worker's perspective, it is quite clear that instability in non-standard employment creates enormous challenges for family life. At the most basic level, inability to rely on a set weekly or monthly income has led more than a quarter of the families in our study to move residences at least once, often numerous times, across one year. Moving residences often leads to changes in child care plans, changes in schools for older children, and greater reliance on extended families' "goodwill" to take them in. These workers often experience frustration with the lack of control they feel in their lives (Pierce, Perry-Jenkins, and Sayer 2008), which in turn is related to diminished mental health over time.

Another common frustration experienced by many of our participants is the inability to secure full-time work. For many, it is the lack of work hours and the lack of benefits connected with part-time work that creates problems. There are countless examples of employees not being allowed to work over 30 hours even when employers are short staffed. Moreover, seasonal jobs, which make up about 20 percent of the occupations in our sample, also contribute to the instability in hours and wages over the course of a year.

Another key point raised by Lambert is the benefit waiting period for workers in hourly jobs. Waiting periods range from 30 days, to six months, to even over a year for full health care benefits to kick in. In addition, accrued paid time off often cannot be used until the waiting period is over. Such policies can pose great problems for working parents. Specifically, for the young parents in our study, it is highly likely that during the first year of a baby's life, the baby will get ill—an event that will occur even more often as infants are exposed to other children in child care settings. Many of the parents in our sample have little or no accrued time off, have used all of their accrued benefits for parental leave, or simply do not have any leave benefits. When a baby becomes ill they have no option that allows them to stay home without receiving sanctions from work. One strategy some parents use is to quit or get fired to deal with the immediate crisis, and then head out to find another job when things settle down.

As noted above, multiple job transitions not only create a daunting methodological challenge but a conceptual one as well. Amick and Mustard (2005) challenge researchers to reconceptualize the study of work as the study of the "working life course." Specifically, these researchers propose that to understand how work is related to health outcomes, we must link unemployment, underemployment, and employment patterns—along with the availability of work—into a coherent working-life-course perspective. As is clear from Lambert's work and some of our own research, multiple job transitions and experiences of un-, under-, and overemployment need to be considered over time to fully assess how various types of work exposure shape an individual's development and family relationships. Moreover, the challenges of understanding how workplace policies may affect employees must take into account the high turnover rates in hourly employment, a challenge Lambert addresses head-on in her research.

The Scheduling Intervention Study

The intervention project currently being conducted by Susan Lambert and Julia Henly is an exciting, creative, and extremely complex effort to identify one specific area for intervention within the retail industry. Although we could highlight many aspects of low-wage work that could be changed, modified, or improved upon, such as pay, benefits, flexibility, and job conditions, they chose to focus on the timing of work, specifically work schedules. At first glance, their intervention appears to be a focused, almost simple idea aimed at work-scheduling policies—namely giving employees more advance notice about their work schedules. One might ask why this intervention is so specific; why not broaden it to address issues of employee control over when and how much they work? Lambert addresses this question and in so doing highlights the ways in which policies or interventions for salaried workers do not always translate well to the unique attributes of hourly work. Specifically, she was concerned that instituting an intervention that gave hourly workers more say about when they work might unintentionally result in a reduction in employee work hours and income. As she suspected, the majority of supervisors in her study indicated that they give more work hours to the employees with greater availability. Thus, employees who limit their availability by specifying preferred work hours may garner more control over their schedules, but in the end they will work fewer hours and reduce their incomes. Although Lambert and Henly have no results to report as yet, the numerous lessons they have already learned as they have worked to create an effective policy that can be implemented across sites will pave the way for future intervention studies.

As we wait to hear the final results of their experiment, their pilot work and methodological planning has already led to some important insights, and it led me to ponder some of the other challenges and potential areas for workplace interventions for low-wage workers. To do this, I turned to some data we have been collecting for the past 10 years. The Work and Family Transitions project has been studying the transition to parenthood for more than 300 low-wage two-parent and single-mother families, with an aim of understanding how work conditions and workplace policies across the transition to parenthood shape the mental health and relationship quality of family members. Our project focuses on working-class employees; specifically, we restricted recruitment to those parents who were employed full-time and whose highest educational degree was an associate's degree or less. The majority of participants held a high school degree. Due to staggered recruitment into the study, we have families negotiating work and parenthood over the first year of their baby's life while some of our other families are already facing their oldest child's transition to the first grade. Thus, we have a great deal of data and many stories about how our families have coped and continue to cope with the challenges of raising babies while holding down full-time, low-wage jobs.

During our interviews we ask our families a number of open-ended questions. The two most important ones in regard to work and family issues are these: (1) "A major goal of our project is to better understand how families juggle the demands of work and family life. What are the most difficult tasks you face in attempting to maintain a balance between work and family life?" and (2) "Have you thought of anything that might help you with the 'juggling act' of combining parenting and working?" This is followed by the prompt, "is there anything that your workplace could do to help with the 'juggling act'?"

A key theme that arose regarding challenges workers face juggling work and family had to do with the issue of *time*—all aspects of time, including work hours, scheduling, time with baby, time with spouse, time for self, flexible time, and sick time. This response makes me believe that Lambert and Henly are on the right track with their intervention; control over one's time gives one control over one's life.

We thought the second question, where we specifically ask the families what would help them manage their work-family challenges, was the place where we would hear about what employers could do to support employees. We were quite surprised by the answers to this question because, most often, parents' first response was to suggest things that they could do to make things better, like sleep less or be more organized, as opposed to something their employer could do. Even when we followed with a prompt asking them to think about how their employers might be able to help, the majority of our families could not think of one way that their workplace could serve as a support. The second most common types of responses were fairly nonspecific comments, such as "give me more time."

In another attempt to brainstorm about what would make a difference in the lives of low-income working families, I sat down with my team of research assistants during one of our project meetings and asked all of them, each of whom has spent hours and hours out in the field conducting interviews, what would make a difference for these families. It will probably come as no surprise that their answers were not focused on "cost containment" or the profit margin. Moreover, my goals in conducting this research were also not aimed at cost containment or profit margins for employers. Herein lies one of the biggest challenges to coming up with workplace policies that might make a difference— employers, employees, CEOs, and social scientists quite simply and quite often have different goals. If the employer's goal is "cost containment," workplace policies are going to look quite different than if the goal is worker morale, worker retention, and worker well-being. This observation is nothing new, yet it bears repeating that when the underlying goals are at odds, it is no wonder we have trouble developing effective policies.

The first question I posed to my research team was whether they thought advance notice about work scheduling would help our parents better manage their work and family responsibilities. We all agreed— the more schedule information, the better. Given that we are studying new families with very young children, workplace scheduling is of extreme importance because parents have to secure child care. Being able to plan ahead relieves a great deal of pressure. Many of our parents, mothers *and* fathers, were employed in health care facilities, primarily nursing homes, and would often pull their monthly schedules off the refrigerator to share with us. That monthly calendar guided their family schedules, and unlike the workers in Lambert's retail sample, scheduling was not their greatest challenge. This is a good reminder that not all hourly jobs are created equal, and the challenges across occupations are likely to be quite unique.

The greatest challenge for our families was the lack of paid parental leave. Unpaid leave for low-wage workers, as provided through the Family and Medical Leave Act (FMLA), is an empty promise for most of the families. Moreover, given the stipulations of the leave policy in terms of length of employment and number of employees, the majority of our participants are not eligible for FMLA benefits. Thus, many just quit their jobs when their babies are born, with the hope of finding a new job or being rehired when they are ready to go back to work. This example highlights how both family life-course and work life-course issues greatly influence the types of challenges workers and families face, as well as the options they have to manage them. For example, caring for infants or elderly parents occurs at different times in one's work career. It is likely that older workers have more seniority and accrued benefits to cope with family demands than younger workers; in turn, the policies that might be most effective for younger workers may be quite different than those meaningful to workers with more seniority.

As my research team continued to discuss what would make a difference for the families in our project, one of my research assistants cleared her throat and prefaced her comment with "I surely don't want to blame anyone here, but shouldn't we also ask what the worker can do?" She was clearly uncomfortable raising this issue, afraid, I suspect, of being accused of "blaming the victim." At the same time, as she said it, everyone on the team nodded their heads. The young mothers and fathers we interview are often in their very first jobs and, yet, their very existence is pinned on that job. I suspect among the group of participants at this conference, if most of us were to think about our very first job (or perhaps some of us can think about our children's first jobs), the majority of us were not trying to support a family on our waitressing tips or cashier's salary. Moreover, many of us had parents or caretakers who reminded us about being on time to work, dressing appropriately, saving some of our earnings, and asking our bosses in advance for time off for appointments.

Many first-time employees make numerous mistakes in their early jobs. For many, those mistakes could be chalked up to a lesson learned in which the only thing affected was their morale or pride. For the majority of young parents in our study, however, making a mistake and losing their jobs could easily lead them down the slippery slope of unemployment, homelessness, and poverty. Many of these working parents have few role models and little job experience. If they oversleep for work or they cannot find a babysitter, they sometimes just do not go to work at all. They have received little training in how to make requests of their bosses or negotiate a day off when their child is ill. One young mother I interviewed worked as a telemarketer and was on her six-month probation period. She had no leave time or sick time accrued yet, and not surprisingly, her baby became ill with an ear infection. She made no attempt to call her boss to ask for more time off or to negotiate some way to deal with her problem; she simply stayed home with her baby. The next week when she walked into work she was fired on the spot, and she was completely surprised by this response from her supervisor.

Our study is not an intervention; however, it was quite clear to me that had I been a friend, an aunt, or some type of mentor to this young woman I might have been able to help her come up with a different strategy. Perhaps a workplace-mentor model might be envisioned, in which more senior employees serve as supports to new workers. These mentors could teach new workers the ropes, educate them about the informal culture of the job, and take them under their wings as they socialize them into the world of work. The fear in raising this type of intervention is that it focuses on changes the employee should make, not the employer. The employer has a critical role to play, and it is my belief that employers' goals for hourly workers must go beyond "cost containment" and the profit margin. As economist Nancy Folbre (2001) notes in her book *The Invisible Heart: Economics and Family Values,* "every society must confront the problem of balancing self-interested pursuits with care for others—including children, the elderly, and the infirmed." In our quest to consider the solutions to better support all working families in this country, the challenge is to take on this task with an eye toward our mutual responsibilities to shape a future society known more for its sense of care and concern for the greater good than for our gross national product and materialism.

NOTE

This research is supported by a grant from the National Institute of Mental Health (R01-MH56777). Special thanks to Amy Claxton, Mary D'Alessandro, Kira Henninger, Jade Logan, and JuliAnna Smith, and for their tireless efforts on the Work and Family Transitions Project.

REFERENCES

Amick, Benjamin C., III, and Cam Mustard. 2005. "Labor Markets and Health: A Social Epidemiological View." In *Work, Family, Health, and Well-Being,* edited by Suzanne M. Bianchi, Lynne M. Casper, and Rosalind Berkowitz King (413–32). Mahwah, NJ: Erlbaum.

Bianchi, Suzanne M., Lynne M. Casper, and Rosalind Berkowitz King, eds. 2005. *Work, Family, Health, and Well-Being.* Mahwah, NJ: Erlbaum.

Folbre, Nancy. 2001. *The Invisible Heart: Economics and Family Values.* New York: New Press.

Pierce, Courtney, Maureen Perry-Jenkins, and Aline G. Sayer. 2008. "Sense of Control Predicts Depressive and Anxious Symptoms across the Transition to Parenthood." *Journal of Family Psychology* 22(2): 212–21.

U.S. Bureau of Labor Statistics. 2006. "Working Poor by Occupation in 2004." http://www.bls.gov/opub/ted/2006/jun/wk4/art04.htm. (Accessed August, 8, 2007.)

PART IV
Future Directions for Research and Policies

13

Work-Life Policies
Future Directions for Research

Jennifer Glass

Imagine that you are a young worker assembling clothes in a factory, who has just discovered she is pregnant. If you lived in the United States, you might begin to worry now about how you were going to manage childbirth and recovery, since your employer is not required to grant you any paid time off. You are thankful that at least you are eligible for the unpaid 12 weeks of leave to which you are entitled under the federal Family and Medical Leave Act (FMLA), but you are worried you may return to find you have been assigned to another work shift or another job. Since it is not likely that you can afford to take 12 weeks of unpaid leave, you might need to start saving now to be able to afford even a few weeks off. You worry about the unannounced overtime that lengthens your shifts, and how you can accommodate that with infant child care that is difficult to find and expensive when found. You might explore your eligibility for TANF (Temporary Assistance for Needy Families) after the baby is born and find you are better off quitting your job and collecting benefits for as long as you can before looking for work again. But this job provides health insurance for you and the baby, and you may never find another job that does.

If you lived in Mexico and were working in a maquila factory along the border, you might begin to strategize how long you can hide your pregnancy. Although federal law entitles you a generous paid leave and a place for your baby in the local child care center through *Seguro Social*, the local child care center has too few spaces and enforcement of the law is weak. Pregnant maquila workers have a way of getting fired for poor performance before their babies can be delivered and the guaranteed paid leave required by federal law must be paid by the employer. Sometimes pregnant workers get caught through the random pregnancy tests that are administered to workers. Without this job, you are likely to fall into the large and unregulated informal sector where no labor protections or benefits exist.

If you lived in Sweden, however, you would rest easy knowing that you are guaranteed 11 months of generous paid leave, followed by the statutory right to work no more than 30 hours per week until your child turns 8. You would know that your local district has a list of child care crèches that provide family care for children under 2, and that your federal housing assistance will increase after the baby is born.

The spread of global capitalism and the incorporation of more and more adults into waged labor worldwide have resulted in a remarkable uniformity in the problems and needs faced by workers with family care responsibilities (Heymann 2006). All need accessible, affordable, and developmentally appropriate child care during work hours. All need adequate paid leave for their families' health care needs and work regulations that give them enough time to provide routine care. All need wages high enough to provide basic food, shelter, and safety for themselves and their dependents. What seems to differ is the capacity of states and labor organizations to respond to these needs with effective policy solutions. While scholars and policymakers agree that working families face significant challenges in competitive labor markets, solutions that treat workers and employers fairly have been elusive in many countries, and nowhere more so than in the United States. In this chapter, I first outline the larger policy context within the United States and the cultural and economic undercurrents that make consensus on national family policy difficult. I then turn to the specific evidentiary needs of business leaders and policymakers that, if satisfied, might move this agenda forward.

Policy Context in the United States

There are a finite number of models for fashioning policies that would assist working families with their dependent care responsibilities. The free-market approach that is currently dominant in the United States leaves

the provision of assistance up to individual employers, with little interference from the state. In theory, employers will analyze the needs of their
workforce, then adjust work practices according to what they feel is affordable and practical, and workers will respond by increasing productivity and
decreasing turnover, giving flexible employers a competitive advantage
over other employers not attending to work-life needs. For a variety of reasons, this free-market approach has not worked. Employers vary tremen-
dously in their susceptibility to global competition for their services and in
their capacity to respond to worker needs, while workers vary dramatically
in their need for work-life accommodations and in their market power
to extract concessions from their employers. What we have as a result is
a patchwork of policies among employers, many only weakly institutionalized and subject to managerial discretion (Beers 2000; Eaton 2003; Glass
and Fujimoto 1995; Golden 2001; Kelly and Kalev 2006), which tends
to leave the lowest paid and most vulnerable workers in the worst straits
(Deitch and Huffman 2003; Glass and Camarigg 1992; Lambert this volume). Many employers offer nothing at all to their employees to help
accommodate family care (Beers 2000; Golden 2001). Even when these
policies are available, workers often fail to use them for fear their use will
mark them as troublesome or less committed workers (Blair-Loy 2003;
Fried 1998). Contrary to common belief, employed mothers frequently
have less access to work-family accommodations than fathers (McCrate
2002) and are more likely to pay a financial penalty for using those accommodations when they are available (Glass and Noonan 2007).

These market failures have been avoided in other Western industrialized countries through different models of social provision (Gornick and
Meyers 2003). These other models of work-family policy provision
include (1) a regulatory approach that forces employers to provide benefits or services to their employees with family care responsibilities and
(2) a governmental provision approach that creates universal programs
for paid leave, child care, health care, and other family and personal needs
for workers, generally funded through payroll or income taxes paid by
all citizens. The modest and unpaid family leave mandated by the 1993
FMLA is an example of the former regulatory approach. Employers were
so resistant to this governmental regulation that large loopholes were
created in the final legislation, disenfranchising about 40 percent of
the labor force by eliminating coverage for businesses employing fewer
than 50 workers and those who work part-time or part-year (Gerstel and
McGonagle 1999). The family leave system of Mexico also models a

regulatory approach, in which individual employers in the formal sector are required to pay for the leaves to which their workers are entitled. As a result, Mexican employers have very strong motivation to exclude pregnant workers from their labor force and discriminate against young mothers in hiring and promotion (Tiano 1994), a pattern that seems to be repeating itself in China and Eastern Europe as formerly state-owned enterprises and collectives that disproportionately employed women under Communism now compete in the free market for workers and consumers (Du, Yang, and Dong 2007).

Medicare is an example of the latter governmental provision approach in the United States, although it is restricted to health care for qualifying citizens over 65. The cradle-to-grave Swedish social security system is an example of governmental provision as well, since benefits are paid directly from the government and are funded through tax revenues. Government provision further divides into direct government services (such as public housing projects and local schools) and publicly funded but *market-provided* care services available by voucher or contract (such as Head Start early childhood education, home health care services, and community mental health services). Proponents of small government who believe that markets function better than government-provided services frequently advocate the latter approach to government provision—when they support government provision at all.

Our existing evidentiary base in the work-family area has clearly documented the failures of the market approach, though we have not yet figured out what types of interventions should replace it. We also have a good comparative grasp of the less-than-perfect but effective social provisioning systems of the European Union nations (see Gornick and Meyers 2003). What we have not yet analyzed completely are two central imperatives: (1) Why did the market approach fail to give workers the flexibility and time they need to engage in family care? (2) Why did government not respond to this market failure through legislation to ensure workers have time to care for their families? The answers to these questions might help us develop a new roadmap for change, in terms of both a well-designed policy program that assists families with diverse jobs and caregiving needs and a well-designed funding mechanism that fairly distributes costs among caregivers, employers, and citizens.

In some respects, the market's failure to adjust jobs to workers' new caregiving needs is hardly surprising—the collapse of the domestic manufacturing economy of the 1960s and 1970s left workers scared of unemployment and employers risk averse in the face of heightened global competition. The short-term profitability of businesses took precedence over their long-term sustainability and capacity to integrate production and reproduction. The shift in employment from unionized manufacturing enterprises to service industries that use part-time and temporary workers left millions of workers short of income, made millions of others more willing to accept inferior working conditions in order to keep a permanent full-time job, and propelled millions of American mothers into the labor force to make up the shortfall (Kalleberg, Reskin, and Hudson 2000). The consequences for American families would not be readily apparent for another generation, until employed parents and dual-earner families became the numerical majority and their tales of time pressures, inadequate leave, and discrimination in the workplace became commonplace (Jacobs and Gerson 2004; Williams 2001).

In a business climate in which workers could find their jobs outsourced to lower-waged workers in developing countries or automated out of existence, demands for paid parental leave, elimination of mandatory overtime, or schedule flexibility must have seemed utopian. Markets generally fail when the market for a product or service is too small or too poor to make provision of that product profitable (think of "orphan drugs" for very rare medical disorders, for example). In this case, employed caregivers within individual firms were often either too small a constituency or too weak in terms of their market power to negotiate work-family concessions from their employers. Women who had just a generation earlier entered managerial and professional ranks were still too small a constituency to demand part-time positions or childbearing leave when they became pregnant, for example. Most employed parents, however, were simply in low-wage jobs in which they were readily replaceable, and so had little bargaining power with which to gain work modifications to accommodate family care.

In this changed economic environment, conservative fears that regulation would lower productivity, hurt job growth, and reduce capital investment in the United States took precedence over the very real difficulties of working families caught between the 24/7 economy and their families' needs for care. Clearly, any analysis of the state of work-family policy in the United States must grapple with the strong antipathy toward employer regulation that exists in both the business community and major political parties. While the rightward shift of both the legislative and judiciary branches of government over the past 30 years is too complex to fully analyze here, political analysts have noted that it has advanced employer interests in this era of heightened global competition for financial capital and jobs (Hacker 2006). The Republican party, meanwhile, began to endorse "traditional family values" in their rhetoric and platform, appealing to a nostalgic view of the housewife/breadwinner family in which women did not both work and raise children and men had little role in family caregiving. Rather than dealing with the real needs of working families, this approach sought to reinforce the wall of separation between the public and private spheres through strategies that encouraged marriage prior to childbearing, encouraged mothers to exit the labor force to care for families, and discouraged divorce. This "housewife in every pot" policy program could not ultimately succeed given the transformed economic environment facing families, especially the erosion of male wages and the simultaneous rise of lower-paid service occupations that drew women into the labor force. But the goal of reducing work-family conflict by returning women to their domestic roles full-time gained some credence among religious conservatives at least. Diagnosing the problem as feminism or women trying to "have it all" enabled employers to view the call for flexible work options and paid leave as inappropriate encroachments on their rights as employers. The party's promise to reinvigorate the entrepreneurial sector of the economy and reduce cumbersome government regulation left decisions about working conditions firmly in the hands of employers, not employees or the state. Moreover, the rhetorical strategy of blaming the state for economic and social problems and envisioning government as the problem rather than the solution to social ills helped create a populace skeptical of all functions of government, including regulation.

Direct government provision fared even worse under this rhetorical strategy. The ideology that lowering taxes and government spending would help families more than government-sponsored provision of education, child care, family leave, and health care prevailed throughout the Republican administrations of the 1980s up to the present. Even in the face of falling real wages, families acquiesced to economic policies that slashed taxes for the wealthy (Bartels 2004), eroded minimum-wage and -hour regulations, and replaced existing government provision with either targeted tax credits to spend in the free market (such as the child care tax credit) or vouchers for privately contracted services (for everything from higher education to mental health services). The unfortunate problem with this leave-it-to-the-market approach is that markets for low-profit services like home health care are often imperfect; the family support services created by market pressures may not be affordable, available, or high quality when workers need them.

The failure of the laissez-faire approach to work-family policy can be seen in the frustrations and angst of American workers in public opinion polls (Galinsky et al. 2005; Heymann 2000), the large "motherhood wage gap" among American workers (Crittenden 2001), and high rates of child poverty (Gornick and Meyers 2003), as well as the high turnover and job churning in the service sector it has produced (Lambert this volume; Schlosser 2001). This has not gone undetected by many employers and trade associations, especially those competing for trained and scarce technical or professional workers, or those concerned over the lost productivity and high training costs created by work-family conflicts. Nor has this gone undetected by politicians who understand the broad crossover appeal of work-family solutions among middle-class voters. Public opinion polls show widespread popular support for work-family policies, including paid family leave, universal pre-K education, and stronger wage and hour laws (not to mention universal health care). At various times, both conservatives and liberals have shown strong support for caregivers' rights in the workplace.[1]

These are all clear signs that the electoral base for an expanded support system for employed caregivers may be reaching a critical mass. From a demographic perspective, both the solvency of the Social Security system and the needs of seniors for government provision depend greatly on the employment rates of baby boomers as they approach retirement age. If the pending wave of boomers can be enticed to stay in the labor force as long as possible, there will be no Social Security or Medicare "crisis," since recipients will be contributing to the funding stream through payroll taxes rather than withdrawing money through their benefits. But keeping boomers in the labor force may require employers to fashion more palatable part-time options and more flexible and generous work schedules and leaves. Work-life policies may be the key to keeping boomers in the labor force as family members age and caregiving needs increase.

At the other end of the age spectrum, young adults show particularly keen interest in work-life issues (Families and Work Institute 2007). Having seen firsthand overworked parents stressed for time and worried about financial insecurity, young workers are more insistent that they control their work lives (Families and Work Institute 2007; Gerson 2002).

Younger workers are also more familiar and comfortable with information technology that makes location less important in getting job tasks performed. Without the expectation that they will secure lifelong employment with a single firm, younger workers may feel freer to negotiate working conditions more to their liking than to their employers' convenience. Expanding worker rights to flexible work hours, guaranteed paid leave and vacation, and part-time parity in benefits will be attractive to this generation of workers who are reluctant to sacrifice family or community pursuits for work.

It remains unclear whether voters actually elect lawmakers sympathetic to work-family reconciliation when available, however. More research is needed to explain the dearth of federal action on paid caregiving leave, work-time regulations, and caregiver support programs in the face of growing popular support. The conspicuous failure of either political party to fully endorse and legislatively push for protections of caregivers in the workforce suggests serious obstacles to reform. The most cynical interpretation is that both major political parties have avoided government regulation or government provision for family care because of their dependency on key business constituencies to finance their campaigns. From a life-course perspective, almost all workers will eventually need some type of care or will provide some type of care to family members, but not all at the same time. The need for protection or assistance on the job ebbs and flows over the life cycle, making the primary constituency for any particular family policy somewhat thin at any specific time point. This soft support on work-family issues may allow politicians to thwart change without paying a huge penalty with voters in the next election. More and better empirical data with which to explore these issues should be a priority.

Sources of resistance or backlash among the general public to federal protection of employed caregivers also deserves further study. Though it has been hypothesized that single or childfree adults resent special protections given to caregivers in the workplace (Burkett 2000), empirical work suggests no pervasive resentment of coworkers with dependent care responsibilities for their children or aging family members (Drago et al. 2001). We also need more analysis of when and how the voter appeal of caregiver protections can be turned into a winning electoral issue. As with the minimum wage and other forms of regulation, research has shown that a legislated "floor" on working conditions is actually good for both workers and businesses (Folbre 2001). Without such a floor, employers who want to treat their employees fairly feel they suffer competitive disadvantages in the short term that prevent their long-term viability. Their competitors will be tempted to do whatever they can to lower labor costs, even if that means working conditions that eliminate caregivers from their labor pool. Welfare-state theorists have developed extensive arguments about the origin and historical development of social welfare programs under capitalism in its different contexts (Gornick and Meyers 2004; Kelly 2003; Orloff 1993). These could be a springboard for scholarly work analyzing the contemporary prospects for a race-, class-, and gender-inclusive expansion of state support for employed caregivers. Where and why do policy initiatives currently succeed in the United States? Where and why do they fail?

Perhaps because the policy context at the national level still seems uninviting, much more experimentation with work-family policy is being done in the states. Tired of waiting for action at the federal level, lawmakers in California and Massachusetts have fashioned paid parental leave programs modeled after disability insurance programs. Required of all workers and paid through relatively modest payroll taxes, the plans provide employees with up to 8 to 12 weeks of compensated leave for the birth, adoption, or serious illness of a family member. Georgia, Iowa, Illinois, and California are also moving toward universal pre-K education for 4-year-olds in their states, recognizing the importance of early cognitive development in children as well as the large numbers of young children in inferior child care settings during the crucial years for vocabulary development and reading readiness. Massachusetts legislators, concerned about the huge public expenses racked up by caring for the uninsured at public hospitals, recently made headlines by instituting the first universal health insurance program for its citizens, requiring them to either provide proof of insurance on their income tax forms or face enrollment in the state-sponsored health care plan. However impressive this action at the state level might be, the devolution of responsibility for work-family issues to the states creates a patchwork system of protections that does nothing to aid citizens stuck in the "wrong" states. Right now, only the larger, wealthier, or more liberal states are taking decisive action on work-family issues. We need better understanding of the social conditions that foster innovation in the states and why states have become better incubators of work-life policies than the federal government. What are some of the drawbacks as well as potential benefits of decentralized solutions to work-life problems?

Beyond Empirical Evidence: How *Should* the Postindustrial Society Come to Terms with the Modern American Family?

The scholarly discourse on work-family policies in the United States can be divided into two waves. The earliest wave predominantly tried to prove the "business case" for family policies in hopes of accelerating the adoption of policies by employers under the current laissez-faire system (Baltes et al. 1999; Kelly 1999). The well-intentioned idea was that empirical work would show that progressive employers that offered work-life supports to their employees would yield large dividends in reduced absenteeism, reduced turnover, and higher productivity among workers. After studies of employer adoption and diffusion of work-family policies began revealing the selective uptake of policies among employers and significant differences in policy availability among employees, even those in the same firm (Eaton 2003; Hochschild 1997), the second wave began, focusing more on the failure of an employer-driven approach to solve the problems of employed caregivers and often ending with a wistful call for European-style family policy (Crittenden 2001; Folbre 2001; Gornick and Meyers 2004; Williams 2001). Absent from much of this discourse was an open debate about the underlying assumptions of either a market-driven or a state-imposed regulatory solution to work-family concerns. The market approach assumes that what is good for families will ultimately be good for business if employers would just listen and look at the evidence rationally. The "win-win" rhetoric of human resource departments suggests that all work-family issues could be resolved through creative and cost-effective business practices. But what if effective solutions to work-family dilemmas (such as paid leave; affordable, high-quality child care; flexible work hours; and limits on overtime) are really not cost effective or do not produce significant gains in productivity or reduced turnover? Or even worse, what if some employment sectors tolerate or actually encourage high turnover and absenteeism, viewing these as strategic mechanisms to keep payroll costs low and avoid paying mandatory benefits such as unemployment insurance (Lambert this volume; Schlosser 2001; Tiano 1994)? The state-imposed regulatory approach, by contrast, assumes that it is the job of employers to protect their employees from harm and that the extension of this right to employee family members and dependents is both logical and justifiable. But why should employers shoulder the burden of care for employee dependents? Does this not simply encourage employers to engage in discrimination against mothers and other caregivers?

Our scholarly discourse often cleverly avoids the larger policy question—just how should the costs of reproducing human life be distributed among family members, individual employers, and society at large? Each group has a clear and compelling interest in the welfare of individual human beings as family members, workers, consumers, and innovators for the future. While these interests are perhaps strongest in the case of dependent children, reproduction in its larger Marxian sense includes the continued replenishment on a daily basis of all human beings, whose human ingenuity and financial capital are needed to keep the economy productive. The health needs of workers, their spouses, and elderly family members fall into this more expansive category, not just the care of minor children. Each group—employers, family caregivers, and unrelated citizens—also has incentives to strategically organize institutions to limit their liability for care work and transfer the costs of care to the other groups.

Economist Nancy Folbre wonderfully summarized this issue in her book *Who Pays for the Kids?* (1994). Having children and caring for your dependents, she argues, is often viewed in American culture as a lifestyle choice, like buying a pet. If you can't afford the time or money to adequately care for a pet, you should not have one. This logic fits in well with both the individualism of American society and the larger market ethos of capitalism. However, you will never have to depend on other people's pets to eventually become your doctor, your sanitation worker, the chef at your favorite restaurant, or (for business owners and managers) your employees. Those pets will not ultimately fund your retirement through Social Security or keep the value of your pension investments high by keeping American businesses profitable. The current and succeeding generations of workers will. At the heart of most European experiments with family policy lies a deep-seated nationalism and pronatalism that recognizes this collective dependency on the welfare of the next generation. Combined with concerns about economic dependency on foreign workers (not necessarily a desire to equitably distribute the cost of care), these philosophies have compelled European countries to develop programs of family assistance that seem astonishingly generous to most Americans.

Folbre's work is a significant start toward articulating the case for public support of caregiving, but an expanded view of the problem would deal not just with kids and not just with the direct costs of their care. Children are sources of future national wealth, but the productivity of today's workers beset by family care responsibilities is also at issue. Take, for example, the single mother who is fired for excessive absenteeism due to her child's medical appointments. Her loss of income necessitates a change in residence to a higher-crime area with inferior schools. Her new rent is partially subsidized by the government, as is her family's health care and food. It takes this mother nine months to find another job with reasonable hours and affordable child care—but the job pays less than her old job and the manager refuses to consider her for a promotion when he discovers she has a child with health problems. She is replaced at her old job by a teenager who has no medical appointments and works overtime off the clock for her employer at the expense of her schoolwork and grades. An employer's preference for workers without caregiving responsibilities has transformed the lives of three people for the worse while increasing government debt. Repeat this scenario thousands of times and one can begin to sense the enormity of the problem created by a market-driven approach to family care.

Here are just a few of the questions that we need to earnestly consider:

1. Are employers entitled to the labor of literate, healthy, productive workers without compensating their caregivers for the cost of this developed human capital?
2. Are employers entitled to the labor of workers without regard to the caregiving obligations they currently hold for family members?
3. Should individuals without caregiving responsibilities enjoy greater labor market success than caregiving workers, despite their abdication from the direct monetary and time costs of reproducing people (and developing their human capital)?
4. Are caregivers entitled to public relief from the direct financial and indirect opportunity costs of care, or would this constitute a reward for caregiving that would diminish the quality of care offered, demean its value, or encourage irresponsible childbearing?

These are not empirical questions as much as ethical and philosophical ones. We know empirically that caring for others directly costs money and indirectly diminishes income-generating capacity (Bianchi, Milkie, and Robinson 2006; Budig and England 2001; Waldfogel 1997). Mothers and their children are the demographic groups most likely to fall below the poverty level, in large part because of inflexible jobs that are impossible to combine with child care. Women who have spent significant amounts of time outside the labor force in order to care for others are the most likely to face inadequate incomes after retirement (McCrate 2002; Rose and Hartmann 2004). From a social justice perspective, these long-term life-course consequences for caregivers are patently unfair. As important from a pragmatic point of view, to what extent do these costs affect the willingness and ability of individuals to care for others? If employers and the general public through government policy both opt out of the costs of reproduction, will families eventually be forced to as well? Fertility researchers have already begun linking the costs of care with declining fertility. Demographers once optimistically viewed below-replacement fertility as a modern strategy favoring "quality over quantity" in children; they now worry that it will seriously undermine old-age support programs and the global competitiveness of nations from Italy to Japan (Morgan 2003).

The inequality produced by the "caregiver wage gap" has more than simple monetary consequences, however. What does it mean if those who avoid caring for others not only accrue more wealth but also more power—which they subsequently use to define the work rules that employed caregivers have to follow? Those astonished by former President George H. W. Bush's unfamiliarity with a grocery store scanner would be appalled by the lack of caregiving experience of most of our elected officials, not to mention the CEOs and top management of the Fortune 500 companies. Is this just the price we pay for living in an imperfect world, or should we work toward a new consensus about the role of government and the role of the private sector in accommodating the reproduction of citizens, on which we all depend? European nations, though differing in their particular policy response to families, have achieved this consensus. The United States has not, perhaps in part because of our tremendous cultural and racial diversity, and perhaps in part because our economy has been relatively immune to the consequences of falling birth rates, high rates of child poverty and ill health, and declining real family income. Exploitation, as any economist will tell you, may nevertheless prove to be efficient.

Evidentiary Needs, or "What Would Get Employers and Policymakers on Board a New Family Policy?"

How can a new consensus on family policy be developed in the United States? What types of evidence can policy researchers produce to move toward universal benefits for caregivers and universal protections from discrimination by employers?

The tacit assumption of almost all the literature on work-family policy is that employers will resist work-life policies that impair managerial discretion or impose any additional costs. Certainly they will avoid any major changes in their own employment practices unless they feel that a cost/benefit analysis shows a competitive advantage in so doing. Employers may also rightly fear that the debate over social provision will end up hurting them through costly new benefits or worker rights that interfere with production or cut into profits. In essence, they believe they will be asked to shoulder an increasing amount of the costs of reproduction relative to caregivers themselves and the general public.

Legislators, on the other hand, are those officials elected to decide what the public interest actually is and how it can best be served. Legislators may avoid work-family policy initiatives because key business groups will withdraw their electoral support or they fear backlash from workers without care responsibilities. But the biggest reason for legislative inaction may be the triumph of neoliberal thinking in federal and state governments. The highest priority in neoliberal thinking is the expansion of the economy and growth in profits. Growing economies produce jobs for constituents; growing profits fuel wage increases. But federal mandates for paid leaves, scheduling flexibility, part-time benefit parity, and other policies might shrink profits, depress wage growth, and hamper new job creation. Surely that is not in the public interest.

These assertions are subject to empirical scrutiny, and the results should become the evidentiary basis for how policy should be implemented. Despite the early research showing that work-family policies can reduce turnover, improve worker loyalty and productivity, and provide other benefits to the employer and the worker, the key question for employers remains whether or not work-life initiatives will at least be revenue neutral and not impair workplace productivity, if not actually boost profitability. Either the existing policy evaluation research is unknown among the population of employers in the United States or is unconvincing. I suspect both are true. Employers want to know that work-family flexibility will not hurt them competitively either domestically or globally. And employers want work-family policies that will lessen, rather than expand, managerial problems with coordination and control over the labor process (including retention of trained workers, coverage of all hours of operation, and customer or client service continuity). Finally, employers want policies that will be cost effective as employees age rather than create escalating numbers of beneficiaries and expenditures. Most existing evaluation research cannot provide reassurance on these points.

It may be that the employment sectors in which work-life policies contribute to productivity, or at least do not impede managerial control, have already introduced such policies. The research community needs better data in national surveys on the availability and use (or impediments to use) of work-family policies in all sectors of the economy to better understand the obstacles to implementation at present. We want to create policy approaches that can be tailored to fit a wide variety of jobs—not just professional or managerial workers, but also manufacturing, clerical, and service workers. We need to better understand the particular vulnerabilities of small businesses and those facing the most serious global competitive threats. At present, our surveys of workers and employers reflect little of the changed environment facing employers and families in the 21st century, so data with which to explore these issues are difficult to find.

We also need to be aware of the diverse needs of caregivers and gather information on the policy approaches that maximize the ability of caregivers to obtain flexibility when they need it and cope with crises as they occur. Similarly, we need to evaluate the eligibility requirements of policies to make sure that we do not disenfranchise workers by limiting our definitions of caregivers or artificially restricting benefits in ways that create conflicts between workers. Finally, we need better intervention research to see how the implementation of workplace flexibility and leave policies can be accomplished in ways that do not water down either coverage or utilization of the policies. As Kelly (2003) notes, there is often a large disjuncture between the stated intention of legislation and its actual implementation in workplaces.

While we have evidence of very successful policy interventions in individual workplaces, much of that literature cannot be generalized across industries, settings, or classes of workers. Further, many of the work outcomes studied are "soft"—employee satisfaction, managerial perceptions of productivity, or turnover intentions of employees, for example. Actual productivity is quite difficult to measure in many occupations, but particularly in managerial and professional occupations. Improving the evidentiary base with which to address these employer concerns will be costly and time consuming. Moreover, it is not clear that the results will always be encouraging. I suspect that many, if not most, work-life policies will not turn out to be "bottom line" profitable for all employers or confer large competitive advantages for very long. There may be an economic rationality in the resistance of some employers to family policy and workplace flexibility. Does this mean that employers will forever be an impediment to work-family policies and programs?

Recent debate over the financing of health care suggests otherwise. Historically hostile toward single-payer plans and payroll taxes to support universal coverage, large employers providing health insurance for their workers are now rethinking their resistance to government provision of health care given the soaring costs of private insurance. Those facing global competitive pressures are especially likely to view employer provision of health insurance as an intolerable burden for the future. Right now we have at least impressionistic evidence that employers realize that firms not providing health insurance for their workers have been free-riding on the family coverage of employers that do, or on the public forms of health insurance provided by Medicaid. Negative publicity over the number of Wal-Mart employees receiving Medicaid was a primary factor in the expansion of that corporation's health care plan, for example. Debates over global warming and energy dependency show a similar softening of business opposition to governmental regulation. The soaring costs of insurance and energy have shown employers that they will all collectively pay for their carbon load on the planet. Collective regulation of energy use through government mandate seems a more appropriate response given that reality.

When appropriate public policy alternatives include stronger public support through payroll or income taxes that alleviate individual employers' expenses for worker benefits, employers may turn out to be key instigators of reform. Welfare-state solutions to work-family dilemmas relieve individual employers of the responsibility for subsidizing family care. Why should large issues such as the provision of child care, paid parenting leave, or sick leave for dependent care be placed at the feet of individual businesses large or small? Alternatives that socialize the financing of care may actually serve business interests better and prevent the exclusion of workers in small or highly competitive businesses with low or volatile profits.

The case of California's successful paid family leave is instructive here. Because it was financed through a very small payroll tax paid by all California workers (similar to disability insurance in that state) rather than employers themselves, business opposition was muted. Because all California workers paid the tax, its impact was very small on workers' purchasing power, but it provided an important benefit to the workers who became parents or suffered family health problems. Employers with large concentrations of young women workers or older workers were not differentially burdened by the provision of paid leave. Nor were employers encouraged to discriminate against these workers in hiring or pay because their benefit costs would be higher.

Legislators, however, have different evidentiary needs before they appear willing to sponsor government-mandated caregiver rights or benefits. Their primary concern seems to be that state-imposed regulation of work hours, leaves, or benefits may discourage employers from creating new jobs or hamper wage growth among existing employees. Work-family researchers have not developed literature to address these concerns, although comparative evidence from Europe has been used to both support and deny the assertion that generous family policies retard economic growth (Gornick and Meyers 2003).[2] Given the strength of neoliberal discourse in the economic policy planning of the federal government, evidence that directly compares the economic performance of comparable employers with and without work-family supports in place is sorely needed. Protocols that test the impact on productivity of government regulation of work hours and schedules versus the impact of government provision of care could help adjudicate which models of state support for working families yield the smallest drag on business performance. But again, the results may be disappointing and show that all types of work-family assistance are, in fact, drags on economic productivity to some extent. The appropriate metric for determining the impact of policies on productivity, however, should include the indirect impacts of family supports on workers' mental and physical health, as well as children's human capital accrual. These indirect benefits may be worth the direct loss of productivity that family benefits for workers produce. At present, we have no creative models that can incorporate and compare these diverse outcomes in a single cost/benefit analysis.

To move the work-family policy agenda forward, scholars ultimately need to create a new discourse that articulates and measures the negative consequences of a market-driven approach to work-family policy, as well as the positive consequences of either employer regulation or government provision of work-family supports. A blueprint for an ethical and fair division of responsibility for human reproduction between caregivers, employers, and the state represents the first step toward building consensus on the goals of work-family policy. Empirical research that details the following should constitute the next phase of scholarly research: (1) which policy alternatives make the biggest difference in the lives of employees in diverse caregiving situations, (2) how these best practices can be tailored to a wide array of jobs in different sectors of the economy, and (3) how compliance by employers can be assured without excessive enforcement costs. Policies that do not reach the workers most in need; that do not provide effective, adequate support; or that hamper the wages or career growth of the individuals that use them are counterproductive and feed the neoliberal logic that less intervention is better. An evidentiary base that delineates the cost of regulation for employers in different industries and global environments and compares those to the costs borne by employed caregivers and their dependents without regulation will go a long way toward convincing policymakers that work-family supports are necessary components of a sustainable economy.

NOTES

1. Eyal Press, "Family-Leave Values." *New York Times Magazine,* July 29, 2007.

2. See also Paul Krugman, "French Family Values," *New York Times,* July 29, 2005.

REFERENCES

Baltes, Boris B., Thomas E. Briggs, Joseph W. Huff, Julie A. Wright, and George A. Newman. 1999. "Flexible and Compressed Workweek Schedules: A Meta-analysis of Their Effects on Work-Related Criteria." *Journal of Applied Psychology* 84: 496–513.

Bartels, Larry M. 2004. "Homer Gets a Tax Cut: Inequality and Public Policy in the American Mind." Unpublished manuscript, Princeton University, Princeton, NJ.

Beers, Thomas M. 2000. "Flexible Schedules and Shift Work: Replacing the 9-to-5 Workday?" *Monthly Labor Review* 123(6): 33–40.

Bianchi, Suzanne, Melissa Milkie, and John Robinson. 2006. *Changing Patterns of Family Life.* New York: Russell Sage Foundation.

Blair-Loy, Mary. 2003. *Competing Devotions: Career and Family among Women Executives.* Cambridge, MA: Harvard University Press.

Budig, Michelle, and Paula England. 2001. "The Wage Penalty for Motherhood." *American Sociological Review* 66: 204–25.

Burkett, Elinor. 2000. *The Baby Boon: How Family-Friendly America Cheats the Childless.* New York: Free Press.

Crittenden, Ann. 2001. *The Price of Motherhood.* New York: Metropolitan Books.

Deitch, Cynthia, and Matt Huffman. 2003. "Family Responsive Benefits and the Two-Tiered Labor Market." In *Work and Family,* edited by Rosanna Hertz and Nancy Marshall (103–30). Berkeley: University of California Press.

Drago, Robert, David Costanza, Robert Caplan, Tanya Brubaker, Darnell Cloud, Naomi Harris, Russell Kashian, and T. Lynn Riggs. 2001. "The Willingness-to-Pay for Work/Family Policies: A Study of Teachers." *Industrial and Labor Relations Review* 55: 22–41.

Du, Fenglian, Jian-Chun Yang, and Xiao-Yuan Dong. 2007. "Why Do Women Have Longer Unemployment Durations than Men in Post-restructuring Urban China?" PMMA Working Paper No. 2007-23. Québec: Poverty and Economic Policy Research Network, MPIA/PMMA Office.

Eaton, Susan C. 2003. "If You Can Use Them: Flexibility Policies, Organizational Commitment, and Perceived Performance." *Industrial Relations* 42(2): 145–67.

Families and Work Institute. 2007. "Generation and Gender in the Workplace." American Business Collaboration Issue Brief. New York: Families and Work Institute.

Folbre, Nancy. 1994. *Who Pays for the Kids? Gender and the Structures of Constraint.* New York: Routledge.

———. 2001. *The Invisible Heart: Economics and Family Values.* New York: New Press.

Fried, Mindy. 1998. *Taking Time: Parental Leave Policy and Corporate Culture.* Philadelphia, PA: Temple University Press.

Galinsky, Ellen, James T. Bond, Stacy S. Kim, Lois Backon, Erin Brownfield, and Kelly Sakai. 2005. *Overwork in America: When the Way We Work Becomes Too Much.* New York: Families and Work Institute.

Gerson, Kathleen. 2002. "Moral Dilemmas, Moral Strategies, and the Transformation of Gender: Lessons from Two Generations of Work and Family Change." *Gender & Society* 16: 8–28.

Gerstel, Naomi, and Katherine McGonagle. 1999. "Job Leaves and the Limits of the Family and Medical Leave Act: The Effects of Gender, Race, and Family." *Work and Occupations* 26(4): 510–534.

Glass, Jennifer L., and Valerie Camarigg. 1992. "Gender, Parenthood, and Job-Family Compatibility." *American Journal of Sociology* 98: 131–51.

Glass, Jennifer, and Tetsushi Fujimoto. 1995. "Organizational Characteristics and the Provision of Family Benefits." *Work and Occupations* 22(4): 380–411.

Glass, Jennifer, and Mary Noonan. 2007. "Effects of Job Flexibility on Wage Growth: Are the Penalties Equal for All Workers?" Paper presented at the 2007 meetings of the Population Association of America, New York, March 29–31.

Golden, Lonnie. 2001. "Flexible Work Schedules: Which Workers Get Them?" *American Behavioral Scientist* 44: 1157–78.

Gornick, Janet C., and Marcia K. Meyers. 2003. *Families That Work: Policies for Reconciling Parenthood and Employment.* New York: Russell Sage Foundation.

———. 2004. "More Alike Than Different: Re-assessing the Long-Term Prospects for Developing 'European-Style' Work-Family Policy in the United States." *Journal of Comparative Policy Analysis: Research and Practice* 6(3): 251–73.

Hacker, Jacob. 2006. *The Great Risk Shift: The Assault on American Jobs.* New York: Oxford University Press.

Heymann, Jody. 2000. *The Widening Gap: Why America's Working Families Are in Jeopardy—and What Can Be Done About It.* New York: Basic Books.

————. 2006. *Forgotten Families: Ending the Growing Crisis Confronting Children and Working Parents in the Global Economy.* New York: Oxford University Press.

Hochschild, Arlie R. 1997. *The Time Bind: When Work Becomes Home and Home Becomes Work.* New York: Metropolitan Books.

Jacobs, Jerry A., and Kathleen Gerson. 2004. *The Time Divide: Work, Family, and Gender Inequality.* Cambridge, MA: Harvard University Press.

Kalleberg, Arne L., Barbara F. Reskin, and Ken Hudson. 2000. "Bad Jobs in America: Standard and Nonstandard Employment Relations and Job Quality in the United States." *American Sociological Review* 65(2): 256–78.

Kelly, Erin L. 1999. "Theorizing Corporate Family Policies: How Advocates Built the 'Business Case' for 'Family-Friendly' Policies." In *Research in the Sociology of Work,* edited by Toby Parcel (169–202). Greenwich, CT: JAI Press.

————. 2003. "The Strange History of Employer-Sponsored Child Care: Interested Actors, Uncertainty, and the Transformation of Law in Organizational Fields." *American Journal of Sociology* 109: 606–49.

Kelly, Erin L., and Alexandra Kalev. 2006. "Managing Flexible Work Arrangements in U.S. Organizations: Formalized Discretion or 'A Right to Ask.'" *Socio-economic Review* 4(3): 379–416.

McCrate, Elaine. 2002. "Working Mothers in a Double Bind." Briefing Paper 124. Washington, DC: Economic Policy Institute.

Morgan, Philip S. 2003. "Is Low Fertility a Twenty-First-Century Demographic Crisis?" *Demography* 40(4): 589–603.

Orloff, Ann Shola. 1993. "Gender and the Social Rights of Citizenship: The Comparative Analysis of Gender Relations and Welfare States." *American Sociological Review* 58: 303–28.

Rose, Stephen, and Heidi I. Hartmann. 2004. *Still a Man's Labor Market: The Long-Term Earnings Gap.* Washington, DC: Institute for Women's Policy Research.

Schlosser, Eric. 2001. *Fast Food Nation: The Dark Side of the All-American Meal.* New York: Houghton Mifflin.

Tiano, Susan. 1994. *Patriarchy on the Line: Labor, Gender, and Ideology in the Mexican Maquila Industry.* Philadelphia: Temple University Press.

Waldfogel, Jane. 1997. "The Effect of Children on Women's Wages." *American Sociological Review* 62: 209–17.

Williams, Joan C. 2001. *Unbending Gender: Why Work and Family Conflict and What to Do About It.* New York: Oxford University Press.

14

Policy Challenges and Opportunities for Workplace Flexibility
The State of Play

Chai R. Feldblum

No one doubts that the makeup of our workforce has changed over the past four decades. In books such as *The Time Divide: Work, Family, and Gender Inequality* by Jerry A. Jacobs and Kathleen Gerson (2004), *The Career Mystique: Cracks in the American Dream*, by Phyllis Moen and Patricia Roehling (2004), and *Being Together, Working Apart: Dual-Career Families and the Work-Life Balance*, edited by Barbara Schneider and Linda Waite (2005), among many others, the data presented on our changing workforce are striking. More women are working today than 40 years ago, our workforce overall is aging, and more people are working past conventional retirement age (Cahill, Giandrea, and Quinn 2005; Toosi 2007; Workplace Flexibility 2010 2006b, 2007b, 2007c).

But the need to manage one's life, together with one's work, has not changed. Many workers are caring for children, parents, spouses, siblings, or other loved ones—responsibilities that are basic, unrelenting, and often mundane, as well as joyful and rewarding. All workers have personal life-maintenance needs, and many workers would like to enhance their training and education or do volunteer work in the community.[1]

Any observer of the American scene can also easily note that the rules, structures, and formats of the workplace are not designed to make it easy for individuals to manage their lives as well as their work (Bailyn 1993; Meiksins and Whaley 2002; Workplace Flexibility 2010 2006b, 2007b, 2007c). This is no surprise. One would reasonably expect that workplaces would be structured to foster *work,* not designed to accommodate potential conflicts between work and other needs. And indeed, for many years those workers who might have had market power to force changes in the workplace usually had spouses at home who could deal with the daily exigencies of life and thus could remove many of the stresses of work-life conflicts.[2]

Times have changed and many workplaces have changed. But overall, as a society we have done a remarkably poor job of forcing or encouraging our workplaces to accommodate to the reality that most workers today will have multiple demands on their time. Workers *do* want to work. But they cannot stop the rest of their lives from happening while they do so.

Obviously, one cannot expect workplaces to lose their basic reason for existence: to produce work. But one simply has to wonder whether there is not a better way to structure our workplaces so that they will do a *better* job of reacting to the multiple demands of our workforces. And one has to wonder whether the primary mechanism by which a democratic society expresses its beliefs and values—the federal, state, and local laws passed by its representatives—might not have some role to play in helping workplaces achieve this more optimal state.

My contribution to the conversation set forth in the various chapters of this book will be to explore the policy challenges and opportunities that exist today with regard to the American workplace as it deals with its changing workforce. I will briefly describe certain advances in the policy conversation that have occurred on the national and state levels over the past five years, and I will identify key limitations and obstacles that continue to exist with regard to policy advances.

My primary focus in this chapter will be to describe an innovative experiment, called Workplace Flexibility 2010, which aims to *intervene* in the current political structure and to serve as a *catalyst* for significant, systematic, and effective policy change.

The Policy Conversation—Then and Now

One way to judge the salience of an issue with regard to its policy potential is to analyze how the issue is discussed and portrayed in the presidential election cycle. Every four years, we have a flurry of media attention on "the important issues of the day"—at least as understood by various presidential candidates.

A comparison of the policy conversations on supporting American families in the 2000 and 2004 elections with the policy conversation that has taken place during the 2008 election demonstrates a small but growing focus on how the structure of work places strains on families. The policy salience of this issue is nowhere near the salience of health care or the economy generally, but it is beginning to merit a separate and distinct focus of conversation within, at least, the Democratic presidential campaigns.

During the 2000 presidential campaign, Vice President Al Gore's policy agenda for supporting working families focused primarily on expanding access to health care and making child care more affordable through tax credits.[3] As an additional side point, Gore touted his strong support for the Family and Medical Leave Act (FMLA),[4] as well as his support for expanding the FMLA to provide workers with "more choices when confronted with the need to work overtime or when parents need to meet with their children's teachers."[5] But that was the extent of Gore's policy focus on work-family issues.

By the 2004 election, John Kerry and John Edwards were speaking more directly to the needs of working families in terms of work-family balance—but their policy solutions still tended to focus primarily *outside* the workplace. The Kerry-Edwards "Plan to Honor Work and Family" claimed as one of its primary goals that of helping all Americans balance the competing demands of work and family.[6] But their agenda to help Americans balance work and family focused on two major initiatives outside of work: increasing the child care tax credit (to cover $5,000 of expenses and to make it available for moderate-income families and stay-at-home parents), and creating a large-scale after-school program for 3.5 million youths (by making some schools remain open until 6:00 p.m.).[7] The only reference to workplace structure was a general commitment by Kerry and Edwards to expand coverage of the FMLA.[8]

By contrast, by the time the 2008 presidential primary season reached its fever pitch in December 2007, all the leading Democratic candidates had developed and presented a set of specific policy ideas governing the workplace with regard to work-life balance. While all the candidates' ideas followed basically the same template (a template that will be analyzed critically below), they reflect a commitment to engaging the federal government in changing workplace structures and rules. And they all reflect a more expansive and detailed set of ideas on the issue than had ever existed before in a presidential campaign.

For example, in October 2007, Senator Hillary Clinton announced her "Agenda for Working Families"—a "work-family agenda for our modern economy" that will support families while working "in partnership with America's businesses to ensure that pro-family work policies and increasing workplace flexibility help improve American competitiveness and economic growth."[9] Clinton's agenda included a goal of having all states institute some form of paid parental leave for employees by the year 2016. A key selling point of her proposal was that states would decide on their own how to structure the leave plans, including how the plans would be financed. The federal government would play a role through the creation of a state family leave innovation fund that would provide $1 billion a year (with increases) to match state expenditures in such leave programs.

Clinton's proposals also included making the federal government a model employer with a generous paid parental leave program; expanding the FMLA to cover employers with 25 or more employees, thereby giving 13 million additional American workers guaranteed unpaid family and medical leave for 12 weeks a year; guaranteeing workers at least seven days of paid sick leave per year that would be paid by their employers; providing employees with the right to request flexibility along the lines of a UK law; promoting model workplaces with grants to support new workplace flexibility programs (including a federal telecommuting initiative); and prohibiting discrimination against parents by employers.[10]

Shortly after Senator Clinton announced her agenda, Senator Barack Obama announced a plan that included very similar proposals. Like Clinton's, Obama's plan included a strategy to encourage states to adopt paid leave systems of their choice. He proposed a $1.5 billion fund to help states with the start-up costs of such plans. Like Clinton, Obama also proposed to expand the unpaid leave provisions of the FMLA to cover businesses with 25 employees or more. He also proposed allowing workers to use their unpaid FMLA leave for elder care and for addressing domestic violence and sexual assault against themselves, their children, or their parents. Obama's proposal allowed parents to use up to 24 hours of FMLA leave to participate in their children's academic activities as well. Finally, Obama proposed requiring employers to guarantee seven paid sick days to their employees, prohibiting employers from discriminating against parents because of caregiving responsibilities, and expanding flexible work arrangements through education and technical assistance for businesses.[11]

Unlike Clinton and Obama, Senator Chris Dodd presented his work-place proposals under the framework of "putting women and families first." As the lead sponsor of the FMLA in 1993, Dodd opted for a contin-uation of this federal model rather than supporting states in developing their own models. Thus, Dodd's proposal to provide paid leave expanded the FMLA to require covered employers to pay for eight weeks of paid leave when an employee cared for a sick family member or took care of a newborn or adopted child.[12, 13]

John Edwards's agenda for work-family balance, as it compared to his positions as part of the Kerry-Edwards campaign, painted the clearest pic-ture of how far presidential candidates have come in terms of promoting workplace flexibility policies. It also illustrated the "arms race" of ideas in a presidential campaign. If an issue appears to have salience with the voters, no one wants to be left out of the game.

Like Clinton and Obama, Edwards opted for the creation of a national family trust to support states in the development of paid parental leave funds rather than using the FMLA framework to require employers to pay for the leave. As the third of the leading candidates to propose a ver-sion of this approach, however, Edwards was well situated to outbid his competitors. Thus, Edwards touted his plan as bolder than those of the others because he set a national goal of states having plans that actually offered eight weeks of paid leave by 2014, and his proposed fund would have provided more federal resources—$2 billion a year—to help states meet that goal.[14]

Like the other candidates, Edwards also proposed expanding the FMLA to include businesses with 25 employees or more and requiring all businesses to provide employees with seven paid sick days per year. Edwards also proposed providing independent contractors and part-time workers with better access to health care and family leave benefits.[15]

Unlike the Democratic candidates, the Republican candidates for the presidential nomination in the 2008 primary contest had not—as of January 2008—proposed any affirmative government policies in the workplace to assist workers in managing their work and life needs. But it was difficult to imagine that, once the general election begun, the Repub-lican nominee would not experience pressure to come up with at least some statement that indicated he was taking the work-life pressures on families across the country seriously. In August 2004, shortly before the election, President George W. Bush responded to similar pressures by proposing a policy approach that had been urged without success for almost a decade by Republicans in Congress.[16] This approach would have amended the Fair Labor Standards Act to allow nonexempt employees to choose compensatory time instead of overtime pay, thereby buying themselves some flexibility on the job.[17]

The broad range of ideas available to the Democratic candidates during the 2008 primary season reflects the breadth in policy proposals that had surfaced on both the state and federal levels between 2004 and 2007. This time period was a particularly fertile one for attention to work-family issues—at least in terms of policy proposals, if not in terms of actual significant movement forward.

On the federal level, three separate bills garnered attention. Chief among these was the Healthy Families Act, introduced initially in 2004 and in each subsequent Congress, in both the Senate and the House of Representatives.[18] The Healthy Families Act requires all employers with at least 15 employees to provide seven days of paid time off for employees to care for their own illness or for the illness of a family member.[19] An employee who works for 30 hours or more per week receives all seven days, while employees who work less than 30 hours a week receive a prorated number of paid days off.[20]

While the Healthy Families Act focuses on sick days, a proposal connected to more traditional FMLA leave, the Family Leave Insurance Act, has also been introduced in the Senate.[21] This bill, introduced in 2007, requires employers already covered under the FMLA (that is, employers with at least 50 employees) and their employees to pay equal premiums into a federally administered fund. The employers are required to pay up to eight weeks of paid leave for employees who take time off for FMLA-covered reasons—care for a newborn or adopted child, care for one's own serious health condition, or care for the serious health condition of a covered family member—and the fund then reimburses the employers for the money expended.[22]

Also, in 2007, the Working Families Flexibility Act was introduced in both the Senate and the House of Representatives.[23] This act allows an employee who works for an employer with at least 15 employees to request a change with regard to his or her scheduling, place of work, or number of hours worked. The employer must meet with the employee to discuss the request and must provide a written response to the request.[24] An employer is permitted to refuse the request as long as it provides a reason for doing so—such as a loss of productivity or the effect of the change on the employer's ability to meet customer demand.[25, 26]

While none of these bills achieved legislative success in the first session of the 110th Congress, hearings were held on the Healthy Families Act on February 13, 2007.[27] In addition, in January 2008 Congress passed an expansion of the FMLA to allow family members who were caring for wounded service members to take up to 26 weeks of unpaid, job-guaranteed leave.[28] And in June 2008, the House of Representatives passed a bill that would grant federal employees up to 4 weeks of paid parental leave after the birth or adoption of a child, or the taking in of a foster child.[29] The bill also authorized the Office of Personnel Management to extend the authorized period of paid leave by an additional 4 weeks. Under the bill, federal employees could continue to use accrued vacation time as part of their leave, but would no longer have to demonstrate medical need to use sick leave to care for a new child.[30]

The activity on the federal level followed on the heels of coordinated activity on the state level over the previous years. In 2003, the Multi-State Working Families Consortium, an organization of labor and community coalitions, started in 8 states and now encompasses 11. The consortium pools resources and information to support the introduction of state or local bills to guarantee paid family leave insurance, paid sick days, and other work-family supports.[31] The National Partnership on Women and Families also works with states and localities to develop and support such legislation.[32]

While success in enacting these bills on the state and local levels has been uneven, a few have passed and others are moving through the process. In 2002, California was the first state to expand its state disability insurance program to provide for six weeks of partial paid leave for employees who take time off to care for a newborn or adopted child or to care for a family member with medical needs.[33] The funds for the new program come from payroll premiums assessed against employees.[34]

In 2007, the state of Washington created a similar program, although restricted to time taken off to care for a newborn or adopted child.[35] The program passed without any final funding mechanism, but with instructions to a task force to recommend a funding mechanism to the legislature for its approval.[36] In January 2008, the task force issued its final report and recommended that the program be funded through the state's general fund for at least the first four years of implementation (Washington State Joint Task Force 2008). These recommendations were adopted into law as part of the supplemental budget passed by the legislature and signed by Governor Christine Gregoire in early 2008.[37]

In addition, on May 2, 2008, New Jersey's governor signed legislation that extended the state's temporary disability insurance (TDI) system to provide up to six weeks of partial wage replacement to employees who take time off to care for a newborn, newly adopted or foster child, or family member with a serious health condition. Eligible employees receive up to two-thirds of their wages, up to a maximum of $524 per week. This cap increases annually with the cost of living and is financed by a tax on employee wages.[38]

Similar bills have been proposed, and are being pursued, in New York and Illinois. The proposal in New York expands the state's existing TDI program but does so by amending the definition of "disability" in the state workers compensation law to include family leave. This change in definition permits employees to get up to 12 weeks of partially paid leave for family care. As under the existing law for disability, eligible employees can get up to half of their wages, but the amount is capped at $170 per week.[39] Although employers and employees jointly fund the existing TDI program, the bill imposes the new "family care cost" solely on employees.[40] The bill has passed the New York Assembly, but has not been voted on by the state Senate.[41]

The proposal in Illinois would create a new family leave insurance program that would provide up to four weeks of partial wage replacement to employees who are caring for a newborn or newly placed adopted or foster child, a family member with a serious health condition, or their own serious health conditions. The program would be funded by both employers and employees, and eligible employees could get up to 67 percent of their wages (up to $380 per week).[42] This bill failed to make it out of committee within the necessary timeframe.[43]

In addition to these paid leave proposals in these states, in which the costs are primarily borne by the employees (with the exception of Illinois, for the moment), there has also been a move toward requiring paid sick days, with the costs to be borne by employers. In 2006, San Francisco became the first locality to require employers to provide some paid sick time to their employees. Employers with more than 10 employees are required to allow their employees to earn up to 72 hours of paid sick time, while employers with fewer than 10 employees are required to allow their employees to earn up to 40 hours of paid sick time.[44]

In March 2008, the District of Columbia followed San Francisco's lead and became the second jurisdiction to mandate that employers provide paid sick leave to workers. The amount of leave an employee earns depends on the number of hours worked and the size of the business, and ranges from three days for full-time workers at businesses with 24 or fewer employees to up to seven days for full-time employees at workplaces of 100 or more.[45]

In 2007 and 2008, 11 states (Connecticut, Maryland, Massachusetts, Minnesota, Missouri, Maine, Vermont, Florida, North Carolina, Pennsylvania, and Illinois) considered bills that would require employers to provide a set number of paid sick days.[46] Most of these bills are similar in scope and structure to the San Francisco and D.C. plans. Each proposal includes requirements for calibrated paid time off based on the number of people employed by the organization, the number of hours worked by the employee, and the number of days the employee has been on the job.[47]

Finally, another recent trend has been to advocate for laws prohibiting discrimination against caregivers in the workplace. In 2007, the California legislature passed a bill prohibiting employers with at least five employees from discriminating against employees on the basis of "familial status."[48] The bill defined having "familial status" as "being an individual who is or who will be caring for or supporting a family member."[49] To prevail in an action brought under this proposed law, an employee would have to show disparate treatment, a hostile work environment, constructive discharge, or another adverse effect of discrimination because of his or her familial status.[50] The bill passed both chambers of the California legislature on primarily party-line votes (with Democrats voting in favor of the bill), but was vetoed by Republican governor Arnold Schwarzenegger.[51] Bills protecting caregivers from employment discrimination have also been introduced in New Jersey, New York, Florida, Pennsylvania, and New York City, but have not been enacted.[52]

Jennifer Glass, in this volume, notes that government can respond to a market failure on the part of employers to provide work-life supports either by mandating employers to provide such supports or by providing such supports directly through government programs. The legislative efforts on the state and federal levels over the past several years and the campaign rhetoric of Democratic candidates in the 2008 election reflect an amalgam of these approaches. These proposals include some direct requirements for employers to pay for a limited number of sick days.[53] With regard to more extensive time off, however, these approaches lean toward government mandating that employees, and sometimes employers, pay into a system that will provide paid time off.[54] Three of the Democratic presidential candidates wanted the states to decide how to fund paid time off, with the federal government providing support solely for administrative and start-up costs.

The Obstacles to Policy Reform

For all the campaign promises, the introduction of bills, the chatter on the Internet, the rallies held, and the onesies sent in support of various bills,[55] we have not seen significant change in the policy arena. Perhaps it is only a matter of time until the various legislative efforts described here become law—or perhaps time by itself will not be enough.

In this volume, Glass argues that both political parties have conspicuously failed to "fully endorse and legislatively push for protections of caregivers in the workforce." She offers the view that the "most cynical interpretation is that both major political parties have avoided government regulation or government provision for family care because of their dependency on key business constituencies to finance their campaigns."

Glass later refines her argument by postulating that the biggest reason for legislative inaction is "the triumph of neoliberal thinking in federal and state governments," which has as its highest priority "the expansion of the economy and growth in profits." This is a problem because "federal mandates for paid leaves, scheduling flexibility, part-time benefit parity, and other policies might shrink profits, depress wage growth, and hamper new job creation." All this would clearly be contrary to the goals of neoliberal governance.

But Glass's main argument is that the existing evaluation research is simply not sufficiently developed, nuanced, and targeted enough to make the case for such forms of governmental intervention. She clearly thinks that policies such as "paid leaves, scheduling flexibility, [and] part-time benefit parity" would be good for society as a means of sharing responsibility for the costs of human reproduction, from which we all benefit. Assertions about the negative impact of federal mandates on profits, wage growth, and new job creation are, she notes, "subject to empirical scrutiny, and the results should become the evidentiary basis for how policy should be implemented." Yet the existing policy evaluation research, argues Glass, simply cannot provide sufficient reassurance to employers that they will not be hurt financially or operationally by such requirements.[56]

I think Glass correctly highlights the significant limitations of the current body of policy evaluation research on the approaches described previously, and I welcome her argument for the shift that must occur in our normative thinking about what society owes to those who shoulder the responsibilities of caregiving. But I want to add a few points with regard to the obstacles I believe exist in achieving policy reform in this arena.

I do not believe it is correct to say that neither political party has pushed for legislative reforms for caregivers in the workplace. To the contrary, based on the mere number of bills introduced on the state and federal levels over the past years, it seems fair to say that members of the Democratic party view this issue as one in which they would like to make their mark and engender some real advances.

But it is also true that successful enactment of these proposals has been difficult to achieve. The reason for that is correctly articulated by Glass: businesses are rationally not interested in having the government dictate to them how to run their workplaces, and they are particularly wary of any dictates that might impose undue financial or operational costs on their businesses. In light of that reality, legislators are loath to impose obligations that might backfire economically on their small-, medium-, and big-employer constituencies. And while providing supports directly through government programs might relieve employers of those obligations, that approach raises the specter of programs that will need to be supported through general taxes.

As a possible way out of this morass, Glass notes the potential of the California model, in which employees pay all the costs of the program, with regard to paid family leave. But business associations have not been any more sympathetic to that approach. Associations of California businesses vigorously opposed California's expansion of the state's temporary disability insurance program in 2002 to include paid family leave, despite the fact that all premiums for the program would be paid by employees.[57] The same was true with regard to opposition from businesses to the New Jersey law and to the pending New York bill, both of which finance the expansions of those states' temporary disability programs to cover family leave solely through employee-paid premiums.[58]

The practical arguments made by these business associations are that the funds come from employee salaries that are paid by the employers, and hence, there may be pressure over time to increase those salaries to offset the premium costs. In addition, businesses are concerned about the indirect costs of setting up and implementing these systems.[59] The ideological argument of these groups is even more straightforward, although they do not often state it as bluntly: businesses should be permitted to decide how to run their operations most effectively without intervention by the government.[60]

The groups advocating the various forms of legislation described in the first part of this chapter do not really believe that the established trade associations will ever support these policy approaches. Rather, they believe there are some (or even many) "good-guy" businesses that believe these policies do make sense, and these are the businesses that need to be surfaced and highlighted in the political debate so they can be heard in the public domain.[61]

I think advocacy groups pushing for paid sick leave, paid family leave insurance, caregiver nondiscrimination laws, and the right to ask for flexible work arrangements (to summarize just the key approaches of the bills and proposals described above) are correct to assume that established business associations will not support any of these policy ideas in their current forms. But these efforts certainly fall within the tried and true approaches of traditional government regulation and will, therefore, presumably play out with the usual alignments of our political process and according to the usual way of doing business.

Under this usual way of doing (political) business, advocates tend to write the strongest piece of legislation they can to address an identified need—usually legislation that regulates businesses to require certain working conditions or that creates a government program to provide the needed benefit. The established trade associations of businesses then invariably oppose the proposed legislation as costly and burdensome. If the political will and votes exist to make the legislation even close to possible passage, the advocacy groups and their legislative allies make enough changes in the bill to gather whatever many remaining votes are needed for passage.[62] Once the bill passes, advocacy groups throw a victory party (regardless of how much the bill has been modified) and business associations moan and groan about how the state (or federal) government is creating a terrible environment in which businesses are being forced to operate.[63]

These are the understood and accepted obstacles to passing legislation along the lines of the policy ideas outlined above. But can one play the game differently? Is it possible to make normative change in the workplace, including change that uses and is supported by public policy, in a way that does not replicate these traditional political fights? If one were able to come up with a different way of doing political business, might the result be even better and more effective policy ideas? Read on for this utopian vision.

The Workplace Flexibility 2010 Enterprise

Reshaping Political Expectations

The Workplace Flexibility 2010 enterprise began in 2003 with a substantial grant from the Alfred P. Sloan Foundation.[64] The goal of the project was to research all existing and potential legal supports or hindrances to workplace flexibility, and subsequently, to develop policy ideas that would work well for both business and employees.[65]

A defining commitment of the enterprise—from its inception—was to search for public policy approaches that would work well for both employers and employees. This key element required *reshaping the political expectations* of those involved in this enterprise. Anyone who has toiled in the field of labor and employment policy and law, including me, simply expects as a normal course of doing business that employer and employee groups will resist each other's public policy efforts. Either group might win or lose in any particular fight, and hence, a bill might advance, be stalled, or be modified, but the expectation is that there *will* always be a fight.

This was certainly the case in 2003, when Workplace Flexibility 2010 came into existence. In the 10 years prior to that time, the policy debate in Washington had addressed only a small and cramped subset of workplace flexibility issues, and legislative action on those issues had itself stalemated.

On the Republican and business side, the primary legislative objective of business trade associations had been to modify the Fair Labor Standards Act (FLSA) to allow employers to offer nonexempt employees compensatory time off in lieu of receipt of time-and-a-half pay for time worked over 40 hours in a given week. Such legislation would have also allowed employers to offer nonexempt employees the ability to "bank" credit hours for compensatory time (even hours that were not worked overtime) and allowed employers to institute a two-week/80-hour schedule, instead of the current one-week/40-hour schedule mandated by the FLSA for purposes of overtime pay.[66]

Legislation to amend the FLSA along these lines was first introduced in 1995, was considered actively by Congress in 1997, and was considered again by Congress in 2003.[67] Congress was closely divided on each occasion and the debate was largely along partisan lines, with Republicans and business associations supporting the bills and Democrats, unions, and progressive family groups opposing them. The legislation came closest to enactment in 1997 but was ultimately stalled by a veto threat by President Bill Clinton and by two successful filibusters mounted by Democratic senators.[68] The legislation has never moved successfully to passage.

On the Democratic, union, and progressive family front, the agenda over the previous 10 years had focused primarily on expanding FMLA to provide pay for such leave, to expand the number of employees covered under the law, and to expand the reasons for which FMLA leave could be taken.[69] None of these bills had moved forward in the Republican-controlled Congress during that decade. In 2003, when Workplace Flexibility 2010 came into existence, the focus of the union and progressive family groups had shifted to pursuing paid family leave bills on the state level (following the successful example of California in 2002) and to pushing for a more narrowly tailored federal bill that would require all businesses to provide seven paid sick days for their employees. Business trade associations vigorously opposed both these state and federal efforts.[70]

In 2003, those of us envisioning Workplace Flexibility 2010 observed two significant problems with the political picture of the time. First, the discussion on workplace flexibility issues was remarkably cramped. It was as if there were a "diet of ideas" in Washington, with discussion occurring only on comp time instead of overtime pay or on requiring businesses to pay for family or sick leave. But changing the workplace in a sweeping and normative manner—which seemed to us the *only* way to truly make a difference in how workers would manage their work and lives together—could not possibly be achieved with just those two ideas on the table.

Second, the debate itself was stalemated. Given that a supermajority was required in the Senate for almost any substantive piece of legislation to pass (Feldblum and Appleberry 2006), it was hard to move anything forward that had the clear and stated opposition of any powerful interest group—be it that of employers or employees.

In this atmosphere, an enterprise that was devoted to developing a broad range of public policies that would work well for both employers and employees was going against the grain. Nevertheless, Workplace Flexibility 2010 has a deep philosophical commitment to this approach, with its roots in both pragmatism and ideology.

At a matter of pragmatism, it is more likely that public policy will be enacted if business trade associations are not vigorously opposing the relevant legislation. But the deeper pragmatic concern, on our part, was that we were seeking a *broad-ranging vision* of public policy that would cut across many categories and laws (e.g., labor, benefits, taxes, government programs, and so on). To enact such truly sweeping and normative reform, business support seems even more essential.

On the ideological level, our commitment is more complicated, yet equally important. The policy conversation for us in the area of workplace flexibility feels different from the policy conversation that needs to take place, for example, in the context of employment laws prohibiting discrimination.[71] In an antidiscrimination context, there are "bad actors" that the law is designed and intended to sanction and deter. Those who support such laws believe there is simply no good reason to treat someone adversely in the workplace simply because of the person's race, sex, religion, disability, sexual orientation, or gender identity. While one might want to engage business in thinking through how to best *prohibit* such discrimination, there is no legitimate reason to engage business in figuring out how to continue facilitating such discrimination.

But workplace flexibility issues feel different. In this arena, we are considering basic workplace standards that will allow time off for employees, but that will also ensure the work still gets done (see, for example, the description below of short-term, episodic, and extended time off as aspects of workplace flexibility). We are also considering innovative partnerships between employees and employers about *how* work gets done (see, for example, the description below of flexible work arrangements as an aspect of workplace flexibility). With regard to both of these areas, it seems appropriate to find out *why* employers are not offering workplace flexibility now. How much of it is financial, how much is operational, and how much is simply old ways of doing business? How much is ingrained in how a business views its workforce for financial purposes, as described by Lambert, and how much is ripe for change, as described by Moen, Kelly, and Chermack (both in this volume)?

Given this reality, it seems appropriate to engage businesses in thinking through *solutions* to the needs of today's workforce. The demographic data are clear that the workforce will continue to require an effective means of managing their work and their lives. If a business's financial plan requires it to ignore those demands affirmatively (as some of Lambert's work suggests), then that is an important fact to bring to the surface.

Conversely, if making workplace flexibility the norm of a business's workplace enables a business to function more effectively, that fact is important to bring to the surface as well. The key is that we will never *know* what the best solutions might be if we do not engage businesses in a truly open, candid, and frank conversation about their needs and the needs of their workers.

From its inception, therefore, Workplace Flexibility 2010 entered the policy arena with the expectation of facilitating a reasonable and productive conversation between employees and employers in the development of public policy. That expectation has been greeted with mild to severe skepticism, even scorn, over the past years. But after five years of Workplace Flexibility 2010 operating on the Washington policy scene— sponsoring briefings, producing reports, and holding meetings—this much is clear: advocates and policymakers across the political spectrum know that we are *serious about* and *committed to* this set of *reframed political expectations*. And, what is most gratifying for us is that many of them seem quite intrigued by the possibilities that this different frame of mind might offer for the development of policy.

Reframing Policy Terminology

Language is powerful in Washington. In 2002, terms such as "comp time," "paid leave," and "intermittent leave" all carried meanings laden with political weight. They did not simply describe a specific need experienced by employees; rather, they telegraphed specific views as to the appropriate role that government should play in meeting those needs.

One of our first goals at Workplace Flexibility 2010, therefore, was to develop a new set of *policy terms*. We wanted to develop language and terms that would not signal one position or another in the current policy debate.[72]

Developing new policy terms also helped communicate to policymakers that Workplace Flexibility 2010 had a targeted, and hence limited, focus for policy analysis. Many contributors to this volume, and in this arena generally, talk about the need for "work-life policies" or "work-family policies." They include within that term policies such as paid sick leave, paid family leave, child care and elder care, and preschool education (Glass this volume). In addition, as one can easily imagine, the size of one's paycheck and simply having a steady paycheck also critically affect the quality of one's work-life management.

This is all true. For Workplace Flexibility 2010, however, our attention has consistently been focused on policies *inside the workplace* that affect work-life management. Policies that take place outside of the workplace are understood by us to be critical components of any holistic public policy, but they are not the focus of our attention. (See figure 14.1.)

For Workplace Flexibility 2010, therefore, "workplace flexibility" does not include issues such as child care, elder care, preschool education, or a living wage. We make this distinction partly to communicate that even

Figure 14.1. Workplace Flexibility as a Component of Workforce Policy

if workplace flexibility were to become a standard of the American workplace, it would not be a panacea unless other pieces of the work-life puzzle were addressed as well. But we do so also to telegraph to policymakers and advocates in Washington our clear and targeted focus: those structures and policies *within the workplace* that make it easier or harder for people to manage their work and life demands.

Having staked out this particular arena as our target, we then proceeded to analyze the needs, obligations, and responsibilities of employees to develop and categorize the elements of what we term "workplace flexibility." We had, as our starting point, a definition that had been developed in 2003 by several grantees of the Alfred P. Sloan Foundation, including this author, in conjunction with the foundation's project officer, Kathleen Christensen:[73]

- the ability to have flexibility in the scheduling of full-time hours;
- the ability to have flexibility in the number of hours worked; and
- the ability to have career flexibility with multiple points for entry, exit, and reentry into the workforce.

As conversations continued around that definition, it also came to include a fourth component:

- the ability to address unexpected and ongoing personal and family needs.

Although not incorporated into the definition itself, conversations around this definition consistently reflected a background assumption: that meeting workplace flexibility needs in an *effective* manner would necessitate taking into account the concerns and requirements of *both* workers and employers. This was not a naïve, rose-colored view of the world. All of us involved in crafting this definition understood that the needs and requirements of employers and employees would sometimes conflict. But we went into the process of defining workplace flexibility with a commitment to taking into account the needs of both employers and employees to the greatest extent possible.

The Sloan definition of workplace flexibility represented a significant step forward in marking the contours of the policies—either governmental policies or voluntary policies of employers—that might help workers manage their work and their lives. Workplace Flexibility 2010 then moved that definitional conversation one step further by developing new policy terms that *mapped* the Sloan definition onto an existing policy conversation—but without conveying, through those policy terms, any expectations of *how* such needs would be met through public policy.

Workplace Flexibility 2010 approached this mapping project by systematically and carefully analyzing the data that existed with regard to the needs experienced by workers and then mapping those needs against federal (and some state) laws and proposed laws that had relevance to those needs.

Based on that analysis, we identified, categorized, and defined *three new policy terms* to capture what was covered under the Sloan definition of workplace flexibility:

- flexible work arrangements,
- time off, and
- career maintenance and reentry.[74]

The first two components of the Sloan definition of workplace flexibility—the ability to have flexibility in the scheduling of full-time hours and flexibility in the number of hours worked—are encompassed in our policy term "flexible work arrangements" (FWAs).

We define an FWA as any arrangement that alters the time, or place, or both that work is conducted regularly in a manner that is as manageable and predictable as possible for both employees and employers.

FWAs include flexibility in the scheduling of hours worked, such as with alternative work schedules (e.g., nontraditional start and end times, flextime, and compressed workweeks) and shift and break schedules. It also includes flexibility in the amount of hours worked, such as part-time work, job shares, part-year work, and phased retirement schedules. Finally, it includes flexibility in the place of work, such as at home, at a satellite location, or in two different locations based on the time of year.[75]

Predictability with regard to when hours are worked is an issue of particular importance to many lower-wage workers (Waters Boots and Danziger 2008). Lower-wage workers are more likely to work in industries and occupations in which schedules are set weekly. Many of these lower-wage workers have very little advance notice of their schedules, requiring them to cobble together child care and other arrangements at the last minute. In addition, while lower-wage workers often desire more hours to earn more income, unscheduled mandatory overtime can be a significant problem. Thus, the FWAs that many lower-wage workers need entail more predictability and control over when they work.

The reasons a worker may wish for an FWA are manifold. One worker may want an FWA because that will allow him to provide better care to an elderly parent or a spouse, while another may want an FWA because there are no funds available for child care or elder care. Yet another worker may want an FWA so that she can attend a weekly class, a weekly Bible session, or a weekly volunteer engagement. And a third worker may want an FWA because that will better address his medical conditions. The definition of an FWA does not itself presuppose any reason for the need or desire for the flexibility.

The fourth part of the Sloan definition of workplace flexibility—the ability to address unexpected and ongoing personal and family needs—is encompassed in our policy term "time off." Within that category, we have conceptualized and named three different types of time off that are necessary to deal with unexpected or ongoing personal and family needs: short-term time off, episodic time off, and extended time off.

"Short-term time off" and "episodic time off" both refer to time off taken in short increments. Short-term time off (STO) is designed to address the ordinary predictable and unpredictable needs of life. Episodic time off (EPTO) is used to address a *recurring* predictable or unpredictable need for time off from work.

STO and EPTO may be needed for different reasons and those reasons will dictate the amount of time needed. For example, with regard to STO, the reason might be the illness of a worker herself, and the STO needed might be three consecutive days. Or the reason might be the illness of the worker's child, and the STO needed might be one day. The reason might be a plumbing emergency at home, the need to go to a court hearing, or a scheduled parent-teacher conference, and the STO required might be anywhere from one to six hours.

All workers—men and women, caregivers and noncaregivers—will presumably need some amount of STO during the course of a year. Even if life does not deal these individuals any significant blows, they will presumably get sick at some point, and if they do not have someone else to deal with other mundane aspects of life, they will need time away from work to address those needs.

What distinguishes EPTO from STO is the *episodic* nature of the time off needed, and in many cases, the additional amount of time needed. For example, a worker who suffers from a chronic health condition or cares for a family member with a chronic condition might need to be absent episodically from work. That episodic time off might be predictable—

for example, scheduled chemotherapy appointments for oneself or scheduled doctor visits for a family member. Or the episodic time off might be unpredictable—for example, a child with unanticipated asthma attacks who has to be taken to the hospital or a worker with migraine headaches that flare up unexpectedly.

A defining aspect of EPTO is that it is needed most by individuals to whom life has already dealt some blow. These workers do not have ordinary headaches on an infrequent basis; they have intense, recurring headaches that make them unable to function during that time. They do not have a child with the general run-of-the-mill set of illnesses; they have a child with a life-threatening chronic illness. What this also means is that the amount of time off that such individuals need is often greater than that needed by the average person who has not been dealt such life blows.

Sometimes the life blow will have a perceived end point—for example, a parent with a terminal illness who requires episodic care. Other times, the end point will be quite far in the future (e.g., until a child grows to adulthood) or may even occur past the point that the individual stops working if the condition affects the individual herself.

These definitions of STO and EPTO convey no information on how *much* STO or EPTO is appropriate to give to workers. Nor do they convey how *public policy* should be crafted to ensure that the STO and EPTO needs of workers are met while simultaneously ensuring that employers will get the necessary work done. Instead, what these terms do is simply *name* a category of need.

"Extended time off" (EXTO) refers to time off taken in long increments. EXTO can be either predictable or unpredictable. For example, EXTO might be required to care for a newborn or a newly adopted child—events that have a generally anticipated timeframe. It might also be required to serve in the military or to receive advanced training and education—events that usually have some degree of lead time associated with them. But EXTO might also be required after a worker or a worker's family member suffers an unexpected accident. In that case, the timing of the EXTO will be impossible to predict and the amount of EXTO needed might be hard to judge as well.

EXTO is needed both by those workers to whom life has dealt some blow—for example, a worker who has an accident or who has a family member with extended caregiving needs—as well as by those who may have sought the change in their life situation—for example, a worker who has a new child.

The need for STO, EPTO, and EXTO is not tied to whether an individual is working full-time or working on an FWA (including working part-time). Presumably, someone with an FWA can better deal with STO and EPTO needs that are predictable. Indeed, data indicates that effective FWAs reduce employees' use of STO and EPTO (Bond and Galinsky 2006; CCH Inc. 2007; Corporate Voices 2005). But an FWA, including part-time work, will not always address STO, EPTO, and EXTO needs.

The third aspect of the Sloan definition of workplace flexibility—the ability to have career flexibility with multiple points for entry into, exit from, and reentry into the workforce—is captured by our policy term "career maintenance and reentry." This form of flexibility addresses the needs of employees who need to or choose to leave the workforce completely for a period of time but who plan to or need to reenter the workforce later. As Kathleen Christensen from the Sloan Foundation often comments, the "off ramps" from the workplace are very accessible and easy to traverse, but it is the "on ramps" that need to be made more accessible and more effective. And the effectiveness of those on ramps may be enhanced by whatever forms of career maintenance are available to those who have exited the paid workforce for some increment of time.

Categorizing, conceptualizing, and defining the policy components of workplace flexibility in this manner has enhanced Workplace Flexibility 2010's analysis in several ways. First, it has allowed us to work systematically through the access and utilization that exists with regard to different aspects of workplace flexibility across job categories and across income levels. This has provided us with a rich and nuanced picture of the varying degrees of need that exist across the American workforce.[76]

Second, we have been able to analyze the range of laws that impact these various components of workplace flexibility in a systematic and rigorous manner. From 2005 through 2007, with the help of a legal working group made up of seven leading management-side lawyers and seven leading employee-side lawyers, we critically analyzed existing and proposed laws that might support or hinder these various components of workplace flexibility.[77]

Third, and of key importance, this approach has allowed us to identify differential policy approaches that might fit the various categories and concomitantly, the different policy obstacles that might arise for each one.

In her contribution to this volume, for example, Glass observes that "there may be an economic rationality in the resistance of some employers to family policy and workplace flexibility. Does this mean that employers will forever be an impediment to work-family policies and programs?"

But why should we lump all "work-family policies and programs" together? Once we separate them into the components described above, we are able to analyze them more clearly. For example, we can ask whether the best way to respond to a market failure in the provision of FWAs is through a traditional approach of regulation or mandate, or whether a completely different policy approach might work better. Similarly, we can ask whether businesses not providing paid time off now will suddenly do so if provided with market incentives, or whether a more regulatory policy approach is needed to achieve that goal.

Separating out the components of "work-family policies and programs" allows us to ask more targeted and rigorous questions. With that, we can better understand the depth of opposition to different policy approaches and begin to leverage the policy opportunities that do exist in this area.

Refining the Policy Obstacles and Leveraging the Policy Opportunities

If all employers provided every component of workplace flexibility to their employees, there would be no need for public policy in this arena. Workplace flexibility would be the ordinary, normal standard of the American workplace and our job would be done.

That is, obviously, not the state of play today. But it is important to differentiate *what* components of workplace flexibility are not being provided by *which* employers to better understand possible opposition to various policy alternatives.

A significant segment of today's workforce does not have access to paid STO, EPTO, or EXTO. This may be because they work in an industry in which such access is limited or because they are part-time workers who are not provided these forms of flexibility.[78] These employers have presumably made a classic cost/benefit business judgment and have decided that they either cannot or need not offer these forms of workplace flexibility. These are not employers who are seeking to compete for labor talent through offering access to such flexibility. Rather, these are employers who are focused on reducing their labor costs. And these are employers who are going to resist strongly any government mandate to provide these forms of flexibility.

There are also many employers who do offer paid STO, EPTO, and EXTO through various employer programs (Workplace Flexibility 2010 2006b, 2007a, b). These are employers who have also made a classic cost/benefit business judgment and have decided that it advances their business interests to offer these forms of flexibility. Indeed, most of these employers do not even think of STO, EPTO, and EXTO as workplace flexibility.[79]

But as a matter of ideology, one can expect most of these businesses to oppose a government mandate that requires other employers to offer such flexibility. These businesses trust that the market will ensure that employers who can afford to offer such flexibility and who need to do so to compete effectively will, in fact, do so. And if businesses choose not to offer these components of flexibility—either because they cannot afford them or because they are under no market pressure to do so—many businesses (including those who do offer such time off) believe it is not the role of the government to regulate those other businesses.

In addition, many of these employers have had experiences with the FMLA, particularly its intermittent leave provisions, that have left them wary of government requirements to provide a benefit—even a benefit that they are already providing.[80] Thus, unless businesses receive something in return for accepting a governmental mandate to provide something they are already providing, it is difficult to imagine why these employers would support such a requirement.

Among employers that offer paid STO, EPTO, and EXTO and that are interested in competing for and retaining labor talent, the desire to develop effective FWAs is often quite strong (Corporate Voices 2005). Indeed, the Alfred P. Sloan Foundation's National Initiative on Workplace Flexibility is comprised of several efforts to support and encourage such voluntary efforts on the part of employers.[81]

But those employers do not necessarily see why government should be involved in this enterprise. They are interested in offering FWAs because it makes sense to them as a business strategy, and they view this arena as something to be negotiated between employers and employees, without interference by the government.

Segmenting the components of workplace flexibility, however, can also provide us the opportunity to imagine creative and effective policy opportunities. Of key importance—it makes it easier for us to imagine a *range* of ways in which government and public policy might have an impact on the availability of, access to, and uptake of various forms of workplace flexibility. By focusing objectively on what we can learn from employers that are offering different components of workplace flexibility, and those that are not, we can develop and target different policy ideas.

At Workplace Flexibility 2010, we have conceptualized five categories of action through which government and public policy might advance workplace flexibility.

- The government can *remove or lower existing legal hurdles* to providing various forms of flexibility. For example, changes to the tax code could make it easier for employers to offer FWAs to employees who are past retirement age and who want to continue working a reduced-hours schedule.
- The government can *support and enhance efforts* on the part of employers who are considering offering workplace flexibility. This could be done through tax changes, outright grants, or awards, and each of these might be targeted to states, to all employers, to some employers, or to employees.
- The government can *exemplify optimal efforts* on the part of those offering workplace flexibility. This could be done through public awareness and education and through the government as a model employer.
- The government can *set minimum standards* that would be required of all or of some employers and that would be enforced by the *government.*
- The government can *establish minimum rights* for all or some employees that would be enforced by *individuals.*

Each of these policy approaches—or some combination of these approaches—might work better for different components of workplace flexibility. By ensuring that the *full* range of government's role is carefully considered for *each* component, we stand the best chance of developing the most thoughtful and workable public policy for advancing workplace flexibility overall.

But how does one ensure that thoughtful and workable ideas actually come to the fore for each component of workplace flexibility? At Workplace Flexibility 2010, we believe this will require a strategic and smart process, a strong commitment from new constituency groups, and a heavy dose of moral outrage from our fellow citizens. With such a tripartite effort, we believe we can leverage the policy opportunities that currently exist in this area. The key policy *opportunity* that exists right now is that people *want* change—they *want* workplaces to work better.

Let's begin with the first prong of the tripartite effort: a strategic and smart process. We discovered, over the 18 months that our legal working group met, that it was possible to have a reasonable conversation about the various components of workplace flexibility if we created a safe "rhetoric-free zone." The safety aspect of the zone was assured by the rules of the group: comments could not be repeated for attribution to a particular person and everyone was expected to listen carefully and respectfully to alternative points of view. And by designating (and running) the meetings as rhetoric-free zones, we found that group members were able to stretch their minds to carefully consider ideas to which they were not intuitively drawn.

Our positive experiences continued with our phased retirement working group, which met in an information and discussion phase from November 2005 through December 2007, and has continued in a policy development stage from May 2008. As with the legal working group, we carefully balanced representation from employer and employee perspectives in the group. In addition, given the technical nature of the issues being considered, we included actuaries, economists, and consultants.[82]

As this book goes to press, the phased retirement working group is considering possible proposals for enhancing phased retirement for both employers and employees. We have no idea whether or to what extent members of the group will choose to endorse the specific policy ideas that Workplace Flexibility 2010 will develop. But we know we have gained significantly already from the balanced and thoughtful conversations of the group regarding the challenges in developing effective phased retirement programs that work well for both employers and employees.

Building on the successes of the legal working group and the phased retirement working group, Workplace Flexibility 2010 launched a national advisory commission on workplace flexibility (the NAC) in April 2008. The NAC is composed of approximately 30 individuals representing a broad range of interests and viewpoints—including high-level former political players, former labor and business advocates, current business executives, and work-family researchers. The NAC members are responding to specific policy ideas being developed by Workplace Flexibility 2010 on each component of workplace flexibility. If possible, the NAC members will come to a consensus on some or all of those ideas. But regardless of whatever formal consensus might be achieved through this process, what each member of the NAC will have contributed is participation in an enterprise of thoughtful dialogue and exchange in the hopes of creating the best public policy ideas possible to advance each component of workplace flexibility.[83]

The second prong of the tripartite effort will be to engage the passions of new constituencies beyond the existing employer and employee groups that currently dominate the policy conversation. If workplace flexibility becomes a standard of the American workplace, that outcome will support and facilitate a range of necessary caregiving for oneself, as well as for one's children, parents, spouses, siblings, and friends. In light of that fact, a large number of constituency groups that care passionately about caregiving should care passionately about advancing workplace flexibility. These include groups that focus on health, disability, children, aging, and family. (And the last should clearly include groups that have a broad and diverse view of the meaning of family—from conservative to progressive family groups.)

But workplace flexibility is not only needed for caregiving. It is needed and appreciated by those who want to volunteer in their communities, to meet their religious needs, to schedule a phased retirement, to deal with a public emergency, or to make our environment greener. Thus, there are yet additional constituency groups that should care passionately about making workplace flexibility a standard of the American workplace: faith-based, volunteer, emergency-preparedness, transportation, and environmental groups.

Workplace Flexibility 2010 has made it a priority to reach out to this broad range of groups and to engage them in conversations about workplace flexibility. Many of these groups have been receptive to the argument that they should care about policy ideas to advance workplace flexibility, because their constituencies and their causes would benefit from workplace flexibility being a standard of the American workplace. Building on this engagement, Workplace Flexibility 2010 will be working with groups across these issue areas as we move forward, soliciting their views and reactions as we develop our specific policy ideas.

And finally, perhaps the third aspect of the tripartite effort will be the one that moves us over the finish line. We need some *moral outrage against the status quo.*

Individuals in our society are beginning to realize that the structures of their workplaces are not individual problems that should be solved individually. The increase in public conversation around these issues, as evidenced by the description of the policy conversation above, reflects the glimmers of understanding that the lack of workplace flexibility is a societal problem and a societal responsibility.

But the complacency in America today is still striking. Why do we think it is legitimate that people do not have access to the STO, EPTO, and EXTO that they need? Why do we think it is acceptable that employers feel no responsibility to affirmatively structure jobs so that they are amenable to FWAs, if possible? Why are we happy living in a society that does not put effort and resources into helping people reenter the workforce after stints of caregiving or after exiting the workforce for other reasons?

The status quo is *unacceptable*. We can do better.

Looking to the Future

The goal of Workplace Flexibility 2010 is to have workplace flexibility be a standard of the American workplace. We want it to be the norm, not the aberration.

In a world in which workplace flexibility is the norm, the aberration will be the 55-year-old man who does *not* take a week off when his elderly mother takes a turn for the worse. In a world in which workplace flexibility is the norm, the aberration will be the 32-year-old father of two who does *not* have a flexible work arrangement. And in a world in which workplace flexibility is the norm, children will be taken to doctors, toilets will get fixed, and elderly parents will get cared for with less anguish than occurs today.

This type of normative change will require an attitude of mutual responsibility and accountability on the part of both employees and employers. Employers will have to be cognizant of the need to take into account the lives of workers and have practices and policies to reflect that. And employees will have to be fully committed to helping the work get done even with the optimal utilization of workplace flexibility.

Throughout it all, government can be a true partner in supporting, enhancing, and undergirding these efforts—with a thoughtful and workable set of public policies. The question is whether we can overcome the policy obstacles and craft that set of policies. A strategic and smart process that allows for the development of creative ideas, a strong commitment from new constituency groups, and a heavy dose of moral outrage—perhaps that tripartite effort will bring us to a successful conclusion.

NOTES

1. See Workplace Flexibility 2010 (2006b, 2007b, 2007c). See also Anna Bahney, "A Life between Jobs," *New York Times,* June 8, 2006, http://travel.nytimes.com/2006/06/08/fashion/thursdaystyles/08vaca.html (accessed December 29, 2007). According to the Census Bureau, the number of married-couple households in which both spouses are employed and handling child care has increased 20 percent between 1980 and 1990 and an additional 10 percent between 1990 and 2000 (U.S. Census Bureau 2008 and unpublished data).

2. In 1970, almost two-thirds of married couples 18 to 64 years of age included one spouse at home, available to handle many of the families' routine and emergency needs. By 2000, 60 percent of married couples had both spouses in the workforce (Jacobs and Gerson 2004, 43).

3. Al Gore for President 2000 web site, "On the Issues: Children and Families," reprinted http://www.4president.us/issues/gore2000/gore2000children.htm (accessed December 27, 2007).

4. The Family and Medical Leave Act (FMLA), enacted in 1993, provides certain employees who work for employers with at least 50 employees the right to receive up to 12 weeks of unpaid, job-protected time off to care for a newborn or adopted child, for their own serious health condition, or for the serious health condition of a covered family member. See 29 U.S.C. § 2601 et seq.

5. Al Gore for President 2000 brochure, "Al Gore's Record as Vice President," reprinted http://www.4president.org/brochures/gore2000brochure.htm (accessed December 27, 2007).

6. John Kerry for President 2004 web site, "John Kerry 2004: On the Issues," reprinted http://www.4president.us/issues/kerry2004/kerry2004economy.htm (accessed December 27, 2007).

7. John Kerry for President 2004 web site, "John Kerry 2004: On the Issues," reprinted http://www.4president.us/issues/kerry2004/kerry2004economy.htm (accessed December 27, 2007).

8. John Kerry for President 2004 web site, "John Kerry 2004: On the Issues," reprinted http://www.4president.us/issues/kerry2004/kerry2004economy.htm (accessed December 27, 2007).

9. Hillary Clinton for President 2008 web site, "Hillary Clinton's Agenda for Working Families: Helping Parents Balance Work & Family," October 16, 2007, press release, http://www.hillaryclinton.com/news/release/view/?id=3743 (accessed December 27, 2007).

10. Hillary Clinton for President web site, "Hillary Clinton's Agenda for Working Families: Helping Parents Balance Work & Family," October 16, 2007, press release, http://www.hillaryclinton.com/news/release/view/?id=3743 (accessed December 27, 2007).

11. Obama for America campaign web site, "Family," http://www.barackobama.com/issues/family/ (accessed December 27, 2007).

12. Chris Dodd President 2008 web site, "Our Families, Our Future: Putting Women and Families First," http://chrisdodd.com/issues/women/ (accessed December 27, 2007).

13. In addition to Clinton, Obama, and Dodd, Senator Joe Biden and Governor Bill Richardson both supported some form of paid family leave. Biden for President web site, 2007, "Joe Biden: Standing with American Workers," http://www.joebiden.com/issues?id=0019 (accessed December 27, 2007, now inactive); Bill Richardson for President web site,

2007, "Addressing Issues of Importance to Women," http://www.richardsonforpresident. com/issues/women/ (accessed December 27, 2007).

14. John Edwards for President web site, "Edwards Announces Bold Plan for Paid Family and Medical Leave," November 13, 2007, press release, http://johnedwards. com/news/press-releases/20071113-paid-leave/ (accessed December 27, 2007). It was interesting to watch the promised federal funds for a trust of this kind move from $1 billion in Clinton's October 16, 2007, announcement, to $1.5 billion in Obama's November 11, 2007, announcement, to $2 billion in Edwards's November 13, 2007, announcement.

15. John Edwards for President web site, "Edwards Announces Bold Plan for Paid Family and Medical Leave," November 13, 2007, press release, http://johnedwards. com/news/press-releases/20071113-paid-leave/ (accessed December 27, 2007). Take Care Net, a coalition of groups and individuals, surveyed all Presidential candidates in 2007 with regard to their positions on a range of proposed policies. Almost all of the Democratic candidates responded; none of the Republican candidates responded (http:// www.takecarenet.org/takecarenetsurvey2007.pdf, accessed December 31, 2007).

16. See, for example, *Working Families Flexibility Act of 1996*, HR 2391, 104th Cong.; *Working Families Flexibility Act of 1997*, HR 1, 105th Cong.; *Family Friendly Workplace Act of 1997*, S 4, 105th Cong.; *Working Families Flexibility Act of 1999*, HR 1380, 106th Cong.; *Family Friendly Workplace Act of 1999;* S 1241, 106th Cong.; *Workplace Flexibility Act of 2001*, S 624, 107th Cong.; *Working Families Flexibility Act of 2001*, HR 1982, 107th Cong.; *Family Time Flexibility Act of 2003*, HR 1119, 108th Cong.; and *Family-Friendly Workplace Act of 2007*, HR 6025, 110th Cong.

17. White House, Office of the Press Secretary, "Fact Sheet: America's Workforce— Ready for the 21st Century," http://www.whitehouse.gov/news/releases/2004/08/ 20040805-6.html, August 5, 2004, press release (accessed December 31 2007).

18. In 2004, in the 108th Congress, the bills were S 2520, introduced by Senator Ted Kennedy, and HR 4575, introduced by Congresswoman Rosa DeLauro. In 2005, in the 109th Congress, the bills were S 932, introduced by Senator Ted Kennedy, and HR 1902, introduced by Congresswoman Rosa DeLauro. In 2007, in the 110th Congress, the bills were S 910, introduced by Senator Ted Kennedy, and HR 1542, introduced by Congresswoman Rosa DeLauro.

19. See *Healthy Families Act of 2007*, S 910, 110th Cong., § 4(3)(B) for the definition of a covered employer, § 5(a) for the definition of provision of paid sick leave.

20. *Healthy Families Act of 2007*, S 910, 110th Cong., § 5(a)(2). See the National Partnership for Women and Families web site for ongoing updates on the Healthy Families Act (http://www.nationalpartnership.org, accessed September 4, 2007).

21. *Family Leave Insurance Act of 2007*, S 1681, 110th Cong. S 1681 was introduced by Senators Christopher Dodd and Ted Stevens.

22. The amount of paid leave is pegged to the employee's salary, with employees who make lower salaries receiving a greater percentage of their salaries in paid leave.

23. *Working Families Flexibility Act*, S 2419, 110th Cong., introduced by Senator Ted Kennedy, and HR 4301, 110th Cong., introduced by Congresswoman Carolyn Maloney.

24. *Working Families Flexibility Act*, S 2419, 110th Cong., § 3 and § 4(b)(A)-(B).

25. *Working Families Flexibility Act*, S 2419, 110th Cong., § 4(b)(C).

26. Britain instituted a "right to request flexibility" policy in 2003 as part of the Work-Life Balance Campaign. The British experience with this approach serves as a model for legislation in the U.S. Karen Kornbluh, "The Joy of Flex," *Washington Monthly,* December 2005, http://www.washingtonmonthly.com/features/2005/0512. kornbluh.html (accessed August 8, 2008).

27. A video of the testimony and a copy of the written transcript from the U.S. Senate HELP Committee's February 13, 2007, hearing on the Healthy Families Act are available at http://www.help.senate.gov/Hearings/2007_02_13/2007_02_13.html (accessed September 4, 2008).

28. *National Defense Authorization Act for Fiscal Year 2008,* HR 4986, § 585; Jerry Geisel, "Congress Approves Bill to Expand FMLA for Military Families," *Business Insurance,* January 23, 2008, http://www.businessinsurance.com/cgi-bin/news.pl?post_date=2008-01-23&id=12062 (accessed January 23, 2008).

29. *Federal Employees Paid Parental Leave Act of 2008,* HR 5781, 110th Cong.

30. President Bush threatened to veto the proposal, calling it "costly" and "unnecessary." Executive Office of the President, "HR 5781—Federal Employees Paid Parental Leave Act of 2008," June 17, 2008, Statement of Administration Policy, http://www. whitehouse.gov/omb/legislative/sap/110-2/saphr5781-r.pdf (accessed August 11, 2008).

31. For a list of states and bills under consideration, see http://www.9to5.org/family valuesatwork/consortium.php (accessed August 11, 2008). Three major groups involved in the Multi-State Working Families Consortium are the 9to5 National Association of Working Women, the NJ Time to Care Coalition, and the Labor Project for Working Families.

32. See http://www.nationalpartnership.org/site/PageServer?pagename=ourwork_ pl_PaidLeave (accessed August 11, 2008).

33. Cal. Un. Ins. Code § 3301(a)(1). The legislation was enacted in 2002. Employee withholding began in January 2004 and benefits became available in June 2004.

34. Cal. Un. Ins. Code § 984.

35. Washington General Sess., 2007, Laws ESSB 5659, § 2 (2).

36. Washington General Sess., 2007, Laws ESSB 5659, § (6).

37. Washington General Sess., 2008, Laws ESHB 2687, §§ 227, 722.

38. New Jersey General Assembly, 2008, S. 786. 213th New Jersey Leg., Reg. Sess.

39. New York State Assembly, 2007, A. 9245 § 5(1)(B). New York Leg. Sess.

40. New York State Assembly, 2007, A. 9245. New York Leg. Sess.

41. The bill was delivered to the state senate on June 22, 2007, but was not acted upon.

42. State of Illinois, 2007, HB 1683, 95th General Assembly.

43. The bill was re-referred to the Rules Committee on March 23, 2007. Bill Status of HB 1683, http://www.ilga.gov/legislation/BillStatus_pf.asp?DocNum=1683&Doc TypeID=HB&LegID=30506&GAID=9&SessionID=51&GA=95 (accessed September 4, 2008).

44. San Francisco, California, 2007, Administrative Code ch. 12 W.

45. Council of the District of Columbia, 2008, *Accrued Sick and Safe Leave Act of 2008,* A17-0324.

46. State of Connecticut General Assembly, 2007, *An Act Mandating Employers to Provide Paid Sick Leave to Employees,* SB 601, January session; State of Maryland General Assembly, 2007, *Healthy Families and Healthy Workplaces Act,* HB 832/SB 828, 423rd Reg. Sess.; Massachusetts General Court, 2007, *An Act Establishing Paid Sick Days,* S 1073, 185th General Court, Reg. Sess.; State of Minnesota, 2007, *Healthy Families/Healthy Workplaces Act,* S.F. 1324/H.F. 1334, 85th Leg. Sess., Reg. Sess.; State of Missouri, 2007, *Healthy Families/Healthy Communities Act,* SB 637, 94th General Assembly, Reg. Sess.; State of Vermont, 2007–2008, *An Act Relating to Paid Sick Days,* H 337, Reg. Sess.; Washington, D.C., 2007, *Paid Sick and Safe Days Act of 2007,* Leg. B17-0197; Maine State Leg., 2007, *An Act to Care for Working Families,* LD 1454, 123rd Leg.; Florida State Leg., 2007, *Healthy Workers, Healthy Families Act,* SB 2192/HB 763, Reg. Sess.; General Assembly of North Carolina, 2007, *An Act to Establish Paid Sick Days to Ensure All Employees in North Carolina Can Address Their Own Health Needs and the Health Needs of Their Families,* HB 1711, Sess. 2007; General Assembly of Pennsylvania, 2007, *Healthy Families, Healthy Workplaces Act,* HB 1155, Sess. of 2007.

47. A review of the proposed legislation reveals the variety of approaches taken considering whether and to what extent to require small employers to provide paid time off, the maximum amount of paid time off that employers must provide per year, and the number of days an employee must work before becoming eligible. The proposals in Maryland, Minnesota, Missouri, and the District of Columbia allow small employers to provider fewer days of paid time off than large employers. Proposals in Massachusetts and Vermont require small employers to provide the same amount of paid time off as large employers. The Connecticut proposal exempts small employers (with fewer than 25 employees) entirely. And although all the state proposals require employees to accrue paid time off through working, they vary in how much total time off may be accrued per year. Most of the state proposals require large employers (defined, in all but Connecticut, as having 10 or more employees) to allow employees to accrue between 5 and 7 days off per year (Connecticut, Maryland, Minnesota, and Missouri), while the proposal in Washington, D.C., requires employers with 6 or more employees to permit employees to accrue up to 10 days per year. The proposals in Massachusetts and Vermont allow employees to accrue up to 7 days of paid time off per year, regardless of employer size. The state proposals (Maryland, Minnesota, and Missouri) with separate requirements for small employers (fewer than 10 employees) require small employers to provide up to approximately 3 days of paid time off per year, while the Washington, D.C., proposal requires small employers (fewer than 6 employees) to provide up to 5 days of paid time off per year. Concerning the number of days an employee must work for an employer to be eligible for paid time off (also known as job-tenure requirements), some of the bills permit paid time off as soon as it is accrued (Maryland, Massachusetts, Vermont), while others impose job-tenure requirements (Connecticut—120 days, Minnesota and Missouri—90 days, Washington, D.C.—60 days).

48. SB 836, 2007 Leg., 1st Sess. (Ca.).

49. "Caring for or supporting" means providing supervision or transportation; providing psychological or emotional comfort and support; addressing medical, educational, nutritional, hygienic, or safety needs; or attending to an illness, injury, or mental or physical disability. A "family member" is a child (a biological, adopted, or foster child; a stepchild; a legal ward; a son or daughter of a domestic partner; or a child to whom the person stands in loco parentis), parent (a biological, adoptive, or foster parent; a stepparent; a legal guardian; or another person who stood in loco parentis to the person when the person was a child), spouse, domestic partner, parent-in-law (parent to spouse or domestic partner), sibling, grandparent, or grandchild (SB 836, § 3).

50. Senate Judiciary Committee Bill Analysis of SB 836, 2007 Leg., 1st Sess., at 10 (Ca.).

51. Arnold Schwarzenegger, SB 727 Veto Message, October 13, 2007, http://gov.ca.gov/pdf/press/2007bills/SB%20727%20Veto%20Message.pdf (accessed September 4, 2008).

52. For New York, see Bill Text Assembly 3214, 230th Leg., Reg. Sess. (N.Y. 2007) and Bill Analysis Assembly 3214 (banning employment discrimination based on "family responsibilities," defined as the legal responsibility to care for a child); for Florida, SB 2628, 109th Legis., Reg. Sess.; and for Pennsylvania, HB 280, 2007 Legis., Reg. Sess. (both prohibiting employment discrimination based on "familial status," defined as a caregiver having someone under 18 years old living with him or her, or his or her designee). For New Jersey, see Bill Text Assembly 2255, 212th Legis., Reg. Sess. (banning discrimination based on "familial status"). For New York City, Int. 565, 2007 Reg. Sess. (banning employment discrimination based on an individual's "actual or perceived status as a caregiver," defined as a person who is contributing to the ongoing care of a person in a dependent relationship with the caregiver).

53. The San Francisco law, the Healthy Families Act, and the bills requiring sick days pending in six states and the District of Columbia would all require that costs for time off be paid by the employer.

54. The California law funds its paid family leave program solely with employee premiums. The proposed New Jersey and New York laws follow the same model. By contrast, the proposed federal Family Leave Insurance Act and the proposed Illinois law fund the program through equal contributions from employers and employees.

55. MomsRising has encouraged a creative campaign of sending baby onesies with a message to legislators considering the bills described in this section. See http://www.momsrising.org/powerofonesie/ (accessed January 1, 2008).

56. As Glass explains, existing research cannot provide reassurance on the issues that matter most to employers: whether "work-family flexibility will not hurt them competitively either domestically or globally," whether "work-family policies . . . will lessen rather than expand managerial problems with coordination and control over the labor process (including retention of trained workers, coverage of all hours of operation, and customer or client service continuity)," and whether work-life policies "will be cost effective as employees age rather than create escalating numbers of beneficiaries and expenditures."

57. Miguel Bustillo, "Paid Leave Bill Ignites Emotions," *Los Angeles Times,* July 29, 2002, A1; Rebecca Vesely, "Paid Family Leave Could Become Reality in California," *Women's E-News,* August 29, 2002, http://www.womensenews.org/article.cfm/dyn/aid/1021/ (accessed September 4, 2008); Mary Ann Milbourn, "California Paid Family Leave Legislation Moves Closer to Passage," *Orange County Register,* August 28, 2002. ("Many business interests, including the California Chamber of Commerce, criticized the law as a 'job killer' that would particularly hurt small businesses.")

58. For opposition in New Jersey, see, for example, Joan Verplanck, President, New Jersey Chamber of Commerce, testimony before the Senate Budget and Appropriations Committee regarding paid family leave S-2249, May 24, 2007; and Jim Leonard, Senior Vice President, New Jersey Chamber of Commerce, statement on paid leave, December 11, 2007, http://www.njchamber.com/News/dec%2007%20pfl%20statement.asp (accessed September 4, 2008). For opposition in New York, see, for example, NFIB/New York State Capitol Update, "Gov. Spitzer Pushes Mandated Family Leave Proposal," June 8, 2007, http://www.nfib.com/object/IO_33781.html (accessed September 4, 2008); Thomas R.

Minnick, Vice President, Human Resources, the Business Council of New York State Inc., testimony before New York Senate Committee on Labor, June 5, 2007, http://www. bcnys.org/inside/labor/2007/familyleavetestimony060507.pdf (accessed September 4, 2008). For opposition in Illinois, where premiums would be funded by both employers and employees, see, for example, NFIB, "Paid Leave and Employee Termination Issues in Illinois," March 7, 2005, http://www.nfib.com/object/IO_20820.html (accessed September 4, 2008).

59. See, for example, Justin Marks, "Paying for Family Leave," *State Legislatures Magazine,* February 2003, http://www.ncsl.org/programs/pubs/slmag/2003/203leave.htm (accessed January 8, 2008). Some businesses are also concerned that once a system for funding is set up, they might be required to pay into the fund down the line. See NFIB, "Paid Leave and Employee Termination Issues in Illinois," March 7, 2005, http://www.nfib. com/object/IO_20820.html (accessed September 4, 2008).

60. See, for example, New Jersey Business and Industry Association, "Paid Family Leave Bill Impacting All Employers Is Back! Act Now to Stop It!" http://www.voter voice.net/core.aspx?Screen=Alert&IssueID=12789&SessionID=$AID=175:SITEID=-1:VV_CULTURE=en-us:APP=GAC$ (accessed January 29, 2008, now inactive).

61. See, for example, Bravo (2007), describing the concept of "identity theft" in which big business associations are not legitimately speaking for all businesses.

62. For example, in California, the paid family leave provision began with contri-butions from both employers and employees. It was only after the bill was changed to require contributions solely from employees that it passed. See Labor Project for Work-ing Families (2003, 8–9). In Washington State, the paid family leave provision began with coverage for leave for a newborn or adopted child, as well as for one's own medical needs or those of a family member. It also required financial contributions from both employ-ees and employers (State of Washington Leg., 2007, SB 5659). The enacted version dropped coverage of medical needs and punted completely on the financing mechanism; see Curt Woodward, "WA Paid Family Leave Becomes Law, Financing Uncertain," *Seat-tle Times,* May 8, 2007, http://seattletimes.nwsource.com/html/localnews/2003699128_ webfamilyleave08.html (accessed September 4, 2008). In New Jersey, paid family leave was originally intended to cover 12 weeks without an exception for small businesses (NJ Assembly, 2000, No. 1577, *An Act Providing Family Disability Leave Benefits and Revising Various Parts of the Statutory Law,* 209th Sess.). The amount of time was reduced to 10 weeks, and that bill was passed by two committees before stalling (New Jersey Gen-eral Assembly, 2007, *An Act Concerning Family Leave and Amending and Supplementing P.L. 1989,* c. 261 A. 2437, 212th New Jersey Leg., Reg. Sess.). The current bill provides for 6 weeks of paid leave. A small-business exemption is still being considered.

63. The president of the Association of Washington Business criticized the pro-posed state paid family leave legislation as a costly, complex, and inefficient mandate. See Don Brunell, "Paid Family Leave Threatens Washington Employers," *Puget Sound Busi-ness Journal,* April 6, 2007, http://seattle.bizjournals.com/seattle/stories/2007/04/09/ editorial5.html (accessed September 9, 2008). After the Washington legislature passed the legislation, the National Federation of Independent Business continued to urge its members to contact their state representatives to eliminate the program. See NFIB, "Family Leave in Washington," 2007, http://www.nfib.com/object/IO_32057.html (accessed September 4, 2008). In California, businesses bemoaned passage of the law. See Alan J. Liddle, "Industry Slams California's Move to Pioneer 55%-Paid Family Leave," *Nation's Restaurant News,* October 7, 2002, reprinted http://findarticles.com/p/articles/mi_m3190/

is_40_36/ai_92724138 (accessed September 4, 2008). And when the Governor of California, Arnold Schwarzenegger, vetoed two bills that would have expanded the family leave provision, he stressed the need to preserve an acceptable business environment in the state. See SB 727 Veto Message, October 13, 2007, http://gov.ca.gov/pdf/press/2007bills/SB%20727%20Veto%20Message.pdf (accessed September 4, 2008).

64. I received a small grant from the Alfred P. Sloan Foundation in summer 2002 to review all laws that might have an impact on workplace flexibility. As part of that review, I looked at all the bills that had been introduced in Congress over the previous 10 years addressing issues of workplace flexibility. Based on that review, I recommended the establishment of a new enterprise that would not yet have taken any positions on existing or proposed legislation. The Alfred P. Sloan Foundation funded an initial form of that enterprise, in November 2003, as the D.C. Workplace Flexibility Policy Initiative. After various modifications, that initiative became Workplace Flexibility 2010 in June 2004.

65. As an enterprise fully funded by the Alfred P. Sloan Foundation from 2004 until 2008, Workplace Flexibility 2010 is prohibited from lobbying. In other words, Workplace Flexibility 2010 does not support any specific piece of legislation in Congress, does not suggest any legislative proposals to Congress, and does no grassroots lobbying on any piece of legislation. With funds provided by the Sloan Foundation, Workplace Flexibility 2010 is limited to the development of policy ideas for general dissemination.

66. See bills in note 16.

67. See bills in note 16.

68. 143 *Cong. Rec.* S5406 (statement of Sen. Coverdell); 143 *Cong. Rec.* S 4508, S 4514 (Cloture Motion); 143 *Cong. Rec.* S 5290, S 5291 (Cloture Motion).

69. U.S. Congress, 1997, HR 191, 105th Cong.; 2001, *Family and Medical Leave Fairness Act and Time for Schools Act,* S 18, 107th Cong.; 2001, HR 1312, 107th Cong.; 2001, HR 2287, 107th Cong.; 2001, *Family and Medical Leave Enhancement Act,* HR 2784, 107th Cong. Several bills were also introduced to provide paid leave for federal employees or to provide states with grants for pilot programs providing paid leave. See, for example, U.S. Congress, 2000, *Federal Employees Paid Parental Leave Act,* HR 4567, 106th Cong.; and 2001, *Family Income to Respond to Significant Transitions Insurance Act,* HR 226, 107th Cong. In addition, during the Clinton presidency, a successful regulatory effort was made to allow states to use their unemployment compensation funds to allow for paid leave under the FMLA: Birth and Adoption Unemployment Compensation Rule, 20 C.F.R. Pt. 604 (2000), published at 65 Fed. Reg. 37210 (June 13, 2000). Members of the business community opposed this effort, arguing that it was a poor use of the unemployment compensation fund. See, for example, Wisconsin Manufacturers and Commerce, "Human Resources Committee Report MB," December 29, 2002, http://www.wmc.org/display.cfm?ID=201 (accessed September 4, 2008). The economy worsened before any state chose to take advantage of the program and in October 2003, the Bush administration's Department of Labor rescinded the regulations. See 2003, *Unemployment Compensation—Trust Fund Integrity Rule: Birth and Adoption Unemployment Compensation, Removal of Regulations,* Final Rule, 68 Fed. Reg. 58,541.

70. See, for example, National Association of Manufacturers, "Family and Medical Leave Act (FMLA)," 2008, http://www.nam.org/s_nam/sec.asp?CID=390&DID=388 (accessed September 3, 2008). ("Numerous bills have been introduced to expand the FMLA for various purposes and to lower the threshold to employers with over 25 employees. The NAM opposes these bills.")

71. I had been actively involved in the development, drafting, and negotiation of the Americans with Disabilities Act of 1990, which prohibits (among other things) discrimination on the basis of disability in employment (see Feldblum 2003). I have also been actively involved in the development, drafting, and negotiation of the Employment Non-Discrimination Act, a bill that would prohibit discrimination on the basis of sexual orientation and gender identity in the workplace.

72. In 2002, the term "workplace flexibility" itself was also strongly associated, inside Washington political circles, with a single policy approach of providing compensatory time instead of overtime pay. But we made the deliberate decision to name our enterprise Workplace Flexibility 2010, with the explicit objective of shifting the public understanding of that term to encompass a broad range of employee *needs*, rather than one policy approach.

73. The basic contours of the definition were first developed by Kathleen Christensen, Anne Harrison Clark, and this author in 2002. They were then refined and agreed upon, through further conversations in 2003, with Ellen Galinsky of the Families and Work Institute, Marcie Pitt-Catsouphes of Boston College, and Patti Giglio of PSG Communications.

74. The identification and categorization of these new policy terms took place between 2004 and 2006, through the efforts of this author, Sharon Masling, Barbara Cammarata, and Katie Corrigan. We initially conceptualized workplace flexibility as consisting of six components: short-term time off, episodic time off, flexible working arrangements, reduced hours, extended time off, and career exit and reentry. In 2007, we reorganized these components into the three major categories set forth in the text.

75. For a more detailed description of FWAs, see Workplace Flexibility 2010 (2006a).

76. It was obviously a challenge for our policy researcher, Dr. Jean McGuire from Northeastern University, to compile data with regard to completely new terms that had not been used in any previous literature. Nevertheless, since the terms overlapped in some respects with other existing terms (e.g., sick leave, intermittent leave under the Family and Medical Leave Act, maternity and paternity leave, disability leave, etc.), Dr. McGuire and her team rose to the challenge and developed a set of fact sheets for each policy component. See Workplace Flexibility 2010 (2006b, 2007b, 2007c).

77. A number of the documents prepared during this process are available at http://www.workplaceflexibility2010.org/ (accessed September 4, 2008).

78. See Workplace Flexibility 2010 (2006b, 2007b, 2007c) for extensive data on access to STO, EPTO, and EXTO.

79. For example, a report issued by Corporate Voices for Working Families on "flexibility" in 2005 focused solely on FWAs (Corporate Voices 2005). Many of the companies surveyed probably offered some forms of paid STO, EPTO, and EXTO, but these were not captured in the analysis. Through Workplace Flexibility 2010's extensive education and engagement with the work-family field of researchers, we have been able to make some inroads into the scope of the definition of workplace flexibility. For example, a report issued by Corporate Voices for Working Families in 2006 on flexibility for low-income workers did discuss the need for STO, EPTO, and EXTO (Corporate Voices 2006).

80. For a description of concerns raised by employers regarding the intermittent leave provisions of the FMLA, see Workplace Flexibility 2010 (2007a).

81. See http://www.law.georgetown.edu/workplaceflexibility2010/docs/Sloan Initiative.pdf for description of the National Initiative on Workplace Flexibility. See

http://www.law.georgetown.edu/workplaceflexibility2010/funding.cfm for links to employer-focused efforts within the initiative (both accessed January 28, 2008).

82. Phased retirement seemed to be a particularly promising route for our consensus-based enterprise, given that the AARP and the Society for Human Resource Management had just published a joint paper titled "Phased Retirement and Flexible Retirement Arrangements: Strategies for Retaining Skilled Workers" (2006). The report concluded that "employers cannot solve the challenges posed by shifting demographics and projected talent shortages on their own. The creation of alliances between employers, policymakers, human resource experts, and employees 50+ can help businesses forge innovative solutions that meet their core values and mission" (14).

83. See http://www.law.georgetown.edu/workplaceflexibility2010/nac.cfm for description of the National Advisory Commission on Workplace Flexibility (accessed September 4, 2008).

REFERENCES

AARP and the Society for Human Resource Management. 2006. "Phased Retirement and Flexible Retirement Arrangements: Strategies for Retaining Skilled Workers." Washington, DC: AARP. http://assets.aarp.org/www.aarp.org_/articles/money/employers/phased_retirement.pdf. (Accessed September 4, 2008.)

Bailyn, Lotte. 1993. *Breaking the Mold: Women, Men, and Time in the New Corporate World.* New York: Free Press.

Bond, James T., and Ellen Galinsky. 2006. "What Workplace Flexibility is Available to Entry-Level, Hourly Workers?" Supporting Entry-Level, Hourly Employees Research Brief 3. New York: Families and Work Institute.

Bravo, Ellen. 2007. *Taking on the Big Boys: Or Why Feminism is Good for Families, Business, and the Nation.* New York: Feminist Press at CUNY.

Cahill, Kevin E., Michael D. Giandrea, and Joseph F. Quinn. 2005. "Are Traditional Retirements a Thing of the Past? New Evidence on Retirement Patterns and Bridge Jobs." Bureau of Labor Statistics, Office of Productivity and Technology Working Paper 384. Washington, DC: U.S. Department of Labor.

CCH Inc. 2007. "Effectiveness and Use of Work-Life Programs 2007." 2007 Unscheduled Absence Survey. Riverwoods, IL: CCH Inc. http://www.cch.com/absenteeism2007/Images/EffUse_WL_AC2007.pdf. (Accessed December 10, 2007.)

Corporate Voices for Working Families. 2005. "Business Impacts of Flexibility: An Imperative for Expansion." Report, November. Washington, DC: Corporate Voices for Working Families. http://www.cvworkingfamilies.org/downloads/Business%20Impacts%20of%20Flexibility.pdf. (Accessed January 28, 2008.)

———. 2006. "Workplace Flexibility for Lower Wage Workers." Report, October. Washington, DC: Corporate Voices for Working Families. http://www.cvworking families.org/downloads/lower%20wage%20flex%20review%20report.pdf?CFID=1565088&CFTOKEN=46342183. (Accessed January 28, 2008.)

Feldblum, Chai R. 2003. "The Art of Legislative Lawyering and the Six Circles Theory of Advocacy." *McGeorge Law Review* 34: 785–850.

Feldblum, Chai Rachael, and Robin Appleberry. 2006. "Law Making: A Case Study of the Family and Medical Leave Act." In *The Work and Family Handbook: Multi-disciplinary Perspectives and Approaches,* edited by Marcie Pitt-Catsouphes, Ellen Ernst Kossek, and Stephen A. Sweet (627–49). Mahwah, NJ: Erlbaum.

Jacobs, Jerry A., and Kathleen Gerson. 2004. *The Time Divide: Work, Family, and Gender Inequality.* Cambridge, MA: Harvard University Press.

Labor Project for Working Families. 2003. "Putting Families First: How California Won the Fight for Paid Family Leave." Berkeley, CA: Labor Project for Working Families. http://www.nationalpartnership.org/site/DocServer/portals_p3_library_PaidLeave_HowCaliforniaWonPaidFamilyL.pdf?docID=576. (Accessed September 4, 2008.)

Meiksins, Peter, and Peter Whaley. 2002. *Putting Work in Its Place: A Quiet Revolution.* Ithaca, NY, and London: ILR Press, Cornell University Press.

Moen, Phyllis, and Patricia Roehling. 2004. *The Career Mystique: Cracks in the American Dream.* Lanham, MD: Rowman & Littlefield.

Schneider, Barbara, and Linda Waite, eds. 2005. *Being Together, Working Apart: Dual-Career Families and the Work-Life Balance.* Oxford: Cambridge University Press.

Toosi, Mitra. 2007. "Employment Outlook: 2006–16; Labor Force Projections to 2016: More Workers in Their Golden Years." *Monthly Labor Review* 130(11): 33–52.

U.S. Census Bureau. 2008. "Table 580: Employment Status of Women by Marital Status and Presence and Age of Children—1970 to 2005." *Statistical Abstract of the United States.* Washington, DC: U.S. Census Bureau. http://www.census.gov/compendia/statab/tables/08s0580.pdf. (Accessed September 4, 2008.)

Washington State Joint Task Force on Family Leave Insurance. 2008. *Final Report.* Olympia, WA: Washington State Legislature. http://www.leg.wa.gov/documents/joint/fli/FinalReport.pdf. (Accessed September 4, 2008.)

Waters Boots, Shelley, and Anna Danziger. 2008. "Lower-Wage Workers and Flexible Work Arrangements." Washington, DC: Workplace Flexibility 2010. http://www.law.georgetown.edu/workplaceflexibility2010/documents/Lower-WageWorkers FWAs.pdf. (Accessed September 4, 2008.)

Workplace Flexibility 2010. 2006a. "Flexible Work Arrangements: The Overview Memo." http://www.law.georgetown.edu/workplaceflexibility2010/definition/general/FWA_OverviewMemo.pdf. (Accessed December 29, 2007.)

———. 2006b. "Workplace Flexibility 2010: Facts on Short Term Time Off." http://www.law.georgetown.edu/workplaceflexibility2010/definition/general/STO_FactSheet.pdf. (Accessed December 29, 2007.)

———. 2007a. "Different Types of FMLA Leave." http://www.law.georgetown.edu/workplaceflexibility2010/law/documents/TopicF-DifferentTypesofLeave.pdf. (Accessed January 28, 2008.)

———. 2007b. "Fact Sheet on Episodic Time Off (EPTO)." http://www.law.georgetown.edu/workplaceflexibility2010/definition/documents/EPTOFactSheet.pdf. (Accessed December 29, 2007.)

———. 2007c. "Fact Sheet on Extended Time Off." http://www.law.georgetown.edu/workplaceflexibility2010/definition/documents/EXTOFactSheet.pdf. (Accessed December 29, 2007.)

15

Work-Life Policies
A "Both/And" Approach

Ellen Galinsky

Jennifer Glass's chapter in this volume, "Work-Life Policies: Future Directions for Research," is an insightful, compelling, and useful analysis of the present situation and what it will take to move forward.

In this chapter, I will explore how we frame and study work-life policies. The point I will be making is that an either/or perspective on work-life policies is problematic. I have chosen this theme, not because it was necessarily missing from the Glass chapter, but because I believe this framing is a serious deterrent to change.

An Either/Or Perspective to Work-Life Issues Is Flawed

One of the frustrations I have had since I began conducting research on the changing workforce, changing family, and changing community is that many of the debates about work-life policies and practices are out of synch with the findings of research.

The public debates about work-life tend to frame the issues as *either/or* issues, whereas the findings of research tend to reveal a much more nuanced picture, a *both/and* view rather than an *either/or* one.

- *Is maternal employment good or bad for children?* It would be hard to argue that the findings of research support this stark view of "good versus bad" but rather, the findings reveal that it is hard to tell how a child will turn out simply because that child's mother is employed (Hoffman and Youngblade 1999; National Institute of Child Health and Human Development [NICHD] 2003a, b). Yet, even recently there were several stories in the media that took this tack—for example, "Work or Stay at Home: It's Still a Quandary" in *USA Today*.[1]

- *Is it quality or quantity time that matters most for children?* Again, the research, including the study that I conducted for *Ask the Children* (Galinsky 1999), shows that both are important. Furthermore, children do not "separate" the amount of time they spend with their mothers and fathers without considering what happens during that time.

- *Is maternal care or child care better for children?* Again, the research shows that it is not a competition, that child care doesn't replace maternal care, and in fact, it can be a support to parent care (Galinsky 1999; NICHD 2003a, b; Zigler and Finn-Stevenson 2007). This either/or framing is equally true in many of the public policy debates I hear. For example, *is relying on the free-market system in the United States good or bad for children and families?* As I will argue here, such a framing is just as problematic as the framework for discussing many of the other issues in work-life research.

It Is True that the Free-Market System in the United States Today Has Many Problems

There is no doubt, as Jennifer Glass argues in her chapter, that in itself, the market system in the United States is inadequate. There are data that reveal these inadequacies, albeit from cross-sectional studies. For example, the ongoing nationally representative studies of both employees and employers conducted by the Families and Work Institute (FWI) reveal that access to workplace flexibility—to talk about one type of work-life assistance—is uneven.

As Susan Lambert similarly reports in her chapter in this volume, data from *employees* in the FWI 2002 National Study of the Changing Workforce (NSCW) indicate that low-wage and -income employees have far less access to flexibility than their more advantaged counterparts (Bond and Galinsky 2006b). Because not all low-wage employees live in low-income households, we focus on low-wage and low-income employees—that is, in the bottom quartile of the earnings distribution, which was less than $9.73 in 2005 dollars, and in families with a total family income below 200 percent of the poverty level.

We found that only 24 percent of low-wage and low-income employees can take a few days off to care for a sick child without losing pay or using vacation days, compared with 54 percent of mid- and high-wage and -income employees. Overall, only 10 percent of low-wage and low-income employees have access to high levels of workplace flexibility. However, even among mid- and high-wage and -income employees, the percentage is also low, with 30 percent having access to high levels of workplace flexibility (see table 15.1).

In addition, even when employers offer flexible time and leave policies, a significant portion of employees believe there would be negative repercussions for using them—39 percent of employees in 2002 felt that they would be jeopardized—less likely to advance in their jobs—if they used the flexibility their employers provided. This percentage has not shifted since 1992, when we first began asking this question in the NSCW (Galinsky, Bond, and Hill 2004).

On the Other Hand, the Provision of Flexibility among Employers Has Stayed the Same or Risen Slightly

As Kossek and Distelberg report in this volume, comparing findings of *employers* from FWI's 2005 National Study of Employers (NSE) with data from FWI's 1998 Business Work-Life Study (BWLS), we found that that the provision of flexibility among employers with 100 or more employees has remained the same or showed small gains over the past eight years (see table 15.2) (Bond et al. 2005).

Furthermore, perhaps contrary to opinion, smaller employers are more likely to provide flexibility than larger ones.

Although large employers have received much more attention for providing work-life assistance than small employers, in fact, these small employers may provide more flexibility. Comparing employers with 50 to 99 employees with those with 1,000 or more employees in the 2002

Table 15.1. Employees Reporting Access to Flexible Workplace Policies and Practices (percent, *n*)

Flexible workplace policies and practices	Low-wage and -income employees	Sig.	Mid- and high-wage and -income employees
Allowed to choose starting and quitting times within some range of hours periodically (traditional flextime)	33 (*n* = 316)	***	45 (*n* = 1,086)
Allowed to choose starting and quitting times daily (daily flextime)	12 (*n* = 310)	***	26 (*n* = 1,083)
Have complete or a lot of control in scheduling work hours	36 (*n* = 321)	n.s.	35 (*n* = 1,089)
Find it relatively easy to take time off during the workday for personal or family matters	62 (*n* = 319)	n.s.	63 (*n* = 1,081)
Have supervisors/managers who accommodate them when family or personal business arises	89 (*n* = 278)	*	93 (*n* = 986)
Allowed some paid time off for personal illness	39 (*n* = 309)	***	79 (*n* = 1,086)
Allowed enough time off for personal illness	28 (*n* = 306)	***	70 (*n* = 1,068)
Allowed a few days off to care for a sick child without losing pay or having to use vacation days	24 (*n* = 141)	***	54 (*n* = 489)
Allowed enough paid time off for sick child care	17 (*n* = 141)	***	49 (*n* = 484)
Allowed to work all or some regular paid hours at home	4 (*n* = 322)	***	11 (*n* = 1,087)
Can decide when they take breaks	33 (*n* = 321)	***	57 (*n* = 1,087)
Are voluntary part-time workers	49 (*n* = 122)	n.s.	35 (*n* = 82)
Could work part-time in same position (if currently full-time)	54 (*n* = 199)	***	34 (*n* = 1,007)
Seldom required to work paid or unpaid overtime with little or no notice	63 (*n* = 318)	**	54 (*n* = 1,084)
Overall workplace flexibility		***	
Low	38		19
Moderate	52		51
High	10		30

Source: Bond and Galinsky (2006b).

*p < .05; **p < .01; ***p < .001; n.s. = not significant

Table 15.2. Employers Reporting Provision of Flexible Workplace Policies and Practices (percent, *n*)

Flexible workplace policies and practices	1998 BWLS	Sig.	2005 NSE
Allow (at least some) employees to periodically change starting and quitting times	68 (*n* = 554)	n.s.	70 (*n* = 428)
Allow (at least some) employees to change starting and quitting times daily	24 (*n* = 552)	*	31 (*n* = 432)
Allow (at least some) employees to move from full-time to part-time work, then back in the same position	57 (*n* = 544)	n.s.	55 (*n* = 421)
Allow (at least some) employees to share jobs	38 (*n* = 547)	n.s.	44 (*n* = 413)
Allow (at least some) employees to compress their workweeks	37 (*n* = 554)	*	44 (*n* = 427)
Allow (at least some) employees to work at home or off site regularly	33 (*n* = 555)	n.s.	35 (*n* = 432)
Allow (at least some) employees to return to work gradually after childbirth	81 (*n* = 548)	n.s.	85 (*n* = 421)
Provide personal health insurance benefits to part-time employees (among employers offering health insurance)	(*n* = 529)	n.s.	(*n* = 373)
Yes, full or prorated	33	n.s.	38
No	67	n.s.	62

Source: Bond et al. (2005).

BWLS = Business Work-Life Study

NSE = National Study of Employers

*p < .05; n.s. = not significant

NSE (see table 15.3), we see that small employers are more likely to provide flexibility than larger ones in 10 of 17 types of flexibility assessed (Bond et al. 2005).[2]

Since the perceptions of employers and employees typically differ (Kossek and Distelberg this volume), we tested whether these differences in access to flexibility among employers of different sizes would hold up if we looked at employee data from the 2002 NSCW.

We found that employees in small organizations did *not* report greater access to various types of flexibility than those in large organizations. We then wondered whether there are differences in the informal

Table 15.3. Smaller and Larger Companies Reporting Provision of Flexibility (percent)

Flexible work arrangements	Allows for some employees	Allows for All or Most Employees			
		Total[a]	Small[b]	Sig.	Large[c]
Periodically change starting and quitting times	68	33	37	**	26
Change starting and quitting times on a daily basis	34	13	17	***	4
Have control over when they take breaks	78	53	52	*	44
Have control/choice over which shifts they work	39	20	21	n.s.	17
Have control over paid and unpaid overtime hours	28	14	16	**	8
Move from full-time to part-time and back again while remaining in the same position or level	53	21	23	**	13
Share jobs	46	13	15	***	4
Work a compressed work week for at least part of the year	39	10	12	n.s.	8
Work part of workweek at home *occasionally*	34	3	3	n.s.	2
Work at home or off-site on a *regular basis*	31	3	4	n.s.	2
Return to work gradually after childbirth or adoption	86	67	66	***	49
Take time off for important personal and family needs without loss of pay	77	60	58	n.s.	63
Phase into retirement	50	28	25	***	14
Take sabbaticals paid or unpaid of six months or more and be to return to a comparable job	49	28	28	*	19

Table 15.3. *(Continued)*

Flexible work arrangements	Allows for some employees	Allows for All or Most Employees			
		Total[a]	Small[b]	Sig.	Large[c]
Take time for education/ training to improve skills	83	55	55	**	42
Take extended career breaks for caregiving or other family/personal responsibilities	73	57	53	n.s.	48
Work part-year on an annual basis	38	16	16	n.s.	12

Source: Bond et al. (2005).

Note: Percentages do not add to 100 percent because response categories are omitted.

a. $n = 1,092$

b. $n = 552$; small companies are those with 50–99 employees

c. $n = 93$; large companies are those with 1,000 or more employees

$*p < .05$; $**p < .01$; $***p < .001$; n.s. = not significant

responsiveness to work and personal/family issues in small versus large organizations. In order to examine these differences, we created scales of five items measuring supervisor support—one measures how supervisors respond when employees are dealing with personal or family issues and four measure a supportive workplace culture (i.e., whether employees have to choose between having a job and having a life) (Bond et al. 2005).

- Only 21 percent of employees in small organizations report a low level of supervisor support compared with 30 percent of those in large organizations.
- Only 16 percent of employees in small organizations report a low level of workplace culture support compared with 26 percent of large organizations.

In sum, the United States' way of relying primarily on a free-market system has its problems, as Jennifer Glass reports, but what of a governmental approach?

Perhaps Surprisingly, There Are Flaws (Though Certainly Not as Large) with a Predominately Governmental Approach

The governmental approach to work-life issues, especially in Europe, is highly touted in the academic literature as well as in the Glass chapter, and rightly so. In fact, Jennifer Glass notes that after the first wave of literature on work-life revealed differential access and selective uptake of work-life policies in the United States, many scholars in the second wave of literature who were exploring the problems of employed caregivers often ended their analyses with a "wistful call for European-style family policy."

But what of the experiences of employees in the European Union and the United States—are European employees more satisfied than those in the United States? Do they experience less work-life conflict? Do they have greater access to work-life assistance?

For many years, we have wanted to compare the *actual* experiences of representative samples of working people around the world and have been looking for opportunities to do so.

We are fortunate that we are beginning to achieve that goal with a project, in which we hope to conduct a comparison of the survey findings from the Fourth European Working Conditions Survey (European Foundation for the Improvement of Living and Working Conditions, 2005) with data from FWI's National Study of the Changing Workforce. The European study covers 31 countries and has sample sizes of approximately 1,000 per country, except in 5 smaller countries where the sample sizes are approximately 600.

To take but one example of this analysis, I will mention control over working hours (see table 15.4). Although the questions on this issue are not identical in the two studies, we have been intrigued by what we have found and think these findings offer some insights into differences between our two populations.

- Unexpectedly, only 7 percent of European respondents report that their working hours are entirely determined by themselves, compared with 15 percent of United States employees who report that they have complete control over the scheduling of their hours.
- On the other end of the spectrum, 65 percent of European employees say that their working hours are set by the company with no possibility of change while 23 percent of United States employees

Table 15.4. Control over Working Times by European and U.S. Employees (percent, *n*)

	n	%	Valid %	Cumulative %
European employees				
How are your working times set?				
They are set by the company with no possibility for changes	13,542	64.5	65.3	65.3
You can choose between several fixed working schedules	2,004	9.5	9.7	74.9
You can adapt your working hours within certain limits	3,773	18.0	18.2	93.1
Your working hours are entirely determined by yourself	1,433	6.8	6.9	100.0
Total	20,753	98.8	100.0	100.0
U.S. employees				
How much control do you have over your working hours?				
Complete	407	14.6	14.6	14.6
A lot	608	21.7	21.8	36.4
Some	700	25.0	25.1	61.5
Very little	437	15.6	15.7	77.2
None	637	22.8	22.8	100.0
Total	2,789	99.8	100.0	100.0

Sources: Bond et al. (2003); European Foundation for the Improvement of Living and Working Conditions, Fourth European Working Conditions Survey (2005).

say that they have no control over the scheduling of their working hours. If one adds those in the United States who say they have little control in the data, this percentage rises to 39 percent.

There have been similar findings in international company-based studies. In *Leaders in a Global Economy,* a study of the 100 top male and the 100 top female executives in 10 multinational companies, FWI, Catalyst, and Boston College found that executives in Western Europe are less likely than executives in North America to say that they have the flexibility they need to manage their work and personal or family lives (Galinsky et al. 2003). Note that all of these regional analyses excluded expatriates and focused only on local nationals. In IBM's 2007 Global Work/Life Survey (unpublished), employees in southern Europe said they were similarly less satisfied with the flexibility they have than employees in other parts of the world did.

Last summer, I was curious about why a group of senior Danish executives wanted to come to the United States to learn about what companies are doing here, since Denmark's public policies are highly admired in the United States. The executives told me why they wanted to come to the United States: they are dissatisfied with how their employees are faring in managing work and family life.

So what is going on? It is obvious that employees in the European Union may *expect* more when it comes to having time for their families and personal lives than in United States, especially in this changing economy, where the United States' brand of overwork is becoming more common internationally (Galinsky et al. 2005).

Gender differences may also play a role. The Leaders in a Global Economy study found that 61 percent of executives in the study are work centric, meaning they prioritize their work over their personal or family lives. Whereas there are no differences between male and female executives in other parts of the world, there are gender differences in Western Europe: 43 percent of male executives in Western Europe, but only 23 percent of the female executives, put work ahead of their personal or family lives "very often."

Regional differences may also play a part, since there is substantial variation among countries and regions in the European Union. FWI will explore these issues further in our analyses.

We Need to Move Beyond an Either/Or Approach to Work-Life Issues Here and Abroad

But the Danish executives had another explanation as well. They have come to the conclusion that they need to move away from an either/or concept of government or the free-market system. Of course, they support their governmental policies and safety net, but they would also like to see companies being more creative in addressing the needs of employees.

I have come to the same conclusion. This may sound obvious when it comes to the United States. No one expects the United States to embrace a government-only approach to work-life issues. But this doesn't seem so obvious to me because a both/and approach calls for reframing everything. It is important to note that I am not talking about the traditional business case nor am I talking about the traditional win-win approach. A both/and approach means that we consider multiple perspectives in how we design, define, and study work-life policies, as well as how we move forward toward change.

If We Are Truly to Heed a Both/And Approach, It Begins with How We *Design* Studies

Because I know them best, I will use examples from Families and Work Institute research to illustrate the both/and approach. In the early 1990s when family leave laws began to proliferate across the states, we designed a study with Ford Foundation funding to assess the impact of various dimensions of state parental leave laws on employers and employees. We looked at the size of the business exemption, the length of the leave offered, and whether there was a temporary disability law in the state that could provide wage replacement to new mothers.

In order to design this study, we asked the governors or the lieutenant governors in each of the four states we were studying to convene the staunchest proponents and the opponents of the new laws to serve as state study advisory groups. We brought them together in each state to ask them what they wanted to know about how the laws were working in their states, then to review the study design, the questionnaires, and the final results (Bond et al. 1991). When the study was released, no one could accuse the findings as being advocacy findings and as such, they had a more powerful impact on deliberations for what became the federal 1993 Family and Medical Leave Act.

A Both/And Approach Also Includes How We *Define* Work-Life Assistance

In a both/and approach, work-life assistance needs to be defined as working for both the employee and the employer. It is true that work-life assistance can clearly favor one group or the other. To use flexibility as an example, there are types of flexibility that favor employers, such as having employees on call—employees who must be ready to come to work *only* when employers need them. Likewise, the employee who leaves work to take care of a family or personal issue *without* making a plan for how his or her work is going to get done represents flexibility that favors the employee.

Although there are areas where there is no common ground, we have taken a both/and approach to defining work-life assistance in a project we are doing with Alfred P. Sloan Foundation funding, called When Work Works. The purpose of this project is to translate research into action. To achieve this, we subcontract with leadership groups comprised of the public and private sectors, which we select through a request for information (RFI) process. Now in 30 communities representing more than one-third of the U.S. population, these leadership groups are providing community education, administering the Alfred P. Sloan Awards for Business Excellence in Workplace Flexibility, and doing media outreach.

How do we take a both/and approach in this project (Galinsky et al. forthcoming)? First, it involves the types of flexibility we assess. We only look at the types of flexibility that have the potential of benefiting both employers and employees—such as flextime, reduced hours, predictability of work hours, part-year work, flex leave, and flex careers. We look at whether these types of flexibility are truly flexible (so-called flexible flex). For example, we look at whether employers offer the opportunity to employees to move from part-time to full-time and back to part-time if they wish, rather than confining employees to a part-time limbo. We also look at whether employers provide leadership opportunities and pro-rated pay and benefits to people who work less than full-time (versus the more typical scenario of decreasing pay but not decreasing workload).

Second, we investigate flexibility from both the employee and employer perspectives. For the awards, we begin by surveying employers about the workplace flexibility they provide. To be considered a finalist, employers have to score in the top 20 percent of employers nationally, using the NSE as a benchmark. We then survey the employees of finalists and require a 40 percent response rate. Two-thirds of the winning score comes from the employees. And we do find that these companies are doing some impressive things. For example among the 247 finalists in 2006, (1) 87 percent of employees say they are allowed to choose their own starting and quitting times on a period basis and 59 percent report access to daily flextime, and (2) 60 percent are allowed to work at home occasionally and 33 percent, regularly. And interestingly enough, there are not the wide gaps in employee and employer perception about what is offered that one typically finds in the literature.

We go beyond access to examine employee usage—as another aspect of the both/and approach. In 2006, we found that 86 to 88 percent of employees with access to flextime use it. And 41 percent of those with access to flexplace work at home on a regular basis.

Finally, of equal importance to a both/and approach, we not only examine access to and use of various types of flexibility, we also look at supervisor support and the supportiveness of the workplace culture. We draw on questions from the NSCW so we can benchmark the findings with this national dataset. For example while 39 percent of employees in the 2002 NSCW feel that there would be jeopardy in using the flexible time and leave policies their employers offer, far fewer, 19 percent of employees in the finalist organizations, report jeopardy. Still this represents one in five employees in good companies—a high percentage.

I am pleased to report that in the forthcoming 2008 NSCW, we parallel this kind of holistic view by examining access to, use of, and demand for many types of flexibility so that we can create better national benchmarks.

The both/and approach applies not only to the selection of variables we look at in research, but to the words we use to describe our work. For example, the use of the word "accommodation" is commonplace in reference to work-life assistance and appears in the Jennifer Glass chapter. Accommodation does not imply a mutual benefit, but rather a favor or a perk.

And this approach also includes who is considered for work-life assistance. Although families are clearly responsible for caregiving and are, thus, typically the focus in the academic literature, a both/and approach, as progressive employers have long realized, must include *all* workers because all workers have needs. In addition, universality gains the greatest traction and creates the least tension among employees.

A Both/And Approach Needs to Extend Beyond Work-Life Assistance to Include the Quality of the Workplace Environment

Jennifer Glass and other speakers at this symposium question the typical business case for work-life assistance. Will work-life assistance truly affect absenteeism, engagement, turnover intention, and other work-related issues?

I think this is the right question. I don't see work-life assistance in a vacuum. If employers provide work-life assistance but otherwise have terrible places to work, why would we expect work-life assistance to have a strong positive effect? This is similar to the point that Kossek and Distelberg make in their chapter and Forrest Briscoe makes in his discussant remarks (this volume). But our definition extends beyond the usual type of work environment considered here.

We are increasingly exploring a number of variables that constitute effective workplaces, variables such as supervisor and coworker support for job success, learning opportunities, job security, input into management decisionmaking, other fringe benefits, and so forth (Bond, Galinsky, and Hill 2004; Jacob et al. 2008). I believe that work-life must be seen as *one* component of an effective workplace. Starting with an effective workplace and then considering work-life makes more sense than simply focusing on work-life by itself. That is why experiments like ROWE (results-only work environment) at Best Buy are focused on how employees work, not work-life, as described in the Moen, Kelly, and Chermack chapter in this volume. And that is why IBM is framing its "people strategy" approach as the "new normal" in working today, not as work-life.

Correlations show that when employees have access to effective workplaces, both they and their employers can benefit. And perhaps unexpectedly, some of these relationships are stronger for low-wage and low-income employees than mid- and high-wage and -income employees (Bond and Galinsky 2006a). For example, access to more learning opportunities, more involvement in management decisionmaking, more generous fringe benefits, more supervisor support for managing personal/family issues, and more flexibility are linked more strongly to job satisfaction for low-wage and low-income employees than for their more advantaged counterparts (see tables 15.5 and 15.6).

Obviously, such research needs to go beyond correlations. And I would also strongly argue that since different employees value different components of an effective workplace, this type of research needs to go beyond a "one size fits all" effective workplace approach.

A Both/And Approach Needs to Involve Community Leaders

Jennifer Glass argues that the changing values of employees and the electorate could be a lever for change, and I agree with this notion. Progressive employers, the kind of employers that instituted work-life assistance in this

Table 15.5. Workplace Flexibility Outcomes of Most Direct Importance to Employers, for Low-Wage and Low-Income Employees (LWI) vs. Mid- and High-Wage and -Income Employees

Drivers of employee effectiveness	Outcomes of Importance to Employers			
	Greater job satisfaction	Stronger job commitment/ engagement	Less negative spillover from home to work (that impairs productivity)	More likely retention
More job autonomy			LWI ↗	
More learning opportunities on the job	LWI ↗			
Employer-provided education/training programs to enhance job skills				LWI ↗
More supervisor support for job success				
More coworker team support for job success		LWI ↗	M&HWI ↗	M&HWI ↗
More trust in managers				
More involvement in management decisionmaking	LWI ↗			
More generous fringe benefits	LWI ↗			LWI ↗
More supervisor support to manage work, personal, and family life	LWI ↗		LWI ↗	
More coworker support to manage work, personal, and family life				
Work-life culture that is more supportive of personal and family life			LWI ↗	
More flexible workplace	LWI ↗		LWI ↗	
Greater overall workplace effectiveness	LWI ↗			

Source: Bond and Galinsky (2006a).

LWI = low-wage and -income employees

M&HWI = mid- and high-wage and -income employees

Table 15.6. Workplace Flexibility Outcomes of Most Direct Importance to Employees, for Low-Wage and Low-Income Employees (LWI) vs. Mid- and High-Wage and -Income Employees

| | Outcomes of Importance to Employees | | |
Drivers of employee effectiveness	Less negative spillover from work to home	Greater life satisfaction	Better mental health
More job autonomy	LWI ↗		
More learning opportunities on the job	LWI ↗	M&HWI ↗	
Employer-provided education/ training programs to enhance job skills		LWI ↗	LWI ↗
More supervisor support for job success	LWI ↗		
More coworker team support for job success			
More trust in managers			
More involvement in management decisionmaking	LWI ↗		
More generous fringe benefits			LWI ↗
More supervisor support to manage work, personal, and family life	LWI ↗		
More coworker support to manage work, personal, and family life	LWI ↗	M&HWI ↗	
Work-life culture that is more supportive of personal and family life			
More flexible workplace	LWI ↗		LWI ↗
Greater overall workplace effectiveness	LWI ↗		

Source: Bond and Galinsky (2006a).

LWI = low-wage and -income employees

M&HWI = mid- and high-wage and -income employees

country, are quite attuned to generational differences (Harrington 2007). They are concerned about younger workers who are more family or dual centric than boomers (Families and Work Institute 2004). An increasing number of employers are concerned about retaining talent as the workforce ages, as Smyer and Pitt-Catsouphes (this volume) point out. So this approach puts some responsibility on the individual employee and employers for raising and responding to these issues.

I think that a both/and approach to research and public policy extends beyond the relationship between an employer and employees. It also includes community leaders. In When Work Works, as I have stated, we require participating communities to create and convene a core leadership community coalition of leaders representing employers, government, and the voluntary sectors to oversee their work.

One could rightly argue that involving several hundred employers, as we have done thus far in When Work Works, is a drop in the bucket, and we would agree. However, we believe that involving community leaders from governments, educational institutions, nonprofits, and employers has the possibility of multiplying these effects to create greater momentum and will be a lever for change. And as Jennifer Glass notes, we are taking a local-to-national approach—because we, like Jennifer Glass, see that much of the change in the United States is bubbling up that way. This is not to say that a national-to-local approach is not also important.

We have found from the RFI process that communities have multiple reasons for wanting to be involved in When Work Works:

- to recruit and retain a multigenerational workforce, especially younger professionals and entrepreneurs (Milwaukee, Birmingham);
- to recruit and retain more women in leadership positions (Salt Lake City, Providence);
- to respond to changing community economic conditions—for example, dealing with the economic downturns in the rust belt, yet wanting to be a good place to work (Detroit) or dealing with the inequities between the haves and the have-nots and reducing poverty in order to create a better community (Savannah); and
- to go greener and reduce traffic congestion (Long Island, Houston).

A both/and approach to bringing about change also involves convening disparate and sometimes "warring" groups and seeing if it is possible to find common ground to affect public policy change. This is the approach that Chai Feldblum (this volume) has described and is using to craft and advance more innovative policy proposals than have surfaced in the recent past.

Finally, a both/and approach involves *seeding* change experiments that are rigorously evaluated. FWI is experimenting with this strategy in the Supporting Work Project with funding from the Ford Foundation. Through a request for proposals, we identified 11 groups around the country that are using employers to connect lower-wage employees to at least two publicly funded work supports (like the earned income tax credit, Food Stamps, the State Children's Health Insurance Program, Child Care Assistance, and others). Nine of these are local and two are national.

We require each site to have a core coalition and diverse leadership group to oversee its work. The sites are working with employers that represent the types of job sites where most low-wage employees work in their communities—restaurants, hotels, retail stores, child care centers, educational organizations, and local governments, to name a few. Each site also differs somewhat in the strategies being used, thus providing an opportunity to conduct a qualitative and quantitative evaluation of what works and what does not. We are using a pre-post design with common measures of both employer and employee outcomes. After this exploratory evaluation, we hope to test the most promising practices with a random assignment design. It is also our expectation that the leadership groups will become advocates for publicly funded work supports for the lower-wage workforce.

In Conclusion

As the times change, so too must our approaches. Arlene Skolnick (2001) has argued that predictable patterns have emerged as the economy shifted in recent history, such as from an agrarian to an industrial base. She says that when expectations no longer fit realities in how we live and work, there is a period of upheaval, of wanting to return to the nostalgically remembered past, of turmoil, and of polarizing and even harshly blaming debate, until a new cultural common sense emerges. She further argues that the shift from the industrial to a global service/knowledge economy is just such a time.

A new time calls for new ways to work. My view is that these new ways need to move beyond "either/or" to "both/and" in how work-life policies are conceived and how research is defined and described, as well as in the strategies for bringing about change.

NOTES

1. Stephanie Amour, "Work or Stay at Home: It's Still a Quandary," *USA Today,* October 2007, 3B.

2. Differences between small and large employers in the 2008 National Study of Employers largely disappeared. For further information, see Galinsky, Bond, and Sakai (2008).

REFERENCES

Bond, James T., and Ellen Galinsky. 2006a. *How Can Employers Increase the Productivity and Retention of Entry-Level, Hourly Employees?* New York: Families and Work Institute.

———. 2006b. *What Workplace Flexibility Is Available to Entry-Level, Hourly Employees?* New York: Families and Work Institute.

Bond, James T., Ellen Galinsky, and E. Jeffrey Hill. 2004. *When Work Works: Flexibility—A Critical Ingredient in Creating an Effective Workplace.* New York: Families and Work Institute.

Bond, James T., Ellen Galinsky, Stacy S. Kim, and Erin Brownfield. 2005. *2005 National Study of Employers.* New York: Families and Work Institute.

Bond, James T., Cynthia A. Thompson, Ellen Galinsky, and David J. Prottas. 2003. *Highlights of the National Study of the Changing Workforce.* New York: Families and Work Institute.

Bond, James T., Ellen Galinsky, Michelle Lord, Graham L. Staines, and Karen R. Brown. 1991. *Beyond the Parental Leave Debate: The Impact of Laws in Four States.* New York: Families and Work Institute.

Families and Work Institute. 2004. "Generation and Gender in the Workplace." American Business Collaboration Issue Brief. New York: Families and Work Institute.

Galinsky, Ellen. 1999. *Ask the Children: What America's Children Really Think about Working Parents.* New York: William Morrow and Company.

Galinsky, Ellen, James T. Bond, and E. Jeffrey Hill. 2004. *A Status Report on Workplace Flexibility: Who Has It? Who Wants It? What Difference Does It Make?* New York: Families and Work Institute.

Galinsky, Ellen, James T. Bond, and Kelly Sakai. 2008. *2008 National Study of Employers.* New York: Families and Work Institute.

Galinsky, Ellen, Kelly Sakai, S. Eby, James T. Bond, and Tyler Wigton. Forthcoming. "Employer Provided Workplace Flexibility." In *Workplace Flexibility: Realigning 20th Century Jobs to 21st Century Workers,* edited by Kathleen Christensen and Barbara Schneider. Mahwah, NJ: Erlbaum.

Galinsky, Ellen, James T. Bond, Stacy S. Kim, Lois Backon, Erin Brownfield, and Kelly Sakai. 2005. *Overwork in America: When the Way We Work Becomes Too Much.* New York: Families and Work Institute.

Galinsky, Ellen, Kimberlee Salmond, James T. Bond, Marcia B. Kropf, Meredith Moore, and Brad Harrington. 2003. *Leaders in a Global Economy: A Study of Executive Women and Men.* New York: Families and Work Institute.

Harrington, Brad. 2007. *The Work-Life Evolution Study.* Boston, MA: Boston College Center for Work and Family.

Hoffman, Lois, and Lisa Youngblade. 1999. *Mothers at Work: Effects on Children's Well-Being.* New York: Cambridge University Press.

Jacob, Jenet I., James T. Bond, Ellen Galinsky, and E. Jeffery Hill. 2008. "Six Critical Ingredients in Creating an Effective Workplace." *Psychologist-Manager Journal* 11(1): 141–61.

National Institute of Child Health and Human Development Early Child Care Research Network. 2003a. "Families Matter—Even For Kids in Child Care." *Journal of Developmental and Behavioral Pediatrics* 24: 58–62.

———. 2003b. "Early Child Care and Mother–Child Interaction from 36 Months through First Grade." *Infant Behavior and Development* 26: 345–70.

Skolnick, Arlene. 2001. *A Time of Transition*. New York: Families and Work Institute.

Zigler, Edward, and Matia Finn-Stevenson. 2007. "From Research to Policy and Practice: The School of the 21st Century." *American Journal of Orthopsychiatry* 77(2): 175–81.

16

Work-Life Policies
The Changing Landscape
of Aging and Work

Michael A. Smyer and Marcie Pitt-Catsouphes

G lass (this volume) provides a thoughtful review of work-life policy issues, emphasizing family formation and early phases of family life. In this chapter, we will highlight four themes that provide a context for considering the gaps in and opportunities for work-life research: the aging workforce, the changing nature of work, the changing nature of families, and the key role that states will play in shaping work-life responses to these trends. To summarize our argument: work-family research must reflect developments in the workforce, workplace, family, and policy arenas. We suggest that progress in work-life research, policy, and practice requires taking each of these elements into account.

The Aging of the United States Workforce

The United States is an aging nation in an aging world (United Nations 2007). As the United Nations recently noted, developed countries, like the United States, are in the third stage of global aging, "rapid aging" that "may pose particular challenges for public policy, as major adjustments in a variety of spheres are required to cope with a declining labour force and an increasing demand for health care and old-age support" (2). Figure 16.1 depicts the now-familiar aging of the United States population.

Figure 16.1. U.S. Population 65 and Older, 1950–2085 (percent)

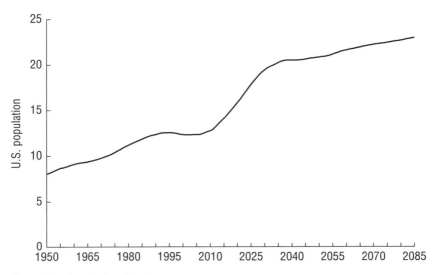

Source: Board of Trustees (2007).
Note: Projections based on the intermediate assumptions of the 2007 Trustees Reports.

David Walker of the U.S. Government Accountability Office (2007) recently reviewed the implications of these trends for the United States economy and for older workers. He noted that the United States is in the midst of a long-term decline in the growth of its labor force, a trend that began in the late 1970s. While our economy has historically experienced labor force growth at a rate of between 1 and 2 percent per year, during the coming decades we can expect growth rates well below 1 percent for the next 60 years. (See figure 16.2.) One implication is that we can expect an older labor force. For example, the Bureau of Labor Statistics projected that by 2008 over half of the United States workforce would be 40 years of age or older (Toosi 2004).

Thus far, we have been considering the aging of the workforce from a societal view. We are also witnessing significant changes in individuals' perspectives on aging and work. Over the last 25 years, we have witnessed a steady increase in the men's and women's labor force participation rates after age 55 (Clark et al. 2004). Simply put, more people are working later in life. As Cahill, Giandrea, and Quinn (2006) noted, higher percentages of men and women have stayed in the labor force for a longer

Figure 16.2. U.S. Labor Force Growth, 1970–2080 (percentage change)

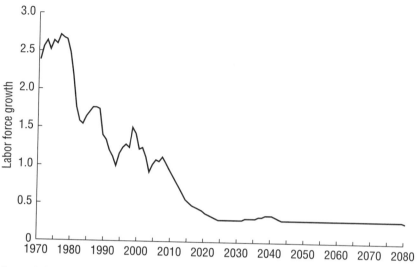

Source: U.S. Government Accountability Office (2007).

Note: Percentage change is calculated as a centered five-year moving average of projections based on the intermediate assumptions of the 2007 Trustees Reports.

period of time. For example, the Urban Institute (Toder et al. 2007) recently estimated significant increases in labor force participation rates for both men and women (see table 16.1) over the ages of 55.

These patterns have implications for employers and employees. For employers, they are an indication that near-term growth in the United

Table 16.1. Labor Force Participation Rates and Percentage Increase for Men and Women 55 and Older

Age	Increase for men, 1992–2007	Men participating, 2007	Increase for women 1988–2007	Women participating, 2007
55–61	7	76	45	64
62–64	24	51	72	43
65–69	55	34	100	26

Source: Johnson et al. (2007) analysis of the March 2007 Current Population Survey.

States labor force may come among older workers (those 55 and above) (Horrigan 2004). For employees, these trends reflect older workers' desire to stay in the labor force past traditional retirement ages—either because they have to work (for health benefits and income) or because they want to work (for social connectedness and a sense of purpose) (Smyer and Pitt-Catsouphes 2007).

The changing workforce demographics have an additional note-worthy element: increasing generational diversity (Pitt-Catsouphes and Smyer 2007). Some have suggested that looming intergenerational conflict is a potential "workforce crisis" (Dychtwald, Erickson, and Morison 2006; Lancaster and Stillman 2002). Others suggest that the level and extent of intergenerational conflict may not be widespread (Burke 2004; Pitt-Catsouphes and Smyer 2007; Shen, Pitt-Catsouphes, and Smyer 2007; Sweet and Moen 2006).

Recent data from James and her colleagues (James, Swanberg, and McKechnie 2007) reflect the complexity of the issues. They surveyed employees in 388 stores and 37 districts of a national retail chain, Citisales (a pseudonym). Using items from Victor W. Marshall's Issues of an Aging Workforce study, they asked employees to assess the characteristics of workers 55 and over on a scale of 1 to 5.

As reflected in figure 16.3, different generations of employees had different views, with the older generations viewing older workers most positively.

James and her colleagues summarize the issue well:

> Managers have a complex balancing act to meet the expectations and needs of a multigenerational workforce. Many employees in the older generations still want and need training, development, and recognition for their work in terms of promotion. However, employees from the youngest generation can become discouraged if they see all the opportunities and promotions going to the workers from the older generations. (James et al. 2007)

Until now, there has been very little research on the elements that contribute to effective management of the multigenerational workforce.

The Changing Nature of Work

For more than a decade, researchers and social commentators have documented the changing nature of work in the American economy (e.g., Bluestein 2006). Several have noted the "flattening" of organizations, the increasing complexity of workflow systems (e.g., Devine et al. 1999), the

Figure 16.3. Retail Employees' Perceptions of Workers 55 and Older, by Generation Surveyed

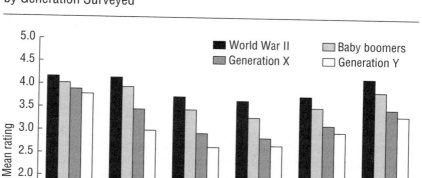

Source: James et al. (2007).

"flattening" world competition (Friedman 2005), and the impact of technology on the organization of collaborations (e.g., Bell and Kozlowski 2002; Czaja 2001; Czaja and Moen 2004).

In addition, many have emphasized that collaborative work is an important element of successful organizations (e.g., Marshall 1995). Kozlowski and Ilgen (2006) recently completed a comprehensive review of research on collaborative work and teams. Unfortunately, they did not consider the impact of changing workforce demographics in their review (Smyer and Pitt-Catsouphes forthcoming). They noted that there are many unanswered questions regarding how aging might affect effective team functioning and how or if age composition affects team processes and outcomes.

While work processes have changed considerably during the last quarter century, the demands that work places on employees have also changed. Johnson and his colleagues (Johnson, Mermin, and Resseger 2007) have documented the percentage of workers facing specific demands at work. For example, in 2006, a small minority of workers faced high general

Table 16.2. Job Demands Faced by Workers, 2006 (percent)

Job demand	Workers facing
High general physical demands	7
Any general physical demands	46
High cognitive ability	35
Some cognitive ability	69

Source: Johnson et al. (2007), based on March 2006 Current Population Survey matched to O*Net.

physical demands at work. In contrast, more than one-third were in roles that required high cognitive ability. (See table 16.2.)

Equally important, Johnson and his colleagues have documented the significant change in workplace demands over the last 25 years. As noted in table 16.3, there has been a dramatic increase in demands for cognitive skills, interpersonal skills, and updating of knowledge and skills.

Again, there is a rich opportunity to assess the combined impact of these work demands and the demographic shifts noted earlier on both work and family functioning.

The Changing Nature of Families

Consider the following case manager's report:

This is a complex case involving family conflict, dementia, homelessness, and transfer of assets. Mr. Lear suffers from the delusion that he is still "King" despite having divested himself completely of his assets in the kingdom. Lear's initial care plan assumed dependency on two adult daughters

Table 16.3. Workers Facing Job Demands, 1971 and 2006 (percent)

Job demand	Workers facing, 1971	Workers facing, 2006	Change
Any general physical demand	57	46	−19
High cognitive ability	26	35	35
Interpersonal skills	25	35	36
Any stress	39	44	14
Updating/using knowledge	11	18	70

Source: Johnson et al. (2007), based on March 2006 Current Population Survey matched to O*Net.

(Goneril and Regan), who have now refused to provide support. Probable elder abuse apparent here. Due to mental incompetence, client has a surrogate decision maker (Edgar). Efforts are currently underway to locate estranged youngest daughter (Cordelia). Because Lear's assets were improperly transferred, we recommend vigorous efforts at asset recovery if he is to have access to community-based services needed.

Respectfully submitted,
W. Shakespeare

Moody's (2007) tongue-in-cheek case write-up reminds us that family caregiving issues have long been a concern. But Moody's (and Shakespeare's) case reflects a simpler time.

Family structure and functioning have been changing at the same time that workplace demands have been in transition. Bengtson and his colleagues recently summarized the trends:

> As a consequence of population aging and globalization, families are changing in both form and meaning. Longer lives and fewer children, high divorce rates and the increase in single parent families, the movement of mothers into the labor force and greater economic insecurity—all have profoundly affected the direction and experience of individual lives. (Putney, Bengtson, and Wakeman 2007)

Rothausen-Vange (2005) reminds us of the diversity of family forms that are encompassed by the term "family," ranging from the "assumed normal family" to single parents to extended, multigenerational kin networks. Van Eeden-Moorefield and Demo (2007) also acknowledge the diversity of family forms and remind us that family diversity includes both structural dimensions (e.g., race/ethnicity) as well as process dimensions (e.g., communication, support).

Two aspects of contemporary family structure and functioning illustrate their relevance for contemporary work-family research: the "beanpole" family structure and caregiving for older relatives. Together, these aspects affect employees' family resources, demands, and concerns for work-family balance.

Bengtson, Rosenthal, and Burton (1990) coined the term "beanpole" to reflect demographic change: "a family structure with a long, thin shape, having more family generations alive than in the past but fewer members in each generation" (Putney et al. 2007). This structural change has been accompanied by a change in the functions that families must play across generations. While contemporary families were changing, the risks of aging were also being shifted increasingly to the individual and her family (Hudson 2007).

These trends may have their largest work-family impact in the area of caregiving for dependents—for both grandchildren and older relatives (e.g., Neal and Hammer 2007; Parrott, Mills, and Bengtson 2000). We will draw on two examples to illustrate the importance of these issues in work-family research.

Recent analyses suggest the scope of adult caregiving (Pandya 2005): there are an estimated 44 million caregivers 18 and older providing care to adults 18 and older; this is approximately 21 percent of the adult population. More than half of these caregivers (59 percent) are currently working or have worked while providing care. The majority of these working caregivers (62 percent) have made adjustments to their work lives to accommodate their caregiving responsibilities. They have used a variety of strategies: reporting late to work, leaving early, taking time off or a leave of absence, or leaving the workforce entirely. These accommodations have not come easily—29 percent of caregivers report that balancing work and family responsibility is one of their major unmet needs.

Shen (2007) recently analyzed data from the National Study of the Changing Workforce (Bond et al. 2002) to assess rates of caregiving among employees at different career stages. His results are informative. (See figure 16.4.)

Note that the percentage of employees involved in caregiving for elderly relatives grows across the lifespan. Of course, those at younger ages may also be providing care for children at the same time.

Havens and McNamara (2007) assessed the impact of one form of workplace flexibility—temporal flexibility—on caregivers. Analyzing data from the Health and Retirement Study (Juster and Suzman 1995), they found that caregivers with temporal flexibility did not use that flexibility to provide additional care.[1] Instead, they spent more time on housekeeping, other routine tasks, and volunteering.

These studies illustrate the types of issues work-family research should increasingly undertake in an aging society.

The Increasing Importance of States

The demographic transition of the United States will be played out at different rates in different regions of the country and in different industry sectors. For example, in 2000, 25 percent or more of the population was

Figure 16.4. Employees with Elder Caregiving Duties during the Past Year, by Age Group (percent)

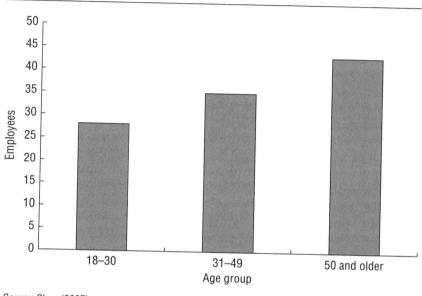

Source: Shen (2007).

55 and over in only four states. By 2010, this will be the pattern in more than three-fifths of the states (Pitt-Catsouphes et al. 2008).

In addition, some states (e.g., Montana, New Mexico, and Wyoming) will experience the greatest rates of increase in their populations 55 to 74 by 2010. Thus, the rates of demographic transition will vary across the states.

At the same time, there is significant variability in the age structure of different industries and occupations (Pitt-Catsouphes et al. 2008). For example, four industries have 45 percent or more of their workforce between the ages of 45 and 61: utilities (53 percent), equipment and appliance manufacturing (48 percent), transportation equipment manufacturing (46 percent), and machinery manufacturing (45 percent). Similarly, there are a handful of occupational roles with 45 percent of their workforce ages 45 and above: management (53 percent), community and social service occupations (49 percent), legal occupations (48 percent), business and financial operations occupations (45 percent), health care practitioner and technical occupations (45 percent), and life, physical, and social science occupations (45 percent) (Pitt-Catsouphes et al. 2008). Of course, these demographic and occupational patterns vary from state to state, providing different challenges and opportunities for each state.

States' policy approaches in two areas can significantly affect work-family functioning: workforce policies and community-based long-term care. States approach workforce issues with a dual perspective: as major employers and as key players in their region's economic development (Pitt-Catsouphes and Shulkin 2007). One example will illustrate the state's role as an employer. We recently interviewed a university president in Colorado about the state of her campus's preparedness for an aging workforce. She quickly responded that recent changes in the state's approach to formerly retired faculty and staff had made a significant difference. Under current state legislation, retirees can be hired for up to 110 days per year without jeopardizing their state-sponsored pensions. This policy change has enabled her to maintain expertise in strategic roles by providing project-specific hiring opportunities. The combination of flexible work options, state policies attuned to changing demographics, and campus leadership poised to retain talent across the lifespan means that this campus can move ahead in several strategic areas.

States are also taking the lead in crafting options for community-based long-term care. Driven in part because of increasing concerns about Medicaid funding in long-term care, states have taken advantage of new options for community-based caregiving. One notable example—the Cash and Counseling Demonstration Project (CCDE)—illustrates this theme (Carlson et al. 2007; Mahoney et al. 2006; Shen et al. 2008). CCDE was undertaken in three states (New Jersey, Arkansas, and Florida) to assess the impact of providing more control over the details of care: who provides it, when, and how. By randomly assigning clients to usual care or the cash-and-counseling approach, researchers were able to document that the CCDE program led to better client outcomes and to no significant cost differences. Based on this evidence, the program was expanded to a total of 15 states.

The states' increasing prominence provides a number of possible policy-relevant research areas. For example, it will be important to assess the impact of workforce policy developments in two ways: changing rates of workplace engagement for older adults and older employees' caregiving. To date, there has been no research linking these themes.

Conclusion

Work-family research has much to contribute to the changing workplace and workforce of the 21st century. We have highlighted four changes that will directly affect the structure and function of work-life balance for employers and employees. Thus far, contemporary work-life research has not adequately reflected these changes. For example, Drago (2007) emphasizes the interplay of family structure, caregiving, and public policy at the federal level. This is an important integration, but he, like Glass (this volume), focuses primarily on caregiving for young children. In addition, he emphasizes federal policy initiatives.

More work is needed on the impact of aging on work functioning and balancing work-family concerns across the lifespan. Similarly, more work is needed on the differential effects of various work demands (e.g., physical skills, cognitive skills, interpersonal skills) on work-life issues. At the same time, states are already providing naturally occurring experiments in approaching workforce issues as both policy laboratories and as employers.

The path ahead requires asking conditional questions: under which conditions, for which type of employees and family constellations, will which type of workplace and public policies have which types of results? This grammatically challenging sentence reflects the differentiated view that contemporary workplaces and contemporary families require. Fortunately, as Professor Glass's work suggests, the field is up to the challenge.

NOTE

The authors appreciate the support of the Alfred P. Sloan Foundation to the Center on Aging and Work.

1. Tay K. McNamara, the Center on Aging and Work/Workplace Flexibility at Boston College, 2007, personal communication with the authors.

REFERENCES

Bell, Bradford S., and Steve W. J. Kozlowski. 2002. "A Typology of Virtual Teams: Implications for Effective Leadership." *Group and Organization Management* 27: 14–49.

Bengtson, Vern, Carolyn Rosenthal, and Linda Burton. 1990. "Families and Aging: Diversity and Heterogeneity." In *Handbook of Aging and the Social Sciences*, edited by Robert H. Binstock and Linda K. George (263–87). San Diego: Academic Press.

Bluestein, David L. 2006. *The Psychology of Working: A New Perspective for Career Development, Counseling, and Public Policy.* Mahwah, NJ: Erlbaum.

Board of Trustees of the Federal Old-Age and Survivors Insurance and Federal Disability Insurance Trust Funds, Social Security Administration. 2007. *The 2007 Annual Report of the Board of Trustees of the Federal Old-Age and Survivors Insurance and Federal Disability Insurance Trust Funds.* Washington, DC: U.S. Government Printing Office.

Bond, James T., Cynthia Thompson, Ellen Galinsky, and David Prottas. 2002. *The National Study of the Changing Workforce.* New York: Families and Work Institute.

Burke, Mary E. 2004. *Generational Differences Survey Report.* Alexandria, VA: SHRM Research.

Cahill, Kevin E., Michael D. Giandrea, and Joseph F. Quinn. 2006. "Retirement Patterns from Career Employment." *Gerontologist* 46(4): 514–23.

Carlson, Barbara L., Leslie Foster, Stacy B. Dale, and Randall Brown. 2007. "Effects of Cash and Counseling on Personal Care and Well-Being." *Health Services Research* 42: 467–87.

Clark, Robert L., Richard V. Burkhauser, Marilyn Moon, Joseph F. Quinn, and Timothy M. Smeeding. 2004. *The Economics of an Aging Society.* Malden, MA: Blackwell Publishing.

Czaja, Sara J. 2001. "Technological Change and the Older Worker." In *Handbook of the Psychology of Aging,* edited by James E. Birren and K. Warner Schaie (547–68). San Diego: Academic Press.

Czaja, Sara J., and Phyllis Moen. 2004. "Technology and Employment." In *Technology for Adaptive Aging: Report and Papers,* edited by R. Pew and S. Van Hemel (150–78). Washington, DC: National Academies Press.

Devine, Dennis J., Laura D. Clayton, Jennifer L. Phillips, Benjamin B. Dunford, and Sarah B. Melner. 1999. "Teams in Organizations: Prevalence, Characteristics, and Effectiveness." *Small Group Research* 30: 678–711.

Drago, Robert W. 2007. *Striking a Balance: Work, Family, Life.* Boston: Economic Affairs Bureau, Dollars and Sense.

Dychtwald, Ken, Tamara J. Erickson, and Robert Morison. 2006. *Workforce Crisis: How to Beat the Coming Shortage of Skills and Talent.* Boston: Harvard Business School Press.

Friedman, Thomas L. 2005. *The World is Flat: A Brief History of the 21st Century.* Waterville: Thorndike Press.

Havens, John, and Tay K. McNamara. 2007. "Civic Engagement: Volunteering, Dynamics and Flexible Work Options." Issue Brief 7. Chestnut Hill, MA: The Center on Aging and Work/Workplace Flexibility at Boston College.

Horrigan, Michael W. 2004. "Employment Projections to 2012." *Monthly Labor Review* 127(2): 3–22.

Hudson, Robert B. 2007. "The Political Paradoxes of Thinking Outside the Life-Cycle Boxes." In *Challenges of an Aging Society: Ethical Dilemmas, Political Issues,* edited by Rachel Pruchno and Michael Smyer (268–84). Baltimore: Johns Hopkins University Press.

James, Jacquelyn B., Jennifer E. Swanberg, and Sharon P. McKechnie. 2007. "Generational Differences in Perceptions of Older Workers' Capabilities." Issue Brief 12. Chestnut Hill, MA: The Center on Aging and Work/Workplace Flexibility at Boston College.

Johnson, Richard, Gordon B. T. Mermin, and Matthew Resseger. 2007. *Employment at Older Ages and the Changing Nature of Work.* Washington, DC: AARP Public Policy Institute.

Juster, F. Thomas, and Richard Suzman. 1995. "An Overview of the Health and Retirement Study." *Journal of Human Resources* 30(Supplement): S7–S56.

Kozlowski, Steve W. J., and Daniel R. Ilgen. 2006. "Enhancing the Effectiveness of Work Groups and Teams." *Psychological Science in the Public Interest* 7: 77–124.

Lancaster, Lynne C., and David Stillman. 2002. *When Generations Collide.* New York: Collins.

Marshall, Edward M. 1995. *Transforming the Way We Work: The Power of the Collaborative Workplace.* New York: American Management Association.

Mahoney, Kevin J., Lori Simon-Rusinowitz, Kristen Simone, and Karen Zgoda. 2006. "Cash and Counseling: A Promising Option for Consumer Direction of Home and Community-Based Services and Supports." *Care Management Journals* 7(4): 199–204.

Moody, H. Rick. 2007. "Aging, Generational Opposition, and the Future of the Family." In *Challenges of an Aging Society: Ethical Dilemmas, Political Issues,* edited by Rachel A. Pruchno and Michael A. Smyer. Baltimore: Johns Hopkins University Press.

Neal, Margret B., and Leslie B. Hammer. 2007. *Working Couples Caring for Children and Aging Parents: Effects on Work and Well-Being.* Mahwah, NJ: Erlbaum.

Pandya, Sheel. 2005. *Caregiving in the United States.* National Alliance for Caregiving and AARP. Bethesda: National Alliance for Caregiving.

Parrott, Tonya M., Terry L. Mills, and Vern L. Bengtson. 2000. "The United States: Population Demographics, Changes in the Family, and Social Policy Challenges." In *Aging in East and West: Families, States, and the Elderly,* edited by Vern L. Bengtson, Kyong-Dong Kim, George C. Myers, and Ki-Soo Eun (191–224). New York: Springer Publishing.

Pitt-Catsouphes, Marcie, and Sandee Shulkin. 2007. "On Your Mark, Get Ready . . . Unfreeze." Boston: National Conference of State Legislatures.

Pitt-Catsouphes, Marcie, and Michael A. Smyer. 2007. "The 21st Century Multigenerational Workplace." Issue Brief 9. Chestnut Hill, MA: The Center on Aging and Work/Workplace Flexibility at Boston College.

Pitt-Catsouphes, Marcie, Sandee Shulkin, Chelsea Lettieri, Michelle Wong, Tay McNamara, and Michael A. Smyer. 2008. "Changing Age Demographics: Opportunity for Visionary State Leadership." State Policy Brief Series. Chestnut Hill, MA: The Center on Aging and Work/Workplace Flexibility at Boston College.

Putney, Norella M., Vern L. Bengtson, and Melanie A. Wakeman. 2007. "The Family and the Future: Challenges, Prospects, and Resilience." In *Challenges of an Aging Society: Ethical Dilemmas, Political Issues,* edited by Rachel Pruchno and Michael A. Smyer. Baltimore: Johns Hopkins University Press.

322   Future Directions for Research and Policies

Rothausen-Vange, Teresa J. 2005. "Family Diversity." Boston: Sloan Work and Family Research Network at Boston College. http://wfnetwork.bc.edu/encyclopedia_template.php?id=1138. (Accessed September 25, 2007.)

Shen, Ce. 2007. Unpublished analysis of data from the National Study of the Changing Workforce. Chestnut Hill, MA: The Center on Aging and Work/Workplace Flexibility at Boston College.

Shen, Ce, Marcie Pitt-Catsouphes, and Michael A. Smyer. 2007. "Today's Multigenerational Workforce: A Proposition of Value." Issue Brief 10. Chestnut Hill, MA: The Center on Aging and Work/Workplace Flexibility at Boston College.

Shen, Ce, Michael A. Smyer, Kevin J. Mahoney, Dawn M. Loughlin, Lori Simon-Rusinowitz, and Ellen K. Mahoney. 2008. "Does Mental Illness Affect Consumer Direction of Community-Based Care? Lessons from the Arkansas Cash and Counseling Program." *Gerontologist* 48: 93–104.

Smyer, Michael A., and Marcie Pitt-Catsouphes. 2007. "The Meanings of Work for Older Workers." *Generations* XXXI(1): 23–30.

———. Forthcoming. "Collaborative Work: What's Age Got to Do With It?" In *Aging and Work,* edited by Sara J. Czaja and Joseph Sharit. Baltimore: Johns Hopkins University Press.

Sweet, Stephen, and Phyllis Moen. 2006. "Advancing a Career Focus on Work and the Family: Insights from the Life Course Perspective." In *The Work and Family Handbook: Multi-disciplinary Perspectives and Approaches,* edited by Marcie Pitt-Catsouphes, Ellen E. Kossek, and Stephen A. Sweet (189–208). Mahwah, NJ: Erlbaum.

Toder, Eric, Richard W. Johnson, Gordon Mermin, and Serena Lei. 2007. "Capitalizing on the Economic Value of Older Adults' Work: An Urban Institute Roundtable." Retirement Policy Program Occasional Paper 9. Washington, DC: The Urban Institute. http://www.urban.org/url.cfm?ID=411658. (Accessed June 30, 2008.)

Toosi, Mitra. 2004. "Labor Force Projections to 2010: The Graying of the United States Workforce." *Monthly Labor Review* 127(2): 37–57.

United Nations Department of Economic and Social Affairs. 2007. *World Economic and Social Survey 2007: Development in an Aging World.* New York: United Nations.

U.S. Government Accountability Office. 2007. *The Challenges and Opportunities of Demographic Change in America.* GAO-07-1061CG. Washington, DC: U.S. Government Accountability Office.

Van Eeden-Moorefield, Brad, and David H. Demo. 2007. "Family Diversity." In *Blackwell Encyclopedia of Sociology Online,* edited by George Ritzer. Malden, MA: Blackwell Publishing. http://www.sociologyencyclopedia.com/public/. (Accessed June 13, 2007.)

17

Limited, Mismatched, and Unequal

Work-Life Policies and Practices in the United States

Kelly D. Davis and Katherine Stamps Mitchell

In the United States today, not only are work-life policies limited, especially compared to other industrialized countries (Kelly 2006), but they are also mismatched with the needs of workers and unequal in availability and use. Although the task of improving policies and practices to support workers is a formidable one, preliminary results from two workplace interventions described by Moen, Kelly, and Chermack and Lambert (this volume) provided a positive outlook on how redesigning work scheduling may be a practice that makes a difference for both employers and employees. Further, several authors offered promising areas for galvanizing change at corporate and governmental levels. Thus, what at first seemed like a bleak outlook became a brighter one. This is an exciting time to use knowledge about work-family correlates and processes garnered from research conducted over the past few decades, as well as lessons learned from existing policy and practice interventions, to make a real difference for individuals, families, and organizations.

In this chapter, we highlight three recurring topics in this volume: (1) U.S. work-life policies and practices being limited and mismatched, (2) "one policy does not fit all," and (3) strategies for instigating change. To conclude, we delineate the strengths of the two workplace interventions described by Moen and colleagues and Lambert, in conjunction with promising areas for future research and advancing policy.

323

Major Themes

U.S. Work-Life Policies and Practices Are Limited and Mismatched

Limited

Work-life supports in the United States are limited in several ways: (1) the number of benefits available, (2) how much existing policies actually offer, and (3) the extent to which various policies and practices are effective in improving the quality of life for individuals and families, at least based on research to date.

First, despite the fact that Americans work more than workers in any other industrialized country,[1] the United States is severely lacking in sheer number of work-life supports. Paid leave is a prime example of how the United States lags behind other countries. There is no national consensus that paid leave is important and only a few innovative states offer such a policy. Ironically, progress is likely hindered by many of the cultural values that epitomize what it means to be American, such as individualism and capitalism (Kossek and Distelberg this volume). For us to see significant increases in the number of supports available, a cultural transformation may be necessary.

Second, the policies in existence are limited in the extent to which they meet the needs of the current workforce, a workforce that is now characterized by more women, dual-earner families, and aging workers than ever before (Kossek and Distelberg; Smyer and Pitt-Catsouphes this volume). Returning to the parental leave example, although the Family Medical Leave Act (FMLA) guarantees job-protected leave after the birth or adoption of a child, there are many drawbacks associated with the policy, such as the leave being *unpaid* and only applicable to individuals who have worked for a company of more than 50 employees for more than a year for a certain number of hours. Consequently, many workers do not even have the option to take leave—paid or unpaid—from work.

Another example of how policies and practices are limited in what they offer is the degree of flexibility an employee actually has in a "flexible" work arrangement. Some employees may only be able to flex their start and end times within a restricted range (e.g., two hours) versus others who have much more latitude over when they work throughout the day—beginning, middle, and end. Additionally, some employees may be permitted to change their schedules for special circumstances, some have to keep the same "flexible" schedule on a regular basis, and others can adjust on a day-to-day basis. Clearly, there is a lot of variation in flexible work arrangements, and less "flexibility" with supposedly flexible schedule arrangements limits the ability of individuals to manage and feel a sense of control over work and nonwork demands.

A third limitation is the lack of evidence establishing how effective policies and practices actually are at the individual, family, or organizational level in the short term and over the long run. Although there seems to be a clear positive association between flexibility and individual productivity and morale at work, the link between flexibility and work-family integration is tenuous. Kossek and Distelberg's (this volume) and Christensen and Staines's (1990) comprehensive reviews indicated there are mixed results regarding the implications of flexible schedules for work-family integration. Specifically, Christensen and Staines revealed that three studies showed flextime was associated with less work-family conflict but one study did not. Additionally, of the two studies they found that investigated the link between flextime and family time, only one study showed flextime was related to more family time. Perhaps flexibility is more limited in making a difference in the family sphere than in the work sphere; however, it is too early to make a firm conclusion. Further investigation is needed regarding the effectiveness of current flexibility options and other available policies and practices. Moen, Kelly, and Chermack's investigation of the results-only work environment (ROWE) (this volume) and Lambert and Henly's (2007) scheduling intervention are the types of studies needed to make a more rigorous evaluation of what is effective for individuals. At this point, it seems premature to determine which policies offer the best opportunity to improve the health and well-being of employees and their families.

Mismatched

Policies and practices can be mismatched in at least two ways. One mismatch occurs when policies on the books do not match what is practiced in the workplace, and another mismatch exists between the structure of work and individuals' needs.

As Zvonkovic (this volume) and others pointed out, often there is a mismatch between policies that are stated in the human resource (HR) handbooks and what is actually implemented or encouraged by supervisors and coworkers. In other words, what may be an official HR policy (that is seen and potentially rewarded by *Working Mother* magazine or another top family-friendly workplace list) may be unofficially discouraged by others at work (Harrington and James 2006). As Kossek and Distelberg (this volume) illustrate with a three-legged-stool analogy, HR policies are not the only indicator of how supportive an employer is of employees' nonwork obligations; formal policies and practices represent only one leg of the stool. The other two legs, or essential components for reducing work-family conflicts, are job design (e.g., structure of work hours) and the norms and culture (e.g., acceptance, encouragement) surrounding the use of supports. In spite of policies being listed as available in the books, the informal work culture may provide a very different picture. In some cases, supervisors and coworkers may explicitly express their dissenting opinion of an alternative work arrangement, for example. Probably more often, though, discouragement is much more subtle; others' disapproval may take the form of glancing at watches when employees arrive at work late or leave work earlier or frowning when employees ask for permission to adjust their schedules. Consequently, the employee may feel these supports are in reality not available.

Underlying these reactions is the discrepancy between an employee's behavior and the ideal worker image, the often revered image of the full-time (predominantly male) worker who is not affected by nonwork activities (see Briscoe; Kossek and Distelberg; Zvonkovic this volume) and willing to work whatever hours it takes to stand out as a highly achieving employee. Being in a workplace where this image is prominent and where "face time" is expected can create a very unsupportive work environment for employees who wish to use policies and practices to meet various obligations and demands successfully. But by creating a culture that respects employees' nonwork roles, employees will be much more likely to use work-life policies and programs (Thompson and Prottas this volume).

Thus, for individuals, families, and organizations to even see the benefits of policies and programs, the culture of the workplace needs to be evaluated and changed if it is lacking support. Unfortunately at this point, as Thompson and Prottas (this volume) write, it is unclear what factors create a supportive work-family culture. Perhaps one factor is the prominent image of the ideal worker in a given workplace. Employers and coworkers may be more supportive when all try to embrace a new worker image that involves a committed yet flexible and adaptable worker who can successfully manage work and nonwork roles. Replacing the outdated image with a new results-oriented image could spur changes in policies and practices that are more accommodating to the diverse needs of individuals. Changing the ideal worker image may require scheduling key meetings at core times, rather than at the beginning or end of the day, rewarding supervisors for creating a flexible work environment, and modeling flexibility by highly visible senior leaders.

Another mismatch (targeted by Briscoe, Lambert, and Moen and colleagues in this volume) is the structure of work and individuals' multiple roles (Zvonkovic this volume). According to Kossek's three-legged stool analogy, a third "leg" is job design, work hours (e.g., 9-to-5 schedule), and employment conditions (Kossek and Distelberg this volume). Obviously the match between the nature of work and needs will vary across jobs and individuals. For example, the mismatch for many middle-class and professional workers may be the tension between the long work hours that may be necessary to meet company goals and get promoted and the reality that these long hours detract from time to maintain a healthy lifestyle (e.g., exercise) or spend time with family and friends. Given the lack of job security, even for white-collar jobs, employees may feel they must work longer and harder to keep their jobs even if it jeopardizes their role performance off the job.

Compared to middle-class and professional workers, working-class individuals probably face a much greater mismatch between the structure of work and their needs. Although salaried workers may doubt their job security, they are more likely to be perceived by employers as talent in which to invest. Hourly workers, on the other hand, are more often perceived as "a cost to be contained" (Lambert this volume). Accordingly, firms are more likely to accommodate professional workers than hourly workers by changing work design in order to retain their "talent." Many working-class jobs are very insecure. Lambert and Perry-Jenkins (both this volume) note other problems that hourly employees may face, many of which are unlikely to be encountered by salaried employees, such as instability of work schedules, lack of benefits (or having to wait up to a year for benefits to begin), and not being allowed to work more than a certain number of hours in a given week. For the latter example, the mismatch is between the number of hours given by employers and employees' need for more hours to earn enough money to cover living expenses. Clearly, one policy or practice will not address these mismatches nor will it assist everyone in the same way, which brings us to the second theme.

One Policy Does *Not* Fit All

There appears to be consensus among the authors of this volume that no single policy strategy emerges as superior to the rest for all Americans because of the tremendous diversity of work contexts and work-life challenges. Perhaps the axiom for work-life policy is "one size does not fit all," a useful mantra offered by Moen and colleagues (this volume). In order for policies to be truly effective, such as by reducing work-nonwork conflicts, it seems necessary to tailor them to organizations and occupations—salaried and hourly—and workforce characteristics, such as socioeconomic background, caregiver status and gender, and life-course stage. Conversely, it also seems that policies should be broad and comprehensive enough to include as many individuals as possible. In other words, there seems to be an underlying tension to develop policies and practices that are not only "broad-brushed and comprehensive, but also implemented in ways that can be customized to empower and meet the special needs of individuals and particular labor market sectors" (Kossek and Distelberg this volume). Below we specify some of the varying needs of employees to consider.

Salaried versus Hourly Employees

The needs of salaried and hourly employees are very different and are often conflicting. The literature suggests that focusing on productivity instead of hours spent at work would alleviate much work-family stress, because workers could schedule their work in ways that would accommodate their individual schedules (Moen et al. this volume). Many recommendations about improving work-life policy include increased flexibility as a primary goal, and for salaried workers, increasing flexibility does seem to be a sound and feasible policy strategy. The focus on flexibility, however, is skewed in favor of professionals to the disservice of hourly employees—schedules of professional jobs are usually more amenable to changes, such as being able to work at home or at unconventional but convenient hours for the employee.

In contrast, many hourly workers must adhere to scheduled working hours in order for the company to function. Hourly jobs often involve work that needs to be done at the workplace (e.g., retail store) during a certain time (e.g., when it is convenient for customers). Thus, in addition to lacking control as to *where* they work, hourly workers commonly lack control over *when* they work. Hourly workers often do not suffer from being overscheduled like salaried employees. Instead, they are much more likely to be under-scheduled and to have little control over the time or timing of their work (Lambert this volume). For hourly workers, flexibility may not be a viable or available solution. Milkman (this volume) refers to a sort of "corporate doublespeak" of the word "flexibility" that neglects hourly workers—companies can say they offer flexibility to their employees, implying that all workers have this option. What is left unsaid, however, is that flexibility is offered only to employees who have jobs that permit it, typically professional (not hourly) jobs. In essence, companies can be given credit for offering flexibility despite the fact that its availability is limited.

Although many salaried employees may benefit from policies that give them more flexibility in their work, hourly employees may be more advantaged by policies that increase their work's predictability, such as scheduling working hours well in advance and scheduling a consistent and dependable number of hours from week to week. Undoubtedly, policy that only makes hourly work more regular and predictable is an oversimplified solution, because a schedule that is too rigid may create other problems, such as employees being scheduled for times when they are not able to work (Lambert this volume). Another reason this is an oversimplified solution is because not even hourly jobs are all the same (Lambert this volume). Furthermore, some flexibility in choosing work hours that allow employees to meet work-life responsibilities must occur in concert with job security, what has been referred to as "flexicurity" (cited in Firestein this volume). For hourly workers in particular, it is essential that increased flexibility in choosing work arrangements does not decrease job security.

The conflicting scheduling needs of salaried and hourly workers is only one example of how work-life challenges may differ by occupational status. Compared to salaried employees, hourly employees (particularly part-time workers) are less likely to have health insurance and other fringe benefits that are important for individuals and families. Indeed, comparisons of the different obstacles that salaried and hourly employees encounter can make many salaried employees' concerns seem almost frivolous compared to the gravity of hourly employees' work-life issues. Yet the work-life obstacles of professionals are not superficial (nor are they the same for the whole group). The needs of employees at all levels need to be addressed, but the solutions may be different.

Socioeconomic Status

Closely related to workers' occupations is their socioeconomic status, around which policies must also be customized. Some of the challenges that make hourly workers especially vulnerable include difficulty accessing affordable, quality child care and little ability to take time off or leave (Enchautegui-de-Jesús this volume). Although middle-class employees may also encounter these difficulties, with their greater economic power, they are in a better position to be able to take an unpaid leave or pay higher costs for better child care. To improve work-life integration for professionals *and* nonprofessionals, the nature of jobs in different occupational and socioeconomic strata needs to be improved (Briscoe this volume). Policies that reach workers of various backgrounds could be a "social leveler" (Milkman this volume)—they could help level the playing field between the working and middle classes (Glass this volume).

Caregiver Status and Gender

Although family caregivers have an enormous need for improvements in work-life policies, they are not the only employees for whom new innovations would be beneficial. The harried working mother is the stereotypical beneficiary of work-life or work-family policies, but policymakers must be careful not to focus on mothers to the exclusion of other groups as targets of work-life policy. Doing so would stigmatize this group further as the group that receives "special" benefits. Yet the fact remains that women continue to be the primary caregivers of children and are often penalized in their work as a result (Kossek and Distelberg this volume). Mothers must be kept in mind when formulating work-life policies, but so must other groups, such as fathers; caregivers for elderly or infirm spouses, parents, or relatives; and noncaregivers.

Noncaregivers should also be kept at the forefront of policymakers' minds. After all, everyone, regardless of family or caregiver status, has a life outside of work that competes with work for their time and attention. Policies can have work-life implications and still be broadly applicable. A prime policy example is paid sick days. Most noticeably, being able to stay home to care for children or parents and not worry about losing a day's pay can greatly reduce stress for caregivers negotiating work and family roles. Nevertheless, single employees can also benefit by having time to get better without risking losing their job or getting a smaller paycheck. Taking a day off rather than forcing the body to work when it needs to recover may prevent worse health complications and promote a faster recovery for employees with and without family responsibilities. *Guaranteed* paid sick days, a policy that has been proposed by Senator Edward Kennedy and Representative Rosa DeLauro and by several states but has not yet passed, is just one example of a policy that would likely benefit workers regardless of caregiving status.

In order to increase workplace support for the availability and use of policies that have positive work-life implications, their applicability to all workers needs to be emphasized. If it is not clear how noncaregivers can benefit, an unintended consequence of work-life policies may be stigmatization of caregivers or alienation of noncaregivers. One way to accomplish this goal is to reframe policy discussion, a topic to which we will return in more detail.

Life-Course Changes in Needs

Another important workforce characteristic that should be considered in policymaking is stage in the life course (e.g., Firestein; Glass; Moen et al. this volume). The needs of young workers, mid-career workers, and workers approaching retirement are different. Workers trying to balance education and a job, parents with young children, middle-aged workers with child and parent care responsibilities, and older workers with less-than-optimal health may all have somewhat different policy needs. If employers want to retain their employees, such as the increasing number of older workers, this will require specific policy changes (Smyer and Pitt-Catsouphes this volume). Therefore, policies will better serve employees and their families if they respond to various life-course needs and allow for unpredictable and ongoing personal and family situations. Such changes will also provide career flexibility with which employees are able to make job transitions as necessary and have multiple points for entry, exit, and re-entry into work (see Firestein; Perry-Jenkins this volume).

Tailoring policies to meet needs for people of various circumstances is ideal, but the reality is that policies cannot be expected to be modified in many different ways to reach more workers when currently, availability and promotion of policies is limited. The challenge for policy advocates will be to consider diversity while developing policies broad enough to benefit as many workers as possible.

Strategies for Instigating Change

There are many innovative solutions to work-life conflict discussed in policy circles, and many valuable ideas are presented in this book. After fitting policies and practices to specific needs, the next obstacle is determining the best way to initiate change. Like the policies themselves, some policy-implementation strategies may be better suited in some situations than others. An important first step, however, is reframing the issue.

Reframe the Issue

There seems to be consensus among the authors in this book that there is a need to reframe the issues. Often work-life policies are perceived negatively as unfairly accommodating workers with families or as only a mothers' issue. For this very reason, the creators of ROWE, as well as Moen and her coauthors (this volume), deliberately refrained from referring to ROWE as a "work-family" or "work-life" initiative. Similarly, Workplace Flexibility 2010 focuses on the workplace, rather than work-life policies per se (Feldblum this volume). Even using the term "flexibility" as a way to avoid work-family language may not always be a solution. As Firestein (this volume) points out, flexibility is a bad word for unions because flexibility is often used as a management tool. The term "flexibility" may already be stigmatized.

Avoiding "work-family" language or, as in the case of flexibility, terms that may be associated with it, may help reframe the issue to what is important—creating policies that help employees and, potentially, employers. The choice of language is yet another piece of the policy puzzle that should be tailored to the relevant audience in order to increase the chances of successful implementation. After correctly reframing the issue, the next policy challenge is deciding where to start advocating.

Determine a "Point of Entry" for Change

There was disagreement among the authors in this book about where to begin instigating policy. Some (e.g., Lambert; Moen et al.) suggested starting at the corporate level by approaching employers with policy recommendations that would benefit both them and their employees, others (e.g., Firestein; Glass; Milkman) recommended government regulation as an ideal method of initiating changes, and still others (e.g.,

Feldblum) delineated the pros of tackling change at several levels. In the following section, we briefly weigh the advantages and disadvantages of promoting policies and practices at various levels.

Federal government. Attempting to pass policy legislation at the federal level is, in our view, the strategy that is least likely to yield change quickly, although federal legislation has the potential to affect much larger numbers of workers than workplace policies. Policy at the federal level can not realistically be expected to be adjusted for workers of many different backgrounds, but it can be expected to create a foundation on which states and workplaces can build. Without minimum requirements, equity for individuals will be much harder to achieve (Kamerman and Kahn 1987). Echoing this sentiment, Kossek and Distelberg (this volume) argue that there should be a national standard for the availability of policies rather than relying on employer choice. Although Galinsky (this volume) is in favor of regulation as part of a comprehensive approach to improving work-life policies, she also draws attention to some of the drawbacks of a regulatory approach by studying workers in the European Union's more regulated government. Perhaps surprisingly, despite more government regulation, European workers do not necessarily experience less work-life stress. Therefore, as far as regulation is concerned, there seems to be agreement in this book that it is more likely to be fruitful to focus regulatory efforts on lower levels.

State government. Many authors in this volume agreed that policy implementation through state governments appears to be an effective way to initiate work-life policy change through regulation, for several reasons. First, passing work-life policy at the state level is perhaps easier (e.g., paid leave in California) than at the federal level, and state-level policies still affect thousands of employers and employees. Second, states can tailor policies to their constituencies better than the federal government can. Implementing policies in different states means they can serve as testing grounds to determine the effectiveness of individual policies, which can then be adopted by other states and the federal government. State-level policies can mandate and support businesses to offer benefits. Businesses may even choose to make nonmandated changes on their own accord after reviewing evidence of policy success at the state level (Milkman this volume). A limitation of this approach, to which Glass (this volume) alerted us, is that individuals who do not have the "luck of the draw" by living in a more innovative state or a state that passes particularly helpful legislation are unfairly left without support.

Unions. Unions have less power as agents of change now compared to the high levels of influence they acquired in the past (Clawson and Clawson 1999). To some extent, the future of unions as effective lobbying organizations is debatable. Although many unions are losing strength, some are still growing. Firestein (this volume) argues that labor unions have been successful in negotiating family-friendly changes in the past and have the best interests of American working families at the forefront of their agendas. Using labor unions as a point of entry is attractive because of the large numbers of hourly workers represented by unions. Having an organized force with common goals is a starting point to lobby for the kinds of regulatory changes Firestein and others propose. A drawback, however, is that many hourly workers are not members of unions, and overall, a shrinking minority of American employees are in unions.

The corporate level. One strategy for making change is to intervene at the workplace level, that is, to make the business case for work-life policies and practices. Both Moen and her colleagues and Lambert (this volume) studied changes enacted by employers. They would agree that a crucial component of getting company buy-in is to make the proposal attractive to them. The proposed policy must at least not hurt their bottom line, and hopefully will have the potential to make employees more productive or reduce turnover. In the workplace, possible strategies are not limited to policies but can also include job redesign. Based on Greenhaus's (this volume) emphasis on work teams, one way to ease work-life conflicts may be to have work teams set goals and develop strategies that accommodate needs of all members of the team. Having a backup strategy for when a coworker has a health appointment, for example, could alleviate some stress and create a more flexible environment. So although the company may not be willing to make companywide changes, it may be willing to let work teams set their own goals and strategies to get work done, similar to the ROWE intervention.

Policy implementation at the corporate level has many advantages. If businesses have a voice when creating the policy, their buy-in will be much greater. By trickling down to managers, this company buy-in may instigate a greater motivation to foster a supportive culture. Another benefit of accomplishing change directly through corporations is flexibility in policy. If a corporation creates and enacts its own policy, the hope would be that the policy is more tailored for the workforce and in turn, more effective in addressing needs. In a "one size does not fit all" world, this is an important consideration.

There are also drawbacks to the business-case approach. Even simple yet promising changes that are likely to improve the productivity and well-being of working-class employees, such as in Lambert's study, may be rejected. Businesses may still be more concerned with putting time, energy, and money toward professional workers rather than hourly workers, "a cost to be contained" (Lambert this volume). Corporations with professional employees may care more about recruiting and retaining high-quality employees, especially if the employees have scarce skills that are difficult to replace or if the company has invested a lot in training them. In contrast, there is a large pool of hourly workers, and if turnover rates are high, the corporation may not be affected. Low-level training may give employers and supervisors the sense that this is a resource that is easy to replenish, especially in times or places with high unemployment. Milkman (this volume), Firestein (this volume), and others advocate concentrating on legislative mandates rather than the business case for lower-wage workers, because the best interests of lower-wage workers and business sometimes are not compatible. In such cases, several authors in this book advocate concentrating efforts on unions and government mandates. Another drawback of the business approach is the fact that it is a small-scale, grassroots effort that only affects one business at a time. Similar to Glass's comments about state-to-state variations in policy, as far as workers are concerned, they get the luck of the draw in terms of whether or not their workplace has attractive work-life policies (Firestein this volume). Finally, if a corporation implements a policy, the corporation can also decide to rescind it (Lambert; Milkman this volume). Munck (2001) described an innovative intervention designed to decrease the face-time culture in a group of full-service hotels. The intervention appeared to work, and employees enjoyed the results-oriented approach, but belt-tightening following the post-9/11 drop in travel led to a decision to abandon the experiment.

Supervisors and managers. The business case refers to implementation at the corporate level, but individual supervisors can also make supportive work-life policy changes and, in fact, may be an integral component of change. Indeed, Kossek and Distelberg (this volume) stated that "supervisors are the gatekeepers to effective implementation of work and family policies." If so, then what kind of burden does this role bring? How much can be expected of managers? Being a manager already comes with responsibility and pressure. As Bailyn (2006, 22) noted,

> this combination, of being assumed to be most competent while being responsible for more tasks, lies behind the pressures of this path. It leads managers to feel they must be available at all times to their employees, and it makes it more difficult for them to delegate responsibilities to other people or to empower their staff.

Management is an even more difficult task when considering the variation in needs of employees by age, gender, and life course (Smyer and Pitt-Catsouphes this volume). What kind of supports or training need to be in place to aid positive work-life change implementation?

Determine Whether (and How) to Meet Multiple Stakeholders' Needs

Perhaps the best approach is creating "buy-in" at several (if not all) the levels mentioned above. Galinsky (this volume) specifically states that we should "consider multiple perspectives in how we design, define, and study work-life policies, as well as how we move forward toward change." If a chain of support is necessary for true success in solidifying change, how do we create buy-in at multiple levels? Can there be a "win-win" (or rather, multiple-win) situation for all involved parties? Getting buy-in from multiple stakeholders is possible, Milkman (this volume) argues, if, rather than trying to address corporate needs (i.e., making the business case), advocates present the case as a human need, something to which people at *all* levels can relate.

Although consensus on a prospective policy is possible, having every level involved completely satisfied with the terms of the agreement may be less than realistic. For example, giving more control over work to employees may mean that managers lose some control (Bailyn 2006). Employers do not want policies that increase managers' responsibilities and problems (Glass this volume), so some type of compromise will be required. Briscoe's (this volume) study of physicians illustrates how tradeoffs are necessary: to obtain more flexibility, physicians had to relinquish some autonomy over their work by sharing patients with colleagues. One difficulty will be finding a balance of tradeoffs that suits all parties. Another difficulty will be addressing conflicting ideologies surrounding the ideal worker image (i.e., how work should be done, stereotypes). Moen and colleagues (this volume) demonstrate in the ROWE intervention that addressing these views is, in fact, feasible but is an ongoing process.

Heretofore, this chapter has demonstrated the need for a greater number of work-life supports in the United States as well as the need for policies and practices that match the current realities of the workforce. After addressing the issue that one policy does not fit all, we reviewed the many ways to address these inadequacies that were offered by authors in this volume. To conclude the chapter, we provide directions for future research and policy initiatives.

Future Research and Policy Implications

The workplace interventions described by Moen and her colleagues and Lambert (this volume) are excellent models for future research in the work-family field and policy initiatives. Both exemplify attempts to change the nature of work to help employees balance responsibilities at work and outside of work. Below we highlight their strengths in conjunction with areas for further investigation.

Develop More "Three-Legged Stool" Interventions

Having a policy "on the books" is not enough; changing the nature of work and promoting a supportive work environment are also crucial elements for sustaining change (Kossek and Distelberg this volume). The ROWE program, described by Moen and colleagues (this volume), incorporated all three "legs," all of which were necessary to uproot deep-seated beliefs about the way work should be done and who is best suited to do this work. Future experiments should measure each of these three components (Kossek and Distelberg this volume; Thompson and Prottas this volume) when evaluating why a program succeeded or failed (and for whom). Policy initiatives not considering informal supports, for example, may be set up for failure; without a supportive work environment, no one may even use the benefits. Thus, keeping these three components in mind in the design stage may save time and money.

Think "Outside the Box"

In some workplaces and for some work groups, all that may be necessary to improve employee and employer well-being is to simply "tweak" an existing practice, as was done in the Scheduling Intervention Study (Lambert this volume). The experiment involved changing how far in advance retail associates received their schedules by increasing the time from one week to one month advance notice, as well as improving communication between employees and supervisors. It may be that a simple solution is all that is needed for a big problem, but this is yet to be determined as Lambert is still in the process of collecting data.

Other times it is necessary to think outside the box—to develop practices that are not a part of current public or private policy. The results-only work environment constitutes a radical change in how work is done and perceived. Rather than building on existing flexible work arrangements, the creators of ROWE designed a whole new approach to getting work done (i.e., control over when and where work is done).

Both approaches—revising existing policies and starting from scratch—are important and may help address the mismatch and inequality in current policies. Furthermore, it is important to note that although change is necessary, some policies and job practices are beneficial. Therefore, it is not always about making changes but also "protecting what works well" (Bailyn et al. 2006).

Measure the Fidelity and Effectiveness of Interventions

Even with randomized experiments, such as Lambert's scheduling intervention, there are potential threats to the internal validity of the program given the real-world context in which it takes place. Outside of the laboratory, businesses experiences change all the time. Changes include employees entering, changing positions, or leaving; corporations moving into new markets; and advances in technology (Moen et al. this volume). As such, workplace interventions may manifest themselves differently depending on the company office or even on the work group that is involved. Therefore, it is important to keep detailed notes regarding the fidelity of the program, that is, how the intervention was intended to work and then how it changed throughout implementation (Horner, Rew, and Torres 2006). Both Moen and colleagues and Lambert attest to the importance of this task. Their research staff took copious notes about the content and delivery of their programs from start to finish. As MacDermid, Remnet, and Pagnan (this volume) noted, the challenges related to intervention fidelity are determining which circumstances may impact the results of the intervention (null or spurious findings) and then deciding how to account for them. Putting these circumstances in context will provide a more realistic picture of the effectiveness of the intervention.

Evaluate the Adaptability of Existing Workplace Interventions

As was emphasized heretofore, one policy or practice often does not benefit all, and accordingly, policies may need to be adapted to benefit different employees' and employers' needs. Toward this goal, current programs should be evaluated in terms of their adaptability—for whom, when, and how. For example, how might ROWE be adapted for Best Buy hourly store associates given their role in interacting with and assisting customers on the floor? If adaptable, will the program be equally, less, or more effective for these employees compared to the corporate professionals? Can ROWE be effective in other industries, such as hospitality and nursing, which require face-to-face contact with guests and patients? Information regarding the fidelity of previous program implementations will likely be vital in deciding how to adapt the program in a different context.

Consider Multiple Contexts and Conditions

When evaluating the impact of a policy or practice, it is important to consider not only the variable of interest (e.g., temporal control or predictability) but also other conditions at work or in the family that may attenuate or improve the effectiveness. MacDermid and colleagues (this volume) questioned the neglect of job demands in the focus of an intervention improving schedule control. They have a valid point in that other work characteristics may influence the impact of a policy or intervention. Measurement of other work conditions may elucidate whether other parts of the job need to be addressed as well.

In addition to considering work conditions, experiences outside of work may account for individual variations in the effectiveness of programs and policies. As Smyer and Pitt-Catsouphes (this volume) and several others noted, the labor force is diverse and continues to change. Thus, the family context (and other salient contexts) and life-course factors should be considered when evaluating effectiveness and adaptability.

Move beyond Associations to Process

Both Moen and colleagues' and Lambert's interventions are designed to study process rather than concurrent associations, a clear strength that should be emulated by future interventions. Both incorporated pre- and post-intervention assessments, providing for an examination of intra-individual changes in selected outcomes. Compared to one-time assessments, longitudinal and process data can capture more information about whether a policy was successful or not and for how long (Moen et al. this volume). Without an experimental design, however, causal connections will remain unclear. Random assignment to control and treatment groups allows researchers to make statements based on the one variable that is manipulated—the intervention program (MacDermid et al. this volume). Understanding what is driving the results can inform future attempts to adapt and implement the program.

Determine Realistic Outcomes for Targeted Change

Finally, we come full circle to the topic of what policies make a real difference for individuals, families, and organizations. To determine the utility of a given policy or practice, we need to measure appropriate outcomes. Outcomes will most likely vary by policy, but there may also be similarities. For organizations, relevant outcomes to assess are return on investment, productivity, retention, and, potentially, health care costs (see Moen et al. this volume for examples). Less obvious, however, is how much change can be expected and how soon it will be apparent after implementing the policy. For individuals, the expectation is that a work-life policy would improve their ability to deal with multiple roles and enhance their life satisfaction. Indeed, Moen and colleagues found that the ROWE program improved employees' perceived control over work and reduced their experience of conflict between work and family after six months. They also found some improvement in employees' health behaviors, such as sleeping and exercising more. It would be interesting to know whether these behaviors translate into actual improvements in health over time. Is it realistic to expect that greater control over work could reduce the risk of cardiovascular disease or ulcers? Future research is needed to determine what individual indicators are likely to change, as well as the possible mediating and moderating explanations.

It is also important to determine what policies have a positive impact on families. Employees are part of a family system (Whitchurch and Constantine 1993) in which each family member's experiences are interrelated. Thus, it is reasonable to expect that effects of a policy targeting one person's workplace could reverberate to home life. For example, Moen and colleagues (this volume) reported that increasing employees' temporal control led to less negative spillover of moods, energy, and behaviors from work to family. How does this relate to the quality and types of experiences among family members at home? One would presume they would be more positive, but this needs to be assessed. Additionally, to avoid mono-reporter bias, collecting data from other household members, including spouses and children pre- and post-implementation, would provide additional evidence regarding effectiveness. Beyond altered family interactions, is it reasonable to expect positive changes in spouses' and children's psychological well-being and physical well-being? This is a worthy area of pursuit, as it would demonstrate that policies have the potential to not only benefit organizations and individuals but also spouses and children—one way to address the needs of society at large.

Concluding Remarks

This volume elucidates the current state of work-life policies and brings together voices from many worlds, including academia, the labor movement, and nonprofit think tanks. Although we cannot conclude by advocating a specific policy or method, we hope this book provides insight into many key issues that will be useful for policymakers, lobbyists, and employers as they attempt to reduce employees' work-life conflict and improve their well-being and performance. Making change—and meaningful change for individuals and families—is no easy task, but it is surmountable. To instigate this change, should we wait for the "right" point of entry or seize any opportunity to make change? We suggest that all be open to making a difference at any level, because as Moen and Kelly discovered, serendipity may create the perfect opportunity to study or develop work-life policies that will make a meaningful difference for organizations, individuals, and families.

NOTE

1. Andrew Curry, "Why We Work," *US News and World Report*, February 2003, 49–52 and 54–56, as cited in Kossek and Distelberg, this volume.

REFERENCES

Bailyn, Lotte. 2006. *Breaking the Mold: Redesigning Work for Productive and Satisfying Lives*, 2nd ed. Ithaca: Cornell University.

Bailyn, Lotte, Ann Bookman, Mona Harrington, and Thomas A. Kochan. 2006. "Work-Family Interventions and Experiments: Workplaces, Communities, and Society."

In *The Work and Family Handbook: Multi-disciplinary Perspectives and Approaches,* edited by Marcie Pitt-Catsouphes, Ellen Ernst Kossek, and Stephen A. Sweet (651–64). Mahwah, NJ: Erlbaum.

Christensen, Kathleen E., and Graham L. Staines. 1990. "Flextime: A Viable Solution to Work/Family Conflict?" *Journal of Family Issues* 11: 455–76.

Clawson, Dan, and Mary Ann Clawson. 1999. "What Has Happened to the U.S. Labor Movement? Union Decline and Renewal." *Annual Review of Sociology* 25: 95–119.

Harrington, Brad, and Jacquelyn B. James. 2006. "The Standards of Excellence in Work-Life Integration: From Changing Policies to Changing Organizations." In *The Work and Family Handbook: Multi-disciplinary Perspectives and Approaches,* edited by Marcie Pitt-Catsouphes, Ellen Ernst Kossek, and Stephen A. Sweet (665–83). Mahwah, NJ: Erlbaum.

Horner, Sharon, Lynn Rew, and Rosamar Torres. 2006. "Enhancing Intervention Fidelity: A Means of Strengthening Study Impact." *Journal of the Society of Pediatric Nurses* 11: 80–89.

Kamerman, Shelia B., and Alfred J. Kahn. 1987. *The Responsive Workplace: Employers and a Changing Labor Force.* New York: Columbia University Press.

Kelly, Erin L. 2006. "Work-Family Policies: The United States in International Perspective." In *The Work and Family Handbook: Multi-disciplinary Perspectives and Approaches,* edited by Marcie Pitt-Catsouphes, Ellen Ernst Kossek, and Stephen A. Sweet (99–123). Mahwah, NJ: Erlbaum.

Lambert, Susan, and Julia R. Henly. 2007. "Low-Level Jobs and Work-Family Studies." In *Work-Family Encyclopedia,* edited by Patricia Raskin and Marcie Pitt Catsouphes. Boston: Sloan Work-Family Research Network, Boston College.

Munck, B. 2001. "Changing a Culture of Face Time." *Harvard Business Review* 79: 125–31.

Whitchurch, Gail, and Larry Constantine. 1993. "Systems Theory." In *Sourcebook of Family Theories and Methods: A Contextual Approach,* edited by Pauline Boss, William Doherty, Ralph LaRossa, Walter Schumm, and Susan Steinmetz. (325–52). New York: Plenum Press.

About the Editors

Ann C. Crouter is the Raymond E. and Erin Stuart Schultz Dean of the College of Health and Human Development and a professor of Human Development at Penn State. Her research, funded by the National Institute for Child Health and Human Development and the Alfred P. Sloan Foundation, focuses on the interconnections between work circumstances and family processes in a variety of populations.

Alan Booth is Distinguished Professor of Sociology, Human Development & Family Studies, and Demography at Penn State. He has been a senior scientist in Penn State's Population Research Institute since 1991. Booth has co-organized the university's National Symposium of Family Issues since its inception in 1993. Booth's research has focused on marital and parent-child relationship quality, nonresidential fathers and their children, adolescents' transition to adulthood, and hormones and family relationships. He is the author of more than 100 scholarly articles and four books, and the editor of 16 volumes. He was editor of the *Journal of Marriage and the Family* from 1985 to 1991.

About the Contributors

Forrest Briscoe is assistant professor of management, Smeal College of Business at Penn State. Briscoe's research asks how organizations and institutions change, especially in relation to the needs of diverse workers. He has recently studied the organizational antecedents of career flexibility among professionals, the transitioning of corporate employees to managed health care, and the rapid diffusion of domestic partner benefits.

Kelly Chermack is a Ph.D. candidate in sociology at the University of Minnesota. Her areas of study include organizational change and innovation, as well as social networks.

Kelly D. Davis is a doctoral candidate in the department of Human Development and Family Studies at Penn State. Her research focuses on how work conditions are related to individual and family well-being. Currently she is examining the connection between work and family experiences, as well as the link between work and health, at the daily level using daily diary and biomarker data from hotel workers and their family members.

Brian Distelberg is a doctoral candidate in the department of Family and Child Ecology at Michigan State University. Brian is a practicing marriage and family therapist, and has experience in researching family- and work-related issues.

Noemí Enchautegui-de-Jesús is visiting assistant professor in psychology and senior research associate, Burton Blatt Institute Centers of Innovation on Disability at Syracuse University. Her research examines the stressors faced by working-poor families of diverse ethnic backgrounds and the impact on family processes and well-being. She also seeks to understand, through the use of qualitative and quantitative data, how family experiences spill over to the work domain and vice versa.

Ellen Ernst Kossek is professor of human resource management and organizational behavior in the School of Labor & Industrial Relations at Michigan State University. She is an internationally recognized scholar who studies workplace flexibility, employer support of work and family, and workplace inclusion and innovation from the manager and employee perspectives. She is associate director of the Center for Work, Family Health and Stress as part of the National Institute of Health's Work, Family, and Health Network. Her newest book is *CEO of Me: Creating a Life That Works in the Flexible Job Age* (with Brenda A. Lautsch, Wharton School Publishing, 2008).

Chai R. Feldblum is professor of law and codirector of Workplace Flexibility 2010 at Georgetown Law in Washington, D.C. She is responsible for codirecting the strategy, legislative-lawyering, policy-research, media, and constituent-outreach components of Workplace Flexibility 2010. Feldblum served as one of the principal lawyers drafting and negotiating the Americans with Disabilities Act during 1988–1990, as well as the ADA Amendments Act during 2007–2008.

Netsy Firestein is founder/director of the Labor Project for Working Families, a national nonprofit organization working with labor unions to negotiate and advocate for better work-family policies, including child care, paid family leave, elder care, and flexible work hours. As a nationally recognized expert on labor and work-family issues, she has more than 20 years' experience working with labor unions on work-family issues and developing contract language.

Ellen Galinsky is president and cofounder of the Families and Work Institute, a Manhattan-based nonprofit organization that conducts research on the changing family, changing workforce, and changing community. She codirects two of the most comprehensive and in-depth nationally representative studies of the workforce (National Study of the Changing Workforce) and the workplace (National Study of Employers). Both are updated regularly and provide extensive information about the changing nature of work and family. Findings are widely used by policy-makers, employers, and the media.

Jennifer Glass is professor in the department of Policy Analysis and Management and the department of Sociology at Cornell University. Her research interests include work and family life, gender stratification, organizations, and mental health. She is currently researching the effects of family-responsive policies on mothers' earnings. Another of her projects explores the influence of religiosity and religious fundamentalism on the labor force behavior and occupational attainment of women.

Jeffrey H. Greenhaus is professor and William A. Mackie Chair in the department of Management at Drexel University's LeBow College of Business. His primary interest concerns career-related issues, with a particular emphasis on the intersection of work and family lives. He has conducted research on the antecedents and consequences of work-family conflict as well as on the factors that contribute to work-family enrichment, the positive side of the work-family interface. He is currently examining the meaning and determinants of work-family balance and the role of gender in work-family processes.

Erin Kelly is associate professor of sociology at University of Minnesota and an affiliate of the Minnesota Population Center. Kelly studies the adoption, implementation, and consequences of antidiscrimination and family-friendly policies. She received the Rosabeth Moss Kanter Award for work-family research in 2000. Kelly and Phyllis Moen are collaborating with other scholars in the Work, Family, and Health Network to study innovative workplace policies that may reduce work-family conflict.

Susan J. Lambert is associate professor in the School of Social Service Administration at the University of Chicago. She is particularly interested in organizational theory and management, the relationship between work and personal life, and lower-skilled jobs and low-wage workers. Lambert is currently coprincipal investigator of a cluster-randomized field experiment that assesses the worker- and store-level effects of a workplace intervention intended to improve scheduling practices in entry-level retail jobs. Lambert has published extensively on issues of labor market stratification, employer practices, and employee well-being.

Shelley M. MacDermid is professor of family studies, director of the Center for Families, and former codirector for the Military Family Research Institute at Purdue University. The institute assists the secretary of defense in studying and developing policies related to quality of life for military families. Her research focuses on relationships between job conditions and family life, with special interests in organizational size, adult development in the context of workplaces, and organizational policies that are more or less supportive of workers' lives.

Ruth Milkman is professor of sociology at UCLA. From 2001 to 2008, she served as director of the UCLA Institute for Research on Labor and Employment. She recently conducted a study of California's paid family leave program, with a special focus on its impact on low-wage workers. She often writes and lectures about the sociology of work and labor. Her most recent book is *L.A. Story: Immigrant Workers and the Future of the U.S. Labor Movement* (Russell Sage Foundation, 2006).

Phyllis Moen holds the McKnight Presidential Chair in Sociology at the University of Minnesota. Moen studies occupational careers, gender, families, and well-being over the life course. She is the founder of the Bronfenbrenner Life Course Center at Cornell University and the 2008 recipient of the Work-Life Legacy Award from the Families and Work Institute.

Colleen Pagnan is a doctoral student in the department of Child Development and Family Studies at Purdue University. Currently, she is a research assistant with the Military Family Research Institute at Purdue. Her research focuses on the relationship between work and family, with a particular focus on the plans and strategies individuals use to achieve career and family goals, the ways that military service shapes family relationships, and policy initiatives that enable individuals to achieve their career and family goals.

Maureen Perry-Jenkins is a professor of psychology at the University of Massachusetts, Amherst. Her work focuses on the ways in which sociocultural factors such as race, gender, and social class shape the mental health and family relationships of employed parents and their children. Her current research involves a 10-year longitudinal study, funded by the National Institute of Mental Health, that examines the transition to parenthood and the transition back to paid employment for working-class, low-wage couples and for African American, Latina, and European American single mothers.

Marcie Pitt-Catsouphes directs the Sloan Center on Aging & Work at Boston College. She is a faculty member at the Boston College Graduate School of Social Work, has an appointment at the Boston College Carroll School of Management, and has a three-year appointment as a visiting scholar at the Middlesex University School of Business in London. Pitt-Catsouphes founded and directed the Sloan Work and Family Research Network and was a 2007 recipient of the Work-Life Legacy Award.

David J. Prottas is assistant professor of management in the School of Business at Adelphi University. He was awarded his Ph.D. in organizational behavior and human resource management in 2006 after spending more than 20 years as a corporate banker for multinational financial institutions with strong work-primacy cultures. His current research focuses on issues related to work-life and self-employment.

Mary Ann Remnet is a doctoral student in the department of Child Development and Family Studies at Purdue University. Her research focuses on challenges specific to National Guard military families and exploring ways to ease and enhance transitions from military service to civilian life after deployment.

Katherine Stamps Mitchell is a doctoral candidate in sociology and demography at Penn State. Her research interests revolve around families and inequality, with a current focus on child well-being. She is now working on a project examining family instability over the course of childhood and adolescent outcomes in high school.

Michael A. Smyer, formerly codirector of the Sloan Center on Aging & Work at Boston College, is provost at Bucknell University. Active in geriatric mental health research for more than 30 years, he is currently focusing on the impact of the workplace and flexible work options for older workers and their family members. He and his colleagues are assessing the impact of cultural, organizational, and policy contexts for the management of a global workforce facing the challenges of aging.

Cynthia A. Thompson is professor of management in the Zicklin School of Business at Baruch College, CUNY. Her research expertise lies in the integration of work and life, particularly the extent to which supportive work-family cultures affect employee attitudes and organizational effectiveness. She has been studying work-family issues for more than 20 years, during which her work has been published by scholarly journals as well as the popular press.

Anisa M. Zvonkovic is chair of the department of Human Development and Family Studies at Texas Tech University. Zvonkovic's research has focused on work and family issues, blending her training in relationship processes with her interest in specific job demands. She has studied workers in a variety of occupations, including commercial fishermen, long-haul truckers, flight attendants, and adoption-agency workers. Her current project, funded by the National Institutes of Health, concerns the effect of jobs requiring travel on workers' family lives.

Index

AARP, 287*n*82

Absenteeism
  child care and, 182
  flexibility and, 20
  hourly employees and, 171
  low level compensation and, 199
  market approach to work-life policy
    and, 240

Accommodations, 21, 124, 301

Adkins, Cheryl L., 39

Administrative Science Quarterly article by
  Karasek, 162

Adoption assistance, 14

Adoption leave, 25–26, 257, 258

Adult caregiving, 316

Advance notice
  hourly employees and, 175, 182–83
  working parents and, 222, 224

Advocacy groups, 262

Advocacy research, 41–42

After-school programs, 253

"Agenda for Working Families"
  (H. Clinton), 254–55

Age variability in industries and
  occupations, 317–18

Aging. *See also* Changing landscape of
  aging and work

global, 309
Urban Institute's estimation of
  workers over age 55, 311
of workforce, 244–45, 251, 313

Alfred P. Sloan Awards for Business
  Excellence in Workplace
  Flexibility, 300

Alfred P. Sloan Foundation, 108, 263,
  268–70, 274, 285*nn*64–65

Alliance of Work-Life Progress, 138

Almer, Elizabeth D., 33

Alternative work schedules, 16, 80–81

Alternative Work Schedules Act of 1982
  (AWSA), 21–22

American Federation of State, County,
  and Municipal Employees, 65–66

American Prospect article by Williams, 32

Americans with Disabilities Act of 1990,
  286*n*71

Amick, Benjamin C., III, 221

Ammons, Samantha, 102, 112–13

Anderson, Elaine A., 21

Anonymity, 114, 161

Applebaum, Eileen, 51

Arbitration, 63

Arkansas, 318

Ask the Children (Galinsky), 290

Association of Washington Business,
    284*n*63
Association of Work-Life Professionals,
    12
Asynchronous commerce, 137
Attorneys, 62, 108, 111
Attrition, 186–88. *See also* Turnover
Automation, 235
AWSA (Alternative Work Schedules Act
    of 1982), 21–22

Baby boomers, 237, 304
Bailyn, Lotte, 51, 336
Baltes, Boris, 20
Bargaining strategies. *See* Collective
    bargaining; Unions
Barriers to benefits access, 173–74
Baughman, Reagan, 23
Baum, Charles L., 27
Beanpole family structure, 315
Being Together, Working Apart:
    Dual-Career Families and the
    Work-Life Balance (Schneider &
    Waite, eds.), 251
Benefits. *See also specific types (e.g., health*
    insurance, retirement)
    barriers to access to, 173–74
    discrimination, 32
    hourly employees and, 169
    results-based administration of, 137
    waiting periods, 173–74, 177, 199, 221
Bengtson, Vern, 315
Best Buy study, 103–27. *See also* ROWE
    intervention
Best companies to work for in America,
    191, 200
    Working Mother's 100 best, 52, 68, 326
Best Contracts database, 63
Best friend at work, 125–26
Bianchi, Suzanne, 32
Bias reporting
    of job flexibility, 17
    of satisfaction of family members, 341
    of white-collar workers, 137
Biden, Joe, 279*n*13

Blackberries, 138
Blair-Loy, Mary, 201
Bloom, Howard S., 186
BLS. *See* Bureau of Labor Statistics
Blue-collar workers. *See also* Hourly
    employees
    flexibility and, 19
    less-than-ample work and, 138
Bonuses, 136
Boston College Center for Work and
    Family, 138
Boundary spanning, 148
Breaks
    flexibility and, 16
    negotiability and, 40
    restrictions on, 210–11
Breaugh, James A., 39
Briscoe, Forrest, 51, 83, 302, 326, 330, 336
Bronfenbrenner, Urie, 114, 123, 126–27
Bureaucratization of medical workplaces,
    86–87
Bureau of Labor Statistics (BLS)
    aging of workforce and, 310
    child care assistance and, 22–23
    employee understanding of FMLA
        and, 27
    family leave and, 28
    low-income workers, occupational
        areas of, 219
    National Compensation Survey, 10,
        12–13
    workplace flexibility and, 15–16, 18–19
Burton, Linda, 315
Bush, George H. W., 243
Bush, George W.
    FLSA amendment proposed, 255–56
    funding of paid leave programs, 285*n*69
    veto threatened to proposed Healthy
        Families Act, 257, 281*n*30
Business trade associations, 262, 263–64
Business Work-Life Study (BWLS), 291

Cahill, Kevin E., 310
California
    discrimination against caregivers in, 259

funding of family leave program in, 283*n54*

newborn or adopted child care leave in, 28, 257

paid family leave (PFL) in, 6, 42, 67, 202–4, 246–47, 261, 264, 284*nn*62–63, 333

Unemployment Insurance Code amendment of State Disability Insurance Program in, 28

universal pre-K education in, 239

California Chamber of Commerce's criticism of paid family leave, 203, 283*n57*

Canada and paid leave, 5

Carbon load, 246

Career flexibility, 86, 272

Career maintenance and reentry, 272

The Career Mystique: Cracks in the American Dream (Moen & Roehling), 251

Career suicide, 52

Caregivers. *See also* Caregiving
accommodations made by, 316
in bureaucratized workplaces, 89
career breaks for, 26
discrimination against, 254, 259, 283*n52*
diversity of needs of, 245
in European Union, 296
extended time off for, 271
fathers as, 3
legislative reforms for, 260–62
paid time off for, 200
physicians as, 85–86
rights of, 237–39, 247
short-term time off for, 270
sick leave for, 330–31
single mothers as, 3
tailoring policies to status and gender of, 328, 330–31
temporal flexibility and, 316
wage gap of, 243

Caregiving, 234–43. *See also* Caregivers; Child care; Elder care
adult, 316
community-based, 318
engaging new constituencies in policy conversations about, 277

failure of market approach to work-life policy, 234–38

flextime and, 21

government regulatory approach to work-life policy and, 6, 238, 240

lawsuits involving, 41

managing work and, 35

NSCW and, 24, 316

NSE and, 23–24

public support of, 241–42

Caring for or supporting, defined, 282*n49*

Cash and Counseling Demonstration Project (CCDE), 318

Centers for Disease Control (CDC), 97, 101

Certified Compensation Professionals, 12

Change. *See also* Changing landscape of aging and work
determining realistic outcomes for, 340–41
point of entry for, 332–36
strategies for instigating, 332–37

Changing landscape of aging and work, 309–22
aging of U.S. workforce, 309–12
changing nature of families, 314–16
changing nature of work, 312–14
overview, 309
states' increasing importance in, 316–18

Chaos, 133–34

Chermack, Kelly
on corporate work-time policy initiative study, 97
Davis and Mitchell comments on, 323, 325, 328, 332, 336, 337, 339
Feldblum comments on, 265
Galinsky comments on, 302
Greenhaus comments on, 141–53
Lambert comments on, 180–81
MacDermid et al. comments on, 133–39
Milkman comments on, 197, 198
Zvonkovic comments on, 155–65

Child care. *See also* Child care assistance
absenteeism and, 182
bargaining strategies for, 72–73
home, 33

hourly working mothers and, 209–10
maternal care vs., 290
in Mexico, 231–33
nonstandard hours of, 210
private, 201
public policy on, 66–67
scheduling predictability and, 182,
190, 224
in Sweden, 232
tardiness and, 182
tax credit, 236, 253
union support of, 63–64
Child care assistance
comparison of U.S. with other
countries, 5–6
demographics of availability and access
to, 22–23
employee perspective on, 22
employer benefits of, 23
employer perspective on, 22
general trends of, 13–14
Children's academic activities, 254
China and employment discrimination
against young or pregnant
women, 234
Christensen, Kathleen, 20, 108, 268, 272,
286n73, 325
Civil Rights Act of 1964, 6
Clark, Campbell, 21
Clawson, Dan, 34–35
Client-based occupations, 88
Client service, 244
Clinton, Bill
FLSA amendment proposed, 264
funding of paid leave programs, 285n69
Clinton, Hillary, 254–55
Cohen, Jeffrey R., 33
Cohen, Philip N., 39
Collaborative cooperation, 134
Collaborative work, 313
Collective bargaining, 61–63. See also
Unions
Commitment
family-supportive culture and, 52
as reason for work-family policies, 14
supervisor support and, 31

Commodified services, 201
Communication. See also Advance notice
of child care needs, 209–10
to request family leave, 210–12
scheduling issues and, 184
of work-family policy, 40–41
Community-based long-term care, 318
Community leader involvement, 303–6
Community mental health services, 234
Commuting, 21, 122
Compensatory time, 263
Competing institutional pressures, 56
Complacency, 278
Compressed workweeks, 16, 19–21
Confidentiality, 114, 161
Conflict, intergenerational, 312
Connecticut and mandatory paid sick
leave legislation, 259, 282nn46–47
Conservative fears of regulation, 235–36
Consistency in research design, 124
Consumer demand
fluctuating schedules and, 186, 197
hourly employees and, 171, 173–76, 199
labor costs linked to, 182, 189
matching work hours to, 179, 220
Contamination in research design,
124, 125
Contingency theory, 57–58
Control of work-life. See Work-life control
Corporate culture, institutional theory
on, 53, 55–56
Corporate Voices for Working Families,
286n79
Corporate work-life intervention. See
ROWE intervention
Corporations, as policy change agents,
334–35
Cost containment
differing goals of employers and
employees and, 224, 226
hourly employees and, 171, 174,
189–91, 198, 327, 335
language of, 220
Costs. See also Cost containment
of California State Disability Insurance
Program, 28

of changes in work design, 90
controlling labor to minimize staffing
     and, 198
of human reproduction, 241, 243–44,
     260
of labor, 170–71, 175, 182
of TDI for paid family leave, 261
Crosby, Faye J., 32
Crouter, Ann C., 33, 123
CultureRx, 107
Customer service, 244

Davis, Kelly D., 33, 323
D.C. Workplace Flexibility Policy
     Initiative, 285n64
Decisionmaking, 150–52
DeLauro, Rosa, 280n18, 331
Demand-control equation, 138
Demo, David H., 315
Democratic party, 253–54, 259–61, 264,
     280n15
Demographics. *See also* Changing land-
     scape of aging and work
   age variability in industries and occu-
     pations, 317–18
   baby boomers and employment, 237
   child care assistance and, 22–23
   declining workforce, 309–10
   elder care and, 24
   fertility levels, 243
   flexibility and, 18–19
   marriage patterns of white-collar
     workers, 201
   married-couple households, increase in
     number of both spouses working,
     279nn1–2
   maternity leave and, 27–28
   poverty level of mothers and
     children, 242
   workforce composition, 52
Denmark's public policies, 298–99
Dependent care assistance plans, 22–23
Design of work. *See also* Professionals
   implications for research and policy
     on, 89–91
   nature of, 84–85

Differentiation, 190–91
Disabilities, 286n71
Discrimination
   benefits, 32
   against caregivers, 254, 259
   disabilities and, 286n71
   employment, 259, 283n52
   gender, 32–33
   against parents by employers, 254
   against part-time workers, 32–33
   policy conversation on, 265
   sexual orientation/gender identity and,
     286n71
   against working mothers, 32
Distelberg, Brian
   Briscoe comments on, 83, 90
   Davis and Mitchell comments on,
     325–26, 333, 335
   Galinsky comments on, 291, 302
   Milkman comments on, 199
   Moen et al. comments on, 106
   Thompson and Prottas comments on,
     51–60
   on work-life policies, 3
   Zvonkovic comments on, 156
District of Columbia and mandatory paid
     sick leave legislation, 258,
     282nn46–47, 283n53
Diversity. *See also* Discrimination
   AWSA and, 21
   ethnicity, 163, 219, 315
   of family forms, 34, 315
   generational, 312, 331
   in research design, 160
Dodd, Chris, 255, 256, 280n21
Domestic labor, 201
Domestic violence, 254
Donaldson, Lex, 57
Drago, Robert W., 319
Dual-career families, 85
Duncan, Greg, 208

Eastern Europe and employment
     discrimination against young or
     pregnant women, 234
Eaton, Susan C., 29, 30

Ecological transition, 123
Economic polarization, 201
Economic risk, 191
Edwards, John, 253, 255, 280nn14–15
Elder care. *See also* Elder care assistance
  availability and access to, 23–24
  bargaining strategies for, 74–75
  employee perspective on, 24
Elder care assistance
  demographics on availability and
    access to, 24
  employee perspective on, 24
  employer perspective on, 23–24
  general trends of, 14
  Obama and, 254
  union support of, 63
Embedded researchers, 135
Emergency family needs, 214–15
Employee, changing definition of, 137
Employee Income Retirement Security
  Act of 1974 (ERISA), 6
Employee perspective
  on child care assistance, 22
  on combining parenting and work,
    223–24
  on elder care, 24
  on instability in nonstandard
    employment, 221
  on maternity leave, 26–27
  on supervisor support of work-family
    employment policy, 31
Employees earning over $15/hour, 19, 23
Employer perspective
  on child care assistance, 22
  on elder care, 23–24
  on flexibility availability, 15–17
  on funding of paid family leave, 203,
    284n59
  on maternity leave, 25–26
  on supervisor support of work-family
    employment policy, 30
  on unemployment compensation
    funds for FMLA leave, 285n69
  on work-life policies, 4–5, 260, 283n56
Employment discrimination, 259, 283n52
Employment instability, 179. *See also* Job
  security

Employment Non-Discrimination Act
  (proposed), 286n71
Employment policy, work-family. *See*
  Work-family employment policies
Enchautegui-de-Jesús, Noemí, 207, 330
Endogamous marriage patterns, 201
Energy issues, 246
Engaged research, 126–27, 133–39
  bridging gap between theory and
    practice, 97
  dilemmas of, 137–39
  overview, 133
  puzzles of, 135–37
  tensions of, 133–35
Entry, exit, and reentry, 65, 268, 272, 331
Episodic time off (EPTO), 270–74,
  286n79
ERISA (Employee Income Retirement
  Security Act of 1974), 6
Estes, Sarah Beth, 21
Ethnicity, 163, 219, 315
Ethnographic research methods, 110,
  112, 161–62, 208–16
European Foundation for the Improve-
  ment of Living and Working
  Conditions, 296
European Trade Union Confederation, 64
European Union
  child care assistance in, 6
  consensus on reproduction accommo-
    dations in, 243
  full-time work in, 7
  paid maternity leave in, 5–6
  work-family policy in, 241, 247,
    296–98, 333
European Working Conditions Survey,
  296–98
Executives. *See* Managers and supervisors
Exempt employees under FLSA, 7, 256
"Experiment of nature," 107, 114, 124
Extended time off (EXTO), 271–74,
  286n79

Face time, 142–43, 152, 156, 326, 335
Fair Labor Standards Act of 1938 (FLSA),
  7, 256, 263

Families
  changing nature of, 314–16
  family member, defined, 282*n*49
  family-member care leave, 26
  responsibilities of, defined, 283*n*52
  status, 259, 283*n*52
Families and Work Institute (FWI), 10,
    12, 286*n*73, 290, 299
Family and Medical Leave Act of 1993
    (FMLA)
  access to information about, 204
  bargaining strategies for, 78–79
  defined, 6
  designing study for, 299
  drawbacks of, 225, 231, 324
  elder care and, 23
  employee understanding of, 27,
    40–41, 204
  employer resistance to, 203–4, 274
  as example of government regulatory
    approach to work-life policy,
    202, 233
  exemptions to, 6
  hourly employees and, 169
  maternity leave and, 25–28
  paid time off and, 212, 225
  passage of, 202–3
  presidential candidates and, 253–55
  scope of, 279*n*4
  subsequent legislation to amend and
    expand, 256, 264
  unemployment compensation funds
    used for, 285*n*69
  union support of, 67
  wounded service members and, 257
Family-friendly workplace. *See also*
    Work-family employment policies
  bargaining strategies for, 71–80
  business case for, 203
  certification system proposed for, 58
Family leave. *See also* Family and Medical
    Leave Act of 1993 (FMLA); *specific
    states*
  bargaining strategies for, 76–77
  business opposition to, 203–4
  hourly employees and, 202, 210–12

negotiability and, 40
politicians and, 255, 279*n*13
popular support for, 203, 237
professional workers and, 202
public policy on, 66–67
as social leveler, 202
in states, 6, 246, 257, 258, 261, 264
union support of, 63, 66–68
Family Leave Insurance Act of 2007 (pro-
    posed), 256, 280*nn*21–22, 283*n*54
Family-supportive culture, 52–53
Family-unsupportive culture, 54–55
"Family Values at Work: It's About Time!
    Why We Need Minimum Standards
    to Ensure a Family-Friendly Work-
    place" (Multi-State Working Families
    Consortium), 68
Fathers
  access to work-family accommoda-
    tions and, 233
  child care and, 5–6
  parental leave and, 25–26, 29
Fear of regulation, 235–36
Federal Employees Flexible and
    Compressed Work Schedules
    Act of 1982, 21–22
Federal government
  flexible or compressed work schedules
    for employees, 21–22
  as model employer, 254
  as policy change agent, 333
  regulatory approach to work-life
    policy, 232–39, 247
Feldblum, Chai R., 251, 286*nn*73–74,
    305, 332–33
The Feminine Mystique (Friedan),
    199–200
Fertility, decline in, 243
Firestein, Netsy, 61, 329, 331, 332,
    334, 335
First-time employees, 225–26
Flattening of organizations, 312
Flattening of world competition, 313
Flexibility plus, 99
Flexibility policies. *See also* Work-family
    employment policies

benefits of, 19–22
career maintenance and, 272
components of, 274–75
consequences of using, 291, 301
demographics of availability and access
    to, 19
employee perspective on, 17–18, 300
employer perspective on, 15–17, 300
hourly employees and. *See* Hourly
    employees
inequalities of access to, 197–205
large vs. small employers and, 291–95,
    306*n*2
leave. *See specific types of leave*
life-course approach to, 65–68
limitations of, 35, 324–25
professional workers and, 83–93
research needs. *See* Future research
    needs
ROWE intervention. *See* ROWE
    intervention
salaried vs. hourly employees and,
    328–31
tripartite approach to, 275–78
unions and. *See* Unions
usage of, 291, 301
Flexible flex, 300
Flexible Work and Well-Being Center
    (University of Minnesota), 97
Flexible work arrangements (FWAs),
    269–70, 272
Flexicurity, 64, 329
Flextime. *See* Flexibility policies
Florida
    CCDE program in, 318
    mandatory paid sick leave legislation
        in, 259, 282*n*46
    prohibiting employment discrimina-
        tion based on "familial status"
        legislation in, 283*n*52
FLSA. *See* Fair Labor Standards Act of 1938
Fluctuating work hours, 175, 176,
    177–78, 199. *See also* Unpredictabil-
    ity in work schedules
FMLA. *See* Family and Medical Leave Act
    of 1993

Folbre, Nancy, 226, 241
Ford Foundation, 299, 305
Foreign workers, economic dependency
    on, 241
Foster care leave, 25–26
Free-market approach. *See* Market
    approach to work-life policy
Friedan, Betty, 199–200
Frye, N. Kathleen, 35
Full-time flex, 175
Full-time work
    categorizing of, 199
    child care assistance and, 23
    defined, 7
    employment leave and, 27–28
    flexibility and, 16, 19
    number of hours worked and, 172, 220
Functional unsupportive cultures, 55
Future research needs, 337–41
    adaptability of interventions and, 339
    approaches to modern American
        family in postindustrial society
        and, 240–43
    context and conditions, consideration
        of, 339
    evidentiary needs to convince
        employers to adopt family-
        friendly policies, 243–48
    improvement of methodology, 35, 39
    measurement of interventions, 338
    overview, 231–32
    policy context in U.S. and, 232–39
    process-oriented outcomes for, 339–40
    realistic outcomes for targeted changed
        and, 340–41
    thinking outside the box and, 337–38
    "three-legged stool" interventions
        and, 337
Fuwa, Makiko, 39
FWAs. *See* Flexible work arrangements
FWI. *See* Families and Work Institute

Galinsky, Ellen, 286*n*73, 289, 333, 336
Gender equality and discrimination,
    32–33. *See also* Women workers

household labor and, 39
job demands and, 162–63
wage inequity, 39
Gender identity, 286*n*71
Generalizability, 124, 184–86, 245
Generational diversity, 312
GenX employees, 56
Georgia
    paid family leave in, 67
    universal pre-K education in, 239
Gerson, Kathleen, 200, 251
Gerstel, Naomi, 34–35
Giandria, Michael D., 310
Glass, Jennifer
    Davis and Mitchell comments on,
        333, 335
    Feldblum comments on, 259–61, 272,
        283*n*56
    flextime impact study by, 21
    on future research needs, 231
    Galinsky comments on, 289, 290,
        295–96, 301, 302, 305
    Greenhaus comments on, 152
    Smyer and Pitt-Catsouphes comments
        on, 309, 319
    Thompson and Prottas comments
        on, 55
Global aging, 309
Global warming, 246
Goodstein, Jerry D., 53
Gore, Al, 253
Government Accountability Office, 310
Government-sponsored work-life pro-
        grams, 57–58. *See also* Family and
        Medical Leave Act of 1993 (FMLA);
        specific states
    benefits of, 202
    in European Union, 333
    flaws in, 296–98
    in U.S., 234, 236–37, 240, 243, 247
Great Britain and Work-Life Balance
        Campaign, 281*n*26
"Great Risk Shift" (Hacker), 191
Greenhaus, Jeffrey H., 141, 150, 334
Gregoire, Christine, 257
Grievance resolution, 63–64

Guaranteed minimum hours, 175, 177,
        181–82

Hacker, Jacob, 191
Harvard clerical union, 65–66
Havens, John, 316
Hawaii and short-term disability for
        maternity leave, 28
Head Start, 234
Health and wellness
    job control and, 98–99
    relationship of work to, 222
    ROWE intervention and, 122, 144
Health insurance
    hourly employees and, 169, 173–74
    as public policy issue, 68
    salaried vs. hourly workers access to,
        200
    universal, 237, 239, 246
    waiting periods for, 173–74, 177, 199
Healthy Families Act of 2004 (proposed),
        256–57, 283*n*53
Henderson, Kathryn A., 24
Henly, Julia, 222, 223, 325
Heterogeneity in research designs, 160
Hierarchical linear modeling (HLM), 39
High-wage and -income employees. *See
        also* Professionals
    effective workplaces and, 302
    flexibility and, 291
Hochschild, Arlie R., 156
Home health care services, 234
Hourly employees, 169–227
    barriers to access faced by, 173–74
    benefit waiting periods and, 173–74,
        177, 199
    challenges faced by, 207–17
    child care and supervision issues,
        209–10
    compared to salaried employees. *See*
        Salaried vs. hourly workers
    conflicts with family and transporta-
        tion needs, 212–14
    emergency family needs and rigidity of
        supervisors, 214–15

employment status of, 173–74
generalizability of study on, 184–86
improving predictability and, 182–86
inequalities among workers and,
    197–205
nonstandard features in standard jobs
    and, 172–73, 220
overview, 169–70, 207–8
predictability vs. rigidity and, 183–84
qualitative studies on, 208–9
realities of, 171–72
role of hourly jobs in corporate labor
    strategies, 170–71
Scheduling Intervention Study and,
    177–88, 222–26. See also Schedul-
    ing Intervention Study
scheduling practices and, 175
in social context, 219–27
stratification of, 176
time off, obstacles associated with,
    210–12
turnover issues, 173–74, 186–88
unintended consequences for, 177
vulnerabilities of, 207–17
Household labor and gender equality
    policies, 39
Huston, Aletha, 208

IBM's 2007 Global Work/Life Survey, 298
Ideal research design vs. corporate
    realities, 124–26
Ideal worker, 29–33, 85, 158, 326–27, 336
Ilgen, Daniel R., 313
Illinois
    family leave insurance legislation in,
        258
    funding of family leave program in,
        283n54
    mandatory paid sick leave legislation
        in, 259
    opposition to paid family leave in,
        284n58
    universal pre-K education in, 239
Incentive bonuses, 136
Income. See also specific socioeconomic
    levels

agrarian jobs and, 157
bureaucratic settings for physicians
    and, 87
instability in nonstandard employment
    and, 221
limiting availability and, 222
predictability of, 179, 182, 189–90
ROWE intervention and, 120
travel and, 159
unpredictability of, 175–76
Independent contractors, 88
Informal work culture, 326
Ingram, Paul, 53
Instability
    of employment, 179. See also Job
        security
    in nonstandard employment, 221
    of work hours, 173, 176, 187–89
Institutional review board (IRB), 110
Institutional theory and work-family
    culture, 53, 55–56
Institution-to-employee spillover, 162
Intensive mothering, 201
Intergenerational conflict, 312
Intersectionality and diversity, 163
Involuntary part-time work, 199
Iowa and universal pre-K education, 239
Issues of an Aging Workforce study, 312

Jacobs, Jerry A., 200, 251
James, Jacquelyn B., 312
Job churning, 237. See also Turnover
Job control, 98–99, 143
Job demands, 162–64
Job-related travel, 158–62
Job satisfaction
    career satisfaction, 89
    effective workplaces and, 302
    family-supportive culture and, 52
    flexibility and, 20
    ROWE intervention and, 122, 144
    supervisor support and, 30–31
    work-family policy effectiveness on, 40
Job security, 172, 327, 329
Job sharing, 16, 19

Job status
    ambiguous, 177
    barriers to benefits access and, 173–74
    hourly employees and, 169. *See also*
        Hourly employees
    number of hours worked and, 172, 220
    stratification of workforce and, 176
Job strain model, 99–100
Johnson, Richard, 313, 314

Kanter, Rosabeth M., 3, 138–39
Karasek, Robert A., Jr., 98–99, 143, 162
Kelly, Erin
    on corporate work-time policy initiative
        study, 97
    Davis and Mitchell comments on, 323,
        325, 328, 332, 336, 337, 339
    Feldblum comments on, 265
    Galinsky comments on, 302
    Greenhaus comments on, 141–53
    Lambert comments on, 180–81
    MacDermid et al. comments on, 133–39
    Milkman comments on, 197, 198
    Zvonkovic comments on, 155–65
Kelly, Erin L., 245, 341
Kennedy, Edward "Ted," 280*n*18,
    280*n*23, 331
Kerry, John, 253
Knussman v. Maryland (2001), 41
Kossek, Ellen Ernst
    Briscoe comments on, 83, 90
    Davis and Mitchell comments on,
        325–26, 333, 335
    Galinsky comments on, 291, 302
    Milkman comments on, 199
    Moen et al. comments on, 106
    on policymaking, 34, 35, 40
    Thompson and Prottas comments on,
        51–60
    on work-life policies, 3
    Zvonkovic comments on, 156
Kozlowski, Steve W. J., 313

Labor costs, 170–71, 175
Labor Department, 25

Labor force. *See* Demographics
Labor Project for Working Families
    Best Contracts database of, 63
    in Multi-State Working Families
        Consortium, 281*n*31
Laissez-faire approach to work-life policy,
    237, 240
Lambert, Susan J.
    Davis and Mitchell comments on, 323,
        325, 327, 334, 335, 337–39
    Enchautegui-de-Jesús comments on,
        207, 209–10, 212, 215–16
    Feldblum comments on, 265
    Galinsky comments on, 290
    on hourly employees, 169
    Milkman comments on, 197–200,
        203
    Moen et al. comments on, 113
    Perry-Jenkins comments on, 219–24
Language
    of cost containment, 220
    in labor/management contract, 61,
        63, 65
    ROWE intervention and, 116, 144
    salaried vs. hourly employees, 170
    stigmatized terms and, 332
    workplace terminology, 266
Lareau, Annette, 201
Large employers
    elder care and, 24
    employment leave and, 28
    flexibility and, 291–95, 306*n*2
Last-minute posting, 175
Lawsuits involving family caregiving, 41
Layoffs, 172
Leaders in a Global Economy (Galinsky),
    297, 298
Leave. *See specific types*
Lee, Mary D., 32
Liechty, Janet M., 21
Life-course theoretical framing, 110
Lifelong employment, 238
Life satisfaction
    family-supportive culture and, 52
    flexibility and, 20
    supervisor support and, 31–32

Long-term care
  community-based, 318
  insurance, 14
Lost productivity. *See* Productivity
Low-income mothers. *See* Working
  mothers
Low-income workers. *See also* Hourly
  employees
  access to flexibility and, 290–91
  effective workplaces and, 302
  predictability of work schedule and,
    269–70
  unaware of paid family leave law, 204
  unpaid leave and, 6
Low-value work, 108, 122, 145
Loyalty, 31, 244

MacDermid, Shelley M., 51, 133,
    338, 339
Maine
  labor-community coalitions in, 67
  mandatory paid sick leave legislation
    in, 259, 282*n*46
Male-breadwinner model, 170, 201
Male gender discrimination, 33
Managers and supervisors
  employee communication. *See*
    Communication
  flexibility access of, 19
  hours worked by, 200
  lack of experience with caregiving, 243
  as policy change agents, 335–36
  rigidity of, 214–15
  salaried, 180
  support of work-family employment
    policy, 29–32
  women as, 200–201
Mandel, Hadas, 39
Market approach to work-life policy
  policy context in U.S., 5–7, 232–35,
    237, 240–43, 247
  problems with, 290–91
Married-couple households, 201,
    279*nn*1–2
Marshall, Victor W., 312

Maryland and mandatory paid sick leave
    legislation, 259, 282*nn*46–47
Masling, Sharon, 286*n*74
Massachusetts
  mandatory paid sick leave legislation
    in, 259, 282*nn*46–47
  paid family leave in, 67
  Unemployment Insurance Code in, 28
  universal health care in, 239
Maternal care vs. child care, 290
Maternal employment. *See* Working
  mothers
Maternity leave
  demographics on availability and
    access to, 27–28
  employee perspective on, 26–27
  employer benefits of, 28–29, 202
  employer perspective on, 25–26
  in European Union, 5–6
  in Mexico, 231–33
  public policy on, 66–67
  in Sweden, 232
Maume, David J., 33
McHale, Susan M., 33
McLoyd, Vonnie C., 208
McNamara, Tay K., 316
Media reporting of work-family policy
  surveys, 13
Medicaid, 246
Medical professionals. *See* Professionals
Medicare, 234, 237
Mental health
  community services for, 234
  flexibility and, 20
  instability in nonstandard employment
    and, 221
  supervisor support and, 31
Mentors, 226
Merton, Robert, 103
Metropolitan-area workers and family
  leave, 28
Mexico and pregnant workers, 231–33
Middle-income workers
  access to flexibility and, 291
  effective workplaces and, 302
  unpaid leave and, 6

Milkman, Ruth, 197, 329–30, 332–33, 335–36
Minimalist market-based approach. *See* Market approach to work-life policy
Minimum hours, guaranteed. *See* Guaranteed minimum hours
Minnesota and mandatory paid sick leave legislation, 259, 282*nn*46–47
Missouri and mandatory paid sick leave legislation, 259, 282*nn*46–47
Mitchell, Katherine Stamps, 323
Mobility, 186–88. *See also* Turnover
Moen, Phyllis
    on corporate work-time policy initiative study, 97
    Davis and Mitchell comments on, 323, 325, 328, 332, 336, 337, 339
    Feldblum comments on, 265
    Galinsky comments on, 302
    Greenhaus comments on, 141–53
    Lambert comments on, 180–81
    MacDermid et al. comments on, 133–39
    Milkman comments on, 197, 198
    Zvonkovic comments on, 155–65
MomsRising, 283*n*55
Moody, H. Rick, 315
Moral outrage against status quo, 277–78
Moss, Philip, 180
Mossholder, Kevin W., 39
Mothers. *See* Working mothers
Moving residences, 221
Multigenerational workforce, 312
Multi-State Working Families Consortium, 67–68, 257, 281*n*31
Munck, B., 335
Mustard, Cam, 221
Myth of separate worlds between work and home, 3
Myth of work stability in past, 157

National advisory commission on workplace flexibility (NAC), 276–77
National Association of Manufacturers, 285*n*70
National Compensation Survey, 10, 12, 26

National family trust for paid parental leave, 255, 280*n*14
National Federation of Independent Business, 284*n*63
National Initiative on Workplace Flexibility, 274
National Institute for Occupational Safety and Health, 97
National Institutes of Health (NIH), 102, 107, 112, 155, 158, 159, 161
National Partnership for Women and Families, 257
    report card on parental leave programs, 28
National Retailers' Work-Life Forum, 185
National Study of Employers (NSE)
    caregiving and, 23–24
    supervisor support and, 30–31
    workplace policy and, 10, 12, 14–17
National Study of the Changing Workforce (NSCW)
    caregiving and, 24, 316
    European Working Conditions Survey and, 296
    flexibility and, 290–91
    supervisor support and, 31
    traveling workers and, 159
    workplace policy and, 10, 12
Negative consequences
    of taking vacations, 33
    of using flexible time, 291, 301
    of using work-family policies, 30–31
Negative spillover
    flexibility and, 20, 156, 340
    ROWE intervention and, 122, 144
    supervisor support and, 31–32
Negotiability of employer policies, 40, 63
Neoliberal thinking, 244, 247, 260
New Hope Child and Family Study, 208
New Hope Ethnographic Study (NHES), 208–16
New Hope Project, 208
New Jersey
    CCDE in, 318
    discrimination against caregivers in, 259

funding of family leave program in, 283*n*54

newborn, adopted, or foster child care leave in, 258

paid family leave in, 67, 204, 284*n*62

prohibiting employment discrimination based on "familial status" in, 283*n*52

short-term disability programs for maternity leave in, 28

TDI in, 68, 261

Unemployment Insurance Code in, 28

New Jersey Chamber of Commerce on paid family leave, 283*n*58

New York

disability insurance legislation in, 258

discrimination against caregivers in, 259

funding of family leave program in, 283*n*54

opposition to paid family leave in, 284*n*58

paid family leave in, 67

prohibiting employment discrimination based on "family responsibilities" legislation in, 283*n*52

short-term disability for maternity leave in, 28

TDI used for paid family leave in, 261

New York City, prohibiting employment discrimination based on "caregiver status," 259, 283*n*52

NIH. *See* National Institutes of Health

9 to 5 National Association of Working Women, 281*n*31

NJ Time to Care Coalition, 281*n*31

Noe, Raymond A., 40

Nonstandard job features, 172–73, 220

Nonstandard work times, 180

Nonsupportive cultures, 54–55

Noonan, Mary C., 21

North Carolina and mandatory paid sick leave legislation, 259, 282*n*46

NSCW. *See* National Study of the Changing Workforce

NSE. *See* National Study of Employers

Obama, Barack, 254

Office of Personnel Management, 257

"100 Best Companies for Working Mothers," 52, 68, 326

Onesies campaign, 260, 283*n*55

Organizational adaptation theory, 53, 56

Outsourcing, 235

Overemployment, 220

Overtime. *See also* Fair Labor Standards Act of 1938 (FLSA)

compensatory time off in lieu of pay for, 263

exempt employees and, 7, 256

flexibility and, 16

mandatory overtime not limited in U.S., 67

Pagnan, Colleen, 133, 338

Paid family leave. *See* Family leave

Paid leave, 5, 6, 42. *See also specific types of leave*

accrued, ability to use, 221

elder care and, 23

FMLA and, 27

Healthy Families Act and, 256–57

hourly employees and, 169, 173–74, 212

legislative efforts toward, 259–60

national consensus on, 324

recurring, 270–71

salaried vs. hourly employees, 200, 202

Parental leave, 29, 225, 254–55, 257. *See also* Family and Medical Leave Act of 1993 (FMLA); Family leave; Maternity leave; Paternity leave

Parenthood, transition to, 223–24

Participatory action research approach, 207

Part-time work

discrimination and, 32–33

employment leave and, 27–28

exclusion from benefits and, 173–74

flexibility and, 16, 19

hourly employees and, 199

involuntary, 199

number of hours worked and, 172, 220

pensions and, 6
physicians and, 86
Paternity leave, 25–26, 29. *See also* Family
    and Medical Leave Act of 1993
    (FMLA); Family leave
Pavalko, Elisa K., 24
Pennsylvania
    mandatory paid sick leave legislation
        in, 259, 282*n*46
    prohibiting employment discrimina-
        tion based on "familial status" in,
        283*n*52
Perry-Jenkins, Maureen, 219, 327
Pets, 241
Pfeffer, Jeffrey, 56
Phased retirement, 16, 276, 287*n*82
Physicians, 84–87, 89, 336. *See also*
    Professionals
Pitt-Catsouphes, Marcie, 304, 309, 324,
    331, 339
Planning ahead, 182–83, 198. *See also*
    Advance notice
"Plan to Honor Work and Family"
    (Kerry-Edwards proposal), 253
Policymaking and workplace flexibility,
    251–322. *See also* Future research
    needs
    "both/and" approach to, 289–308
    buy-in by multiple stakeholders,
        336–37
    changing landscape of aging and work,
        309–22. *See also* Changing land-
        scape of aging and work
    community leaders, involvement of,
        302–6
    comparison of presidential candidates
        (2000–2008), 252–60
    "either/or" perspective, 289–90
    flexibility policies currently in place,
        291–95
    free-market system, problems of,
        290–91
    future agenda for, 33–42, 278
    goals for, 298–99
    governmental approach, problems of,
        296–98
    implementation improvement needs,
        39–41
    obstacles to reform, 260–63, 283*n*56,
        284*n*59
    overview, 251–52
    "point of entry" for change, 332–36
    process-oriented outcomes for, 339–40
    quality of workplace environment and,
        301–2
    realistic outcomes for targeted changed
        and, 340–41
    refining policy obstacles and leveraging
        opportunities, 273–78
    reframing of issues, 34–35, 332
    reframing policy terminology, 266–73
    research studies, design of, 299
    reshaping political expectations, 263–66
    strategies for instigating change, 332–37
    thinking outside the box and, 337–38
    work-life assistance, definition of,
        299–301
    Workplace Flexibility 2010 enterprise,
        263–78. *See also* Workplace Flexi-
        bility 2010 enterprise
Pollitt, Katha, 32
Powell, Gary N., 150
Predictability, 191, 198, 269–71, 329. *See
    also* Hourly employees; Scheduling
    Intervention Study
Pregnant women. *See also* Maternity leave
    discrimination against, 231–34
Pre-K education, 237, 239
Premeaux, Sonya F., 39
Presidential campaigns and issues,
    252–56
Presser, Harriet B., 180
Pretax dollars, 22
Productivity
    AWSA and, 21
    flexibility and, 20
    market approach to work-life policy
        and, 240
    as relevant outcome, 340
    work-family conflict and, 237
    work-family policy and, 14, 40,
        244–45

Professionals, 83–93
  bureaucratized medical workplaces
      and, 86–87
  family leave and, 202
  flexibility and, 20, 180, 197–98
  implications for research and policy on
      flexibility of, 89–91
  nature of design of work of, 84–85
  nonphysician professionals, 87–89
  overview, 83–84
  women as, 200–201
  work-life flexibility of, 83–93
Profit margin, 224, 226
Project on Global Working Families, 66
Prottas, David J., 51, 326
Public policy. *See also* Policymaking and
      workplace flexibility
  health care and, 246
  hourly employees and, 169
  political expectations and, 263–65
  union activism and, 66–68
Puget Sound Share the Success initiative,
      186
Purdue's Center for Families, 138

Qualitative and quantitative research
      methods, 101, 142, 144, 152, 161–62
Quality vs. quantity time with children,
      290
Quasi-experiment, 114, 124
Quinn, Joseph F., 310

Randomization, 133–34
Recruitment
  AWSA and, 21
  as reason for work-family policies, 14, 40
  ROWE intervention and, 106
Recurring time off, 270–71
Reduced compensation professionals, 173
Regulatory approach to work-life policy,
      232–39, 247, 254, 316–18
Religious observances, 21
Remnet, Mary Ann, 133, 338
Repercussions. *See* Negative consequences

Replacement pay, 26, 28
Replication. *See* Generalizability
Republican party, 236, 255, 263–64,
      280n15
Research. *See also specific studies*
  advocacy, 41–42
  on design of work and professional
      flexibility, 89–91
  diversity in design of, 160
  ethnographic methods of, 110, 112,
      161–62
  family and personal life in, 158
  on firm adoption of work-life policies,
      53, 54–55
  future research needs. *See* Future
      research needs
  heterogeneity in design of, 160
  importance of relationships in, 110
  on organizational responsiveness,
      55–57
  participatory action approach, 207
  qualitative and quantitative methods
      of, 144, 152, 161–62
  recommendations on work-family
      policy, 35–39
  for ROWE intervention, 97–102
  utility of, 135
Resource dependence theory, 53, 56, 58
Ressler, Cali, 103, 107–8, 110, 114, 125
Results-only work environment (ROWE)
      study. *See* ROWE intervention
Retail employees. *See* Hourly employees;
      ROWE intervention
Retention
  AWSA and, 21
  child care assistance and, 23
  flexibility and, 20
  as reason for work-family policies, 14
  as relevant outcome, 340
  ROWE intervention and, 106
  supervisor support and, 31
  work-family policy effectiveness
      on, 40
Retirement benefits
  inadequate income due to caregiving,
      242

inequalities between hourly and
    salaried employees, 200–201
pensions and ERISA coverage, 6
phased, 16, 276, 287*n*82
Return on investment, 340
Rhetoric-free zone, 276
Rhode Island and short-term disability
    for maternity leave, 28
Richardson, Bill, 279*n*13
Rigidity
    predictability vs., 183–84
    of supervisors, 214–15
Rivera, Dennis, 62
Roehling, Patricia, 251
Rosabeth Moss Kanter Award for Excel-
    lence in Work-Family Research,
    138–39
Rosenthal, Carolyn, 315
Rothausen-Vange, Teresa J., 315
ROWE intervention, 97–165
    adaptability and, 339
    ambiguous identities of those conduct-
        ing study, 116–19
    concept of study, 142–43
    corporate level changes and, 334
    defined, 107
    effective workplaces and, 302
    engaged research and, 126–27, 133–39
    family and personal-life perspective
        and, 158
    findings of, 120–23, 144–45
    fitting in vs. getting in, 115–16
    formulation of research problem,
        98–101
    future research recommendations,
        150–52
    gaining access for research, 103–10, 143
    gaps between research and corporate
        realities, 124–27
    Greenhaus assessment of, 141–53
    ideological and philosophical issues of,
        155–57
    impact of individual employee charac-
        teristics on outcomes, 147–49, 197
    impact of research on outcomes,
        145–47, 157–58

job demands and, 162–64
lessons learned, 158–62
limited work-life policies and, 325
meeting multiple stakeholders' needs
    and, 336
minimal intrusiveness of study, 119
moving targets, nature of research on,
    111–12
overview, 141–42
reframing of policy issue, 332
relationships, importance of, 110–11
research challenges during, 102–3
research design for, 101–2, 112–19, 144
serendipity in research on, 103–6
thinking outside the box, 338
three-legged stool and, 337
timelines for, 104–5, 107–11
Zvonkovic comments on, 155–58
Ryan, Ann Marie, 40

Sabbaticals, 16
Salancik, Gerald R., 56
Salaried vs. hourly workers, 170, 198,
    200, 220–22, 327, 328–29
Sampling strategies, 160
San Francisco and mandatory paid sick
    leave legislation, 258, 283*n*53
Satisfaction. *See* Job satisfaction; Life
    satisfaction
Scheduling. *See also* Hourly employees
    alternative work, 16, 80–81
    of availability, 177
    of childcare, 182, 190, 224
    communication with supervisors
        and, 184
    control of, 136
    flexibility of, 269
    fluctuating with consumer demand,
        175, 197
    notice. *See* Advance notice
    turnover and, 186
    working mothers and, 182, 210–12
Scheduling Intervention Study, 177–88
    generalizability of, 184–86
    overview, 178–79

Perry-Jenkins comments on, 222–26
predictability and, 182–84, 337–38
role of labor strategies and practices
    and, 179
targets for, 179–82
turnover data for, 186–88
Schneider, Barbara, 251
Schwarzenegger, Arnold, 259, 285n63
Seasonal jobs, 222
SEIU 1199/Employer Child Care
    Fund, 64
Self-direction, 98–99
SEM (structural equation modeling),
    35–36
Semyonov, Moshe, 39
Seniority, 169, 176, 225
Senior-level executives, 19
Serendipity, 103–7, 159, 341
Service Employees International Union
    (SEIU), 62–64
Service members, wounded, 257
Service workers, 19
Seven-minute rule, 116
Sex discrimination, 32–33. See also
    Women workers
Sexual assault, 254
Sexual orientation, 286n71
Shadowing, 114, 118–19, 143
Shen, Ce, 316
Short-term disability programs for
    maternity leave, 28
Short-term time off (STO), 270–74,
    286n79
Sick leave
    for caregivers, 330–31
    city policies on, 258
    demerits given for taking, 174
    employee perspective on, 26
    guaranteed, 331
    hourly workers and, 202, 211
    politicians on, 254
Simons, Tal, 53
Single, Louise E., 33
Single mothers, 3, 202, 223–24. See also
    Women workers; Working mothers
Skolnick, Arlene, 306

Small employers
    elder care and, 24
    employment leave and, 28
    flexibility and, 291–95, 306n2
    FMLA and, 6
    paid leave exemption for, 284n62
Smyer, Michael A., 304, 309, 324, 331, 339
Social capital, 136
Social Security, 237, 241
Society for Human Resource Management,
    287n82
Socioeconomic status, 330
    class inequalities, 201
    job demands and social class, 163
Spillover from work to home, 18, 122, 156,
    303–4. See also Negative spillover
    institution-to-employee spillover,
        162–63
    of working mothers, 208–9
Stability of work hours, 176, 181–82. See
    also Instability
Staines, Graham L., 20, 325
Starting and quitting times, 15–16, 18,
    20–21
State family leave innovation fund, 254
State governments. See also specific states
    family leave laws, 6, 246, 257, 258, 261,
        264
    as policy change agents, 333
    regulatory approach to work-life
        policy, 239, 254, 316–18
    report card on parental leave
        programs, 28
Stevens, Ted, 280n21
STO (Short-term time off), 270–74,
    286n79
Stone, Pamela, 201
Stratification of workforce, 176–77
Stress
    family-supportive culture and, 52
    work-family policy and, 40
Stress process theory, 100
Structural contingency theory, 57–58
Structural equation modeling (SEM),
    35–36
Supervisors. See Managers and supervisors